MINNESOTA
Gardener's
Guide

MINNESOTA STATE

HORTICULTURAL SOCIETY'S

MINNESOTA
Gardener's
Guide

Melinda Myers
Edited by Chuck Levine

**COOL
SPRINGS
PRESS**

Nashville, Tennessee
A Division of Thomas Nelson, Inc.
www.ThomasNelson.com

Myers, Melinda.
   [Minnesota gardener's guide]
   Minnesota State Horticultural Society's Minnesota gardener's guide / Melinda Myers; edited by Chuck Levine.
     p.   cm.
   Includes bibliographical references (p.   ).
   ISBN 1-888608-64-1
   1. Landscape plants -- Minnesota 2. Landscape gardening -- Minnesota
   I. Title: Minnesota gardener's guide. II. Levine, Chuck. III. Title.
  SB407 .M977 2001
  635.9'51776–dc21
                        2001004056

Published by Cool Springs Press, a Division of Thomas Nelson, Inc., P.O. Box 141000, Nashville, Tennessee 37214

First printing 2001
Printed in the United States of America
10 9 8 7 6 5 4 3 2 1

Horticultural Nomenclature Editor: Chuck Levine, Minnesota State Horticultural Society, Falcon Heights, Minnesota

On the cover (clockwise from top left): Tulip, Purple Coneflower, Yarrow, Bleeding Heart.

Visit the Thomas Nelson website at: www.ThomasNelson.com

DEDICATION

To my Board of Directors for helping me chart new territory and for all my friends who make each new adventure one to remember.
—Melinda Myers

I dedicate my portion of this book to my wife Tarri and my children Rachel, Jacob, and Noah who have allowed me the time to be the gardener I wanted to be. To my parents, Sherwin and Gloria for encouraging me to be whatever I wanted to be; to the folks at the Minnesota State Horticultural Society who have given me this opportunity; and lastly to the many students, teachers, and friends who have inspired me.
—Chuck Levine.

ACKNOWLEDGMENTS

A special thanks to my daughter Nevada who makes every day worthwhile; and to my husband Wes with his gentle spirit, for tolerating yet another project that consumed much time and space in our lives. And to my parents, Betty and John, who gave me a strong foundation of love and support to help me through life.

Thanks to all the enthusiastic northern gardeners, horticulturists, professionals, and associates that inspired me in my profession and personal life. Your generosity, knowledge and spirit have made going to work a pleasure.

My appreciation to Marjee Righeimer and the Minnesota State Horticulture Society for entering into this partnership. Your dedication to serving gardeners and insights were useful in preparing this book and for our future endeavors.

And a huge THANK YOU to Angela Reiner my managing editor. Your humor and understanding made this project happen. Thanks to Cindy Games who can always make me laugh while moving every project forward, Roger Waynick for the opportunity, and everyone else at Cool Springs who worked hard to get this book published.

—*Melinda Myers*

MINNESOTA
Gardener's
Guide

CONTENTS

Introduction 8

The Garden Environment 12

Annuals 26

Bulbs 82

Groundcovers 114

Ornamental Grasses 148

Perennials 170

Photographic Gallery of Featured Plants 231

Roses 248

Shrubs 264

Trees 314

Turfgrass 376

Vines 386

Sources 405

Index 436

INTRODUCTION

W hen I moved north, over 20 years ago, I was amazed to find such a horticultural paradise in a place I had only seen as a winter wonderland on TV. I remember watching the weather reports and wondered how people, let alone plants, could survive such a harsh climate. My first trip to the Twin cities, fortunately in summer, showed me a state filled with lush green trees and colorful gardens. And there were lots of people outside enjoying it all.

Minnesota has a long history of green and growing. In the 1860s, Minnesota's new homesteaders were few in number, but blessed with many green thumbs. They brought their desire for beauty and love of the plants with them as they moved west to their new homeland.

Many green thumb gardeners showed off their harvest at the 1866 Minnesota State Fair. The good showing inspired a group of growers to form the Minnesota Fruit Growers Association. As the interest in other plants grew, the group expanded their mission and changed their name to the Minnesota State Horticultural Society. Over the years their minutes were published and soon transformed into a gardening magazine that is now known as *Northern Gardener*.

At the turn of the century, gardeners turned their focus from food production to ornamental plants. The increase in flower planting and use of tropical plants inside and out changed the gardening scene with a short break to grow Victory Gardens for the WWII effort. Community and backyard gardeners continue this tradition and benefit from the joy of growing their own fresh-from-the-garden produce.

The big explosion in landscaping came after WWII. As the veterans returned home, built new houses, and started raising families, the interest in landscape grew. Large expanse of grass was used to fill the space and create play areas for the children. Shrubs ringed the houses and gardens were filled with annuals and a few perennials.

In 1955, the Men's Garden Club (an affiliated club of MSHS) decided that northern gardeners needed more help and guidance for gardening in the rigors of Minnesota weather. They undertook the development of a landscape arboretum to increase research for hardy ornamentals, create an interest in plants, provide a horticulture library and promote plant testing throughout the state.

The arboretum was soon deeded over to the University and has continued with the original mission. To date, hundreds of plants have been introduced, additional ornamentals have been evaluated, and thousands of Minnesota gardeners have been inspired by their plantings and educational efforts. The impact of the University of Minnesota Landscape Arboretum and The Minnesota State Horticultural Society (*Northern Gardener*) can be seen in parks, greenways, and home gardens. The expanded use of perennials and native plants has changed the suburban landscape from an expanse of lawns and sheared Yews to an array of flowering trees, shrubs, ornamental grasses, and flowers.

Next time you drive through the city or your neighborhood, look for remnants of our gardening past and signs of things to come.

USING THIS BOOK

Minnesota Gardener's Guide is designed to help you make the connection with nature and achieve some gardening success of your own. I wrote the book with you, the gardener, in mind. I tried to include answers to the questions gardeners are always asking me. I selected plants that are easy to find here and are often used in gardens and yards. The information included in the pages of this volume should help you grow a healthy and attractive landscape.

The book is divided into chapters by plant categories. These include annuals, bulbs, groundcovers, ornamental grasses, perennials, roses, shrubs, trees, turfgrass, and vines. I mixed the native plants in with plants not native to Minnesota within the appropriate category. I thought that arrangement would make the book easier to use for planning your landscape. You may be surprised to learn how many of our common garden plants are natives!

Start by reading "The Garden Environment" (p. 12), which covers some of the gardening basics. It contains soil information, pest control techniques, and an overview of our weather conditions. Reading "The Garden Environment" section first will help you make better use of the information in subsequent chapters. Each chapter includes an introduction with general information unique to that group of plants. Read the chapter introductions before turning to the plant entries. Every plant entry within the chapter features a plant profile for quick reference. The following symbols indicate full sun, partial shade and shade:

Full Sun   Partial Shade   Shade

ADDITIONAL BENEFITS

Some of the beneficial characteristics of many of the plants are indicated by symbols:

 Attracts Butterflies   Produces Food for Wildlife

 Attracts Hummingbirds   Good for Cut Flowers

 Produces Edible Fruit   Long Bloom Period

 Fragrance

NATIVE PLANT

Each plant that is native to Minnesota is marked by the following symbol next to its common name:

DID YOU KNOW?

Many plant entries end with a "Did You Know?" information box that offers information about the plant's uses, nomenclature, history, or other information that is little known or just plain interesting.

Introduction

GETTING THE MOST OUT OF YOUR GARDEN

Minnesota Gardener's Guide is just a starting point. Use the basic information I have provided along with your own experience to increase your gardening success. Whether you're a beginner or a more experienced gardener, membership in the Minnesota State Horticultural Society (MSHS) is the premier resource for northern gardeners like you! It is the mission of MSHS to encourage the science and practice of northern gardening through the public's enjoyment, appreciation, and understanding of plants.

Start keeping a garden journal to record this information—it doesn't have to be fancy. It's just a place to record your gardening successes and failures. Yes, your failures. I've learned more from my failures than my successes! Record significant weather events. The impact of droughts, floods, and extreme heat and cold can show up years later. Buy a weather calendar or almanac and let the meteorologists keep track of some of the climate data for you.

Thomas Jefferson, a horticulturist as well as our third president, inspired me to keep a garden journal. I read that he kept a garden journal for 50 years, entering the name, date, and source of every plant he purchased, how it grew, and when and why it was removed. I have not mastered his discipline, but as my memory fades, I am getting more motivated!

With all that said, the most important thing is to relax and have fun. If a plant dies (and it happens to all of us), look at this as an opportunity to try something new. If you put a plant in the wrong spot, move it to a new location. Gardening should be enjoyable, not a weekly chore. And when you get discouraged, think about what Thomas Jefferson said: "Though an old man, I am but a young gardener."

Weather

WHEN I FIRST MOVED north, someone told me, "If you don't like the weather, wait five minutes and it will change." They were right. Minnesota weather, like much of the upper Midwest weather, is variable and often challenging for gardeners.

We base our plant selection and care on average weather conditions and expected extremes. Then weather exceptions come along, like the drought of 1988, the floods of 1993 and 1997, severe storms and hail, and too many others to list.

In the twenty plus years I have lived in the north, I have yet to experience "normal" weather. There always seems to be some type of weather extreme to keep gardeners and horticulturists challenged and humble. An overview of our average weather conditions, however, may help you better plan and care for your garden.

Let's start with frost dates. On the back of every seed packet and throughout this book you will read, "Start seeds ____ number of weeks prior to the last spring frost." That date varies from May 2 to May 17 in the southern parts of Minnesota and from May 18 to June 6 in northern Minnesota. (See maps on pages 246, 422, and 423.)

Now count the days between the last spring frost and the first fall frost. That will give you the number of growing days for your region. The frost-free season varies from 107 to 160 days in southern Minnesota and from 90 to 120 days in the northern part of the state. These are average frost dates based on one hundred years worth of data. Soil temperature and the frost tolerance of each plant should determine your planting date. I remember losing quite a few plants when we had a killing frost several weeks after the "normal" last frost.

Average growing temperatures and seasonal extremes will influence plant growth and development. Some plants need warm temperatures to thrive and flower. Others become stressed or stop flowering in hot weather. Winter temperature extremes are among the major factors that influence winter survival. The U.S. Department of Agriculture hardiness zones are based on the average annual minimum temperatures. Minnesota has USDA Zones 2b through 4b. That is the rating system used by most gardeners and this book. The Arnold Arboretum also publishes a hardiness map used by some nurseries. Check the front of plant catalogs to determine which hardiness map and ratings they use.

Rainfall is also important for growing healthy plants. Most plants need an average of 1 inch of water each week. Plants need more water during the hot, dry days of summer and less during cooler periods. The type of plants grown and the care you provide influences the amount and frequency of watering. Some plants, like Yucca and Coneflowers, are more drought tolerant and can go longer between watering. Others, like Astilbe and Hostas, need moist soil and will scorch if the soil dries. Select more drought-tolerant plants if you are unable to water during dry periods. Mulching will also reduce the need to water by keeping the soil cool and moist.

Select plants that tolerate your landscape's climate to increase survival and minimize maintenance. But what about those gardeners who like to push plants to the extremes? Well, we can't change the weather, but we can modify it by creating microclimates or modifying our gardening practices.

Modifying the Climate

Microclimates are small areas that have slightly different growing conditions than the surrounding areas. Large bodies of water and nearby vegetation can alter frost dates and moderate temperatures. On the other hand, cold air sinks, creating frost pockets in valleys and other low areas. Woodlands and shelterbelts can block the northwest winter winds and reduce winter damage to sensitive plants. These areas can also shade the landscape, keeping temperatures cooler.

The Garden Environment

Use the following ideas to create microclimates. Plant windbreaks or install decorative fencing to block damaging winter winds. Grow heat-loving plants near brick buildings and walls. Even a flat warming stone in the perennial garden can add warmth for a nearby plant. Use an outdoor thermometer to track the temperatures in different parts of your garden. Record this information for future use.

Mulch can also be used effectively. Organic mulch used on the soil keeps roots cooler in the summer and warmer in the winter and minimizes soil temperature fluctuations that can stress plants. Winter mulches can be used to protect the aboveground portion of the plant. Roses, Rhododendrons, and other tender plants are frequently mulched for winter protection. Apply straw, marsh hay, or evergreen branches once the ground freezes. The purpose is to keep the soil temperature consistent throughout the winter. This prevents early sprouting that often occurs during our frequent, but short, midwinter thaws. Mulching also prevents drying of stems and evergreen leaves. The mulch blocks winter wind and sun to reduce moisture loss. Minnesota gardeners have access to the best winter mulch: a reliable snow cover. Even as you tire of shoveling this winter, remember that all that white stuff is protecting your plants.

Maybe it's not the cold winter that limits your gardening, but rather the short growing season. You can easily lengthen the growing season by several weeks or even a month or more. Gardeners traditionally use cold frames to get a jump on the growing season. These structures require talent to build and room to store, and they also need venting and watering. I never seem to have the time to do all that. Season-extending fabrics such as ReeMay® and other spun-bonded fabrics can make this task easier. Plant annuals or frost-sensitive perennials outside several weeks earlier than normal and loosely cover the planting bed with a season-extending fabric. The covers keep the plants warm and protect them from spring frost. Air, light, and water can all pass through the fabric, so it doesn't need to be removed for watering or ventilation. Remove the covering once the danger of frost has passed. You can also use these fabrics, bed sheets, or other material to protect plants from the first fall frost. Cover plants in the late afternoon or early evening when there is a threat of frost. Remove the frost protection in the morning. The season extenders can be left in place day and night if the meteorologists predict several days of cold, frosty weather. I find the first fall frost is often followed by two weeks of sunny, warm weather. Providing frost protection will give you a few more weeks of enjoyment before our long winter arrives.

Soil

Soil is the foundation of our landscape. Not many gardeners enjoy spending the time, energy, or money it can take to build this foundation. I have to admit it's more fun to show someone a new plant than to show off my properly prepared soil. But it's a good idea to have and follow the recipe for productive soil.

The Basics

Let's start by looking at Minnesota's native soils. There are twenty-five major soil areas and six hundred soil classifications in Minnesota. I'm going to greatly simplify this discussion with some broad generalities. I hope the soil scientists out there will forgive me!

Soil is composed of mineral material, organic matter, water, and air. The mineral matter comes from the weathering of bedrock. Bedrock in parts of Minnesota are limestone, so those soils tend to be alkaline, often called sweet, with a high pH. Other parts of the state have granite bedrock and the soils tend to be acidic, or sour, with a low pH. The weathered bedrock combines with organic matter from dead plants, manure, and other decomposing materials. The empty spaces are filled with either water or soil. It takes 100 years to make 1 inch of topsoil.

The size, shape, and quantity of the mineral particles determine the soil texture. Clay particles are tiny and flat like plates. Water is trapped between these plate-like particles making clay soils, those with a high percent of clay particles, slow to dry. Sand particles are larger (and more angular) compared to the clay. The water runs around the particles and through the soil. This is why sandy soils, those with a high percentage of sand particles, dry out faster than clay soils. Silt particles are larger than clay and smaller than sand. They feel smooth but are not sticky. Loam soils have equal parts of sand, silt, and clay particles. These soils are better drained than clay soils and have better water-holding capacity than sandy soils.

Minnesota Soils

Soils in Minnesota range from mostly clay to sandy to some type of loam to the gravel and rocks dumped by the glaciers. The soils in the Red River Valley area are among the best agricultural soils in the United States.

That's how our state's soils began. We have greatly changed our soils since we started building homes, buildings, and parking lots. In fact, some plant and soil scientists don't call this soil, but rather "disturbed materials." When buildings are constructed, the topsoil is scraped off the lot and removed. Once the basements are dug, much of the clay, sand, or gravel subsoil is spread over the lot. Some of the building materials, many of them made from limestone, accidentally get mixed into this "soil." An inch or two of topsoil is spread, sod is laid—and is the yard ready to be landscaped? Not at all. This conglomeration is usually poorly drained, very alkaline or acidic, and hard on most plants. Fortunately, many municipalities and customers are requiring builders to stockpile the topsoil for reapplication to the site.

Modifying the Soil

Given all this information, what do you need to do to improve your soil? Adding 2 to 4 inches of organic matter such as compost, peat moss, or aged manure will improve the drainage of heavy clay soil and increase the water-holding capacity of sandy soil. Work this material into the top 6 to 12 inches of soil. Improve the soil whenever you establish a new garden, plant your annuals and perennials, or transplant perennial flowers and groundcovers.

Do not add sand to clay soil. You need an inch of sand for every inch of soil you are trying to amend. If you add less than that, you will end up with concrete. Don't add lime to improve the drainage of alkaline soil. Lime improves drainage, but it also raises the soil pH. That increases problems with nutrient deficiencies in alkaline soil. Gypsum works only in soil high in sodium. Minnesota soils are not naturally high in sodium, so gypsum won't be effective at improving the soil drainage.

Gardeners growing plants in poorly drained, disturbed sites have a bigger challenge. These soils will take years to repair. Many gardeners give up and bring in additional topsoil. Make sure the topsoil you buy is better than what you already have. Purchase a blended or garden mix. Many garden centers and nurseries sell small quantities of topsoil. For large quantities, contact a company that specializes in topsoil. Friends, relatives, or a landscape professional may be able to recommend a reliable firm. Otherwise, check the telephone listings under Soil or Topsoil.

A 2-inch layer of good topsoil spread over disturbed material will not help much; water drains through the good soil and stops when it hits the bad material. A better solution is to create planting beds throughout the landscape. Large, raised planting beds and berms at least 12 inches high will give plants a good place to start growing.

Testing the Soil

Now that you have improved the soil drainage and structure, you need to develop a fertilization program. That starts with a soil test. Contact your University of Minnesota Extension Office (listed in the appendix, beginning p. 412). Extension personnel can provide you with the necessary forms and information for soil testing, or you can contact a state-certified soil testing laboratory listed in the phone book.

Take separate soil samples for each type of planting: one for the lawn, another for flowers, and a third for trees and shrubs. Remove several plugs of soil from the garden area to be tested. Take the soil from the top 4 to 6 inches from different areas throughout the garden. Mix these soil plugs together and allow the mixture to dry. Send 1 cup of this soil mix to the lab for analysis. Your results will be in the mail within two to three weeks.

The soil test report tells you how much and what type of fertilizer to use for the type of plant you are growing. It also tells you the soil pH and what, if anything, should be done to adjust it.

Amending Soil pH

Soil pH affects nutrient availability. Urban soils tend to be alkaline. Iron and manganese are not readily available in these high-pH soils. The nutrients are in the soil, they are just not available to the plants. That creates problems for acid-loving plants such as rhododendrons, red maples, and white oaks. It is very difficult to lower the soil pH. Incorporating elemental sulfur and organic matter can slightly lower the pH. Using acidifying fertilizers, chelated iron and manganese, and organic mulch will help. But all of these methods can take years to lower the pH and have a minimal impact. It is much easier on you and the plant to grow species adapted to high-pH soils.

Acidic soils occur in sandy, wet organic soils in Minnesota. The phosphorus, calcium, and magnesium are tied up in these soils and are unavailable to the plants. Many gardeners add lime to raise the soil pH. Follow soil test recommendations carefully. It takes years to correct improperly limed soils. Never lime alkaline soils.

Selecting a Fertilizer

Your soil test report will tell you what type of fertilizer to add. The main nutrients are nitrogen, phosphorus, and potassium. The percentage of each of these nutrients contained in a fertilizer are represented by the three numbers on the bag. For example, a 15-10-5 fertilizer has 15 percent nitrogen, 10 percent phosphorus, and 5 percent potassium.

Nitrogen stimulates leaf and stem growth. It is used in relatively large amounts by the plants. This mobile element moves through the soil quickly. You can use slow-release forms to provide plants with small amounts of nitrogen over a longer period of time. These products also reduce the risk of fertilizer burn. Excess nitrogen encourages leafy growth and discourages flowering. It also leaches through the soil, harming our lakes, streams, and ground water.

Phosphorus is the middle number on the bag. Phosphorus stimulates root development and flowering. This nutrient is used in small amounts by the plants and moves very slowly through the soil. Excess phosphorus can interfere with the uptake of other nutrients and damage our lakes and streams.

Potassium is used in even smaller amounts by plants. It is essential in many plant processes and helps the plants prepare for winter.

Urban soils tend to be high in phosphorus and potassium. That comes from years of using complete fertilizers, like 10-10-10 and 12-12-12. Excessive amounts of one nutrient can interfere with the uptake of other nutrients. You can't remove the excess nutrients, but you can stop adding to the problem by following your soil test recommendations.

Test your soil every three to five years, or as problems arise. That will allow you to adjust your fertilizer program to your soil and the plants you are growing. This practice will save you money, improve plant growth, and help our environment.

Pest Management

Once your plants are growing, some unwelcome visitors may enter the landscape. These pests come in the form of weeds, diseases, insects, and plant-devouring wildlife. A healthy plant is your best defense against pests. Even with proper planting and care, you may need to intercede to help plants through difficult times.

Weed Control

You will simplify your life by eliminating existing weeds before planting. They can be removed with regular cultivation one season prior to planting. Another option is to cover the planting area with black plastic for at least one full growing season to "smother the weeds." A more attractive method involves wood chips and newspaper. Prepare the soil, and then spread several layers of newspaper covered with wood chips over it. You may need an extra set of hands to keep the newspapers from ending up in the neighbor's yard. The newspaper helps smother the weeds, but eventually breaks down and improves the soil. Plant through the mulch into the soil below. Or use a total vegetation killer such as Roundup for quicker results. You can plant treated areas in one to two weeks. Remember, these products will kill any green plant they contact. Be sure to read and carefully follow label directions.

I have had good luck mulching around trees or converting lawn areas into gardens using the following technique:

Kill the grass and weeds using a total vegetation killer, leaving the dead grass in place to act as the first layer of mulch. Cover the dead grass with wood chips, twice-shredded bark, or another organic material. The dead grass eventually decomposes, adding organic matter to the soil. The dead grass continues to control the weeds. Plant right through the mulch and dead grass.

Planting is easier the year after the dead grass layer has decomposed. You need to start with good soil for this planting method to work.

Mulch the soil after planting. This step will prevent many weed seeds from sprouting. Any that do creep through will be easy to pull. Heavily mulched soils may need some additional nitrogen fertilizer. Cultivation with a hoe or weeding tool will also work to control weeds. Be careful not to damage the roots of your garden plants.

Dealing with Diseases

Leaf spots, stem rots, mildew, and blights are just a few of the diseases found on plants. Growing the right plant in the right location will reduce the risk of infection. Proper soil preparation will help reduce rot problems. Remove infected leaves as soon as they appear. Fall cleanup will reduce disease infection the following season. Most disease problems develop in response to the weather. You will have problems some years and not others. Plants are usually more tolerant of these problems than the gardener. Contact the Minnesota State Horticultural Society, University of Minnesota Extension Service, certified arborists, or other landscape professionals for help in identifying and controlling these problems.

Managing Insects

As you battle the insects, remember that less than 3 percent of all the insects throughout the world are classified as pests. Many more are beneficial and desirable to have in your garden. Keep in mind insecticides also kill aphid-eating ladybugs and the caterpillars that turn into beautiful butterflies. Try some environmental (and often fun) control techniques before reaching for the spray can. Always read and follow label directions carefully before using any pesticide.

Aphids are small teardrop-shaped insects that come in a variety of colors. They suck the plant juices causing the leaves to yellow, wilt, brown, curl, and become distorted. They also secrete a clear sticky substance on the leaves called honeydew. It doesn't hurt the plant, but a black fungus, called sooty mold, may develop on the honeydew. You can wait and let the ladybugs move in and devour this pest or try spraying the plants with a strong blast of water. You can also use insecticidal soap, which is effective for killing softbody insects, but is gentle on the plant and the environment. You may need several applications to control large populations.

Mites cause similar damage. You need a hand lens to see these pests. Like aphids, they suck plant juices and cause leaves to bronze, wilt, and brown. Don't wait to see the webs before you treat the mites. Sprays of water and insecticidal soap will help control this pest.

Slugs are slimy creatures that eat holes in the leaves of hostas and other garden plants. They feed at night, so you will notice the damage before you see the slugs. Slugs love cool, dark, damp locations and multiply quickly in wet weather. Stale beer in a shallow dish makes a great slug trap. A fellow gardener shared a good tip with me: *Lay a partially filled beer bottle on its side in the garden. Tuck it out of sight under the plant leaves. The bottle keeps the beer from being diluted by rain, so it won't need frequent replacing.* The slugs really do crawl in the small hole, drown in the beer, and die. Or try one of the new and more environmentally-friendly products such as Sluggo® and Escargot®. These contain Iron phosphate which kills the slugs, but doesn't harm the environment. Commercial slug baits are also available, but they are more toxic, and should be used with care around children, pets, and wildlife.

Animals in the Garden

Wildlife can be a nice addition to the landscape—until they start eating all the plants. Start by eliminating hiding and nesting areas, such as brush piles. Fence desirable plants. Sink fencing several inches into the ground to keep out meadow mice (also known as voles. This rodent kills young plantings by feeding on the trunks of trees and shrubs and the crowns of some perennials. Fences must be at least 4 feet high to keep out rabbits and over 10 feet high to keep out deer. This type of deer fencing is not very practical. Many gardeners are having luck fencing small planting beds with 4- or 5-foot-tall black or green fencing. You can see through to the garden while keeping out the deer, who seem to avoid small, fenced areas.

Scare tactics and repellents may provide some control, but I find urban wildlife very tolerant of the sounds and smells of humans. Vary the repellents and scare tactics for better results. And work with your neighbors—make sure one of you isn't feeding the wildlife while the other is trying to eliminate it from the neighborhood.

Next Year's Garden

If all these methods fail, there is always next year. Someone passed along to me a great definition of a green thumb gardener: *The green thumb gardener is someone who grows a lot of plants, kills a few without mentioning it to others, and keeps on planting!* So, take heart. If you've lost a few plants, you're probably on your way to a green thumb.

"Gardeners are not made by

sitting in the shade."

—Rudyard Kipling

"We have no wealth but the wealth of
nature. She shows us only surfaces,
but she is a million fathoms deep."

—Ralph Waldo Emerson

Annuals

THE PROMISES OF SPRING and its colorful flowers help many a Minnesota gardener survive the snow and cold of our long, dreary winters. And that's exactly what annuals provide—beautiful hues all season long.

Botanically speaking, annuals are plants that complete their life cycle (from seed to producing seeds) in a single season. Horticulturally speaking, they can be true annuals or nonhardy perennials that are replanted each year. Creating an attractive annual garden involves planning, proper planting, and a little follow-up care.

THE PLAN

Take some time to plan before you go plant shopping. I think all gardeners are guilty of buying bargain plants or hard-to-resist selections, instead of the right plant for the intended location. I like to plan my gardens all year-round. I visit botanical gardens, attend garden tours, scour garden catalogues and magazines, and talk with other gardeners to get new ideas. I then try to apply some or parts of various ideas in my own garden designs. You may want to start a section in your garden journal listing what flower combinations work, new plants you want to try, and those to avoid. If you don't have a garden journal, now is a good time to start one.

Next, gather your family or other gardening partners together. Find out what everyone wants from the garden. You may want to include flowers for cutting, drying, or crafts. And don't forget about wildlife. Annuals are great lures for birds and butterflies, which add motion and color to your garden, and may help get nongardeners interested in the landscape.

Chapter One

Think about creative combinations when you make your choices. I like to mix herbs, like 'Purple Ruffle' Basil, and decorative vegetables like 'Bright Lites' Swiss Chard in with my annuals. Their color and texture, not to mention their culinary value, make them great additions to the annual garden.

As you look through the catalogs and garden centers, note the All American Selections (AAS) logo. AAS winners have performed well in test gardens across the country. The plants were selected for their superior performance by independent AAS judges. We are lucky to have five of the AAS Display gardens here in Minnesota. You can stop by and visit the Display gardens located at University of Minnesota Landscape Arboretum in Chanhassen, the North Central Experiment Station in Grand Rapids, the Lyndale Park Gardens in Minneapolis, the West Central Experiment Station in Morris, or the University of Minnesota trial gardens in St. Paul.

Evaluate your annual garden's location. How much sun and shade will the plants receive? What's the soil like in this particular spot? If the soil is like modeling clay or as porous as a sandy beach, invest some time and money to improve it before you plant. A couple of inches of organic matter mixed into the top 6 to 12 inches of soil makes a big difference. (For more details, see the section on improving soil in "The Garden Environment," page 17.)

Now select plants that serve the desired function and tolerate, or preferably thrive in, the growing conditions. Note the height and width of each plant, and then make a sketch of your flower garden. Place tall plants in the center of island beds or at the back of flower borders. Shorter plants should be planted near the edge, and everything else can go toward the middle. Plant in rows for a more formal look and in masses or drifts for a more informal feel.

Don't limit your use of annuals to flower beds. Try them in containers, as a splash of color along the edge of a shrub bed, or intermingled with vegetables.

GETTING STARTED

Annuals can be started from seeds or purchased as transplants. Some annuals, like Zinnias and Marigolds, can be planted directly outside in the garden. Others, like Geraniums, take a long time to mature and blossom. These should be started as seeds indoors for best results. Starting your own plants from seeds takes extra work, but gives you a greater selection of new and different plant varieties.

Many gardeners prefer to buy transplants from their local garden center, greenhouse, or nursery. The extra expense provides the advantage of ready-to-plant and soon-to-bloom annuals. Select transplants with full-size green leaves and stout stems. Avoid insect- and disease-infected plants. And this is a case where bigger isn't necessarily better. Smaller plants that aren't rootbound will suffer less transplant shock than larger-blooming rootbound transplants.

PLANTING

Prepare your plants for the garden before you put them in the ground. Plants moving from the shelter of the greenhouse or your home need a little help preparing for the great outdoors. This process is called hardening off. Move the plants outdoors into partial shade. Gradually decrease watering and stop fertilizing. At the same time, increase the amount of light the plants receive

Chapter One

each day. In two weeks, the plants will be ready to move to their permanent location. Many garden centers do this job for us. Ask if you're not sure.

Carefully remove the plants from the container. Gently massage the roots before planting, which will encourage them to grow out of the rootball and into the surrounding soil. Place the plant in the ground at the same level it was growing in the container.

Water your new planting thoroughly, wetting the top 6 inches of soil. This will encourage deep, more drought-tolerant roots. Check new plantings several times per week. Once established, plants need about 1 inch of water. During dry periods, provide the needed water once a week to plants growing in clay soil and half the weekly rate twice a week to plants in sandy soil. Mulch once the soil warms.

Ageratum

Ageratum houstonianum

Other Name: Flossflower
Size: 6 to 15 inches tall by 6 to
   12 inches wide
Flowers: Blue, lavender, white, and pink
Bloom Period: Spring through frost
Color photograph on page 232.

Light Requirements:

Additional Benefits:

Ageratums have provided neat and tidy edging plants for gardeners for many years. The compact types form tight mounds covered with flowers all season long. Planted in large numbers, these annuals will provide a mass of color. The blue cultivars are often combined with red and white annuals for a patriotic display. These attention-getting annuals combine well with Dusty Miller, Salvia, Geraniums, and Marigolds. The taller types are more open, forming looser flower heads. They work well as fillers in perennial gardens or as part of an informal flower border. All Ageratums perform well in container gardens.

WHEN TO PLANT

Ageratums can be purchased as transplants or started from seeds indoors. Start seeds indoors in mid-March. Sprinkle the fine Ageratum seeds on the surface of moist, sterile, seed starter mix. Gently tamp the seeds to ensure good seed-soil contact, but do not cover the seeds. They need light to germinate. Keep the soil warm, about 70 to 75 degrees, and moist. Seeds will sprout in five to ten days. Hardened-off transplants can be planted outdoors after all danger of frost is past.

WHERE TO PLANT

Ageratums make great additions to flower gardens, containers, rock gardens, or shrub borders. The planting area should receive a full or partial day of sun. Ageratums prefer moist, well-drained soil. Adding organic matter will improve the water-holding ability of sandy soil and the drainage of heavy clay soil.

HOW TO PLANT

Space compact plants 6 inches apart. Taller cultivars can be spaced up to 9 inches apart. Plant the transplants at the same depth they were growing in the container.

CARE AND MAINTENANCE

If placed properly, ageratums require little maintenance. Make sure the soil is slightly dry before watering. Too much water can lead to root rot. Occasional deadheading will keep the plants blooming throughout the season. Leggy plants can be cut back halfway to encourage more attractive growth. Powdery mildew may be a problem, but it can be avoided by planting in a sunny area with good air circulation.

ADDITIONAL INFORMATION

Add Ageratums to the landscape to help attract butterflies to your yard. It only takes a few Ageratums in a planter or as an edging plant to lure butterflies to the garden. Tall types of Ageratum can be used for cut flowers.

ADDITIONAL SPECIES, CULTIVARS, OR VARIETIES

Most often, the compact types are simply sold as blue, white, or pink Ageratums. Selecting a named cultivar will help ensure you get the size, flowering, and growth habit desired. The 'Hawaii' Series is compact (6 inches), with blue, royal blue, or white flowers. 'Blue Danube' is slightly larger (7 inches), with a uniform growth habit. 'Swing Pink' is a compact (6 to 8 inches), pink-flowering cultivar. 'Leilani Blue' is a new variety for cutting. Plants reach 14 to 16 inches tall, 10 to 12 inches wide. The flowers are big, fluffy, mid-blue, and do not need deadheading.

 Did You Know?

The name Ageratum comes from Greek meaning not old. This feature is truly reflected by the long-lasting blooms, although as the white flowers fade, they can look a little unkempt.

Alyssum

Lobularia maritima

Other Name: Sweet Alyssum
Size: 4 to 8 inches tall by 10 to
   15 inches wide
Flowers: White, pink, or lavender
Bloom Period: Spring through frost
Color photograph on page 232.

Light Requirements:

Additional Benefits:

Sweet Alyssum is a longtime favorite of gardeners. If you have not tried it or no longer grow it, consider adding Alyssum to your garden. The lovely fragrance makes a nice addition to any landscape. Alyssum is one of those annuals that may reseed in your garden. It's never happened to you? Maybe you cultivated it out before planting your new annuals. This is one case where procrastination is rewarded with scattered plants of Alyssum.

WHEN TO PLANT

Alyssum can be purchased as a transplant or started from seeds indoors. Start seeds indoors in mid-March. Sprinkle the seeds on the surface of moist, sterile, seed starter mix. Gently tamp the seeds to ensure good seed-soil contact, but do not cover them. Alyssum needs light to germinate. Keep the soil warm, 70 degrees, and moist. Seeds will sprout in about eight days. Alyssum seedlings are susceptible to damping-off, a fungal disease. Avoid this problem by using a sterile mix and keeping it moist, but not too wet. Seeds can be sown directly outdoors after the last hard frost. These plants will bloom much later than those started indoors. Hardened-off transplants can be planted outdoors after all danger of frost is past.

WHERE TO PLANT

Its delicate features and profusion of blooms make Alyssum an eye-catching plant, whether it is used in the flower garden or a planter. Try using Alyssum as an edging plant in your annual flower beds or rose gardens. It mixes well with other container plants as it spills over the edge of the planter. Alyssum can also be used to provide some color while softening the look of steppers and planting walls. And don't forget to add Alyssum plants to your butterfly garden.

How to Plant

Plant Alyssum transplants 6 to 8 inches apart for complete and quick cover. Plant transplants at the same depth they were growing in the container. Water thoroughly and allow the soil to dry slightly before watering again. Over-watering and deep planting can lead to damping-off. Spread seeds on well-prepared soil when you are planting directly outdoors. Lightly tamp them to ensure seed-soil contact. Water to keep the soil slightly moist until the seeds germinate, then reduce watering to avoid damping-off.

Care and Maintenance

Alyssum is low maintenance, free flowering, and basically pest free. Plants need very little care when grown in moist well-drained soil. Extreme heat may cause the plants, especially the purple ones, to stop flowering. Clip back leggy plants and wait. Plants will begin flowering as soon as temperatures cool.

Additional Information

Alyssum is at its peak in cool weather, and will even tolerate a light frost, giving you a good fall show. Try direct seeding Alyssum around spring-flowering bulbs. As the foliage fades, the Alyssum will grow, covering the declining foliage and filling in the empty space.

Additional Species, Cultivars, or Varieties

Plants are often sold simply as white, pink, or purple Alyssum. Several cultivars are generally available in the garden centers. Two commonly seen white cultivars are 'New Carpet of Snow', a 3- to 4-inch spreading plant, and 'Snow Crystals', a low grower with larger flowers and good heat tolerance. The 'Easter Bonnet' cultivars are compact, uniform in size and come in pink, violet, or mixed colors. 'Rosie O'Day' is a 4-inch low-growing spreader with lavender-rose flowers.

Annual Pinks

Dianthus chinensis

Other Names: Garden Pinks, Indian Pinks, Rainbow Pinks
Size: 6 to 12 inches tall and up to 12 inches wide
Flowers: Red, pink, white, and bicolored
Bloom Period: Summer through fall
Color photograph on page 232.

Light Requirements:

Additional Benefits:

Garden Pinks are an old-time favorite that have many relatively new, award-winning cultivars. Their informal growth habit, lightly scented flowers, and blue-green foliage make them a nice addition to the flower garden. It seems gardeners either love or hate this plant. If you have cool temperatures and well-drained soil, Annual Pinks will bloom all season long. Otherwise they tend to become unkempt and need a little grooming or a trip to the compost pile. Use Annual Pinks for early- and late-season interest. Garden Pinks also provide nectar for butterflies when little else is blooming.

WHEN TO PLANT

Pinks are available as seeds or transplants. Hardened-off transplants will tolerate a light frost and can be moved outdoors several weeks prior to the last spring frost. Start Garden Pinks from seeds indoors about 8 to 10 weeks before the last spring frost. The seeds need moist 70-degree temperatures to germinate within a week.

WHERE TO PLANT

Cool summer temperatures and well-drained soil are the keys to success. Grow Annual Pinks in an area that receives full to partial sun. An east location, where plants are shaded from the hot afternoon sun, works well. Avoid poorly drained locations. Gardeners with heavy clay soil should add organic matter to improve drainage. Avoid overwatering since too much moisture will kill these plants.

HOW TO PLANT

Plant transplants of the smaller cultivars about 6 inches apart. Larger ones can be spaced up to 12 inches apart. Or try planting the seeds directly in the garden for a late-season flower display. Plant seeds outside after all danger of frost has passed.

CARE AND MAINTENANCE

Believe it or not, our summers can actually get too hot for Annual Pinks. Trim back unsightly plants during hot weather. Cool temperatures and occasional deadheading, or the removal of faded flowers, will keep this plant blooming all season long. You may need to increase care if the weather turns hot. Cut unsightly plants back halfway and wait. Once temperatures cool, the plants will reward you with fresh new growth and flowers. Avoid high-nitrogen fertilizers that can discourage flowering and cause tip burn on the leaves. With a little protection and cooperation from nature, these plants will sometimes survive our winters.

ADDITIONAL INFORMATION

The attractive, fragrant flowers helped name this plant. The botanical name, *Dianthus*, comes from the Greek meaning divine flower. The common name, Pinks, doesn't refer to its flower color, but rather to the frilly edges of the flowers. The flower edges appear to be cut with pinking shears.

ADDITIONAL SPECIES, CULTIVARS, OR VARIETIES

There are several All American Selection-winning Annual Pinks. The 'Telstar' Series was selected for its early bloom, compact growth habit, and heat tolerance. The 'Parfait' Series also provides a compact growth habit with single-frilled flowers. The 'Carpet' Series, available in five colors or as a mix, will give you a 6- to 8-inch-high carpet of bloom.

 Did You Know?

The annual carnation (Dianthus caryophyllus) *is a close relative of Garden Pinks. It has fragrant, showy flowers. Cultivars of this plant are used by florists as cut flowers. Select one of the more heat-tolerant types such as the 1982 AAS winner, 'Scarlet Luminette'.*

Begonia

Begonia semperflorens-cultorum

Other Names: Wax Begonia,
  Fibrous-rooted Begonia,
  Bedding Begonia
Size: 6 to 12 inches tall and wide
Flowers: White, red, or pink
Bloom Period: Summer to frost
Color photograph on page 232.

Light Requirements:

Additional Benefits:

Begonia is a standard plant for park, municipal, business, and home landscapes. This durable choice provides attractive foliage and a season of bloom with minimal care. Wax Begonia leaves are glossy and come in green or bronze. The bronze-leafed cultivars tend to be more sun tolerant. Individual flowers are small and can be single or double. Though the blooms are diminutive, they are large in number. No matter what type you choose, Wax Begonias will give an impressive display.

WHEN TO PLANT

Most gardeners buy transplants. Hardened-off transplants can be placed outside in late May or early June, after all danger of frost is past. Patient gardeners with steady hands and good eyes may want to try starting Begonias from seeds. The tiny seeds (2 million per ounce) need about 4¹/₂ months to develop into flowering plants. Begonia seeds need light, moisture, and 70-degree temperatures to germinate.

WHERE TO PLANT

Begonias can grow in a wide range of light conditions. They prefer partial shade, but will tolerate full sun if the soil is kept moist. In heavy shade, be careful not to overwater. Shaded soil is slow to dry and it is easy for gardeners to overwater. Adding organic matter to most Minnesota soils will increase the health and vigor of the plants. Begonias look great when used as an edging plant, en masse in a flower bed, or as an annual groundcover. Try using them in containers and hanging baskets. They perform well in many of the new planters, such as the hanging bag, pole, and vertical wall planters.

How to Plant

Wax Begonia transplants can be purchased in flats or small 3- to 4-inch pots. Plant Begonias at the same depth they were growing in the container. Space small cultivars about 6 to 8 inches apart. Larger cultivars can be planted 8 to 12 inches apart. Proper spacing will help prevent disease problems.

Care and Maintenance

Begonias need very little care. Make sure the soil is moist but not overly wet. The small flowers will give you a great display without regular deadheading. Wax Begonias are susceptible to several fungal diseases. Powdery mildew, botrytis blight, leaf spots, and stem rots are the most common. Most of these can be avoided with good soil preparation and proper spacing of the plants. Avoid over-head watering and use good sanitation to help reduce disease problems. Remove diseased flowers and leaves as soon as they appear. I find deadheading during wet weather helps reduce botrytis blight and leaf spot diseases.

Additional Information

Begonias can be wintered indoors. Take cuttings from healthy plants in late August or September. Root the cuttings in moist vermiculite or perlite. Once rooted, the cuttings can be planted in any well-drained potting mix. Grow them in a sunny window with good air circulation. You can also bring the whole plant indoors. Dig and repot plants before the first frost. Grow Begonias as houseplants in a sunny window. I prefer the cutting method. The smaller plant takes up less indoor growing space, and there is less risk of bringing unwanted pests indoors.

Additional Species, Cultivars, or Varieties

Check garden catalogs and local garden centers for the many Begonia cultivars. The 'Cocktail' Series has bronze leaves, comes in a variety of colors, and tolerates full sun.

Cleome

Cleome hasslerana

Other Names: Spider Cleome,
   Spider Flower
Size: Up to 6 feet tall and 2 feet wide
Flowers: White, pink, rose, purple
Bloom Period: Summer through fall
Color photograph on page 232.

Light Requirements:

Additional Benefits:

When driving through any Minnesota city you are bound to witness the beauty of these large, delicate flowers. Plantings of Cleomes along city boulevards and in county parks are designed to catch the eyes of passersby. And that they do. The blooms are held over attractive foliage, making this tall plant an excellent backdrop to flower borders or a striking centerpiece in an island bed. If you have a new landscape, consider using these plants as a temporary shrub. You will have a large plant, beautiful flowers, and time to let your other plants fill in the empty space.

WHEN TO PLANT

Start seeds indoors about six weeks before the last frost. Seeds can be purchased or collected from existing plants. Place collected seeds in the freezer for one week before planting. Provide seeds with light and warm (80 degrees) temperatures for germination. Transplants can be planted outdoors after all danger of frost is past.

WHERE TO PLANT

Cleomes prefer full sun but will tolerate partial shade. They grow in a variety of soils. Although they are very tolerant of heat and drought, they will also benefit from ample moisture. Cleomes are large plants that require space. Try using them as a background plant, or as the focal point of a flower garden. Do you have a brand new yard? Cleomes provide the size and color often lacking in undeveloped landscapes. They can be used to fill in voids left between properly spaced young shrubs. Perhaps you need a little time to decide on your permanent plantings. Cleomes can give you a big display while you make up your mind.

How to Plant

Cleome transplants are usually sold in 3- or 4-inch pots. Purchased or home-grown transplants should be hardened off, and then planted outdoors after all danger of frost is past. Remember, these are big plants that need lots of space. Allow at least 2 feet between plants. Cleomes often reseed themselves in the garden. These seedlings should be thinned or moved to the desired planting location.

Care and Maintenance

Cleomes require very little maintenance. You may have to weed out a few unwanted plants the following year.

Additional Information

The common name, Spider Flower, aptly describes the flower. The long stamen extends beyond the petals giving the plant a light, airy appearance. The long, thin seedpods are also attractive and add to the 'spidery' look. Cleome is a great cut flower with an interesting fragrance, often described as skunk-like. Use Cleomes to help attract butterflies to the landscape.

Additional Species, Cultivars, or Varieties

'Sparkler Blush' is the AAS selection for 2002. The flowers are huge 4- to 6-inch clusters in pink with a flush of white. They have a nice uniform growth habit, long bloomtime, and terrific heat and sun tolerance. Plants reach $3^{1}/_{2}$ to 4 feet. 'Helen Campbell' and the 'Queen' Series are long-time favorites. 'Helen Campbell' is 4 feet tall with white flowers. The 'Queen' Series is also 4 feet tall, but has larger flowers of rose, purple, pink, white, or cherry.

 Did You Know?

The former botanical name, Cleome spinosa, *describes the small spines at the base of the leaves. Keep this in mind when placing and weeding around the plants. One gardener told me all her guests received a prickly hug from the cleomes growing next to her front door.*

Cockscomb

Celosia argentea

Other Name: *Celosia cristata*
Size: 6 to 30 inches tall
Flowers: Red, yellow, gold, orange, pink
Bloom Period: Summer through fall

Color photograph on page 232.

Light Requirements:

Additional Benefits:

B right, bold, and tough, Cockscomb is a good choice for hot, dry areas. Even when grown in tough sites, this plant provides a bold splash of color outdoors in the garden or indoors in a vase. The flowers can be crested like a rooster's comb, or plumed like a feather. They come in warm colors of red, yellow, gold, orange, and pink. In fact, the botanical name, *Celosia,* refers to the flower color. It is Greek for burned. Cockscomb leaves are green or bronze and set beneath the flowers.

WHEN TO PLANT

Start Cockscomb seeds indoors eight weeks prior to the last spring frost. The seeds need light, moisture, and 70- to 75-degree temperatures to germinate. Lightly cover the seeds to prevent them from drying out. Transplants can be moved outdoors after all danger of frost is past. Don't be too anxious to move the plants outdoors. Cool soil and air temperatures can stunt the plants.

WHERE TO PLANT

Cockscomb performs best in full sun and well-drained soil. Add organic matter to heavy clay or rocky soil for best results. A mass planting of Cockscomb makes a bold statement in any landscape. I find the crested types a bit more challenging to blend with other flowers. Try using the short, crested types as edging plants. Use the taller types of plume, or crested, Celosia in the middle or the back of the flower border. Celosia's drought tolerance makes it a good candidate for container gardens. Be sure to include a few in the cutting garden for fresh or dried use.

HOW TO PLANT

Hardened-off transplants can be placed outdoors after the last frost. Space small cultivars 6 to 8 inches apart and larger ones 12 to

15 inches apart. Cockscomb can be seeded directly outdoors, although plants started outdoors will bloom much later. Wait until the soil is warm to plant seeds outdoors. Lightly cover the seeds and keep them moist. Thin plantings to the proper spacing for the type of Celosia grown.

CARE AND MAINTENANCE

If properly placed, Celosias need very little care. Poorly drained soil can result in stem rot and leaf spot. Mites may be a problem in hot, dry weather. A strong blast of water from the garden hose or insecticidal soap is often enough to keep mites under control. Occasionally deadhead or harvest flowers to keep the plants blooming all season long.

ADDITIONAL INFORMATION

The dense Celosia flowers make great hiding places for insects. Lightly spray the blooms with water before bringing them indoors. This will help dislodge any unwanted guests. Celosias are easily dried by hanging the blossoms upside down. The flower color seems to intensify as it dries.

ADDITIONAL SPECIES, CULTIVARS, OR VARIETIES

'Jewel Box' is a dwarf crested type. It comes in a variety of colors and grows 5 to 6 inches tall. 'Apricot Brandy' and the 'Castles' Series are both AAS winners with plume-type flowers and plants of medium height. 'Prestige Scarlet' is a 1997 AAS winner. It is a 12- to 15-inch-tall plant with large and small red-crested flowers. Celosia spicata cultivars such as 'Flamingo Feather' and 'Pink Candle' have smaller, barley-like flower spikes. They are outstanding in the landscape and make excellent cut flowers.

 Did You Know?

The crested-flower types of Celosia are the result of fasciation, a process of abnormal cell growth. The fasciation produces enlarged flattened stems with lots of buds. Fasciation also occurs in other plants such as Lilies, Cacti, and Willows.

Coleus

Solenostemon scutellarioides

Other Name: *Coleus × hybridus*
Size: 6 to 24 inches tall by 12 inches wide
Flowers: Grown for colorful leaves
Bloom Period: Colorful foliage provides
season-long interest
Color photograph on page 232.

Light Requirements:

Many of you may know Coleus as a houseplant first and a bedding plant second. That's the case for me. An easy-to-grow indoor plant, Coleus is equally at home in the garden. This annual is grown for its colorful foliage, not its flowers. Breeding efforts have resulted in a wide variety of leaf shapes, colors, and variegated patterns. Minimal flowering and self-branching types are also available. These features result in less maintenance and a better-looking plant. Try Coleus in flower beds or containers. Planted en masse they put on quite a show.

WHEN TO PLANT

Coleus plants can be purchased as transplants or started from seeds and cuttings. Start seeds indoors eight weeks before the final spring frost. Seeds need light, moisture, and 70-degree temperatures to germinate. Cuttings can be taken any time indoors. Allow at least four weeks for cuttings to develop a sustainable root system before planting them outdoors. Coleus is very frost sensitive, so wait until late May or early June when all danger of frost is past before placing hardened-off transplants outdoors.

WHERE TO PLANT

Coleus prefers moist soil with lots of organic matter. Add compost, peat moss, or another organic material to the soil prior to planting. This is especially necessary when growing Coleus in full sun. Coleus performs best in partial shade, although it will tolerate shade and full sun. Plants grown in heavy shade can become thin and leggy. The leaves of those grown in full sun may fade and even scorch. Make sure plants grown in full sun receive sufficient moisture. Mulching will help keep the roots cool and moist.

How to Plant

Buy Coleus as bedding plants in flats or small, 3- to 4-inch pots. Plant Coleus transplants at the same depth they were growing in the container. Space 10 to 12 inches apart.

Care and Maintenance

Remove flowers as soon as they appear. This will encourage new branches to form, giving you a fuller, more compact plant. The self-branching types of Coleus produce only a few flowers and require very little pruning. Slugs may be a problem on Coleus grown in the shade. Shallow dishes filled with beer are effective traps for slugs.

Additional Information

Coleus will die with the first fall frost. In Minnesota, there are often several good growing weeks after this. So make plans to remove and replace the Coleus, or live with the voids left by the frost-killed plants. There is nothing more unsightly than an entry garden filled with dead plants. You can keep enjoying your plants year-round. Take cuttings of healthy Coleus in August or September. Cuttings will root quickly in moist vermiculite or perlite. Plant cuttings in any well-drained potting mix. Grow Coleus in a sunny window keeping the soil slightly moist. Cut the plants back throughout the winter to encourage branching. The cuttings can be rooted and used to start additional plants.

Additional Species, Cultivars, or Varieties

Check garden centers and catalogs for the wide variety of Coleus cultivars available. The plants in the 'Wizard' Series are self branching and do not require pinching. The 'Saber' Series gets its name from the long, saber-like leaves. 'Fiji' Series Coleus plants have fringed leaves. 'India Frills' has small, colorful, irregular leaves on a full, compact plant. 'Palisandra' has very dark, nearly black foliage.

 Did You Know?

Sun-loving Coleus, old and new cultivars that show greater sun tolerance, have recently become quite the rage. Look for 'Solar Sunrise', 'Cranberry Salad', and the 'Hurricane Series'.

Cosmos

Cosmos species

Other Names: *Cosmos sulphureus,*
  Cosmos bipinnatus
Size: 12 to 72 inches tall and 12 to
  24 inches wide
Flowers: Yellow, orange, red, white,
  pink, rose, and purple
Bloom Period: Summer until frost
Color photograph on page 232.

Light Requirements:

Additional Benefits:

Neat and tidy, loose and wild, or somewhere in between: all these descriptions fit Cosmos. The species and cultivar you grow will determine the look you get. *Cosmos sulphureus* produces single and double yellow, orange, or orange-red flowers throughout the summer. *Cosmos bipinnatus* has finer-textured leaves and large single flowers of pink, white, red, or purple. Longtime favorites of gardeners, Cosmos blooms make great cut flowers. The taller cultivars are best used as fillers or background where the surrounding plants can provide support.

WHEN TO PLANT
Seeds can be started indoors four weeks before the last spring frost. That is the same time to start your cucumbers and melons. Seeds need moist, 70-degree starting mix to germinate. Transplants can be moved outdoors after all danger of frost is past.

WHERE TO PLANT
Cosmos does best in full sun and well-drained soil, although it will tolerate hot, dry conditions. Add these plants to the garden and you will be sure to attract butterflies. Dwarf Cosmos plants are suitable for the flower garden and container plantings. Taller cultivars, especially those of Cosmos bipinnatus, can become floppy and do better when mixed with other plants.

HOW TO PLANT
Cosmos seeds can be planted directly outside. Plant seeds or transplants after the last spring frost. Seeds should germinate in five to ten days. Thin seedlings to 12 inches. Cosmos can also be purchased

as bedding plants in flats. Plant hardened-off transplants 12 inches apart.

CARE AND MAINTENANCE

Minimal care is needed to keep the plants producing beautiful flowers. Avoid overfertilizing since too much nitrogen will give you tall, leafy plants that tend to fall over. Pinch back tall cultivars of *Cosmos bipinnatus* early in the season to promote fuller, sturdier plants.

ADDITIONAL INFORMATION

Once you plant Cosmos you will be rewarded with seedlings the following year. Keep in mind that seedlings of hybrids will not always look like or grow the same size as the original plant.

ADDITIONAL SPECIES, CULTIVARS, OR VARIETIES

The 'Sonata' Series of Cosmos produces dwarf plants 12 to 18 inches tall with white, pink, and red flowers. Another *C. bipinnatus* cultivar to consider is 'Sea Shells'. This 36-inch-tall plant has fluted flowers of white, pink, and crimson that resemble a shell. If you want a cosmos plant to use for bedding, consider one of the dwarf *Cosmos sulphureus*. The 'Ladybird' Series produces semi-double flowers of orange, scarlet, and yellow on 12-inch plants. 'Sunny Delight' was the 1987 AAS winner. It has bright red flowers with a yellow center. The plants are 12 to 14 inches tall.

Did You Know?

The name Cosmos *is from the Greek kosmos meaning beautiful. The* bipinnatus *refers to the bi-pinnate, or feathery, leaves. In the other species,* sulphureus *refers to the sulphur-yellow flowers.*

Dusty Miller

Senecio cineraria

Other Name: *Cineraria maritima*
Size: 6 to 15 inches tall
Flowers: Silver-white colored foliage
Bloom Period: Foliage effective all
  season long
Color photograph on page 232.

Light Requirements:

Additional Benefits:

The silvery-gray foliage of Dusty Miller provides a nice contrast in the flower garden. The leaves can be slightly lobed or deeply divided and lacy, depending on the cultivar. It is often used as an edging plant in rose gardens. The fine-textured silvery foliage contrasts nicely with the glossy green leaves of the roses. The light-colored leaves stand out in the night landscape. And for the multitalented gardener—try pressing the leaves for craft projects.

WHEN TO PLANT

Seeds should be started indoors about ten weeks before the last frost. Use a well-drained, sterile seed starting mix. Spread the seeds on the surface of the mix and water. Do not cover the seeds. Keep the planting mix at 75 degrees. Do not overwater; these plants are susceptible to dampening-off disease, a fungal problem. Plant hardened-off transplants outdoors after all danger of a hard frost is past. Dusty Miller can tolerate a light frost.

WHERE TO PLANT

Dusty Miller prefers full sun and well-drained soil. It will tolerate light shade, but NOT wet feet. Add organic matter such as peat moss or compost to heavy clay soil. Combine Dusty Miller with other annuals in containers. Use the silver foliage as a foil for other plants. Place Dusty Miller behind a dark blue or a deep purple flower. The contrast will make the dark-colored flowers more noticeable. Or use the silvery foliage to provide visual relief or continuity in a multicolored flower bed. Dusty Miller is often used as an edging plant. Use it with care. I have seen its bold features create an out-of-place formal edge when it was used in an informal garden.

HOW TO PLANT

Plants are available at garden centers as bedding plants in flats. Harden off purchased or home-grown transplants prior to planting outdoors. Space the plants 8 to 10 inches apart.

CARE AND MAINTENANCE

This is a low-maintenance, easy-to-grow plant when it is placed in the right spot. Avoid stem and root rot with proper watering. Water the soil thoroughly and allow it to dry slightly before watering again. You may need to trim back some of the unruly plants to keep them full and compact. Many of the newer cultivars have been bred to maintain a compact growth habit without shearing.

ADDITIONAL INFORMATION

Dusty Miller will tolerate light frosts. Include a few in the garden where they can be enjoyed in the fall. Dusty Miller will give you enjoyment long after your other annuals have been killed by frost. These frost-tolerant plants have been known to occasionally survive Minnesota winters. I know gardeners who have kept the same plant for several years. A protected location, a mild winter, and luck seem to be the keys to success with Dusty Miller.

ADDITIONAL SPECIES, CULTIVARS, OR VARIETIES

Select a cultivar that has the foliage, texture, and size you want. 'Silver Queen', 'Silver Dust', and 'Silver Lace' are all compact, 6- to 8-inch-tall plants with lacy foliage. 'Silver Lace' has the most finely divided leaves. 'Cirrus' is slightly taller, with rounded, only slightly lobed leaves.

 Did You Know?

Have you ever seen a Dusty Miller bloom? They can produce small, cream or yellow, daisy-like flowers. In Minnesota, the flowers usually don't appear until the late fall of an unusually long growing season, or the second year on plants that survived the winter. You should trim off the flowers to keep the plants and foliage attractive. I occasionally leave a few flowers so I can enjoy the seldom-seen blooms.

Flowering Tobacco

Nicotiana alata

Other Name: Ornamental Tobacco
Size: 10 inches to 5 feet tall and 6 to 24 inches wide
Flowers: White, red, pink, lavender, green, and yellow
Bloom Period: Summer until frost
Color photograph on page 232.

Light Requirements:

Additional Benefits:

Looking for a showy alternative to Geraniums? This free-flowering plant will produce a floral display all season long. Flowering Tobacco has star-shaped flowers with long throats. These are perfect blooms for attracting hummingbirds. The flower clusters are held above the leaves, creating a colorful display that moves with the breeze. Many of the Flowering Tobacco plants are fragrant, which is another big plus.

WHEN TO PLANT

Start seeds indoors about eight weeks before the last spring frost. Flowering Tobacco seeds need light, moisture, and 70-degree temperatures to germinate. Sprinkle the seeds on the surface of the starting mix. Lightly tamp and water the seeds. Hardened-off transplants can be moved outdoors after all danger of frost is past.

WHERE TO PLANT

Flowering Tobacco prefers full sun to partial shade. It prefers moist, well-drained soil, but will tolerate an occasional dry spell. Shorter cultivars can be planted en masse as bedding plants or used in containers. Larger cultivars serve as specimen or background plants. Even these larger cultivars can be effectively used in container plantings. Include any of the Nicotianas in the cutting garden. Though they are a little sticky to the touch, they hold up well as cut flowers. Try adding a few Flowering Tobacco plants to the perennial garden. Their informal growth habit and smaller flowers help them fit right in.

HOW TO PLANT

You can purchase Nicotianas as bedding plants in flats from most garden centers. Transplants should be spaced 8 to 12 inches apart depending on the cultivar. The larger cultivars need a little more space, since their lower leaves may grow more than 12 inches long. Flowering Tobacco plants will reseed themselves in your garden. Most of the seedlings tend to be taller, wider, and more fragrant than their hybrid parent.

CARE AND MAINTENANCE

Flowering Tobacco is easy to grow. Once it is established, it can tolerate dry periods. Even properly watered plants may appear wilted in the hot afternoon sun. So before you water, wait until the temperature cools to see if the plants recover. Though free flowering all season long, an occasional deadheading will help keep the display fresh and full. Healthy plants will tolerate the few diseases and insects that can attack. With the increased use of Flowering Tobacco, we are seeing an increase in damage by Colorado potato beetles. These insects eat holes in the leaves, and large populations of Colorado potato beetles can be quite damaging. Mechanical controls are often sufficient. Some of you may remember picking these insects off vegetable plants when you were children. It is an effective nonchemical way to control these pests. Plus, I find insects are a great way to get some children into the garden.

ADDITIONAL INFORMATION

Some Nicotiana cultivars are very fragrant. Their light fragrance fills the evening air, making Flowering Tobacco a welcome addition in any garden. I always include a few plants near the garage or my front door for a fragrant welcome home.

ADDITIONAL SPECIES, CULTIVARS, OR VARIETIES

The 'Nikki' Series is popular and readily available. They generally have good fragrance, come in a variety of colors, and grow 18 to 24 inches tall. The 'Domino' Series is more compact and starts flowering earlier than the 'Nikki' Series. *Nicotiana sylvestris* is a big plant that produces fragrant white flowers. The face of the flower is smaller and the throat is longer than Flowering Tobacco. The plant grows 5 feet tall and does not need staking. This is one that is sure to make your neighbors take a second look. *Nicotiana langsdorfii* 'Variegata' is a distinctive variety with lime green blossoms that hang downwards. The leaves are splashed with white.

Fuchsia

Fuchsia × hybrida

Other Name: Lady's-Eardrops
Size: 8 inches to 3 feet tall by 12 to
  24 inches wide
Flowers: Pinks, reds, purples, white
Bloom Period: Summer until frost
Color photograph on page 232.

Light Requirements:

Additional Benefits:

Fuchsias are traditional favorites for shade-tolerant hanging baskets. The single, semidouble and double pendulous flowers create a lovely display. Most gardeners are less familiar with the upright forms. These are nice additions to the shade garden.

WHEN TO PLANT

Most gardeners start with purchased or overwintered plants. Fuchsia can be moved outdoors after all danger of frost is past. Cuttings can be taken and rooted in the early spring. These plants can be hardened off and moved outdoors after all danger of frost is past. Fuchsias can also be started from seed. You will need to order them from one of the specialized garden catalogues.

WHERE TO PLANT

Fuchsias need full to partial shade. Avoid hot sun and windy locations. The trailing types can be planted in hanging baskets and containers. Try mixing Fuchsias with other shade-tolerant plants to create a different look. Use tree-trained Fuchsias as specimen or patio plants. You will need a place to winter them indoors. Upright forms can be used in containers or as bedding plants. Some of the Micro-fuchsias and Minifuchsias are good accents for small areas and blend more readily with other plants. All Fuchsias attract hummingbirds.

HOW TO PLANT

Fuchsias are available as hanging baskets or in 3- to 4-inch pots. The smaller plants can be potted up in hanging baskets or other containers. Plant your own hanging basket using three plants for an 8-inch pot and four plants for a 10-inch pot. The upright types can be planted in the ground. Space larger upright cultivars 12 inches apart.

CARE AND MAINTENANCE

Fuchsias require moist soil. Check the soil moisture in hanging baskets and containers at least once a day. Check pots twice a day during hot weather. Water containers thoroughly, allowing excess water to run out the drainage holes. Fertilize planters frequently throughout the summer. Use any flowering plant fertilizer according to the label directions. Pinch back faded flowers to keep the plants blooming all summer long. Fuchsias will stop flowering during hot weather. Once the weather cools, the flowers will return.

ADDITIONAL INFORMATION

Fuchsias can be overwintered indoors like geraniums. Dormant stored Fuschias should be brought out of storage in late February. Prune them back to old wood and grow them as houseplants.

ADDITIONAL SPECIES, CULTIVARS, OR VARIETIES

Check garden centers for the many types of trailing Fuchsia. 'Thalia' is the most available upright type. It has long, tubular, orange-red flowers. Check the specialized garden centers for some of the newer Microfuchsias and Minifuchsias. 'Firecracker' is a brand new variegated Fuchsia. It produces huge bunches of rich orange-scarlet flowers. The very large leaves are variegated in olive-green and cream with pink to dark pink veining. 'Golden Marinka' is a variety with yellow and green variegated foliage, while the blooms are pink and purple.

 Did You Know?

Make your own Fuchsia tree with a 10-inch pot, a single-stem plant, and a stake. Plant the Fuchsia and tie it to the stake. Remove any side branches that form. Do not remove the leaves. Pinch out the growing tip when stem reaches the desired height. Allow branches to form along the top 8 to 12 inches of the stem. Lower leaves will drop off exposing the stem. Pinch as needed to shape the tree.

Geranium

Pelargonium × hortorum

Other Names: Zonal or Bedding Geranium
Size: 12 to 20 inches tall by 12 inches wide
Flowers: Red, pink, rose, violet, salmon,
  white
Bloom Period: Summer until frost
Color photograph on page 232.

Light Requirements:

Additional Benefits:

The Geranium is one of the most popular bedding plants. Its long history and popularity helped it become the city flower of Milwaukee, Wisconsin. Geraniums form a mound of decorative foliage at the base. The leaves are rounded with scalloped or toothed edges and may be solid green or variegated. Either type may have a zone (a ring around the middle of the leaf) of bronze-green or red. The showy flowers are held above the leaves and can be single, semidouble, or double.

WHEN TO PLANT

Sow seeds 12 to 16 weeks prior to the last spring frost. Seeds need a moist, 70- to 75-degree starting mix to germinate. Plants can also be started from cuttings taken in the spring. Most gardeners, however, purchase Geranium plants at the garden center. Hardened-off transplants can be planted outdoors after all danger of frost is past.

WHERE TO PLANT

Geraniums prefer full sun and moist, well-drained soil. They work well in containers and hanging baskets. A mass planting of geraniums will provide a season-long floral display. Try interplanting other annuals like Heliotrope for a little different look.

HOW TO PLANT

Geraniums are available from garden centers in 3- or 4-inch pots. Plant the Geraniums at the same depth they were growing in the container. Space the plants 8 to 12 inches apart.

CARE AND MAINTENANCE

Geraniums do best when they are kept cool and moist in well-drained soil. Mulch the soil to keep roots cool and moist, and the plants at peak performance. Deadhead frequently to keep the plants blooming. Geraniums grown in containers need a little extra care. Check the soil moisture at least once a day. Fertilize planters frequently with any flowering plant fertilizer. Follow label directions. Though easy to grow, Geraniums do have several pest problems. Check plants frequently for signs of damage. Bacterial leaf spot, stem rot, and botrytis blight are some of the more common diseases. Avoid these problems by purchasing disease-free plants, planting them in well-drained soil and watering properly. Remove damaged leaves as soon as they appear.

ADDITIONAL INFORMATION

Geraniums can be wintered indoors. Many gardeners dig up, pot, and bring their plants inside. Grow Geraniums in a bright, sunny window and keep the soil moist. Don't be alarmed if the plant drops most of its leaves. It will soon send out new leaves more suited for its indoor location. Another option is to take cuttings from healthy plants in late August or September. Root the cuttings in moist vermiculite or perlite. Once rooted, plant the Geranium cuttings in any well-drained potting mix and grow as a houseplant. A common, but less successful, method is dormant storage. Most of our basements are too warm for this method to work. In mid-March, bring the plants up to a warm, sunny location. Prune back to 4 inches, water, and fertilize as soon as new growth appears.

ADDITIONAL SPECIES, CULTIVARS, OR VARIETIES

There are new Geranium cultivars introduced every year. Check seed catalogs and garden centers for the cultivar best suited for your garden situation. The trailing Geranium used in hanging baskets is the Ivy Geranium (*Pelargonium peltatum*). This plant has waxy leaves and performs best in full sun and cool conditions.

Did You Know?

Scented Geraniums are also Pelargonium *species with a variety of leaf shapes, textures, and fragrance. Place these plants where you will brush against them for a fragrant surprise.*

Impatiens

Impatiens wallerana

Other Names: Busy Lizzie, Patient Lucy, Sultana

Size: 6 to 18 inches tall by 12 to 24 inches wide

Flowers: White, red, pink, orange, purple

Bloom Period: Summer through frost

Color photograph on page 233.

Light Requirements:

Additional Benefits:

Impatiens provides a sea of color for the shade garden. That's why it's such a popular annual. With its mound of green leaves covered with 1- to 2-inch-diameter single or double blooms, this free-flowering plant will reward you with color from summer through frost. Impatiens makes an impressive flowering groundcover under trees and shrubs. In containers and planters, it can be used to brighten up a shady spot on the deck or patio. Mixed with Ferns and Hostas, it adds season-long color to the perennial shade garden.

WHEN TO PLANT

Start Impatiens from seeds 12 weeks before the last spring frost. Seeds need light, moisture, and 70-degree temperatures to germinate. Be patient; it takes two to three weeks for the seeds to sprout. Impatiens is subject to damping-off disease. Use a sterile starting and don't overwater. Hardened-off transplants can be moved outdoors in late May or early June after all danger of frost is past. Don't move them outdoors too soon. They are very sensitive to frost.

WHERE TO PLANT

Impatiens plants do best in partial to full shade. Keep the soil moist but not waterlogged. Impatiens can take some sun when they are grown in moist, organic soil. Mulch the soil to keep the roots cool and moist. Impatiens can be planted in containers or in the garden. Use the plants en masse for a wave of color, as a groundcover, or mixed with other annuals and perennials in the garden.

HOW TO PLANT

Impatiens is available as a bedding plant in flats or as a hanging basket. Plant the Impatiens at the same depth it was growing in the

container. Space small cultivars 8 inches apart and larger cultivars 12 inches apart.

Care and Maintenance

Impatiens plants are easy-care annuals. Most are free flowering and won't need deadheading. The more water and fertilizer you provide, the bigger the plants grow. Dwarf plants won't stay small if you give them extra water and nutrients. Leggy or tired plants can be clipped back. Leaf spot diseases and slugs can sometimes be a problem.

Additional Information

Impatiens will die with the first fall frost. So make plans to remove and replace it, or live with the void left by the frost-killed plants. You can winter your plants indoors. Take cuttings from healthy Impatiens plants in August or September just like Geraniums (see page 53).

Additional Species, Cultivars, or Varieties

There are many cultivars of Impatiens and the number increases yearly. Most cultivars were bred to be free-flowering, compact plants. A few of the newer introductions feature yellow flowers and the more informal growth habit of the species. The 'Accent' Series offers dwarf plants, 8 inches tall, producing large flowers of many colors. 'Blitz' Impatiens produces even bigger flowers on larger, 14-inch plants. I have had good luck growing these in the sun. Impatiens 'New Guinea' is often called the Sun Impatiens. It has attractive foliage with fewer but larger flowers. I find it grows best for most gardeners in partial shade. *Impatiens balfourii* is quite different from the standard Impatiens used for bedding everywhere. This species from the western Himalayas grows to three feet high and has pink and white flowers. It naturalizes shady areas.

 Did You Know?

Our native plant, Jewelweed (Impatiens capensis *and* Impatiens pallida)*, is a tall relative of the Garden Impatiens. It can grow to 5 feet tall producing yellow and orange flowers.*

Lobelia

Lobelia erinus

Other Name: Edging Lobelia
Size: 4 to 8 inches tall by 6 to
   18 inches wide
Flowers: White, blue, rose, purple
Bloom Period: Summer to fall
Color photograph on page 233.

Light Requirements:

Additional Benefits:

Lobelia has traditionally been used in containers or as an edging plant. Cultivars can be upright types, forming mounds 4 to 8 inches tall, usually 6 inches tall. The trailing types can spread as much as 18 inches. This makes them good candidates for containers or for cascading over boulders and garden walls. The fine-textured leaves and delicate flowers add a soft touch to any garden.

WHEN TO PLANT

Start Lobelia from seed ten to twelve weeks prior to the last spring frost. Seeds need light, moisture, and 70-degree temperatures to germinate. Hardened-off transplants can be planted outdoors after all danger of frost has passed.

WHERE TO PLANT

Lobelia prefers full sun, cool temperatures, and moist, well-drained soil. Mulch the soil or plant Lobelia in partial shade to keep the roots cool and moist. An east location will provide sufficient light while avoiding the heat from the afternoon sun. Lobelias are used as bedding and edging plants. They tend to go into a midsummer heat slump, so use them in areas where this will be less noticeable. I use them in containers or rock gardens mixed with other plants so the other flowers will draw attention away from the resting Lobelias.

HOW TO PLANT

Lobelias are available from garden centers as bedding plants in flats. Plant lobelias at the same level they were growing in the container. Space plants about 6 inches apart.

CARE AND MAINTENANCE

Lobelias grow and flower best in cool weather. They often shut down and stop flowering altogether in hot weather. Lightly prune Lobelias after the first flush of flowers to encourage new leaf and flower growth. Leggy plants can be pruned back halfway. Continue to water and fertilize as needed.

ADDITIONAL INFORMATION

Lobelias can provide splashes of color throughout the landscape. They mix well with annuals planted in the ground or in containers. Their delicate texture makes them easy to blend with perennials in the garden. Container plantings with a mixture of Lobelia, Geraniums, Dusty Miller, and Spike are a traditional favorite.

ADDITIONAL SPECIES, CULTIVARS, OR VARIETIES

Select the cultivar with the growth habit and flower color you prefer. 'Crystal Palace' is a compact type with dark blue flowers and bronze foliage. This plant seems to leap out of the garden and demand your attention. 'Blue Moon' is a true blue that grows 6 inches tall. 'Rosamund' has cherry-red flowers on a 4- to 6-inch plant. Trailing types include the 'Cascade' and 'Fountain' Series. Both have a variety of colors including blue, white, and red. 'Sapphire' is a trailing plant producing blue flowers with white eyes.

 Did You Know?

The Garden Lobelia is a relative of our native Cardinal Flower, Lobelia cardinalis. *This upright perennial plant produces beautiful spikes of red flowers. They can be found in wet areas of our southern forests. It is also sold for use in perennial or natural gardens.*

Madagascar Periwinkle

Catharanthus roseus

Other Names: Rose Periwinkle, Vinca, *Vinca rosea*

Size: 8 to 18 inches tall by 8 to 12 inches wide

Flowers: White, pink, rose, red, rose-purple

Bloom Period: Summer to fall

Color photograph on page 233.

Light Requirements:

Additional Benefits:

Though it is delicate in appearance, Madagascar Periwinkle is a sturdy plant that will tolerate some of the toughest garden conditions and keep flowering. Heat, drought, and pollution won't stop the blooms, which are framed by glossy green leaves. Try using this plant when you want the look of Impatiens in hot, sunny areas. They have the same neat, tidy, and mounded appearance as Impatiens.

WHEN TO PLANT

Start seeds 10 to 12 weeks prior to the last spring frost. Seeds need moist, dark, and warm conditions to germinate. Keep the starting mix at a temperature of 70 degrees. Be careful not to overwater. Vinca will rot in cool, wet soils. Be patient: it takes 15 to 20 days for the seeds to germinate. Madagascar Periwinkle can also be started from cuttings. Root cuttings in the spring. Hardened-off transplants can be placed outdoors after all danger of frost is past.

WHERE TO PLANT

Madagascar Periwinkle does best in full sun or partial shade. Though it prefers moist, well-drained soil, it can tolerate heat and some drought. Madagascar Periwinkle makes a nice flowering annual groundcover. The dwarf cultivars can be used as an edging plant. They can be planted alone or mixed with other plants for attractive in-ground or container gardens.

HOW TO PLANT

Madagascar periwinkles are available as bedding plants in flats or in 3- to 4-inch pots. Place the plants at the same depth they were growing in their containers. Space the plants 8 to 12 inches apart.

CARE AND MAINTENANCE

Madagascar Periwinkle requires very little care. The plant prefers moist, well-drained soil, but will not tolerate wet roots. It needs very little grooming to maintain its attractive appearance. Leaf spot disease and slugs may be problems during wet weather. Madagascar Periwinkle can be wintered indoors. They will even flower indoors if grown in the right conditions. Take cuttings from healthy Madagascar Periwinkle plants in August or September just as you do with Geraniums. Cuttings will root quickly in moist vermiculite or perlite. Plant rooted cuttings in any well-drained potting mix. Grow Madagascar periwinkle in a sunny window keeping the soil slightly moist. Cut back leggy growth as needed throughout the winter. Pruning encourages branching. These cuttings can be rooted and used to start additional plants.

ADDITIONAL INFORMATION

I like to plant the bicolor Madagascar Periwinkles with Dusty Miller. The dark-green glossy leaves of Vinca make the lacy white leaves of the Dusty Miller stand out. The white leaves of Dusty Miller also echo the white in the bicolor Madagascar Periwinkle flower. This helps each plant to complement and flow with the other.

ADDITIONAL SPECIES, CULTIVARS, OR VARIETIES

'Jaio Scarlet Eye' is the 2002 AAS winner. It has 2-inch rosy-scarlet blossoms with a white eye and makes a big impact in pots. The 'Pretty in Pink', 'Pretty in Rose', and 'Parasol' Madagascar Periwinkles are all AAS winners. The 'Pretty' Series plants are compact, free flowering, and 12 inches tall. 'Parasol' is a 12- to 18-inch plant that produces the largest flowers. They are white with a rose eye. The 'Cooler' Series is readily available. It is 8 to 10 inches tall.

 Did You Know?

Madagascar Periwinkle is native from Madagascar to India. The botanical name comes from the Greek catharanthus, *which means a pure flower.* Roseus *means rose-colored flower.*

Marigold

Tagetes species

Other Names: Dwarf French Marigold
(*Tagetes patula*), American Marigold,
African Marigold, Aztec Marigold
(*Tagetes erecta*)

Size: 6 to 36 inches tall by 6 to
15 inches wide

Flowers: Yellow, orange, gold, bronze,
creamy white

Bloom Period: Summer through fall

Color photograph on page 233.

Light Requirements:

Additional Benefits:

Marigolds are one of the easiest annuals to grow. With very little care, you will be rewarded with season-long blooms. I think every gardener has grown at least one Marigold. And it seems as though every schoolchild has started Marigolds to give to his mom for Mother's Day. The French and African Marigolds are the most popular. Both produce a colorful display. Their round flowers and warm colors command attention in any landscape.

WHEN TO PLANT

Marigolds are easy to start from seeds indoors or outside in the garden. Start seeds indoors about four weeks before the last spring frost. Keep the starting mix moist and at a temperature of 70 degrees. Seedlings will appear in about 5 to 7 days. You can also start seeds outdoors after the last spring frost. Hardened-off transplants can be planted outdoors after all danger of frost is past.

WHERE TO PLANT

Marigolds prefer full sun and moist, well-drained soil. They will tolerate drought, but not extreme heat. Mulch the soil to keep the roots cool and moist. Use the French and Signet Marigolds as edging plants. The larger-flowered, taller African Marigolds work well as background plants. Use any of the Marigolds as bedding plants to create a colorful display. Their warm colors and bold texture make them stand out in the landscape or in a flower vase indoors. Try growing Marigolds in containers. Butterflies will seek out Marigolds no matter where they are grown. Include some single-flowered Marigolds. The butterflies like them even better.

HOW TO PLANT

Marigolds can be directly sown in the garden after all danger of frost is past. Prepare the planting bed. Lightly cover the seeds with soil and keep it moist until the seeds germinate. Transplants are available from garden centers as bedding plants in flats. Space plants 6 to 18 inches apart in the garden.

CARE AND MAINTENANCE

Marigolds perform well with minimal care. Though drought tolerant, they will perform best in moist, well-drained soil. Remove faded flowers to encourage branching and continual blooms. French Marigolds will stop flowering during hot weather, but once temperatures cool, they will resume blooming. African Marigolds are a little more heat tolerant, although the flowers won't look as nice in extreme heat. Contrary to popular belief, rabbits and woodchucks love Marigolds. Marigolds are usually problem free, although they can be damaged by slugs, spider mites, aphids, and aster yellows disease.

ADDITIONAL INFORMATION

Try planting yellow Marigolds with Blue Salvia. The contrasting colors and flower forms are quite striking in the garden. I also like to use 'Purple Ruffle Basil' with Marigolds. Use one of the yellow or golden Marigolds with maroon-tipped flowers. It echoes the Purple Basil.

ADDITIONAL SPECIES, CULTIVARS, OR VARIETIES

The French Marigold, *Tagetes patula*, is a compact plant, 6 to 18 inches tall. The flowers can be single or double, and up to 2 inches across. The African Marigold, *Tagetes erecta*, is usually taller, 10 to 36 inches, with large 2- to 5-inch flowers. Triploids are a cross between the French and African Marigolds. They are more heat-tolerant and keep flowering in hot weather. The Signet Marigold, *Tagetes tenuifolia*, is a compact plant with fern-like leaves. It produces small, single flowers all season long. 'Lemon Gem' Signet Marigold has a lemony fragrance and small edible flowers.

Moss Rose

Portulaca grandiflora

Other Names: Rose Moss, Sun Plant
Size: 4 to 8 inches tall by 6 inches wide
Flowers: White, yellow, orange, red, rose,
    lavender
Bloom Period: Summer through fall;
    flowers close in afternoon
Color photograph on page 233.

Light Requirements:

Additional Benefit:

Moss rose is a great choice for hot, dry locations. These plants thrive and flower in areas where most annuals would be lucky to survive. Their narrow, fleshy leaves give them a moss-like appearance. The flowers can be single or double. The double ones resemble a rose, thus the name, Moss Rose. Avoid planting Moss Roses in areas only enjoyed in the evening. Since the flowers close in low light, there won't be much of a display to see at that time. However, this feature makes them an interesting addition to the garden. It might help you get some of those reluctant young gardeners interested in plants.

WHEN TO PLANT

Start Moss Rose seeds indoors six weeks before the last frost. The seeds are very fine and should not be planted deep. Sprinkle the seeds on the planting mix surface and water them in. Keep the mix slightly moist and at a temperature of 70 degrees. Seeds can also be planted directly outdoors after the danger of frost is past. Hardened-off transplants can also be placed outdoors after the last spring frost.

WHERE TO PLANT

Plant Moss Rose in areas with full sun and well-drained soil. They prefer hot, dry conditions, making them perfect candidates for rock gardens, hanging baskets, containers, and other hot spots in the landscape. They can also be used as a groundcover or edging plant. Try direct seeding Moss Rose near early-fading perennials. As these perennials die back, the Moss Rose will fill in the void. Remember the Moss Rose closes in the late afternoon and evening. Use these plants in areas where you can enjoy their flowers during the day.

How to Plant
Start seeds outdoors after all danger of frost is past. Prepare the planting bed. Sow seeds on the surface of the soil and water them in. Transplants should be spaced 6 to 12 inches apart. Once you have grown Moss Rose, you will be rewarded with seedlings the following season. These can be dug and moved to their permanent planting location.

Care and Maintenance
If placed properly, the Moss Rose needs very little care. Avoid overwatering since wet soil can lead to root and stem rot problems.

Additional Information
Are you having trouble handling the fine Moss Rose seeds? Here's a trick that may help. Mix the seeds with fine sand. Sprinkle this mixture onto the starter mix surface and water in. The sand makes it easier to handle the seeds and will also help to space them.

Additional Species, Cultivars, or Varieties
Many of the new cultivars have been bred to stay open later in the day or during cloudy weather. The flowers of 'Afternoon Delight', 'Sundance Mix', and the 'Sundial' Series will stay open for most of the day. The 'Sundial' Series was specifically bred for better flowering in cool, gray climates as ours can sometimes be. 'Calypso Mixture' is probably the most readily available double-flowering Moss Rose. It comes in a variety of colors.

Did You Know?
The botanical name Portulaca grandiflora *comes from Latin.* Porto *means to carry and* lac *means milk. This refers to the milky sap found in many of the species. And I bet you guessed what* grandiflora *means. That's right: large flowers.*

Nasturtium

Tropaeolum majus

Other Name: Indian Cress
Size: Bush types up to 12 inches tall
and 12 to 14 inches wide; vining
types up to 8 feet long
Flowers: Yellow, orange, red, white
Bloom Period: Summer to frost
Color photograph on page 233.

Light Requirements:

Additional Benefits:

Nasturtium is a good plant for sunny, dry areas. The circular, large leaves with radiating veins are quite attractive. Unfortunately, they sometimes hide the flowers. The large orange, yellow, red, and white flowers have nectar-filled spurs that attract hummingbirds.

WHEN TO PLANT

For best results, direct seed Nasturtium outdoors in the garden after the last spring frost. Nasturtium seeds are easy to start, but difficult to transplant. Seeds can be started indoors. Plant them 1/4 inch deep in any sterile starter mix, and keep the mix at a temperature of 65 to 70 degrees. Hardened-off transplants can be moved outdoors after the last spring frost.

WHERE TO PLANT

Grow Nasturtiums in full sun, in a well-drained location. Add organic matter to heavy clay soil to improve drainage. Nasturtium does best in poor, rocky soil. This makes the plants the perfect choice for rock gardens, containers, and other difficult sites. The low-growing types make attractive edging plants and groundcovers. Seed Nasturtiums in the garden next to early-fading perennials. As the perennials die back, the Nasturtiums will fill in the empty spot.

HOW TO PLANT

Direct seed Nasturtiums in the garden. Prepare the planting site. Cover the seeds with 1/4 inch of soil. Keep soil moist until seeds germinate. Hardened-off transplants can be planted outdoors after all danger of frost is past. Plant Nasturtiums 8 to 12 inches apart.

CARE AND MAINTENANCE

The old saying, "be nasty to your Nasturtiums" is certainly true. Too much fertilizer and water can diminish the health and beauty of this plant. Excess nitrogen results in lots of large leaves and no flowers. Overwatering can lead to disease problems. Once plants are established, they need little care. In extreme heat they may stop flowering, but once the weather cools, the blooms will resume. Aphids are the most serious pest of this plant. A strong blast of water or several weekly sprays of insecticidal soap will take care of these insects. Watch for mites, cabbage worms and thrips. Hand pick or apply Bacillus thuringiensis (Bt) to control cabbage worms. The aphid treatment will also keep mites and thrips under control. Leaf spot disease can be a problem. Avoid overwatering.

ADDITIONAL INFORMATION

Nasturtium leaves, flowers, and seeds are edible. They have a nice spicy flavor. In fact, the common name, Nasturtium, is Latin for "Cress." This refers to the pungent flavor of the plant. Use the leaves and flowers in salads or as a garnish. They spice up the flavor and appearance of any meal—even for a less-than-enthusiastic cook like me. Special care must be taken if you plan on treating pests on the Nasturtiums bound for the dinner table. The pest control methods mentioned above are all safe; just wash the plants before eating them. Be sure to read and follow label directions before treating any plant with a pesticide.

ADDITIONAL SPECIES, CULTIVARS, OR VARIETIES

My new favorite is the 'Alaska' Series. These Nasturtiums have green leaves with creamy speckles. 'Whirleybird' is a spurless cultivar. Its single and semidouble flowers face up. They are held above the leaves and put on a good floral display. The annual canary vine, *Tropaeolum peregrinum*, reaches heights of 8 feet. The small yellow flowers are fringed like a bird's wing.

Pansy

Viola × wittrockiana

Size: 4 to 8 inches tall and 9 to 12 inches wide

Flowers: White, blue, purple, yellow, dark red, rose, apricot, brown

Bloom Period: Spring to early summer and fall

Color photograph on page 233.

Light Requirements:

Additional Benefits:

Although Pansies are an old-time favorite, they are experiencing a renewed interest and expanded role in the landscape. Whether used in containers or in the garden, Pansies can add flowering interest to spring and fall plantings. Their fragrant flowers can be used for cutting or pressed for crafts. Add Pansies to your butterfly garden. They provide needed nectar for winged visitors, whether early or late in the season.

WHEN TO PLANT

Start Pansy seeds indoors in January. Place the seeds in moist media and chill in the refrigerator for one week. Seeds need moist, dark, 65-degree conditions to germinate. Lower the growing temperature to 50 degrees once the seeds sprout. Hardened-off transplants can be planted outdoors in April, as soon as the snow has melted and the soil is dry enough to work.

WHERE TO PLANT

Most gardeners think Pansies need shade. They really prefer full sun, but perform best in cool temperatures. That's why Pansies make such excellent spring and fall bedding plants. Plant Pansies in full sun or partial shade in moist, well-drained soil. Mulch to keep the soil cool and moist. Pansies work well in planters alone or mixed with other plants. Use them as a groundcover around spring flowering bulbs. This doubles your flower display and helps mask the fading bulb foliage. Mix them in with your perennial plants. The more heat-tolerant cultivars can be used as bedding plants.

HOW TO PLANT

Pansies can be purchased as bedding plants in flats, in 3- to 4-inch pots, or in planted containers. Plant Pansies at the same depth they were growing in their original containers. Space plants 6 inches apart in the garden, although they can be planted closer in containers. Pansies occasionally survive the winter. I have had both plants and seedlings appear in my garden the following season.

CARE AND MAINTENANCE

Pansies are a snap to grow in cool temperatures. The easiest method is to grow them as a spring bedding plant. As temperatures warm and pansies decline, replace them with a heat-tolerant annual. A new crop of Pansies can be added to the garden in fall. Deadhead Pansies for maximum blooms. Select a heat-tolerant cultivar when using Pansies for season-long interest. Even those may stop blooming during hot weather. Remove faded flowers and keep the soil moist. Unkempt plants can be pruned back. Once temperatures cool, flowering will resume. Pansies are generally pest free. Slugs and fungal leaf spots may be problems in wet weather.

ADDITIONAL INFORMATION

Past breeding efforts have focused on developing more heat-tolerant Pansies. Breeders are developing more cold-tolerant Pansies that will reliably survive our winters, such as 'Second Season'. We will be able to plant these Pansies in the fall for enjoyment then and the following spring.

ADDITIONAL SPECIES, CULTIVARS, OR VARIETIES

'Imperial', 'Maxim', 'Springtime', and 'Universal' are heat-tolerant Pansy cultivars. Johnny-jump-up, *Viola tricolor*, is a close relative. It produces small flowers with "faces" made of blue, gold, and deep violet. Once planted, it will make itself at home throughout your garden.

Did You Know?

Pansy flowers are edible. They can be used in salads or as garnishes. Do not use flowers from pesticide-treated plants. I like to freeze the flowers in ice cubes or rings. It makes even the most inept cooks, like me, look like gourmet chefs!

Petunia

Petunia × hybrida

Size: 6 to 18 inches tall by 6 to 36 inches wide

Flowers: Pink, red, violet, lavender, yellow, salmon, white

Bloom Period: Summer through frost

Color photograph on page 233.

Light Requirements:

Additional Benefits:

I remember helping my mother deadhead the cascading Petunias in our front planters. The sticky stems and my youth made this seem like torture. Fortunately, many of the new Petunias have minimized the need to deadhead and maximized the beauty. I now include Petunias somewhere in my planters or garden. I enjoy their fragrance, and they help bring butterflies and hummingbirds to my garden.

WHEN TO PLANT

Start Petunias from seeds indoors ten weeks prior to the last spring frost. Petunias need moisture, light, and 70 degree temperatures to germinate. Hardened-off transplants can be placed outdoors after the danger of frost is past.

WHERE TO PLANT

Petunias need full sun to partial shade and well-drained soil. In full shade, the plants get leggy and fail to flower. Use Petunias in containers and hanging baskets or as edging and bedding plants. I often use this tough plant for schoolyard and community greening projects.

HOW TO PLANT

Petunias can be purchased as bedding plants in flats. Plant Petunias at the same depth they were growing in the container. Spacing depends on the type of Petunia grown. Check the plant tag for specifics on the Petunias you purchase. In general, miniatures can be planted 6 inches apart, bedding types 10 to 12 inches apart, and the trailing types up to 24 inches apart when used as a groundcover.

CARE AND MAINTENANCE

Other than deadheading, Petunias are very low maintenance. Remove faded flowers and clip back leggy stems to keep the plants full and flowering. Stem rot can be a problem with Petunias grown in poorly drained soil. Botrytis blight can cause flowers and leaves to brown, but regular deadheading and removal of infected plant parts is usually sufficient to control this disease. Flea beetles and aphids can also infest Petunias, as well as tobacco mosaic virus, spread by aphids. Control the aphids and remove infected plants to keep this disease under control.

ADDITIONAL INFORMATION

There are several major categories of Petunias. The Grandifloras have fewer, but larger, single or double flowers. I find they need deadheading and suffer rain damage more readily than the others. The Multifloras have more, but smaller, single or double flowers. Many of the newer cultivars hold up in the rain and require less deadheading. The Millifloras produce lots of small, single flowers on compact plants. These work well in containers mixed with other plants. Trailing types work well in containers and hanging baskets. The amount of grooming needed depends on the cultivar selected.

ADDITIONAL SPECIES, CULTIVARS, OR VARIETIES

Check seed catalogs and garden centers for the many Petunia cultivars. The 'Daddy' Series is an early-flowering Grandiflora with pink, purple, or lavender-blue flowers. The 'Carpet' Series has Multiflora Petunias with a compact growth habit. As their name suggests, they make an excellent groundcover. The 'Wave' Series are vigorous Multifloras that grow and flower all season long. Stems can reach 36 inches in length, making them ideal for hanging baskets.

 Did You Know?

There is a new Petunia look-alike on the market. 'Million Bells' (Calibrachoa) is a fast-growing compact plant that produces lots of small Petunia-like flowers from summer through frost. It is self-cleaning, reducing the need to deadhead. Try it in hanging baskets, in containers, or as a groundcover.

Salvia

Salvia splendens

Other Names: Scarlet Sage, Red Salvia, Firecracker Plant
Size: 8 to 30 inches tall by 8 to 12 inches wide
Flowers: Red, orange, pink, blue, lavender
Bloom Period: Summer until frost
Color photograph on page 233.

Light Requirements:

Additional Benefits:

Nothing grabs the garden visitor's attention like Red Salvia. The intense color and large flower spikes make it stand out in the landscape. It is an excellent plant for making large spaces appear smaller. Use it as a focal point to accent a hard-to-find entrance, garden art, or another landscape feature. These flowers also attract the attention of wildlife. Both hummingbirds and butterflies enjoy them. Salvia is often used to provide the red in patriotic red, white, and blue gardens. They combine well with most of the commonly grown annuals.

WHEN TO PLANT

Start Salvia from seeds indoors about six to eight weeks before the last spring frost. Sow the seeds in a sterile starter medium and water in. Do not cover since these seeds need light to germinate. Keep the planting mix moist and the temperature at 70 degrees. Do not overwater. Salvia is subject to damping-off disease. Hardened-off transplants can be planted outdoors after all danger of frost is past.

WHERE TO PLANT

Salvia prefers full sun, moist, well-drained soil, and cool temperatures. The plants will tolerate partial shade. Shorter Salvias grow well in containers or in the garden as edging and bedding plants. The taller Salvias make a nice backdrop in the garden. Include them in your cutting and wildlife gardens.

HOW TO PLANT

Salvias are available as bedding plants in flats or in 3- to 4-inch pots. Plant salvias at the same depth they were growing in the containers. Space smaller cultivars 8 inches apart and larger cultivars 10 to 12 inches apart.

CARE AND MAINTENANCE

Mulch Salvias to keep the roots cool and moist. Deadhead to encourage branching and continual blooming. You can minimize this chore by regularly cutting flowers for indoor use. It accomplishes the same results and somehow seems less like work. Salvias may suffer from downy and powdery mildew. Plants grown in full sun and properly spaced are less susceptible to these problems. Remove infected plant parts to reduce the spread of these diseases.

ADDITIONAL INFORMATION

Red Salvia is an attention getter in the garden, although the intense red can be overpowering in the landscape. Temper this by planting Red Salvia in front of evergreens or mixed with Dusty Miller. Or try growing the AAS winner 'Lady in Red'. The red flowers on this compact plant are more open and less overpowering. I find it blends better with perennials and less formal landscapes.

ADDITIONAL SPECIES, CULTIVARS, OR VARIETIES

Check catalogs and garden centers for the cultivar that best suits your needs. 'Carabinere', 'Empire', and 'Firecracker' Series are all compact plants, 10 to 12 inches tall, and come in a variety of flower colors. 'Strata' is another AAS winner. This medium-sized Salvia has long flower spikes of blue and white flowers. Mealycup Sage, *Salvia farinacea*, makes a good dried flower. The shorter, 18-inch 'Victoria' cultivar produces violet-blue flower spikes. They may be substituted for lavender in wreaths and arrangements. I find the subtler features of this plant are easier to blend with perennials and my informal style of gardening.

 Did You Know?

The Garden Sage, Salvia officinalis, *is a perennial cousin of Red Salvia and is used in cooking. The attractive foliage makes this an ornamental addition to the landscape as well. I have included the 'Tricolor' cultivar in my plantings. Its wrinkled leaves of white, purple, and pink make an attractive addition to herb and flower gardens alike.*

Snapdragon

Antirrhinum majus

Other Names: Common Snapdragon, Garden Snapdragon
Size: 6 to 48 inches tall by 6 to 24 inches wide
Flowers: White, yellow, bronze, purple, pink, red
Bloom Period: Summer to frost
Color photograph on page 233.

Light Requirements:

Additional Benefits:

Snapdragons are an old-time favorite with new cultivars providing a modern update. These stately plants hold spikes of colorful flowers over whorls of narrow green leaves. The Snapdragon is an impressive flower outdoors in the garden or inside in a flower vase. Put your nose in close and you may be rewarded with a light fragrance.

WHEN TO PLANT

Start Snapdragons from seeds indoors about ten weeks before the last spring frost. Seeds need light, moisture, and a temperature of 70 degrees to germinate. Snapdragons can be direct seeded outdoors in the spring as soon as the soil is workable. Hardened-off transplants will tolerate frost, but do best when planted outdoors after all danger of frost is past.

WHERE TO PLANT

Snapdragons prefer full sun, but will tolerate some light shade. Plant them in an area with moist, but well-drained, soil. Use dwarf cultivars as a groundcover, in a container, or as an edging plant. Include medium cultivars in annual and perennial gardens. The tall cultivars make great background plants where it is easier to hide the stakes.

HOW TO PLANT

Snapdragons are available from garden centers as bedding plants in flats. Plant transplants at the same depth they were growing in the containers. Space small Snapdragon cultivars 6 inches apart, medium cultivars 8 to 10 inches apart, and tall cultivars at least 12 inches apart.

CARE AND MAINTENANCE

Snapdragons require regular deadheading to stay in bloom. Remove faded flowers before too many seedpods form on the flower stem. Seedpods are the round balls that form where flowers once appeared. Taller cultivars may need staking. Use grow-through stakes, dead twigs, or other plants to support the tall Snapdragons. Snapdragons may stop blooming in extremely hot weather. Prune plants back and wait for an impressive fall display. Aphids and mites may cause leaves to curl, yellow, and eventually brown. A strong blast of water from the garden hose or several weekly applications of insecticidal soap will usually control these pests. The fungal disease *rust* may also cause problems. Reduce rust problems by growing plants in full sun, properly space them and avoid overhead watering.

ADDITIONAL INFORMATION

Snapdragons will reseed in your garden. I find this a welcome surprise in my informal flower gardens. The plant itself may even survive mild winters. Get the longest vase life from Snapdragons by picking the flowers when the blossoms on the lower third of the flower stem are fully open. The middle blossoms will be partially open and the top will be colorful buds.

ADDITIONAL SPECIES, CULTIVARS, OR VARIETIES

Many newer Snapdragons have open flowers for a showier flower display. The 'Floral Carpet' Series and the improved 'Floral Showers' Series are dwarf Snapdragons, 6 to 8 inches tall. The 'Sonnet' Series is a medium (22-inch) Snapdragon available in various colors. It makes a good cut flower and does not need staking. The tall 'Rocket' Series was developed for heat tolerance and makes a great cut flower. 'Frosted Flames' and 'Powy's Pride' are both variegated forms that make quite an impact in the garden.

 Did You Know?

Did you know snapdragons can talk? Remove a single blossom from the stem. Gently squeeze the sides. The flower will open and shut.

Spike

Cordyline indivisia

Other Name: Dracaena	**Light Requirements:**
Size: 24 inches tall by 15 inches wide	
Flowers: Grown for foliage, not flowers	
Bloom Period: Foliage effective all season	
Color photograph on page 233.	

Spike plants are a Minnesota favorite. The traditional container planting includes a Spike in the middle surrounded by a couple of Geraniums, a few Dusty Millers, Alyssum, and Vinca vine. Its popularity is growing across the country. I am seeing more and more planters and gardens incorporating this plant for vertical interest.

When to Plant

Plant Spikes outdoors after all danger of frost is past. Planted containers can be moved indoors and back outside as weather permits. That allows you to get a jump on the season.

Where to Plant

Spikes prefer full to partial shade and moist, well-drained soil. Avoid wet soil and heavy shade where the plants are more likely to develop root rot. Spikes have traditionally been used in containers, where they serve as a vertical accent. This feature can also be used in the garden. I have seen Spikes planted en masse in the center of an island bed for an impressive show. Other gardeners use individual Spikes throughout their annual plantings, creating a scattering of vertical interest.

How to Plant

Spikes are available from garden centers in 2- or 3-inch pots. Plant these at the same depth they were growing in the container. Usually a single Spike is planted in the middle of the container. Space spikes 12 to 15 inches apart when planted en masse.

Care and Maintenance

Spikes are very low-maintenance plants. They will thrive in properly maintained planters. Check the soil moisture in containers at least once a day. Water containers thoroughly, allowing excess water to run out the drainage holes. Fertilize planters frequently throughout the summer. Use any flowering plant fertilizer to keep the flowering plants blooming with the spike growing. Follow label directions.

ADDITIONAL INFORMATION

Spikes can tolerate cool temperatures in the 40-degree range. Many enthusiastic gardeners winter their plants indoors. One of my students shared a picture of a 4-year-old Spike. It was 4 feet tall and lived in a half whiskey barrel planter. Her strong friends move it indoors each winter. I take the easy way out, enjoying my Spikes until the cold weather kills them or the snow flies. Then I recycle them in the compost pile and start with new plants the next spring. Are you tired of Spike and looking for a different plant to provide vertical interest? Try Bronze Fennel, ornamental grasses, *Verbena bonariensis*, or other upright plants. Be creative. Your imagination is your only limit.

ADDITIONAL SPECIES, CULTIVARS, OR VARIETIES

'Purpurea' has leaves suffused bronze-purple. Check with specialty garden centers in the next few years to see what is available in your area.

 Did You Know?

Many people call the Spike a Dracaena. These are actually 2 different groups of plants. Though they look similar on the outside, the difference lies within. The Cordyline *contains many ovules (part of the reproductive structure) and the* Dracaena *contains a single ovule.*

Sunflower

Helianthus annuus

Other Name: Common Sunflower
Size: 15 inches to 15 feet tall by 12 to
    24 inches wide
Flowers: Yellow, white, bronze, with
    yellow, brown, purple, or
    crimson center
Bloom Period: Summer until frost
Color photograph on page 233.

Light Requirements:

Additional Benefits:

The Sunflower, native to North America, is a longtime garden
favorite. It has recently moved out of the back of the vegetable
garden into the flower garden. Breeding programs have resulted in a
variety of flower sizes, colors, and plant heights that make excellent
cut flowers and readily blend into the garden.

WHEN TO PLANT

Start Sunflowers from seeds outside after all danger of frost is past.
Prepare the planting bed. Cover the seeds with 1/2 inch of soil and
water well. Sunflowers can also be started indoors four to six weeks
before the last spring frost. The seeds need moist starter mix and
68 to 86 degree temperatures to germinate. Seedlings should appear
in ten to fourteen days. Hardened-off transplants can be planted
outdoors after all danger of frost is past.

WHERE TO PLANT

Sunflowers like full sun and well-drained soil. The lower leaves of
Sunflowers can become unsightly. Plant shorter plants in front of the
Sunflowers to mask the lower leaves. You may also want to include a
few Sunflowers in your vegetable garden. The seeds are edible; you
just need to beat the wildlife to them. Acrobatic squirrels and colorful birds can put on quite a show while harvesting the seeds. One
friend reported seeing a hummingbird feeding at his Sunflowers.

HOW TO PLANT

Plant Sunflower seeds 6 inches apart and 1/2 inch deep in the garden.
Thin the plants when they are about 3 inches tall. Leave about 24
inches between the remaining plants. Transplants are available from

garden centers in 3- or 4-inch pots. Space transplants at least 24 inches apart in the garden.

CARE AND MAINTENANCE

Sunflowers are very low-maintenance plants if grown in full sun with well-drained soil. Leaf spot and powdery mildew can cause the leaves to become unsightly. Proper spacing will help reduce problems with these non life-threatening diseases. Aphids may also cause damage.

ADDITIONAL INFORMATION

Many garden centers offer Dwarf Sunflowers for fall planting. These can be planted in containers or vacant spots in the garden. The Dwarf Sunflowers make a great fall display combined with Mums in the garden or pumpkins on the porch. Sunflower seeds are easy to harvest and fun to eat. Cover the mature flower heads with cheesecloth or other fine mesh. Remove the flower with 1 to 2 feet of the stem attached when the back of the flower head is brown. Hang it upside down to dry until the flower head is dry and papery. Harvest the seeds and store them in an airtight jar in the refrigerator.

ADDITIONAL SPECIES, CULTIVARS, OR VARIETIES

More and more Sunflower cultivars are available. 'Teddy Bear' is a 24-inch-tall dwarf cultivar with 5-inch-diameter double yellow flowers. They look more like Dahlias than Sunflowers since they do not have the traditional dark center. 'Valentine' is 5 feet tall and produces lemon-yellow flowers with dark centers. 'Italian White' is 4 feet tall and produces creamy white flowers with dark centers.

Did You Know?

You can grow your children a playhouse. Plant tall Sunflowers in a circle in your garden. Leave a little extra space between plants for the "door." Plant Squash, Beans, or Morning Glories between the Sunflowers. These climbers will use the Sunflowers as a trellis, forming the walls of the playhouse.

Verbena

Verbena × hybrida

Other Name: Garden Verbena
Size: 10 to 15 inches tall by 12 to
   20 inches wide
Flowers: White, lavender, purple, blue,
   pink, red, apricot
Bloom Period: Summer through frost
Color photograph on page 234.

Light Requirements:

Additional Benefits:

With all the cultivars and related species available, there is bound to be a Verbena that is right for your garden. There are upright and spreading types on the market, and included within these groups are plants with broad, wrinkled, hairless, or fernlike leaves. The flower clusters come in a variety of colors and are quite showy. Include these in your garden or container plantings.

WHEN TO PLANT

Start verbena seeds indoors twelve weeks prior to the last spring frost. Verbenas can sometimes be tricky. Chill the seeds for 7 days before seeding. Plant the seeds in a well-drained sterile starter mix and maintain a temperature of 70 degrees. Keep the starter mix on the dry side to avoid damping-off disease. Hardened-off transplants can be planted outdoors after the last spring frost.

WHERE TO PLANT

Plant Verbena in areas with full sun and well-drained soil. Add organic matter to heavy clay soil to improve drainage. Verbenas are attractive in the garden or in containers. Try a few of the spreading types in hanging baskets mixed with *Helichrysum* (Licorice Vine) or Lotus Vine. Verbenas make good edging plants, bedding plants, and groundcovers. Include some in the rock and butterfly gardens.

HOW TO PLANT

Verbenas are available from garden centers as bedding plants. Plant them at the same depth they were growing in the containers. Space upright-type plants 12 inches apart. Spreading types should be spaced 18 inches apart.

CARE AND MAINTENANCE

Verbenas need some maintenance to keep them flowering all season long. Remove faded flowers to encourage branching and continual blooms. Verbena will stop blooming during hot, dry spells. Provide adequate water, and once the weather cools, the flowers will return. Verbenas are also subject to powdery mildew. Proper spacing and full sun will help reduce the risk of this disease.

ADDITIONAL INFORMATION

There are several related annual and perennial Verbenas. One of my favorites is Brazilian Verbena, *Verbena bonariensis*. This plant can reach heights of 6 feet when in bloom. The stiff stems have leaves on the bottom 12 to 15 inches of the plant. The plants develop small flower heads on long, 3- to 4-foot, leafless flower stems. The flowers wave in the breeze and are very attractive to butterflies. I like to mix Brazilian Verbena in with other plants and ornamental grasses. The flowers are a nice surprise in the garden. Mixing it into the garden also hides the foliage that can become unsightly. They also reseed readily.

ADDITIONAL SPECIES, CULTIVARS, OR VARIETIES

There are several award-winning cultivars. Check catalogs and your local garden center for the availability of newer cultivars. 'Peaches and Cream' is a heat-tolerant Verbena that grows 12 inches tall and produces salmon and apricot flowers. It is an AAS and Fleuroselect Gold Medal winner. The 'Romance' Series are compact plants with a dense spreading habit. They are available in a variety of colors. 'Imagination' is another AAS winner. It is one of the cutleaf spreading types, and looks great in hanging baskets. 'Tapien' and 'Temari' are also spreading types. They are heat and cold (to 14 degrees) tolerant and flower freely with little or no deadheading.

Zinnia

Zinnia elegans

Size: 6 to 36 inches tall by 18 to 24 inches wide

Flowers: White, yellow, green, red, orange, apricot, rose, red, violet

Bloom Period: Summer to frost

Color photograph on page 234.

Light Requirements:

Additional Benefits:

The variety of flower types, colors, and plant heights available make the Zinnia a popular plant in Minnesota gardens. Zinnia flowers can be single or double. The Dahlia-flowered Zinnia has large double flowers. The petals tend to cup, giving it a more rounded appearance. The Cactus-flowered Zinnia has twisted petals and resembles the Cactus-flowered Dahlia. Single Zinnias are not as bold as the doubles, and are easier to blend with other flowers. All Zinnia flower types make good cut flowers.

WHEN TO PLANT

Start Zinnias from seeds indoors about six weeks before the last spring frost. Plant the seeds in a sterile starter mix keeping it moist and at a temperature of 70 degrees. Zinnias can be direct seeded in the garden after all danger of frost is past. Hardened-off transplants can also be planted outdoors at that time.

WHERE TO PLANT

Zinnias are perfect plants for the hot, dry locations in your landscape. Plant them in areas with full sun and well-drained soil. Add organic matter to heavy clay soil to improve drainage. Tall Zinnias make nice background plants, while others can be used as bedding plants. Smaller cultivars work well in containers. Use Zinnias, especially the single ones, to attract butterflies to your garden.

HOW TO PLANT

Zinnias are available from garden centers as bedding plants in flats. Plant transplants at the same depth they were growing in the containers. Small cultivars can be planted 6 to 8 inches apart and the larger cultivars at least 12 inches apart. Zinnias can also be direct seeded in the garden. Prepare the soil and plant seeds 3 to 6 inches apart. Thin to final spacing once the seeds are 3 inches tall.

CARE AND MAINTENANCE

Proper plant selection, siting, and spacing are critical to the health and appearance of Zinnias. If you have grown this plant, you know powdery mildew is its biggest problem. Select mildew-resistant cultivars whenever possible. Plant zinnias in full sun with proper spacing to reduce this and other disease problems. Remove faded flowers to encourage branching and continual blooms.

ADDITIONAL INFORMATION

The linear-leafed Zinnia, *Zinnia haageana,* also listed as *Zinnia angustifolia* and *Zinnia linearis,* is one of my favorites. This Zinnia has narrow leaves with 1½-inch-wide single flowers. Cultivars are available in 6- to 12-inch heights. The plant is mildew resistant. 'Crystal White' is a 1997 AAS winner. It is 8 to 10 inches tall and has white flowers with a yellow center. 'Orange Star', also called 'Classic' or 'Classic Golden Orange', is another mildew-resistant cultivar of this plant. It grows 10 inches tall and is topped with single orange flowers. These Zinnias work well as bedding plants, in rock gardens, or mixed with perennials.

ADDITIONAL SPECIES, CULTIVARS, OR VARIETIES

There are many Zinnia cultivars on the market. Check catalogs and garden centers for available cultivars. The 'Peter Pan' Series is an AAS winner. It has large, up to 4-inch flowers on 8- to 10-inch-tall plants. The 'Thumbelina' Series, an AAS winner, has single or semidouble flowers on 6-inch-tall plants and makes a good container or edging plant. The tall 'Ruffles' Series has ruffled flowers, as the name implies. This AAS winner also has good disease resistance. The flowers are 3 to 3½ inches wide and double. Include this one for excellent cut flowers. 'Profusion Cherry' and 'Profusion Orange' were selected as All America Selections Gold-Medal Winners in 1999 for their low maintenance and disease resistance. Their narrow leaves and single flowers make them a nice addition to both annual and perennial plantings. Provide proper spacing and good drainage to avoid stem rot problems.

CHAPTER TWO

Bulbs

A FTER SURVIVING THE COLD AND SNOW of a Minnesota winter, the gardening season never seems long enough. Extend your garden's bloom time by incorporating spring-flowering bulbs into your landscape. But don't stop there. Try including some of the hardy and nonhardy summer- and fall-blooming bulbs. They can add color and interest to your annual, perennial, and container gardens.

For the purposes of this book, I am using the term "bulb" to include plants grown from true bulbs, rhizomes, corms, tubers, and tuberous roots. They may be hardy or nonhardy. Hardy bulbs can be left in the ground year-round. Nonhardy bulbs are planted outdoors each spring. You can remove them from the ground and store them indoors over the winter. The trick is finding storage areas cool enough to keep the bulbs dormant.

Most bulbs prefer moist, well-drained soil. Work several inches of peat moss, compost, or other organic matter into the top 12 inches of soil before planting. Organic matter helps improve the drainage in heavy clay soil and increases the water-holding capacity of sandy soil. Fertilize bulb plantings according to soil test recommendations. In general, bulbs receive enough nutrients from a regular garden fertilization program.

SELECTING HARDY BULBS
Most of us think about adding bulbs to the garden with the first big daffodil display in the spring. Unfortunately, we usually forget about planting them until the next spring when the daffodils are again in bloom. Luckily, many mail order companies have started sending out their bulb catalogues in the spring. It's an easy way to order the bulbs while you are inspired by the spring bloom and have them delivered in the fall in time for planting. Watch for other bulb catalogues later in the season and stop by the garden centers as soon as

the bulbs go on display for the greatest selection. Select firm, blemish-free bulbs. Avoid those with nicks, cuts, or soft areas. Store bulbs in a cool, dark place until it is time to plant. Bulbs should be stored in perforated plastic or mesh bags. Do not store them in closed plastic bags where they can rot.

PLANTING AND CARE OF HARDY BULBS

Plant most hardy bulbs in the fall when temperatures are consistently cool, usually late September or early October. However, you can plant bulbs until the ground freezes. I think we all have planted a few in the snow and frosty soil.

In general, bulbs should be planted at a depth two or three times the vertical diameter of the bulb. Space them at least three to four times the width of the bulb apart. Water the newly planted bulbs. Avoid planting bulbs near your home's foundation, especially the south side, near a dryer vent, or close to other artificial heat sources. Bulbs planted in these spots could sprout early.

Most of us have experienced the problem of a "premature spring." Every January or February, we get a week of warm weather and bulbs start peeking through the ground just in time for the next cold wave. Prevent this by using winter mulch. Cover the ground with evergreen branches, straw, or marsh hay after the soil lightly freezes. Discarded Christmas trees work great.

Remove the mulch when the air temperature hovers above freezing and bulb growth appears. You can add a low-nitrogen fertilizer to bulb gardens in the early spring as the leaves appear. Don't forget to water if we have a dry spring. Remove faded flowers but leave the leaves intact. The leaves produce the needed energy for the plants to return and flower next year.

Allium

Allium species

Other Names: Flowering Onion,
    Ornamental Onion
Size: 6 inches to 5 feet tall
Flowers: White, purple, blue, pink, yellow
Bloom Period: Early through late summer
Zones: Varies; Zone 3 or 4
Color photograph on page 234.

Light Requirements:

Additional Benefit:

Eye-catching Alliums are guaranteed to get your garden a second
look. Include an assortment of Alliums in the landscape for summer-
long enjoyment. These flowers also work well in fresh and dried flower
arrangements. Select Alliums that are hardy to your area and provide
the look you want in your yard.

WHEN TO PLANT

Plant Allium bulbs in the fall. Wait until late September or early
October when temperatures are consistently cool. Alliums can be
planted until the ground freezes. This is also a good time to dig and
divide or move existing plantings.

WHERE TO PLANT

Most Alliums need full sun and well-drained soil. A few species
will tolerate partial shade. Add organic matter to heavy clay soil
to improve drainage. Smaller Alliums can be used in rock gardens.
Some species will reseed and naturalize. Most Alliums look good
mixed with perennials. The giant onion, *Allium giganteum*, is a good
background plant, although I find the large flower head difficult to
blend. Try surrounding this bold element with finer textured plants
like Threadleaf Coreopsis. Or use an equally bold-textured plant like
a Yucca to create contrast in form.

HOW TO PLANT

Alliums are most readily available as bulbs from garden catalogs.
Some garden centers may carry a few of the more commonly grown
Alliums such as the giant onion and drumstick chives. Ornamental
onion is often sold as a perennial plant at more specialized garden

centers. Plant the bulbs at a depth of two to three times their diameter, but no deeper than 4 inches. Spacing of the bulbs varies with the species. Plant container-grown Alliums at the same level they were growing in the pot.

CARE AND MAINTENANCE

Bulb rot is a common problem in cool, damp soil. You can't control the rain, but you can adjust your watering schedule. I occasionally see frost-damaged tips on early-sprouting Alliums. It doesn't hurt the plant, it just worries the gardener. Mulch Allium plantings with evergreen boughs, straw, or marsh hay after the soil lightly freezes. The mulching will help more tender Alliums make it through our tough winters.

ADDITIONAL INFORMATION

The large flowers are tempting for little fingers. We now plant ours where we can see them but the neighborhood children can't pick them.

ADDITIONAL SPECIES, CULTIVARS, OR VARIETIES

The giant onion (*Allium giganteum*) is the most well known of the flowering onions. The 5-to-6-inch-diameter purple flower head tops a 3-to-4-foot-tall plant. The Drumstick Chives plant (*Allium spaerocephalon*) is equally impressive but on a smaller scale. The 2-to-3-foot-tall plant will be filled with many 2-inch-diameter purple flowers. The large number of blooms makes quite a display, while the smaller flower size makes them easier to blend with other plants. Ornamental onion (*Allium senescens glaucum* or *Allium montanum glaucum*) is only 6 inches tall. It provides a lot of interest for a small plant. The attractive, slightly twisted, gray-green foliage is effective all season long. The flowers are 1 inch in diameter, round, and come in lilac or mauve. It blooms from late summer into fall.

Caladium

Caladium × bicolor

Other Names: Fancy-leaved Caladium,
   Angel Wings, Elephant's Ear,
   Caladium × hortulanum
Size: 1 to 2 feet tall
Flowers: No flowers; but colorful leaves
   in combinations of red, pink, white, green
Bloom Period: Leaves attractive summer
   through frost
Zones: All; not winter hardy
Color photograph on page 234.

Light Requirements:

The colorful leaves of Caladium can add life to shade and indoor gardens. The arrowhead-shaped leaves are held on long stems, which makes each leaf stand out in the garden. The leaves are a colorful mix of white, red, pink, and green. Some cultivars, like 'White Christmas', are white with green veins. Other cultivars, like 'Pink Beauty', have red veins with speckles of bright green, pink, and white throughout the leaves.

WHEN TO PLANT

Caladiums can be started from tubers. Start tubers indoors in mid-March. Plant them with the knobby side up in a well-drained potting mix. Keep the potting mix moist and at 70 degrees. Tubers can also be planted directly outdoors after all danger of frost has passed. These plants will take longer to create the desired display. Hardened-off transplants can be planted outdoors after all danger of frost is past.

WHERE TO PLANT

Caladiums are colorful foliage plants for full and partial shade locations. The leaves will scorch—turn brown—when Caladiums are grown in full sun. Mulching will help keep the soil cool and moist, reducing scorch problems. Caladiums make excellent bedding plants. Use them en masse or mixed with other shade-tolerant plants.

HOW TO PLANT

Plant container-grown Caladiums at the same depth they were growing in the pot. Space small cultivars 12 inches apart and larger

cultivars 18 to 24 inches apart. Plant tubers no more than 2 inches deep outdoors. Space cultivars a little closer together, 10 to 18 inches apart, for earlier impact in the garden.

CARE AND MAINTENANCE

Caladiums are basically pest free. Plants may suffer scorch, or leaf browning, if they are grown in full sun or if the soil is allowed to dry out in hot weather. Mulch to reduce this problem. Caladiums grown in planters need regular care. Check the soil moisture in planters at least once a day; twice a day during hot weather. Water containers thoroughly, allowing excess water to run out the drainage holes. Fertilize planters regularly throughout the summer according to label directions. Dig Caladiums up after the first light frost. Allow tubers to dry in a well-ventilated location. Store tubers in peat moss in a cool basement.

ADDITIONAL INFORMATION

Caladiums can be grown as houseplants all year long, although many gardeners like to summer their plants outdoors. Caladiums can be summered outdoors in their containers or planted in the garden. Reduce maintenance by leaving the Caladium in its container. Sink the pot into soil, making sure the lip of the container is even with the soil surface. Remove the pot from the garden before the first frost. This reduces the stress on the plant and makes your job easier. Check for insects before moving it indoors.

ADDITIONAL SPECIES, CULTIVARS, OR VARIETIES

Caladiums are available as fancy- and lance-leaved types. The fancy-leaved Caladiums have large leaves and are the most popular. The narrow lance-leaved types are usually dwarf and more sun tolerant.

 Did You Know?

Another plant shares the common name of Elephant Ears. It is also known as Taro (Colocasia). This is the same plant used to make poi in the tropics.

Calla Lily

Zantedeschia aethiopica

Other Names: Arum Lily, Garden Calla, Trumpet Lily, Lily of the Nile
Size: 24 to 36 inches tall by 24 inches wide
Flowers: White
Bloom Period: Late spring to early summer
Zones: All; not winter hardy
Color photograph on page 234.

Light Requirements:

Additional Benefits:

Calla Lilies are a favorite cut flower and garden plant. These long-lasting blooms are commonly sold by florists and used in bridal bouquets and funeral arrangements. The fragrance is an added benefit. In the garden, calla flowers can brighten up a shady location. Their arrowhead-shaped leaves make a dramatic statement whether the plant is in a container, in a flower garden, or near a water garden.

WHEN TO PLANT

Plant rhizomes indoors in mid-March for an earlier outdoor flower display. Grow them in a container with well-drained potting mix. Cover the rhizomes with 3 inches of soil. Water sparingly until growth appears, then increase the watering and fertilize them. Another option is to plant rhizomes in the garden after all danger of frost is past. Hardened-off transplants can also be moved outdoors after the danger of frost is over.

WHERE TO PLANT

Plant Calla Lilies in partial to full shade. However, they will tolerate full sun if the soil is kept moist. Calla Lilies prefer moist, organic soil. Add organic matter to heavy clay soil for improved drainage and to sandy soil for increased water retention. Calla Lilies will grow in shallow pools or ponds and they look nice when planted in or near water gardens. They also work well in containers alone or mixed with other plants. Try using them in perennial and annual gardens. Once the Calla Lily has finished flowering, you can count on the leaves to provide continued interest in the garden.

How to Plant

Calla Lilies are available from garden centers in 3-, 4- or 6-inch pots. Plant container-grown Calla Lilies at the same level they were growing in the pot. Rhizomes can be purchased from catalogs or garden centers. Plant rhizomes 4 inches deep and 18 inches apart in the garden.

Care and Maintenance

Calla Lilies are fairly low-maintenance plants. Remove faded flowers for a tidier appearance. Leaf spot fungal disease may be a problem in wet years. Remove infected leaves to control this problem. Dig up Calla rhizomes in the fall after the first light frost. Allow the rhizomes to dry. Store them in peat moss or perlite at a temperature of 50 degrees.

Additional Information

Calla Lilies can be grown as houseplants. Keep plants in a warm, sunny window in the winter. Water just as the soil starts to dry out. Increase the watering as the light intensity increases in spring through the summer. These plants can be summered outdoors as a container plant or in the garden. Planting the Calla Lily container and all in the ground reduces maintenance and stress on the plant. Sink the pot into the soil, making sure the lip of the container is even with the soil surface. Lift the pot out of the garden before the first frost. Check it for insects before moving it indoors. If you have sensitive skin, wear gloves when handling Calla Lilies. Contact with the sap may irritate sensitive skin.

Additional Species, Cultivars, or Varieties

Check catalogs and garden centers to see what cultivars are available. 'Green Goddess' has green leaves and white spaths tinged green. 'Little Gem' is a very fragrant dwarf, 12 to 18 inches tall. Calla Lily 'Crowborough' produces large, 4-inch flowers and is supposed to be more sun tolerant. Try some of the related species for more colorful leaves and flowers. *Zantedeschia albomaculata* has green arrowhead-shaped leaves with white spots. *Zantedeschia elliottiana* has yellow flowers and green leaves with silvery-white spots.

BULBS

Canna
Canna × generalis

Other Names: Canna Lily, Indian Shot
Size: 1 to 5 feet tall
Flowers: Orange, yellow, white, red, pink
Bloom Period: Midsummer through frost
Zones: All; not winter hardy
Color photograph on page 234.

Light Requirements:

Additional Benefits:

You can't drive through Como Park without seeing the large, impressive Cannas. These bold plants fill city boulevards and flower beds. Their large green or bronze leaves are covered with big, brightly colored flowers. It only takes a few plants to make a statement. Consider including Cannas in your container or flower gardens.

WHEN TO PLANT
Rhizomes can be planted directly outdoors in the garden after the last spring frost. Start Canna rhizomes indoors in mid-March for earlier outdoor bloom. Cut rhizomes into pieces with at least two or three eyes (buds) per section. Place the rhizomes in a shallow flat filled with 1/2 peat moss and 1/2 vermiculite or perlite. Keep the mix warm and moist. Transplant the rhizomes to individual pots once they have formed several leaves. Only starting a few Cannas? Start them right in a 4- or 6-inch pot filled with a well-drained potting mix. Hardened-off transplants can be planted outdoors after all danger of frost is past.

WHERE TO PLANT
Plant cannas in full sun and in well-drained soil. Use smaller cultivars as bedding plants. Larger cultivars make nice background plants for other flowers. Use cannas in the middle of formal island flower beds. Mix them with spider cleome or surround them with annual fountain grass to soften their bold texture.

HOW TO PLANT
Plant rhizomes 3 to 4 inches deep and 1 1/2 to 2 feet apart. Cannas can also be purchased as transplants in 4- to 6-inch pots. Plant hardened-off transplants outdoors after all danger of frost is past.

CARE AND MAINTENANCE

Cannas are relatively low-maintenance plants with no serious pest problems. Water during dry periods. Remove faded flowers to maintain a neat appearance and encourage continuous blooming. Dig up the rhizomes in the fall after a light frost. Cut off the stem leaving several inches above the rhizome. This makes a convenient carrying handle. Remove any loose soil. Pack the rhizomes in peat moss and store them in a cool, 45- to 50-degree location. Divide rhizomes in the spring before planting them.

ADDITIONAL INFORMATION

Several gardeners have successfully grown Cannas in water gardens. The Water Canna *Thalia dealbata* is commonly grown as an aquatic plant. It has large, Canna-like leaves, but smaller flowers and can reach heights of over 6 feet. You can also find these specimens at the Chicago Botanic Gardens.

ADDITIONAL SPECIES, CULTIVARS, OR VARIETIES

The 'President' Canna has been popular for many years. This 3-foot-tall plant produces scarlet red flowers with glossy green leaves. The striped leaves of 'Pretoria' have gained this plant much recognition. This 6-foot-tall plant has green leaves with yellow stripes and orange flowers. There are several annual-type Cannas. 'Tropical Rose' is an All-America Selection award winner and is probably the best known of this group. 'Cleopatera' has large purple blotches weaving through large green leaves. The foliage on 'Phasion' or 'Tropicana' is purple with dramatic stripes of yellow and red evenly spaced throughout the leaf. Atop the 7-foot tall stems are orange flowers. 'Stuttgart' is a boldly variegated form with green and white blocked patterns on the foliage.

 Did You Know?

The Canna has long been valued for its functional attributes. The black seeds are so hard they were used for shot by natives of the West Indies. The Queensland Arrowroot, Canna edulis, *is edible. It was used as food and is the source of arrowroot starch.*

Crocus

Crocus vernus

Other Name: Dutch Crocus
Size: 6 inches tall
Flowers: White, purple, striped
and yellow
Bloom Period: Early spring
Zones: All
Color photograph on page 234.

Light Requirements:

Additional Benefit:

Crocus is one of the first flowers to greet you in the spring. It is an easy-to-grow plant that can add weeks of enjoyment to your garden. The small plants hold their flowers above the narrow, grass-like leaves. Its early bloom period and variety of color make Crocus one of the most commonly grown spring-flowering bulbs. Add some to your garden or try forcing a few indoors in the winter for a sneak preview of spring.

WHEN TO PLANT

Plant Crocus corms in the fall. Wait until late September or early October when temperatures are consistently cool. Crocuses can be planted until the ground freezes.

WHERE TO PLANT

Crocuses grow well in full sun or partial shade. They prefer well-drained soil, but seem to tolerate all Minnesota soils. Add organic matter to heavy clay soil to improve drainage. Crocuses make an impressive spring display when planted en masse under trees, in groundcovers, naturalized in the lawn, or throughout perennial and rock gardens. A well-manicured lawn is not the place to naturalize Crocuses. You need to let the Crocus foliage grow after the flowers fade. That means you must delay cutting your grass or cut it high at the start of the mowing season.

HOW TO PLANT

Order Crocus corms from bulb catalogs in the spring or summer prior to planting in the fall. Crocus corms are also available from garden centers in late summer or early fall. Place corms 3 inches deep and 4 inches apart. Plant them in groups of at least fifteen to twenty.

CARE AND MAINTENANCE

Crocuses are low-maintenance plants. Flowers will close on cloudy days or in heavy shade. Corm rot is a problem in poorly drained soil. Add organic matter to heavy clay soil to avoid this problem. Animals are the biggest problem the Crocus faces. Squirrels, mice, and chipmunks will dig, move, and eat Crocus corms. Rabbits love to nibble on the flowers and buds. Commercial and homemade repellents may provide relief. A variety of scare tactics may also keep these critters under control. Bulbs in small plantings can be protected with hardware cloth installed over them when they are put in the ground.

ADDITIONAL INFORMATION

Showy Crocus, *Crocus speciosum,* is a fall-flowering Crocus. It flowers in fall before the leaves are fully developed. This plant is easy to grow and hardy statewide. Autumn Crocus (*Colchicum*) is another popular fall-blooming plant, with the look of a Crocus. Plant these corms in late August. The plant produces leaves in early spring, which die back to the ground in 6 to 8 weeks. In September, the flowers appear without leaves. Plant Autumn Crocus among groundcovers. You will surprise garden visitors with Autumn Crocus flowers among your Vinca or Winter creeper groundcover. They also work well in annual, perennial, and rock gardens and are hardy to Zone 5.

ADDITIONAL SPECIES, CULTIVARS, OR VARIETIES

Check bulb catalogs and garden centers for the many different Crocus cultivars. Golden Crocus, *Crocus chrysanthus,* is a close relative. It flowers earlier than the Dutch Crocus, helping to extend the flowering season.

 Did You Know?

The saffron that is used to flavor and color food comes from a crocus. Saffron is made from the dried stigmas of the Saffron Crocus, Crocus sativus. *Ever wonder why it's so expensive? It takes 7 thousand flowers to make 3 ounces of saffron!*

Daffodil

Narcissus species and hybrids

Other Names: Narcissus, Jonquil
Size: 6 to 24 inches
Flowers: Yellow, white, orange, pink, green
Bloom Period: Early to mid-spring
Zones: All
Color photograph on page 234.

Light Requirements:

Additional Benefits:

Daffodils are guaranteed to brighten up any spring landscape. Select several different cultivars for variety and extended bloom. The Daffodil's distinctive flowers stand out from their strap-like leaves. This makes them great in the garden, in a flower vase, or in a pot forced for indoor enjoyment.

WHEN TO PLANT

Plant Daffodil bulbs in the fall. Wait until late September or early October when temperatures are consistently cool. Planting at that time allows the roots to become established before winter, but you can keep planting Daffodils outdoors until the ground freezes.

WHERE TO PLANT

Plant Daffodils in areas with full sun or partial shade and well-drained soil. Add organic matter to heavy clay soil to improve drainage. Daffodils can be planted in perennial gardens, around trees and shrubs, or naturalized in woodland landscapes. Use smaller species in rock gardens.

HOW TO PLANT

Plant Daffodil bulbs 5 to 6 inches deep and 6 to 12 inches apart. In areas with sandy soil, plant Daffodils up to 8 inches deep. Use closer spacing for smaller cultivars and quicker display. The wider spacing works for larger cultivars and naturalizing. The greater the spacing the longer you have before the bulbs become overcrowded.

CARE AND MAINTENANCE

Daffodils are one of the easiest-to-grow bulbs. Even the animals leave this poisonous bulb alone. Remove the faded flowers for a tidier look and leave the foliage on the plant for at least six weeks after flowering. Bulb rot can be a problem in poorly drained soil. Poor flowering can also be a problem. Excess shade, overcrowding, overfertilizing, and cold-temperature injury to the buds can prevent flowering. Move the Daffodils, divide them, and avoid high-nitrogen fertilizers to fix the first three problems. Cold damage is a little more challenging. You can't change the weather, but you can winter mulch plants prone to early sprouting or move them away from the house and other artificial heat sources.

ADDITIONAL INFORMATION

So is it a Daffodil, Jonquil, or Narcissus? Gardeners use all three names for this plant. Narcissus is the scientific name that is often used as its common name. Daffodil is a common name introduced and spread by English-speaking people. Jonquil is actually a species of this plant, *Narcissus jonquilla.* So what do you say if you have three narcissus? The American Daffodil Society voted to use the same word for both singular and plural purposes. So you can have one or many Narcissus.

ADDITIONAL SPECIES, CULTIVARS, OR VARIETIES

There are more Daffodils than you can imagine and many of them don't even look like a typical Daffodil. Some have very short trumpets while others are double. Daffodils may be all one color or have different colored perianth (flat petals behind the trumpet) and trumpets. Some Daffodils are better for naturalizing, others are more fragrant, and still others may be better for forcing. Check out the many different Daffodil species and cultivars in bulb catalogs and garden centers.

Did You Know?

Daffodils make great cut flowers. But keep them separate from other flowers. The plant sap that leaks from the Daffodils' cut stems will plug the cut ends of other flowers. This blocks their intake of water and shortens their vase life.

Dahlia

Dahlia hybrids

Other Name: Garden Dahlia
Size: 1 to 5 feet tall
Flowers: White, pink, red, orange, yellow
Bloom Period: Midsummer to frost
Zones: All; not winter hardy
Color photograph on page 234.

Light Requirements:

Additional Benefits:

Have you ever been to a Dahlia show? I am always amazed at the wide range of flower sizes, types, and colors available. But don't let the high-quality exhibition flowers scare you away. With proper planting and routine maintenance, you can put on your own Dahlia show right in the garden.

WHEN TO PLANT

Plant Dahlia tuberous roots indoors in mid-March for early bloom outdoors. Each section must have at least one eye, the point of new growth. Plant in any well-drained potting mix. Tuberous roots can be planted directly in the garden after the last spring frost. Hardened-off transplants can be placed outdoors after all danger of frost is past.

WHERE TO PLANT

Plant Dahlias in a location with full sun to light shade in moist, well-drained soil. Tall Dahlias make excellent background plants. Those grown for cutting and exhibition are often planted in rows for ease of maintenance rather than their landscape value. Medium and short Dahlias can be planted in small groupings throughout annual and perennial gardens.

HOW TO PLANT

Dahlias are available as tuberous roots from catalogs and garden centers. Prepare the top 12 inches of the soil before planting. Plant the tuberous roots 4 inches deep. Lay the tuber on its side with the eye pointing up. Stake tall cultivars at planting time to avoid injuring the tuberous root. Cover the tuber with soil. Dahlia plants are available in 4- to 6-inch pots from garden centers. Place the plants several inches deeper in the ground than the Dahlias were growing in the container.

CARE AND MAINTENANCE

Mulch Dahlias to keep the soil cool and moist. Make sure the plants receive adequate moisture and nutrients throughout the growing season. Pinch out the growing tips and deadhead for shorter, bushier plants. These plants will give you an impressive display in the garden with their many small flowers. Additional care is needed to produce large show blossoms. To get the larger blooms, train the plants to one major stem, removing side shoots as they develop. Next, remove all the flower buds that develop along the stem. Leave one bud on the end of each stem. You will have fewer, but much larger, blossoms. Most diseases can be avoided with proper site selection and care. Insects such as mites, aphids, leafhoppers, and thrips can cause damage. Insecticidal soap will control these pests.

ADDITIONAL INFORMATION

Move Dahlias into storage after the first light frost. Start by cutting the Dahlia stems back to 1 foot above the soil surface. Dig, being careful not to damage the tuberous roots and gently remove any loose soil. Allow them to air dry for several hours. Remove any damaged or diseased areas and cut the stem back to 3 to 4 inches above the tuberous roots. Store in a cool (35 to 40 degrees), dry place for the winter. Pack the stems in sand to prevent the tuberous roots from drying out. Divide Dahlias in the spring before planting. Leave at least one eye for every division.

ADDITIONAL SPECIES, CULTIVARS, OR VARIETIES

Dahlias are classified by flower size and type. Flower types vary from the single daisy-like flowers to the double-flowering decorative types. The Cacti flowers have twisted petals; the ball Dahlias look like pom-poms, and the Water Lily Dahlias resemble Water Lily flowers.

 Did You Know?

Bedding Dahlias are grown from seed and planted as annuals. These smaller plants are less expensive and can be used in containers, as bedding plants, or mixed with other flowers.

Gladiolus

Gladiolus × hortulanus

Other Name: Gladiola
Size: 1 to 5 feet
Flowers: White, yellow, pink, red,
   orange, purple, blue, green
Bloom Period: Summer
Zones: All; not winter hardy
Color photograph on page 234.

Light Requirements:

Additional Benefits:

Popular as a cut flower, the Gladiolus is often relegated to the back of the garden. Consider incorporating this plant into your landscape. Its attractive flowers can create a colorful vertical accent in the flower garden. The flowers will also help bring hummingbirds to the landscape. So try planting it where it can be seen.

WHEN TO PLANT

Start planting Gladiola corms outdoors in the spring as soon as the soil is workable. Gladiola will bloom in 60 to 120 days, depending on the cultivar selected. Use a variety of cultivars to extend your bloom time. You can also continue planting every two weeks through the end of June, which will extend your bloom and cutting time throughout the season. Use the earlier-blooming cultivars for your late-June plantings.

WHERE TO PLANT

Plant Gladiola in areas with full sun and well-drained soil. Their strong vertical forms can be difficult to blend in the garden, but take advantage of this feature when using them. One gardener planted a group of Gladiola in her garden and used a piece of white lattice as a grow-through stake. The strong features of the lattice structure balanced the sturdy vertical features of the Gladiola. Try softening the Gladiola with fine-textured plants such as Baby's Breath, Threadleaf Coreopsis, and Cosmos.

HOW TO PLANT

Plant Gladiola 3 to 6 inches deep and 3 to 6 inches apart. The larger the corms, the deeper and further apart they should be planted.

CARE AND MAINTENANCE

Gladiola need 1 inch of water per week during the growing season. You may need to supplement rainfall during dry spells. Gladiola suffer from a variety of insect and disease problems. Reduce problems by purchasing and storing only pest-free corms. Many gardeners treat corms with insecticides and fungicides prior to storage. Read and follow all label directions before using any pesticide. Label the stored corms as pesticide treated. That will remind you to wear gloves when handling these corms.

ADDITIONAL INFORMATION

Dig up the corms in the fall after the leaves have turned brown. Cut the stem just above the corm. Discard any damaged or diseased corms. Remove loose soil and allow the corms to dry in a well-lit location for several days. Store the corms in shallow, well-ventilated boxes. Label them and place the boxes in a warm, 80-degree location for 3 to 4 weeks. Once they are cured, divide the corms and discard any that are old or shriveled. Now, move them into storage in a cool, 40-degree, well-ventilated location.

ADDITIONAL SPECIES, CULTIVARS, OR VARIETIES

The large-flowered hybrids grow 2 to $4^1/2$ feet tall. They produce long flower spikes with large flowers and come in a variety of colors. The miniature and butterfly hybrids are $1^1/2$ to 4 feet tall. Each corm produces several slender flower spikes filled with small flowers. The primulinus hybrids are $1^1/2$ to 3 feet tall. Each corm produces a single slender stem covered with lots of flowers.

 Did You Know?

Here's how to get the most out of your cut flowers. Harvest Gladiola in the early morning or evening. Select flowers with the lower third of the flowers open, the middle third just starting to open, and the upper third in bud. Leave at least 4 leaves on the plant to prepare the corm for next season.

Grape Hyacinth

Muscari botryoides

Other Name: Common Grape Hyacinth
Size: 6 to 9 inches tall
Flowers: Blue, white
Bloom Period: Early spring
Zones: All
Color photograph on page 234.

Light Requirements:

Additional Benefits:

Though small in size, the Grape Hyacinth can create great interest in the landscape. Plant them in large masses for an impressive spring display. Mix them with other, taller bulbs, such as Daffodils and Tulips. Kuegenhoff Gardens in the Netherlands has used them in winding patterns, like a river, throughout their plantings. Be sure to bring a few indoors as forced or cut flowers so you can enjoy the fragrance.

WHEN TO PLANT

Plant Grape Hyacinth bulbs in the fall. Wait until late September or early October when temperatures are consistently cool. Grape Hyacinths can be planted until the ground freezes.

WHERE TO PLANT

Grape Hyacinths will grow in most locations, but they prefer full sun to partial shade, and cool, moist, well-drained soil. Grape Hyacinths can be planted en masse under trees and shrubs. Try naturalizing them in wooded landscapes or grassy areas. Use small cultivars in the rock garden. And don't forget to force a few to enjoy indoors.

HOW TO PLANT

Order Grape Hyacinths from bulb catalogs in the spring or summer prior to fall planting. Grape Hyacinths are also available from garden centers in late summer or early fall. Keep the bulbs in a cool, dark place until you are ready to plant them. Plant the bulbs 3 inches deep and 4 inches apart. Plant them in groups of at least 15 to 20 for good impact.

CARE AND MAINTENANCE

Grape Hyacinths are low-maintenance plants. The leaves will persist and continue to grow all season. That's not a problem; you just need to plan for it in your garden. Grape Hyacinths multiply quickly. They will need dividing every four or five years. Lift and divide overgrown plantings in the late summer or fall. I gave my father one bag of Grape Hyacinth and three years later, he gave me back three bags and said he would never need any more!

ADDITIONAL INFORMATION

I let the seed pods develop on my Grape Hyacinths. I think the translucent pods add interest in the garden and to dried flower arrangements. The vigorous Grape Hyacinths will not be weakened by letting the flowers go to seed. The only disadvantage is that you will have even more plants since they will reseed.

ADDITIONAL SPECIES, CULTIVARS, OR VARIETIES

Plant *Muscari botryoides album* for a white-flowering Grape Hyacinth. Plant the plumed Grape Hyacinth, *Muscari comosum* 'Plumosum', for a really different look. The flowers on this Grape Hyacinth are shredded and look like plumes or tassels. The Armenian Grape Hyacinth, *Muscari armeniacum,* is a larger and more vigorous plant than the common Grape Hyacinth. It is often sold as Grape Hyacinth in some catalogs and garden centers. It is only hardy in Zone 4, while the common Grape Hyacinth is hardy throughout Minnesota.

Did You Know?

Muscari *comes from the Turkish name for this plant.* Botryoides *means like a bunch of grapes, which certainly describes the flowers.* Comosum *means with a tuft, and, you guessed it,* Plumosum *means feathery.*

Hyacinth

Hyacinthus orientalis

Other Names: Dutch Hyacinth, Common Hyacinth, Garden Hyacinth
Size: 6 to 10 inches
Flowers: Blue, violet, white, rose, pink, yellow, salmon, apricot
Bloom Period: Spring
Zones: All
Color photograph on page 234.

Light Requirements:

Additional Benefits:

Hyacinths are sure to brighten up a landscape or room with their large flowers and sweet fragrance. Use this plant outdoors in the garden or force it indoors. Either way, it will make a colorful addition to your spring bulb display.

WHEN TO PLANT

Plant Hyacinth bulbs in the fall. Wait until late September or early October when temperatures are consistently cool. Although planting in the fall allows the roots to become established before winter, Hyacinths can be planted until the ground freezes.

WHERE TO PLANT

Plant Hyacinths in areas with full sun and moist, well-drained soil. Add organic matter to improve the drainage of clay soil and increase the water-holding capacity of sandy soil. The stiff habit and large flowers give the Hyacinth a formal look. Use mass plantings for an impressive spring display. I use small groupings of Hyacinths scattered throughout my gardens to blend better with my informal landscape.

HOW TO PLANT

Order Hyacinths from bulb catalogs in the spring or summer prior to fall planting. Hyacinth bulbs are also available from garden centers in the late summer or early fall. Select medium-sized bulbs, which will produce nice-sized flowers that are less likely to require staking. Keep the bulbs in a cool, dark place until you are ready to plant.

Plant the bulbs 6 inches deep and 6 to 9 inches apart. Even a small grouping of 6 or 9 bulbs can put on a good show.

CARE AND MAINTENANCE

Hyacinths are generally short-lived in our area. They need cool summers and moist, well-drained soil to flourish and multiply. These conditions are found in the Netherlands, but not Minnesota. Remove faded flowers to allow all the energy to go into the bulb instead of into seed formation. Flowers will tend to get smaller each year. Replace Hyacinths every three or four years for the best flowering display. Hyacinths are subject to bulb rot. Plant them in well-drained locations and add organic matter to heavy clay soil to avoid this problem.

ADDITIONAL INFORMATION

Hyacinths are frequently used for forcing. They require at least 10 to 12 weeks of cold (35- to 45-degree) temperatures to initiate the flowers. Many bulbs are precooled for indoor forcing. This means you can pot them and watch them grow. Plant Hyacinths in containers with well-drained potting mix. Precooled bulbs can be placed in a shallow bowl with pebbles or in a glass forcing jar filled with water. Gardeners with sensitive skin should wear gloves when handling Hyacinth bulbs. They can cause skin irritation and aggravate skin allergies.

ADDITIONAL SPECIES, CULTIVARS, OR VARIETIES

Check bulb catalogs and garden centers for available cultivars. Select the cultivars that best suit your garden.

 Did You Know?

Hyacinthus is named after Hyakinthos of Greek mythology. The legend tells that that this young Spartan was accidentally slain by Apollo. Hyacinths grew where his blood was shed.

Iris

Iris hybrids

Other Names: Bearded Iris, German Iris
Size: 4 to 48 inches tall
Flowers: Wide range of colors
Bloom Period: Late spring to early summer
Zones: All
Color photograph on page 235.

Light Requirements:

Additional Benefits:

The stately beauty of the Iris can fill in the blooming void between spring-flowering bulbs and early summer perennials. Its wide range of heights and colors makes this versatile plant work in any garden. The flowers consist of three inner segments or standards, which are usually upright. The three outer drooping segments are called falls. Iris flowers add beauty both indoors in a vase or outdoors in the garden.

WHEN TO PLANT

Plant Iris rhizomes in midsummer through early fall, which will allow the plants to develop roots before winter. Late plantings should be mulched after the ground lightly freezes.

WHERE TO PLANT

Plant Iris in full sun in well-drained soil. Mix Iris with perennials for late spring and early summer interest. Healthy, sword-shaped leaves can provide a vertical accent in the summer garden.

HOW TO PLANT

Plant rhizomes just below the soil surface. Each rhizome should contain at least one fan of leaves. Plant Iris singly or in groupings of three. Set the rhizomes 6 to 24 inches apart with the leaf fans facing outward. Smaller cultivars can be spaced closer, but larger, fast-growing cultivars should be spaced farther apart. The closer the Iris are planted the sooner they will need dividing.

CARE AND MAINTENANCE

Selecting the proper site and planting correctly will help reduce maintenance. Taller cultivars will need staking with Iris stakes, which are available in catalogs and garden centers. They support the flower without detracting from its beauty. Remove spent flowers.

Poor flowering can result from excess fertilizer, low light, and overcrowding. Avoid high-nitrogen fertilizers that promote leaf growth and discourage flowering. Divide overcrowded Iris in midsummer. Cut leaves back to 6 inches. Dig rhizomes and cut them into smaller pieces containing at least one set of leaves and several large roots. Discard any damaged or insect-infested rhizomes. Iris borer is the biggest pest that affects Bearded Iris. Physically remove any borers found during summer transplanting. Fall cleanup is the best prevention. Removing the old foliage in the fall eliminates the egg-laying site of the adult moth.

ADDITIONAL INFORMATION

The Miniature Dwarf Bearded Iris is the first to bloom. It is 4 to 10 inches tall, which makes it a good choice for the rock garden. The Standard Dwarf Bearded Iris blooms about seven to ten days later. It is 10 to 15 inches tall. The Intermediate Iris is the next to bloom and grows to 15 to 28 inches tall. The Tall Bearded Iris is over 28 inches tall and the last to bloom.

ADDITIONAL SPECIES, CULTIVARS, OR VARIETIES

Select the height, bloom time, and color that best fits your landscape. Don't forget about fragrance. Some Iris can provide fragrance to the early spring garden. Include a variety of Iris to extend the flowering period. The Siberian Iris, *Iris sibirica,* is tolerant of moist soil, partial shade, and is less susceptible to Iris borer. The plant grows 2 to 4 feet tall with long, grass-like leaves, which look good all summer. I find it a good alternative to ornamental grass. The reblooming, remontant Iris will often produce a second set of flowers in the fall. Check Iris catalogs for a hardy cultivar. The blue Iris seen growing wild throughout our state is Blue Flag, *Iris versicolor.* It is native and tolerant of moist to wet soil.

 Did You Know?

Though never proved, it was once believed that Iris had medicinal properties. The root of Iris florentina (Orrisroot) *was used as a breath freshener and perfume.*

Lily

Lilium species

Other Names: Garden Lily, Hardy Lily

Size: 2 to 6 feet tall

Flowers: White, yellow, orange, red, pink

Bloom Period: Early to midsummer

Zones: Some types and cultivars in all zones

Color photograph on page 235.

Light Requirements:

Additional Benefits:

The classic Lily is as at home in the informal garden as it is in a more formal setting. Lilies are a little more challenging than Daffodils and Crocuses, but the flowers will convince you they are worth the effort. Be sure to include enough plants for cutting. The beautiful, fragrant flowers are a great addition to any arrangement.

WHEN TO PLANT

Plant Lily bulbs in the fall. Wait until late September or early October when temperatures are consistently cool. Precooled Lily bulbs sold in the spring can be planted outdoors as soon as the soil is workable. Lily plants can be planted whenever they are available during the growing season.

WHERE TO PLANT

Plant Lilies in full sun and well-drained soil. Add organic matter to heavy clay soil to improve the drainage. Use Lilies in large masses or as individual plants scattered throughout the garden. Tall Lilies make excellent background or specimen plants. Mix any of the Lilies with other perennials. They are quite attractive growing up through or behind shorter plants.

HOW TO PLANT

Order Lily bulbs from catalogs in the spring or summer prior to fall planting. Precooled bulbs can be ordered in the winter for spring planting. Lily bulbs are also available from garden centers in the late summer or early fall. Precooled bulbs are available at nurseries in the spring. Keep the bulbs in a cool, dark place until you are ready to plant them. Plant Lily bulbs at a depth two to three times their height. Use the minimum planting depth for Lilies growing in clay soil. The deeper the bulb is planted the greater the risk of bulb rot. Plant Lilies at least three times their width apart.

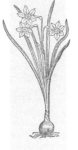

CARE AND MAINTENANCE

Mulch the soil to keep Lily roots cool and moist. Avoid overwatering, especially in clay soil. Lilies are subject to bulb rot. Proper soil preparation and watering will help prevent this problem. Deer, rabbits, and groundhogs will eat the plants down to ground level. A combination of repellents and scare tactics may help keep these pests at bay.

ADDITIONAL INFORMATION

A longtime garden favorite is the Tiger Lily *Lilium lancifolium* (formerly *Lilium tigrinum*). The Tiger Lily produces lots of orange-red flowers with spotted recurved petals. It's easy to grow and multiplies quickly in the garden. Tiger Lilies tolerate some shade and moist soils. The upper stems will produce black balls called bulbils. These drop to the ground and start new plants, or you can harvest them and plant them where you choose. Be patient; it takes several years to get a blooming plant from a bulbil.

ADDITIONAL SPECIES, CULTIVARS, OR VARIETIES

Select a cultivar that is hardy to your part of the state. The Asiatic and oriental hybrids are the most readily available. The Asiatic cultivars tend to be hardier than the oriental types. Their flowers are usually unscented and their leaves are wider. The oriental hybrids usually produce lots of fragrant flowers. Many florists are forcing the Asiatic and oriental hybrids into bloom for Easter. This Easter Lily alternative can then be added to the perennial garden.

 Did You Know?

Don't compost your Easter Lily when it has finished blooming. Keep your Lily growing in a sunny window throughout the spring. Plant it outdoors in a sunny, well-drained location in late May. Winter mulch. With a little luck, you will have flowers next July.

Squills

Scilla siberica

Other Names: Siberian Squill, Blue Squill

Size: 6 inches tall

Flowers: Blue, white

Bloom Period: Early spring

Zones: All

Color photograph on page 235.

Light Requirements:

Picture a sea of true blue flowers in the midst of the bluegrass in your front lawn. This is just one of the many uses of the Siberian Squill. Its true blue color is hard to beat in the early spring garden. These early-blooming bulbs are easy to grow and hardy throughout Minnesota. Brighten up your early spring garden with this blue beauty.

WHEN TO PLANT

Plant bulbs in the fall. Wait until late September or early October when temperatures are consistently cool. Squills can be planted until the ground freezes.

WHERE TO PLANT

Plant Squills in full sun or in a partially shaded location. They prefer well-drained soil. Add organic matter to heavy clay soil to improve drainage and to sandy soil to increase water-holding capacity. Naturalize squills in lawn areas and wooded landscapes, include them in rock gardens, or plant large drifts around trees and shrubs. Plant them in areas where they have room to grow. Squills multiply quickly and can take over the spring garden.

HOW TO PLANT

Order Squills from bulb catalogs in the spring or summer prior to fall planting. Squill bulbs are also available from garden centers in the late summer or early fall. Keep the bulbs in a cool, dark place until you are ready to plant. Plant the bulbs 3 inches deep and 4 to 6 inches apart. Plant them in groups of at least fifteen to twenty for good impact.

CARE AND MAINTENANCE

If properly placed, Squills are low-maintenance and basically pest-free plants. Crown rot can cause plants to wilt, yellow, and die.

Improve soil drainage prior to planting to avoid this problem. Most gardeners have too much success with their Squills, complaining that their plants have taken over the garden and moved into the lawn. I think the lawn may be a better place for this plant. It brightens up our spring lawn without damaging the grass. Squills also tolerate mowing once the flowers have faded. Bulbs can be lifted and divided every 4 to 5 years.

ADDITIONAL INFORMATION

Once you have experienced the delight of Squills, you may want to add some additional early-blooming small bulbs to your landscape. Snowdrops, *Galanthus nivalis,* and Winter Aconite, *Eranthis hyemalis,* are the first bulbs to bloom in my garden. Both are shade tolerant and naturalize readily. The Winter Aconite is first to bloom. It is 3 to 4 inches tall with yellow, cup-shaped flowers. The Snowdrops appear next with their pure white flowers on 6-inch plants. Glory-of-the-Snow, *Chionodoxa luciliae,* will appear right before the Siberian Squill. The star-shaped flowers are bright blue with a white center. These early bloomers can tolerate the cold temperatures we seem to get each spring after our early spring plants start blooming.

ADDITIONAL SPECIES, CULTIVARS, OR VARIETIES

Scilla Sibirica 'Alba' is a white-flowering Siberian Squill. 'Spring Beauty' has large, blue flowers. They are held above the leaves on taller spikes than the straight species. Two-leaved Squill, *Scilla bifolia,* is another true blue flowering Squill. It grows 3 to 6 inches tall and naturalizes well in sun or partial shade.

Did You Know?

Pretty to look at, safe to touch, but do NOT eat. All parts of Squills contain digitalis-like substances that are toxic if eaten. This feature helped Squills get their botanical name. Apparently Hippocrates used this Greek word to mean to wound *or* harm, *just as the plants can do if ingested.*

Tuberous Begonia

Begonia × tuberhybrida

Size: 10 to 24 inches tall by 18 to 24 inches wide
Flowers: Orange, red, yellow, pink
Bloom Period: Summer till light frost
Zones: All; not winter hardy
Color photograph on page 235.

Light Requirements:

Additional Benefit:

Bold, beautiful, and made for the shade, Tuberous Begonias can add a lot of color and texture to container and shade gardens. These plants can be upright or pendulous in habit. The large green leaves provide an attractive backdrop for the flowers, which are usually double and can be up to 6 inches in diameter.

WHEN TO PLANT

Plant tubers indoors in mid-March. Place tubers rounded-side down (hollow side up) in a shallow flat filled with 1/2 peat moss and 1/2 vermiculite or perlite. Keep the mix warm and moist. Transplant tubers to individual pots once several leaves have formed. Only a few Tuberous Begonias? Start them right in a container or hanging basket filled with a well-drained potting mix. Hardened-off transplants can be planted outdoors after all danger of frost is past. Tuberous Begonias are very frost sensitive, so don't plant them outdoors too early.

WHERE TO PLANT

Plant Tuberous Begonias in partial sun to shady areas with moist, well-drained soil. Tuberous Begonias work well in hanging baskets and containers. Plant them en masse for a colorful display in the shade garden. Avoid windy locations where the stems may break.

HOW TO PLANT

Tuberous Begonias are available from garden centers in 3- to 4-inch pots. Hardened-off transplants should be planted at the same depth as they were growing in the containers. I do not recommend planting tubers directly outside in the garden. If they are planted outside too early, the tubers will rot. If they are planted after all danger of frost is past, you miss the majority of the flowering season.

CARE AND MAINTENANCE

Mulch to keep the soil cool and moist. Remove faded flowers for improved appearance. Tuberous Begonias are susceptible to powdery mildew and botrytis blight. Proper spacing will increase air circulation and reduce disease problems. If this is a continual problem, try planting the begonias in an area with a little more light. Botrytis blight and downy mildew are common problems in wet seasons. Remove faded or infected flowers and leaves as soon as they appear to help reduce the spread of this disease. Tuberous Begonias will not survive outdoors in Minnesota. After the first light frost, carefully dig up the tubers. Allow them to dry for several days. Remove dead leaves and loose soil and store them in peat moss at 45 to 50 degrees.

ADDITIONAL INFORMATION

Tuberous Begonias are frequently grown in containers and hanging baskets. Check the soil moisture in hanging baskets and containers at least once a day. Check pots twice a day during hot weather. Water containers thoroughly, allowing excess water to run out the drainage holes. Fertilize planters frequently throughout the summer.

ADDITIONAL SPECIES, CULTIVARS, OR VARIETIES

The 'Non Stop' Series is a seeded type that has received a great deal of attention. It is a compact plant that grows 12 inches tall and wide. It produces 3-inch-wide double flowers of red, pink, apricot, orange, white, or yellow.

 Did You Know?

You can bring your Tuberous Begonias indoors for the winter. Bring the plants indoors before the first fall frost. Place them in a sunny window or under artificial lights. Keep the soil moist. One of my students has kept the same plant alive and growing year-round for 4 years.

Tulip

Tulipa species and hybrids

Size: 4 to 36 inches tall	**Light Requirements:**
Flowers: All colors	
Bloom Period: Early through late spring	
Zones: All	**Additional Benefits:**
Color photograph on page 235.	

Tulips are a sure sign of spring for most gardeners. Whether forced in a pot or grown in the garden, Tulips can provide color and interest throughout the season. Select early-, mid-, and late-spring blooming Tulips for a continuous display.

WHEN TO PLANT

Plant Tulip bulbs in the fall. Wait until late September or early October when temperatures are consistently cool. Tulips can be planted until the ground freezes. Plant Tulips as late as possible to avoid fall sprouting.

WHERE TO PLANT

Plant Tulips in full sun in well-drained soil. Tulips can be planted en masse or scattered throughout the perennial garden in small groupings. Include small species and cultivars in rock gardens. Don't forget to plant extra Tulips for cutting.

HOW TO PLANT

Order Tulips from bulb catalogs in the spring or summer prior to fall planting. Tulip bulbs are also available from garden centers in the late summer or early fall. Plant bulbs 5 to 6 inches deep and 6 to 9 inches apart. Plant Tulips 8 inches deep in well-drained sandy soil.

CARE AND MAINTENANCE

Leave the foliage in place for at least six to eight weeks after the Tulips bloom. Mulch the soil to keep bulbs cool and moist in the summer. Excessive heat can result in poor flowering the following spring. Tulips are subject to several rot diseases. Add organic matter to poorly drained soils prior to planting to reduce the risk of rot disease. Deer and rabbits are major pests of this plant. They will eat the

flowers and trample the plants. Squirrels, mice, and chip-munks will dig, move, and eat Tulip bulbs. A combination of repellents and scare tactics may help keep these critters at bay. Small plantings can be protected with hardware cloth installed at planting time. Tulip hybrids tend to be short lived. Include some of the longer-lived species or perennializing Tulips in your garden. Or plan on replacing the short lived hybrids every few years.

ADDITIONAL INFORMATION

You may have heard about "tulipomania." In the early 1600s, the Dutch became obsessed with the Tulip. It was seen as a status symbol, and people started trading money, possessions, and even family businesses for these bulbs. A virus caused a streak in the flower color, which increased the excitement over and value of the Tulip.

ADDITIONAL SPECIES, CULTIVARS, OR VARIETIES

Check bulb catalogs and garden centers for the many avail-able cultivars. Select the sizes, bloom types, and colors that best fit your landscape design. The early Tulips tend to be shorter, while the late spring Tulips are taller, reaching heights of 36 inches. Tulips come in single and double flowers. Some of the late double-flowered Tulips are so full they look like Peonies. The Lily-flowered Tulips have reflexed, pointed petals while those of the Parrot Tulip are fringed. Be sure to include a few early-, mid-, and late-sea-son Tulips. They will provide you with daily surprises and bloom all season long.

Did You Know?

Tulips are native to Turkey, not Holland as many people think. It's a common mistake since most of our Tulips are now produced in the Netherlands. The name Tulip comes from tulband, *the Turkish word for turban. It was originally used to describe the flower and later adopted as the plant's name.*

113

CHAPTER THREE

Groundcovers

GROUNDCOVERS ARE A GREAT ALTERNATIVE to grass for shady locations or hot, dry areas, and they also create a better environment for our trees and shrubs. They are less competitive than grass with the trees and shrubs for water and nutrients—and groundcovers help keep the tree roots cool and moist.

All of the advantages of groundcovers make them a very appealing choice for home owners. But before you tear out your lawn, let's talk about installation and maintenance.

Many established groundcovers are relatively low maintenance, but remember that no plant is maintenance free. As much as I prefer groundcover to grass, you can mow down or spray weeds in the lawn. You have to pull the weeds that invade your groundcovers.

Increase your success and decrease maintenance by investing time and effort during planting and establishment of groundcovers. First, eliminate the existing grass and weeds. You can remove weeds with or without the help of chemicals. Cut an edge around the area to be planted in groundcover. Use a sod cutter to remove the grass and weeds or treat the area with a total vegetation killer. Remember, these products kill anything green that they touch. Wait seven to ten days, check the label after treatment before tilling the site. And always read and follow label directions carefully.

Take a soil test. It will tell you how much and what type of fertilizer to add. Work the recommended fertilizer and 2 inches of organic matter such as compost, aged manure, or peat moss into the top 6 to 12 inches of the soil. This will improve drainage in heavy clay soil and increase the water-holding capacity in sandy soil.

Many groundcovers are planted under trees and shrubs. Planting in these areas requires extra care. Do not add soil on top of the roots or till the soil surrounding established trees and shrubs. That can injure or kill the trees and shrubs. Start by killing or removing the grass around established plantings.

Dig a hole larger than the rootball and plant the groundcover in the existing soil. Broadcast the recommended fertilizer over the soil surface and water in. Next, mulch with an organic material such as shredded leaves, twice-shredded bark, pine needles, or cocoa bean shells. As the mulch breaks down, it will improve the soil below. Be patient; it takes plants longer to fill in this type of planting.

Groundcovers growing under trees and shrubs may need a little extra fertilizer and water to help them compete with tree roots. But don't overdo it. Too much water and fertilizer is also bad for your plants. Your soil test will also tell you what type of fertilizing you should do once the plants are established.

Weeds are the biggest problem these plants face. Mulch ground-cover plantings to reduce weed infestation, or plant the groundcovers a little closer so they will fill in quickly to crowd out the weeds. Planting closer means more plants and more money, and the ground-covers may need dividing sooner. Remove weeds as soon as they appear, especially when the groundcovers are getting established. Once the groundcover fills in, there will be fewer weeds. Water new plantings thoroughly. Allow the top 6 inches of the soil to dry slightly before watering again. When they are established, many groundcovers can survive on natural rainfall.

Does all this sound like too much work? Just picture this: a carpet of green or variegated leaves covered with fragrant and colorful flowers. Bluegrass can't do that. So invest some time and hard work now for years of beauty.

Barren Strawberry

Waldsteinia ternata

Other Names: Dry Strawberry or
   Yellow Strawberry
Size: 4 to 6 inches tall by 18 inches wide
Flowers: Yellow
Bloom Period: May through June
Zones: 4 and 5
Color photograph on page 235.

Light Requirements:

Additional Benefit:

B arren Strawberry is a tough, low-growing groundcover. Its evergreen leaves provide year-round interest. In the spring, the plants
are covered with bright yellow flowers, which turn into small, dry,
brown fruits. These don't look like Strawberries and are not edible. Try
using Barren Strawberry in shady areas and under trees and shrubs.

WHEN TO PLANT
Plant Barren Strawberries in the spring for best results. Winter mulch
late plantings after the ground freezes to help this groundcover
through the first tough winter.

WHERE TO PLANT
Grow Barren Strawberries in full sun or partial shade. They prefer
moist, well-drained soil, but will tolerate a wide range of conditions.
Established plants growing in partial shade are drought tolerant,
while those growing in full sun should be watered during extended
dry spells. Barren Strawberries make good groundcovers in tough
locations and under trees and shrubs.

HOW TO PLANT
Prepare the soil prior to planting. Work 2 inches of organic matter
into the top 6 to 12 inches of soil. That will improve drainage in
heavy clay soil and increase the water-holding capacity in sandy
soil. Do not add to or till the soil surrounding established trees and
shrubs, as this could damage critical feeder roots. Dig a hole larger
than the rootball and plant Barren Strawberry in the existing soil.
Mulch with organic matter. As the organic matter breaks down, it
will improve the soil below. Barren Strawberry plants are available
from garden centers and perennial nurseries in flats and containers.

Plant them at the same level they were growing in the pots. Space plants 1 foot apart. Divisions can be made and planted in the spring once the plant has finished blooming.

CARE AND MAINTENANCE

Once established, Barren Strawberries are low-maintenance plants. The only real serious pests are weeds. Mulch new plantings to conserve moisture and reduce weeds. Remove weeds as they appear. This is an important though often time-consuming task during the first few years. Once the Strawberries fill in, they will crowd out the weeds and cut down on the time you spend weeding. Lift and divide overgrown plants, which often have dead centers or fail to bloom. Use a shovel or garden fork to dig out the plants. Cut the clump into several sections and replant the divisions at 12-inch intervals in a prepared spot.

ADDITIONAL INFORMATION

False Strawberry, *Duchesnea indica,* is often confused with Barren Strawberry. This plant does produce red strawberry-like fruit, which is tasteless but ornamental. False Strawberry is less desirable than Barren Strawberry. This aggressive grower can overtake the landscape. Some states list it as a noxious weed.

ADDITIONAL SPECIES, CULTIVARS, OR VARIETIES

Waldsteinia fragaroides is a closely related species that is also sold as Barren Strawberry. It is a larger plant with dull green leaves and a looser, more informal look. This Barren Strawberry is native to Minnesota. It would be a good choice for gardeners interested in using native plants.

 Did You Know?

The botanical name Waldsteinia *is for the Austrian botanist Count Franz Adam Waldstein-Wartenburg. I'm glad they only used part of his name!* Ternata *means in threes and refers to the three leaflets that make up the Barren Strawberry's leaves.* Fragaroides *means like. It looks like* Waldsteinia ternata.

Barrenwort

Epimedium × rubrum

Other Name: Bishop's Hat
Size: 8 to 12 inches tall and wide
Flowers: Red
Bloom Period: May
Zones: 3b through 4b
Color photograph on page 235.

Light Requirements:

Additional Benefit:

Barrenwort's changing character can provide year-round interest in your landscape. The new growth emerges in green with a touch of red. The heart-shaped leaves are held on wiry stems, giving them a delicate, airy appearance. The red flowers emerge in May or June as the new leaves develop. In the fall, the leaves will turn reddish bronze. Old leaves persist through the winter, adding interest to the winter perennial garden.

WHEN TO PLANT

Plant Barrenwort in the spring for best results. This gives it plenty of time to get established before winter. Mulch late plantings for winter after the ground lightly freezes. Divide plants in the spring or early summer after the new leaves are full size.

WHERE TO PLANT

Plant in full to partial shade. These plants will tolerate full sun as long as the soil is kept moist. Barrenwort needs moist, well-drained soil. Use it in small groupings, mixed with other shade lovers, in rock gardens, or under trees where grass won't grow.

HOW TO PLANT

Barrenwort plants are available from garden centers and perennial nurseries in flats and containers. Prepare the site prior to planting. Plant Barrenworts at the same level they were growing in the pots. Space plants 9 to 12 inches apart. Divisions can be made and planted in the spring or early summer after the new leaves are full size.

CARE AND MAINTENANCE

Barrenworts are slow growers, which gives fast-growing weeds an opportunity to move into the planting. Mulch new plantings to reduce weeds and conserve moisture. Pull weeds as they appear. Avoid cultivating near the plants, which could damage the Barrenwort's shallow roots. Weed control is very important and often time-consuming during the first few years. Once the Barrenworts fill in, they will crowd out the weeds and reduce the time you spend on this task. Water the plants during dry periods. Mulching will help conserve moisture and lengthen the time between waterings. Water plantings thoroughly when the top 4 to 6 inches of the soil start to dry out. Fertilize Barrenworts growing under trees that are competing for nutrients. Use a low-nitrogen fertilizer in the spring. Use a complete fertilizer, which also contains phosphorus and potassium, if other nutrients are lacking in your soil. Follow soil test recommendations or directions on the fertilizer container. Cut back old foliage in the late winter or early spring before new growth begins. This will make the flowers more visible.

ADDITIONAL INFORMATION

Epimedium is a long-lived plant. It can remain in the same location for many years. Division is needed only if you want to start new plants for other areas.

ADDITIONAL SPECIES, CULTIVARS, OR VARIETIES

Sulphur bicolor barrenwort, *Epimedium* × *versicolor* 'Sulphureum', grows 10 to 12 inches tall and has yellow instead of red flowers. This cultivar is more tolerant of dry, shady sites than the other Epimediums.

Did You Know?

Barrenwort's delicate blooms can be used as cut flowers. Use them in small containers alone or as a filler with other flowers. Pick partially opened flowers in the morning or evening for best results. The flowers will last quite a few days in fresh water.

Bishop's Weed

Aegopodium podagraria 'Variegatum'

Other Names: Silveredge Goutweed, Variegated Bishop's Weed

Size: 1 foot tall

Flowers: White

Bloom Period: June

Zones: All

Color photograph on page 235.

Light Requirements:

Bishop's Weed is lovely to look at, but make sure you really want it before you put the first plant in the ground. This aggressive grower has green leaves with white variegation. The white markings help brighten up heavily shaded areas in the landscape. The flowers rise a foot above the leaves and remind me of the flower of Queen Anne's lace. This is a tough plant that should be reserved for the most difficult situations.

WHEN TO PLANT

Plant container-grown Goutweed any time during the growing season. It can be divided and the divisions can be planted in early spring or early fall.

WHERE TO PLANT

Bishop's Weed can tolerate a wide range of conditions. This plant will grow in full sun to full shade. Its leaves will tend to scorch or brown when it is grown in full sun. Bishop's Weed grows in all types of soil, including wet and dry. It grows well in deep shade and is able to compete with the trees for water and nutrients. Bishop's Weed is a substitute for the grass that won't grow under Norway Maples. I prefer to limit its use to contained areas, such as planting beds between the house and sidewalk. Surrounding it with concrete is the best way to keep it under control.

HOW TO PLANT

Bishop's Weed will grow in any soil with or without proper preparation. Plants are available from garden centers and perennial nurseries in flats and containers. Plant them at the same level they were growing in the pot. Space plants at least 1 foot apart. They will fill in the area within two years. Divisions can be made and planted in early spring or early fall.

CARE AND MAINTENANCE

Bishop's Weed tends to look unkempt and develop brown leaves in August. Prevent this problem by mowing the plant back to 6 inches two or three times during the summer. That will eliminate the flowers while keeping the plants compact and tidy. This fast-growing groundcover can easily outgrow the weeds. Remove any weeds that do manage to grow through the planting. Prune out any green shoots as soon as they appear. Your biggest maintenance task will be controlling this plant. Remove stray plants as soon as they leave the confines of their planting beds. Stray plants can be dug or spot treated with a total vegetation killer. Edge planting beds prior to chemical treatment. That will prevent the chemicals from damaging the plants you want to keep.

ADDITIONAL INFORMATION

Bishop's Weed plants are long lived. They can grow for many years in the same location with little care. In fact, this plant has become naturalized in many parts of North America.

ADDITIONAL SPECIES, CULTIVARS, OR VARIETIES

The species *Aegopodium podagraria* is solid green and even more aggressive than the variegated cultivar. I would avoid using this plant in the landscape.

 Did You Know?

The common names give us some insight into this plant. This plant is so persistent that people believed it would even make a bishop swear, thus the name Bishop's Weed. Anyone trying to control an out-of-control planting would probably agree. The roots and leaves were used to treat gout, hence the name Goutweed.

Bugleweed

Ajuga reptans

Other Name: Ajuga
Flowers: Violet, blue-purple, rarely
  red or white
Bloom Period: May through June
Zone: 4
Color photograph on page 235.

Light Requirements:

Bugleweed is a beautiful evergreen groundcover. The strap-like leaves create a thick mat of green, bronze, or variegated foliage. New and interesting cultivars are continually appearing in garden centers. The foliage creates a nice backdrop to the spikes of its purple-blue May flowers. Use this plant where it can be enjoyed year round.

WHEN TO PLANT

Plant container-grown Bugleweed in the spring or early summer to allow the plants to become established before our tough winters.

WHERE TO PLANT

Bugleweed can be grown in sun or shade but flowers best in full sun. Use this plant as a groundcover in beds with moist, well-drained soil. Avoid open or exposed areas where this plant may suffer winter kill. Bugleweed is a quick mat-forming plant that works well under trees, in rock gardens, or as a groundcover in large beds. Avoid growing it next to lawn areas where its aggressive nature can be a problem.

HOW TO PLANT

Bugleweed plants are available from garden centers and perennial nurseries in flats and containers. Plant them at the same level they were growing in the pot. Space plants 12 inches apart. Divisions can be made any time, but you will get the best results if plants are divided in spring or early summer.

CARE AND MAINTENANCE

Bugleweed is a quick-growing plant that will eventually crowd out the weeds. Mulch new plantings to conserve moisture and reduce weeds. Remove weeds as they appear. Cut or mow off faded flowers to prevent reseeding and to keep the plants looking good. Lift and divide crowded plants. These fast growers may need to be divided as often as every 2 to 3 years. Overgrown plants often have dead centers or fail to bloom. Use a shovel or garden fork to dig out the plants. Cut the clump into several sections. Replant the divisions at 12-inch intervals in a prepared site. Bugleweed is susceptible to crown rot. Avoid this disease by growing plants in well-drained soil. Divide the plants every 2 to 3 years to avoid overcrowding and to reduce the risk of crown rot.

ADDITIONAL INFORMATION

Bugleweed seems to march out of the planting beds and right into the lawn. It often seems as though Bugleweed prefers the lawn location. Regularly edge the planting beds to slow the spreading Bugleweed. Remove stray plants as soon as they appear. Broadleaf weed killers applied to the lawn will help control the invading Bugleweed.

ADDITIONAL SPECIES, CULTIVARS, OR VARIETIES

Bugleweed comes in a variety of leaf and flower colors. Select a cultivar that is hardy to your location and complements the landscape design. *Ajuga reptans* 'Alba' has white flowers and light green leaves. 'Catlin's Giant' is one of the largest Bugleweed cultivars. It has 8-inch bronze leaves and blue flowers. The leaves of 'Burgundy Glow' are green, white, and dark pink. 'Chocolate Chip' is a natural dwarf with chocolate colored foliage and lacy blue flowers to 3 inches tall.

Did You Know?

Bugleweed is a member of the Mint family. It spreads in all directions by stolons. These horizontal stems lay on the soil surface producing new plants along the way. One plant can fill a 3-square-foot area in a season.

Deadnettle

Lamium maculatum

Other Name: Spotted Deadnettle
Size: 8 to 12 inches tall
Flowers: Rose-purple
Bloom Period: May through midsummer
Zones: 4
Color photograph on page 235.

Light Requirements:

Deadnettle is such an ugly name for such a pretty plant! The green and white foliage brightens up shady locations all season long. The delicate rose-purple flowers rise above the leaves for added beauty in May and June. Deadnettle works equally well in large or small groundcover plantings.

WHEN TO PLANT

Plant container-grown Deadnettle plants any time throughout the growing season. Divide plants in early spring for best results.

WHERE TO PLANT

Grow Deadnettle in partial to full shade locations. The leaves may scorch or brown if grown in full sun. It prefers moist, well-drained soil and will become open and a bit leggy in dry conditions. Deadnettle makes an excellent groundcover for shaded areas. Use it under trees where grass won't grow. I also like to use it as an edging plant or in rock gardens. It can be a little aggressive for some garden settings, so pick its neighbors carefully. The attractive foliage of Deadnettle has made it a popular addition to hanging baskets and containers.

HOW TO PLANT

Prepare the soil prior to planting. Work 2 inches of organic matter into the top 6 to 12 inches of soil. That will improve drainage in heavy clay soil and increase the water-holding capacity in sandy soil. Do not till the soil surrounding established trees and shrubs, as this could damage critical feeder roots. Dig a hole larger than the rootball and plant Deadnettle in the existing soil. Mulch the soil with organic matter. Deadnettle plants are available from garden centers and perennial nurseries in flats and containers. Plant them at the same level they were growing in the pot. Space these clump-forming plants 12 inches apart. Divisions can be made and planted in the early spring.

CARE AND MAINTENANCE
Spotted Deadnettle is basically pest free. Mulch new plantings to conserve moisture and reduce weeds. Weed control is critical in the first year, so remove weeds as they appear. Once established, Deadnettle will quickly fill in, keeping weed growth to a minimum. Water new plantings during dry periods. Prune back plants growing in dry shade to encourage fuller, more compact growth. Lift and divide overgrown plants, which often have dead centers or fail to bloom. Use a shovel or garden fork to dig out plants. Cut the clump into several sections. Replant divisions at 12-inch intervals in a prepared site.

ADDITIONAL INFORMATION
Deadnettle is similar to Variegated Yellow Archangel. In fact, it was once considered a species of Lamium. Both plants have similar growing requirements and uses. Deadnettle grows in a clump form, while Variegated Yellow Archangel is more spreading.

ADDITIONAL SPECIES, CULTIVARS, OR VARIETIES
'Beacon Silver' and 'White Nancy' are probably the two most popular deadnettle cultivars. 'Beacon Silver', also sold under its German name, 'Silbergroschen', has pink flowers. Its silver leaves with narrow green borders really stand out in the shade. 'White Nancy' looks like 'Beacon Silver' but has white flowers.

 Did You Know?

Spotted Deadnettle makes a nice addition to container plantings. The variegated foliage is an attractive backdrop for other plants. Move plants to the garden in the fall, or sink the container in the ground to overwinter. An even easier choice is to recycle the plants in the compost pile.

Ginger

Asarum canadense and *Asarum europaeum*

Other Names: Wild or Canada Ginger, and European or Shiny-Leaf Ginger
Size: 6 to 12 inches tall
Flowers: Greenish-purple or brown
Bloom Period: Early May
Zones: 3 to 5
Color photograph on page 235.

Light Requirements:

Additional Benefit:

Can't grow anything under that Spruce Tree? Try Wild Ginger. Both European and Wild Ginger can take heavy shade and moist conditions that most plants won't tolerate.

WHEN TO PLANT
Plant container-grown plants in early spring. Divisions can be made and planted before growth begins.

WHERE TO PLANT
Both European and Wild Ginger prefer full to dense shade, but will tolerate partial shade. Plant them in moist soil with lots of organic matter. They prefer an acid soil. Use them as groundcovers under trees and shrubs. The glossy green leaves of European Ginger reflect the light and help brighten shady locations. Wild Ginger is hardier and is a good choice for native woodland gardens. Both European Ginger and Wild Ginger combine well with Ferns, Hosta, Astilbe, and other shade-tolerant plants. Grow the European Ginger in a protected location for best results.

HOW TO PLANT
Ginger plants are available from garden centers and perennial nurseries in containers. Plant them at the same level they were growing in the pot. Space plants 8 to 12 inches apart. Divisions can be made in early spring before new growth begins.

CARE AND MAINTENANCE
Mulch new plantings with shredded leaves, twice-shredded bark, pine needles, or another organic matter. The mulching will help conserve moisture, reduce weeds, and add organic matter to the soil as

it breaks down. Water Ginger during dry periods. Water thoroughly, wetting the top 6 inches of the soil. Water again when the soil just starts to dry. Remember, shaded areas dry out more slowly than full-sun locations. Check the soil moisture before watering. Remove weeds as they appear.

ADDITIONAL INFORMATION

The Ginger flower often goes unnoticed. It is a greenish-purple or brown bell-shaped flower. The large leaves mask the flowers lying on the soil surface. Though hidden from above, the ground-dwelling insects are able to find and pollinate the flowers. Next spring, take a minute to peek under the Ginger leaves and see these unusual flowers.

ADDITIONAL SPECIES, CULTIVARS, OR VARIETIES

Wild Ginger, *Asarum canadense*, is native to the deciduous forests of Minnesota. It is hardy throughout the state. It has large, 5- to 6-inch-wide, kidney-shaped leaves. The leaves are deeply veined and slightly pubescent, providing textural interest in the garden. Wild Ginger dies back for the winter, leaving a void until early spring. European Ginger, *Asarum europaeum*, is an evergreen and is only hardy in Zone 4. It has smaller, glossy green leaves. Plant European Ginger in a protected location out of the winter wind and sun. Mulch plantings that will not be covered with snow throughout the winter. Mulching and proper planting will reduce the risk of winter injury. Other species and varieties worth experimenting with include, *Asarum naniflorum* 'Eco Dècor', *Asarum speciosum* 'Buxom Beauty' and *Asarum arifolium*.

 Did You Know?

The wild and European Gingers are not related to Zingiber officinale, *the Ginger used in cooking. The common name comes from the spicy fragrance given off by cut leaves, flowers, and rhizomes. Early European settlers candied or dried the roots of Wild Ginger for cooking.*

Houttuynia

Houttuynia cordata 'Chameleon'

Other Name: *Houttuynia cordata* 'Tricolor'
Size: 6 to 9 inches
Flowers: White
Bloom Period: Late June
Zone: 4b
Color photograph on page 235.

Light Requirements:

Houttuynia creates colorful mounds of heart-shaped leaves. The 2- to 3-inch leaves are a mixture of yellow, green, bronze, and red. The color is effective all season long. The small, white flowers are an added benefit in late June. Southern Minnesota gardeners looking for a change may want to add this plant to their landscape.

WHEN TO PLANT

Container-grown Houttuynia can be planted any time during the growing season. Plant in the spring and early summer for best results. Divisions can be made in the spring and cuttings can be taken and rooted in the summer.

WHERE TO PLANT

Grow Houttuynia in full sun or partial shade, although you will have better leaf color on plants grown in full sun. The leaves tend to fade to green and maroon in shady locations. Houttuynia prefers moist soil and will tolerate wet conditions. Use Houttuynia as a groundcover, edging plant, or in a rock garden. It looks nice when used next to water in the landscape. This plant seems to either struggle or take over the garden. So keep an eye on new plantings. Some gardeners plant Houttuynia in a pot and sink the pot in the soil, which helps slow down its spread.

HOW TO PLANT

Houttuynia will tolerate moist to wet soil. Adding organic matter to the soil will increase growing success and winter survival. Houttuynia plants are available from garden centers and perennial nurseries in containers. Plant them at the same level they were growing in the pot. Space plants 12 inches apart. Divisions can be made and planted in the spring.

CARE AND MAINTENANCE

Houttuynia is marginally hardy in Minnesota. It seems to either thrive or die in this area. Mulch new plantings to conserve moisture and reduce weeds. Remove weeds as they appear. Thriving plants will quickly crowd out the weeds. Lift and divide overgrown plants. Use a shovel or garden fork to dig out the plants. Cut the clump into several sections and replant the divisions at 12-inch intervals in a prepared site. Slugs may eat holes in the leaves. Beer-baited traps do a good job of controlling this pest.

ADDITIONAL INFORMATION

Houttuynia may need a little help getting through tough Minnesota winters. That's especially true for plants in wet locations. Mulch Houttuynia plants with straw, marsh hay, or evergreen branches in the fall after the ground freezes. That will help insulate the roots and increase the chance for survival.

ADDITIONAL SPECIES, CULTIVARS, OR VARIETIES

The straight species *Houttuynia cordata* has solid, dark green leaves. It is a larger plant, 18 inches tall, and can be more invasive. The cultivar 'Plena' has double white flowers.

 Did You Know?

Houttuynia is native to Japan. It was named for the Dutch naturalist Martin Houttuyn. Cordata refers to the heart-shaped leaves. Crush a leaf and take a whiff. The bruised foliage has a citrus smell. Some people like it while others think it smells like cheap perfume.

Lily-of-the-Valley

Convallaria majalis

Size: 8 inches tall
Flowers: White
Bloom Period: May to mid-June
Zones: All

Color photograph on page 236.

Light Requirements:

Additional Benefits:

Lily-of-the-Valley is an old-time favorite. Its fragrant, white, bell-shaped flowers and adaptability have helped this beauty remain part of modern landscapes.

WHEN TO PLANT

Plant Lily-of-the-Valley pips (shoots that appear on the rhizome) in the spring. Container-grown plants can be planted any time during the growing season.

WHERE TO PLANT

Lilies-of-the-Valley grow almost anywhere. They prefer partial to full shade and moist, well-drained soil, although they will tolerate most soil conditions. Lily-of-the-Valley is an effective groundcover in shady areas where nothing else will grow. It is one of the few plants that will grow in the small, shaded areas between homes. Use it in the heavy shade under trees and shrubs. Give plants a yearly application of fertilizer to help them compete with tree and shrub roots. Use Lily-of-the-Valley on a shady slope to cover the soil and reduce erosion. It is a great cut flower that has been a favorite of brides for many years. Keep in mind that any plant this tough is usually a weed problem in good garden settings. Do not grow this plant along with less assertive plants.

HOW TO PLANT

Though a tough plant, Lily-of-the-Valley benefits from proper soil preparation. Lilies-of-the-Valley are available from garden centers and perennial nurseries in containers. Plant them at the same level they were growing in the pot. Space container-grown plants or divisions with several pips 6 to 8 inches apart. Single pips should be spaced

3 to 4 inches apart. With proper care, the planting area will be filled in by the end of the second season.

CARE AND MAINTENANCE

Remove foliage in the spring before new growth begins. Mulch and water the plants during dry periods to keep them looking good all summer long. Plants grown in dry, sunny locations tend to brown out in midsummer. The plants will survive, but will look bad. Leaf spot and stem rot can be problems during wet seasons. These diseases cause brown spots to develop on the leaves and stems. Severe infestations can cause the plants to die back to ground level. Remove and destroy infected foliage. Remove all leaves in the fall to reduce the source of disease for next season. Divide the plants in the spring every four or five years to maintain a good flower display. Dig, divide, and replant the pips in properly prepared soil.

ADDITIONAL INFORMATION

Lily-of-the-Valley is an invasive plant that can be a problem in Minnesota forests. Avoid using this plant in landscapes near native woodland areas.

ADDITIONAL SPECIES, CULTIVARS, OR VARIETIES

There are quite a few cultivars available. The hybrids are often less aggressive than the species. Try 'Flore Pleno' if you want double white flowers. For a bigger plant, try 'Fortin's Giant'. It has longer leaves and bigger flowers. The variety *Rosea* has pink flowers. For interesting foliage, try 'Albo-striata', 'Aureovariegata', or 'Variegata'. They all have some type of yellow, cream, or white variegation on their leaves.

Did You Know?

All parts of the Lily-of-the-Valley are poisonous. Even the water used for the cut flowers is toxic. You may want to remove the poisonous red berries if there are children in your area.

Moneywort

Lysimachia nummularia

Other Names: Creeping Jenny
Size: 2 to 4 inches tall
Flowers: Yellow
Bloom Period: June
Zones: All
Color photograph on page 236.

Light Requirements:

The adaptability and fine texture of Moneywort make this a useful groundcover. The bright green leaves are round like coins. In June, the planting will be brightened with yellow flowers. The green leaves persist late into the fall. This attractive groundcover can provide a long season of interest in a variety of growing conditions.

WHEN TO PLANT

Plant seeds and divisions in early spring. Container-grown plants can be planted any time during the growing season.

WHERE TO PLANT

Moneywort will tolerate a wide range of conditions. It prefers shade with moist to wet organic soil. Plants grown in full sun need to be kept moist. Use Moneywort as a groundcover under trees and shrubs. I have it creep through my perennial gardens. The larger, robust plants can hold their own with this groundcover. I just pull it away from the less aggressive plants in my garden. Use it to soften structures in the landscape. Let it cascade over a wall, crawl between steppers, or climb in a rock garden. Though aggressive, it can easily be pulled to keep it in bounds. Broadleaf weed killers will keep it under control if it creeps into the lawn. Avoid using this plant near natural wetlands and waterways where it has become invasive.

HOW TO PLANT

Moneywort plants are available from garden centers and perennial nurseries. Plant them at the same level they were growing in the pot. Space plants 15 to 18 inches apart. Divide existing plantings in the spring. I had Moneywort plant itself in my yard. We left a flat of divisions sitting in the backyard waiting to be planted.The stems grew over the flat and into the surrounding soil. We now have a backyard filled with this groundcover.

CARE AND MAINTENANCE

Moneywort is a fast-growing plant. It can take over an area if the growing conditions are right. Monitor the planting, pruning back and pulling plants that have overstepped their bounds. Hand pulling or broadleaf weed killers will control plants that creep into the lawn. Water Moneywort during dry spells. Mulch plantings to conserve moisture and reduce weeds. Remove weeds as they appear. Moneywort will quickly fill in the area and eliminate this maintenance task. Lift and divide overgrown plants. Use a shovel or garden fork to dig them out. Cut the clump into several sections. Replant the divisions at 12-inch intervals in a prepared site.

ADDITIONAL INFORMATION

Moneywort is an invasive plant that has naturalized in the eastern United States. It may become a problem in Minnesota wetlands and springs. Avoid using this plant in landscapes near these types of natural areas.

ADDITIONAL SPECIES, CULTIVARS, OR VARIETIES

A yellow leaf form is available. Use *Lysimachia nummularia* 'Aurea' in full sun and moist soil for the best leaf color. This plant is less vigorous than the straight species. Remove any of the more aggressive green sprouts that appear.

 Did You Know?

The name Lysimachia *comes from King Lysimachos back in 300 B.C. He was said to have tamed a bull with a piece of loosestrife. In Greek, his name means ending strife.* Nummularia *means with coin-shaped leaves. And can you guess where the money of Moneywort came from?*

Mother of Thyme

Thymus serpyllum

Other Names: Creeping Thyme,
Thymus angustifolius
Size: 1 to 6 inches tall
Flowers: Purple
Bloom Period: Summer
Zones: All
Color photograph on page 236.

Light Requirements:

Additional Benefits:

Mother of Thyme is a close relative of the Thyme most used for cooking. Its creeping growth habit makes it a good groundcover for sunny, dry locations. Add attractive leaves and a summer-long bloom, and you have a groundcover fit for most landscapes.

WHEN TO PLANT

Start seeds of Thyme indoors in early spring. The seeds need light and 55- to 60-degree temperatures to germinate. Established plants can be lifted and divided in the spring. Plant container-grown Thyme throughout the growing season. I like to get it in the ground early so it has time to get established before winter. You can also take cuttings of new growth and root and plant them in the summer.

WHERE TO PLANT

Grow Thyme in full sun and well-drained soil. It will tolerate light shade, but does best in full sun and poor, dry soil. Use Thyme as a groundcover on slopes, in rock gardens, near walkways, and between steppers where it can be seen. The lovely fragrance and attractive flowers add to its landscape value. Thyme will tolerate light traffic. In fact, a little foot traffic will release its fragrance. I like to surprise my visitors with the lovely aroma as they pass over my Thyme-edged steppers. In the past few years, I have seen many Thyme "lawns." People have used Thyme with stone walkways in place of the traditional Bluegrass lawn.

HOW TO PLANT

Thyme is available from garden centers and perennial nurseries in containers. Plant them at the same level they were growing in the pot. Space plants 6 to 18 inches apart. Divisions can be made and planted in the spring or early summer.

CARE AND MAINTENANCE

Established Thyme needs very little care. Winter dieback can be a problem in extremely cold winters or poorly drained locations. Fortunately, stems will often root and survive even when the parent plant dies. Prune back plants in the spring before flowering begins. Be careful not to disturb the rooted stems you want to keep. Spring pruning will remove any winter damage and give the plants a neat appearance. Do not fertilize unless your plants show signs of nutrient deficiencies. Excess fertilizer results in tall, weak, and unattractive growth. Root rot can be a problem when Thyme is overwatered or grown in poorly drained soils. Lift and divide overgrown plants. Use a shovel or garden fork to dig out plants.

ADDITIONAL INFORMATION

Bees love Thyme flowers. This is a nice bonus for those of us who are not highly allergic to the bees. Use one of the less floriferous Thymes, such as woolly, or clip off the flowers if bee allergies are a concern.

ADDITIONAL SPECIES, CULTIVARS, OR VARIETIES

There is great confusion over this plant. It is listed under several different botanical names. That may be why there is some variability in the plants sold as Creeping or Mother of Thyme. For a little flower color variety, try 'Albus' with white flowers, 'Coccinea' with red flowers, or 'Pink Chintz' with pink flowers. 'Elfin', as its name implies, is small, 2 by 5 inches, and slow growing.

 Did You Know?

Thymus *has long been used as a fragrant groundcover. Europeans grew it in their landscapes. As women's skirts brushed over the Thyme, its fragrance was released. It was a nice way to cover up problems that regular bathing and deodorants now handle.*

Pachysandra

Pachysandra terminalis

Other Name: Japanese Spurge
Size: 6 to 8 inches
Flowers: White
Bloom Period: April to May
Zone: 4b
Color photograph on page 236.

Light Requirements:

Pachysandra is probably one of the most commonly used ground-covers. Its glossy green leaves provide year-round interest. In the spring, the leaves are topped with white flowers. It is a good ground-cover for shady areas with appropriate soil conditions.

WHEN TO PLANT

Plant divisions and rooted cuttings of Pachysandra in the spring or early summer. Container-grown plants can be planted any time during the growing season. Earlier plantings allow transplants to get established before winter.

WHERE TO PLANT

Grow Pachysandra in light to full shade. Plants will yellow when grown in full sun. Winter wind and sun can also cause yellowing. Avoid this problem by planting this evergreen groundcover in a pro-tected location. Pachysandra needs moist, well-drained soil for best results. Grow this groundcover under trees and shrubs. It can also be used in small or large groundcover beds on flat or sloped surfaces.

HOW TO PLANT

Pachysandra needs moist, well-drained soil to thrive. Prepare the soil prior to planting. Work 2 inches of organic matter into the top 6 to 12 inches of soil. That will improve drainage in heavy clay soil and increase the water-holding capacity in sandy soil. Do not till the soil surrounding established trees and shrubs; this could damage critical feeder roots. Dig a hole larger than the rootball and plant Pachysandra in the existing soil. Mulch the soil with organic matter. Pachysandra plants are available from garden centers and perennial nurseries. Plant them at the same level they were growing in the pot. Space plants 12 inches apart.

Care and Maintenance
Mulch new plantings to conserve moisture and reduce weeds. Remove weeds as they appear. This is very important and often a time-consuming task the first few years. Once the Pachysandra fills in, it will crowd out the weeds. Yearly mulching will also help improve the soil. Mulch and fertilize plants as needed in the spring.

Additional Information
Leaf blight, root rot, and Euonymus scale can be devastating problems. Proper soil preparation, placement, and care will help prevent these problems. Remove blight-infected leaves as soon as they appear. Water in the morning or late afternoon to avoid wet leaves at night. Treat Euonymous scale when the young shell-less scales are active. This coincides with the beginning of Japanese Tree Lilac and Catalpa bloom. Use insecticidal soap at that time and then twice more at ten- to twelve-day intervals.

Additional Species, Cultivars, or Varieties
Allegheny Spurge, *Pachysandra procumbens,* is a close relative of Japanese Pachysandra. It is native to more southern areas of the United States. This Spurge is hardy to the southern part of Minnesota. Over the winter, the leaves can become tattered or totally drop from this plant. It is taller and less vigorous than the Japanese Pachysandra and works best in small areas. The 'Green Carpet' cultivar of Japanese Pachysandra is a low-growing plant. The compact growth and deep green leaves make this the preferred choice for many landscapers. The less vigorous 'Variegata' has mottled white foliage. Use this choice for small locations or to create contrast in shade gardens.

Potentilla

Potentilla species

Other Names: Spring Potentilla, Three-Toothed or Wineleaf Cinquefoil **Size:** 3 to 10 inches **Flowers:** White or bright yellow **Bloom Period:** May to June **Zones:** 3 to 4 *Color photograph on page 236.*	**Light Requirements:** **Additional Benefit:**

Potentilla is a good groundcover for those of you gardening in rocky and sandy locations in the state. The species you select will determine the look you get in the landscape. Some Cinquefoils lose most or all of their leaves for the winter, while others are evergreen. Flowers are typically yellow or white, although there are some newer red-flowering cultivars. Select the Potentilla that is hardy to your location and fits best in your setting.

WHEN TO PLANT

Plant container-grown Potentillas throughout the summer. Divisions can be made and planted in the spring.

WHERE TO PLANT

Grow Potentillas in full-sun locations, although they will tolerate light shade. They need good drainage for best results. Use Potentilla for rock gardens, on dry slopes, or as a groundcover in open, rocky areas.

HOW TO PLANT

Potentilla needs good drainage. Proper soil preparation is critical before planting Potentilla in clay soil. Work 2 inches of organic matter into the top 6 to 12 inches of soil. That will improve drainage in heavy clay soil and increase the water-holding capacity in sandy soil. Potentilla plants are available from garden centers and perennial nurseries. Plant them at the same level they were growing in the container. Space plants 6 to 12 inches apart, depending on the species used. Divisions can be made and planted in the spring. Space divisions 6 to 12 inches apart.

CARE AND MAINTENANCE

Water new plantings as needed until they are established. Some species are drought tolerant once established, while others benefit from watering during extended dry periods. Mulch new plantings to conserve moisture and reduce weeds. Remove weeds as they appear; this is a very important though time-consuming task during the first few years. Once the Potentillas fill in, they will crowd out the weeds. Some species benefit from pruning. This can be done whenever the plants appear unkempt. Lift and divide overgrown plants, which often have dead centers or fail to bloom. Use a shovel or garden fork to dig out the plants. Cut the clump into several sections and replant the divisions at 12-inch intervals in a prepared site.

ADDITIONAL INFORMATION

The Potentilla groundcovers are related to the popular summer-blooming shrub. A close look at the flowers will help you see the similarity.

ADDITIONAL SPECIES, CULTIVARS, OR VARIETIES

Spring Cinquefoil, *Potentilla verna,* formerly known as *Potentilla tabernaemontani,* grows 2 to 3 inches tall and has yellow flowers in late spring. This deciduous plant loses its leaves in the winter. Use it in dry wall plantings or as a low-growing groundcover. It is hardy in Zone 4. Wineleaf Cinquefoil, *Potentilla tridentata,* can also be used as a groundcover, in rock gardens, and on dry slopes. It is native to Minnesota and can be found along the shore of Lake Superior. This evergreen spreader is 2 to 6 inches tall with white flowers. Wineleaf Cinquefoil is hardy throughout Minnesota.

 Did You Know?

The name Potentilla *comes from the Latin word* potens *which means powerful. The word refers to the medicinal properties this group of plants is supposed to possess.*

Sweet Woodruff

Galium odoratum

Other Name: Woodruff
Size: 6 to 8 inches
Flowers: White
Bloom Period: May and June
Zone: 4
Color photograph on page 236.

Light Requirements:

Additional Benefits:

Don't let the delicate appearance of Sweet Woodruff fool you. Its bright green, fragrant leaves will cover the ground from early spring through late fall. The white flowers cover the plant for several weeks. Consider adding a little patch to your garden or a large planting under some trees and shrubs.

WHEN TO PLANT
Divide and plant divisions of Sweet Woodruff in early spring for best results. However, the plants do seem to tolerate division almost any time during the growing season. Plant container-grown Sweet Woodruff throughout the season.

WHERE TO PLANT
Sweet Woodruff performs best in full to partial shade. Plantings tend to burn out in full sun and dry locations. Woodruff prefers moist, well-drained soil, but tolerates a wide range of conditions. Use Woodruff as a groundcover under trees and shrubs. In shady spots, it makes a nice edging or rock garden plant. Place it somewhere you can enjoy the fragrance and blooms. I have mine under a Serviceberry tree near my front door. The fragrance greets me on warm summer evenings. It's a little landscape aromatherapy to end my work day.

HOW TO PLANT
Sweet Woodruff plants are available from garden centers and perennial nurseries. Plant them at the same level they were growing in the pot. Space plants 12 inches apart.

CARE AND MAINTENANCE
Keep the soil near new plantings moist, but not wet. Once the plants are established, they will need watering only during dry periods.

Mulch new plantings to conserve moisture and reduce weeds. Remove weeds as they appear. The Woodruff will quickly cover the area, reducing your weeding time. Mine grew into the lawn and crowded out the bluegrass. That was fine, since I wanted to expand that planting bed anyway. You can prevent this problem by digging out the edge of the spreading Woodruff. Woodruff maintains an even and attractive growth habit throughout the summer. You can clip it back several times during the summer to create a more formal appearance. Poor flowering and a fungal leaf spot may be a problem on rare occasions. Apply a low-nitrogen fertilizer in the spring to improve flowering. Remove disease-infected leaves. In severe cases, you will need to remove infected plants, add organic matter, and wait for the surrounding plants to fill in the bare spots.

ADDITIONAL INFORMATION

Lift and divide overgrown plants, which often have dead centers or fail to bloom. Use a shovel or garden fork to dig out plants. Cut the clump into several sections and replant the divisions at 12-inch intervals in a prepared site.

ADDITIONAL SPECIES, CULTIVARS, OR VARIETIES

Sweet Woodruff was formerly listed as *Asperula odorata*. This group of plants is often called Woodruff. Both Galium and Asperula have been called Bedstraw. *Galium odorata* is the best choice for use as a groundcover. To avoid confusion, use both the common and botanical names when ordering this plant.

Did You Know?

Sweet Woodruff has long been valued for its fragrance and flavor. The dried leaves and stems are used in potpourris and sachets. Fresh leaves and flowers are used to flavor May wine and other spring drinks.

Variegated Yellow Archangel

Lamium galeobdolon 'Variegatum'

Other Name: Yellow Archangel
   Lamiastrum galeobdolon 'Variegatum'
Size: 12 to 18 inches tall
Flowers: Yellow
Bloom Period: Late May to June
Zone: 4
Color photograph on page 236.

Light Requirements:

N eed a plant for dry shade? Variegated Yellow Archangel could be the plant you are looking for. It will quickly fill in those difficult shaded locations. Its variegated leaves will help brighten the deep shade and the bright yellow flowers will liven up the landscape in late May through June. Just plant it where you can keep an eye on it— Variegated Archangel tends to move around the landscape without waiting for your permission.

WHEN TO PLANT
Plant container-grown Variegated Yellow Archangel any time during the growing season. Divide established plants in early spring.

WHERE TO PLANT
Grow Variegated Yellow Archangel in partially to fully shaded locations. It prefers moist, well-drained soil while adjusting to its new location. Established plants are tolerant of well-drained to dry soil. This is one of the few plants that can take dry shade. Use this aggressive grower in difficult areas. The poor conditions will help to contain its rampant growth. Or plant variegated archangel in contained areas, such as planting beds between the house and sidewalk. The variegated leaves help brighten up shady locations, and contrast nicely against the dark green leaves of other plants. It can also be used in planters, hanging baskets, or as a houseplant.

HOW TO PLANT
Variegated Yellow Archangel will grow just about anywhere it is planted. These plants are available from garden centers and perennial nurseries in flats and containers. Plant them at the same level they were growing in the pot. Space the fast-growing plants

142

2 to 3 feet apart. Divisions can be made and planted in early spring.

CARE AND MAINTENANCE

Yellow Archangel is basically pest free. This fast grower can hold its own with the weeds. Mulch new plantings to conserve moisture and reduce weeds. Remove weeds as they appear. In a short time, the Yellow Archangel will be able to crowd out the weeds with little help from you. Shear plants back to 6 inches in midsummer to promote compact growth. Containing this plant will be your biggest maintenance task, although proper siting will help reduce this problem. Contain the plants by pruning back any stems that grow out of the planting bed. Plants that creep into the lawn can be dug or controlled with broadleaf lawn weed killers. Lift and divide overgrown plants in early spring. Use a shovel or garden fork to dig out plants. Cut the clump into several sections and replant the divisions 2 to 3 feet apart.

ADDITIONAL INFORMATION

The Variegated Yellow Archangel can be found listed under several botanical names. *Lamium galeobdolon* is once again the accepted name. You may also see it listed as *Lamiastrum galeobdolon* or *Galeobdolon luteum*.

ADDITIONAL SPECIES, CULTIVARS, OR VARIETIES

Herman's Pride Archangel, *Lamium galeobdolon* 'Herman's Pride', is a popular cultivar. It has narrower green leaves with regular silver variegation. This cultivar has more of a clump form than a spreading form. It is less aggressive than 'Variegatum'.

Did You Know?

Yellow Archangel is included with the Spotted Deadnettles, Lamiums. *A closer look at the flowers made the botanist rename this plant* Lamiastrum *for a short time, which means "somewhat resembling* Lamium."

Vinca

Vinca minor

Other Name: Periwinkle

Size: 6 inches

Flowers: Blue

Bloom Period: May

Zone: 4

Color photograph on page 236.

Light Requirements:

The periwinkle blue flowers of Vinca can brighten the sometimes dreary days of May. Its glossy evergreen foliage makes this a plant with year-round interest. Use it to cover a small piece of ground or as a groundcover under trees and shrubs. I grow several different varieties of Vinca in my garden tucked in under plants, around boulders, and in other spots that need livening up.

WHEN TO PLANT

Plant Vinca divisions in the spring for best results. Container-grown plants can be planted any time during the growing season.

WHERE TO PLANT

Vinca performs best in partial to full shade. It will tolerate full sun, but the leaves will be dull and pale green. Grow plants in an area protected from winter wind and sun. Vinca grows best in moist, well-drained soil. The plants will not tolerate wet conditions. Use Vinca as a groundcover under trees and shrubs. It also works well in rock gardens and sloped areas. I like to mix spring- and fall-blooming bulbs in with this groundcover. It gives you added bloom and makes for a nice surprise in the landscape.

HOW TO PLANT

Moist soil with good drainage is critical for growing success. Prepare the soil prior to planting. Do not till the soil surrounding established trees and shrubs, which will damage critical feeder roots. Dig a hole larger than the rootball and plant Vinca in the existing soil. Mulch the soil with organic matter. Vinca is available from garden centers and perennial nurseries in flats and containers. Plant them at the same level they were growing in the pot. Space plants 6 to 14 inches apart. It will take 2 years for the plants placed at 12-inch intervals to fill in a bed. Pinch back Vincas at planting time. This encourages branching and will give you a denser cover. Divisions can be made and planted in the spring.

CARE AND MAINTENANCE

Mulch new plantings to conserve moisture and reduce weeds. Remove weeds as they appear. This is very important and often time consuming the first few years. Once the Vinca fills in, it will crowd out the weeds. Water plants during dry periods. Fertilize as needed in the spring. Keep the plants looking good by shearing them in the spring. Sheared plants tend to be thicker and more vigorous. Lift and divide overgrown plants. Use a shovel or garden fork to dig out plants. Cut the clump into several sections and replant the divisions 6 to 14 inches apart in a prepared site.

ADDITIONAL INFORMATION

Vinca is susceptible to several diseases including canker, leaf spot, and root rot. Avoid these problems by growing Vinca in areas with good air circulation and good drainage. Remove any infected leaves as soon as they appear.

ADDITIONAL SPECIES, CULTIVARS, OR VARIETIES

More and more cultivars are becoming available. Check with your local garden center or perennial nursery for cultivars available in your area. There are several white-flowering forms including 'Alba' and 'Bowles White'. 'Alba Variegata' has white flowers with green- and yellow-variegated leaves. 'Argenteovariegata' has light violet-blue flowers with white and green leaves. Try 'Atropurpurea' if you want dark purple flowers. 'Illumination' has bright golden foliage edged in dark green.

 Did You Know?

Vinca is starting to appear in our natural forest areas around the state. Watch for and remove stray plants. Those near natural areas should avoid this plant.

Wintercreeper

Euonymus fortunei

Other Name: Wintercreeper Euonymus
Size: 2 to 18 inches tall
Flowers: Greenish-white; not effective
Bloom Period: June or July; not effective
Zone: 4
Color photograph on page 236.

Light Requirements:

Additional Benefit:

Trailing types of Wintercreeper can be grown as groundcovers. The small leaves and trailing growth habit can soften walls, raised beds, and other structures in the landscape. Wintercreeper will root wherever its stems touch the ground, which makes it easy to propagate new plants. Wintercreepers are semi- or fully evergreen. The trailing types tend to produce few, if any, flowers or fruits.

WHEN TO PLANT

Container-grown plants can be planted any time during the growing season. Spring planting will result in established plants with the greatest chance for winter survival.

WHERE TO PLANT

Plant Wintercreeper in areas with full or partial shade and moist, well-drained soil. They will tolerate full sun in the summer, but can be damaged by winter sun and wind. Variegated and less hardy cultivars benefit from winter protection. Mulch exposed plants or grow them in areas protected from the winter wind and sun. Use Euonymus as groundcovers under trees and shrubs, or in large planting beds. The small-leafed varieties look nice in rock gardens, while the variegated types make nice specimen plantings.

HOW TO PLANT

Trailing Wintercreeper plants are available from garden centers and perennial nurseries in flats and containers. Plant them at the same level they were growing in the pot. Space plants 12 to 24 inches apart.

CARE AND MAINTENANCE

Proper cultivar selection and plant placement are the best ways to reduce maintenance and keep this plant healthy. Select cultivars and varieties that are hardy for your location. Prevent winter injury by growing this plant in a protected site or east exposure, where it will be safe from winter wind and sun. Scale insects and crown galls are the worst pest problems. Scale insects are sucking insects that feed on plant juices. They form a hard shell that makes treatment difficult. Treat the shell-less immature scale with an insecticide when the Japanese Tree Lilacs are just starting to bloom. Repeat the application twice at ten- to twelve-day intervals. Read and follow all label directions carefully. Crown gall is caused by a bacteria. Infected plants develop golf ball-like nodules on the roots and stems. Remove and destroy badly infected plants. Light infections can be controlled with sanitation. Prune out and destroy gall-infested stems. Disinfect tools with denatured alcohol between cuts.

ADDITIONAL INFORMATION

Prune trailing forms of Wintercreeper in the spring. Use your lawn mower for quick results. Set your rotary mower on the highest setting and cut the Wintercreeper.

ADDITIONAL SPECIES, CULTIVARS, OR VARIETIES

Purpleleaf Wintercreeper, *Euonymus fortunei* var. *coloratus*, is the most popular and readily available trailing Euonymus. It is hardy in Zone 4b. The evergreen leaves turn purple in winter. It grows 6 to 18 inches tall and benefits from winter protection. Check your local nursery for available cultivars.

 Did You Know?

Wintercreeper is starting to appear in wild areas around the state. Select a sterile type that is less of a threat to our native areas. Watch for stray plants. Those near natural areas may want to avoid this plant.

Ornamental Grasses

I N THE LAST FIFTEEN TO TWENTY YEARS, ornamental grasses
have become an important part of the American gardening scene.
With their long, narrow leaves, these distinctive plants provide
motion and sound in a landscape. A gentle breeze makes the tall
Moor Grass flowers dance and the Switchgrass rustle.

Most ornamental grasses bloom at some point during the growing
season. The flowers on some, such as Blue Fescue, are secondary to
the foliage, while those of others, such as Silver Grass, steal the show
from the greenery. The blooms also add winter color to an otherwise
barren garden since the dried leaves and flowers often remain intact
on the plant. They also can be enjoyed in a vase indoors.

One of the biggest and most desired ornamental grasses is pampas
grass. If you have traveled to California, the southeastern United
States, or the arid dome in Milwaukee Wisconsin's Mitchell Park
Conservatory (the Domes), you have seen this plant. It grows up to
10 feet tall, producing large white, silver, or pink flowers. Many
plants go by the name pampas grass, but the variety I just described
is Cortaderia selloana, and is not hardy in Minnesota.

It is important to select ornamental grasses that are best suited to
the growing conditions in your area. Most grasses prefer full sun and
well-drained soil. A few, like Hakonechloa, will tolerate shade and
moist soils. Some of these grasses are relatively new to the upper
Midwest. Many Minnesota gardeners, gardening professionals, and
researchers have been evaluating ornamental grasses and their
cultivars for winter hardiness. Those of you in Zone 3 may have to
do some testing on your own. Try a few of the hardiest grasses in
protected sites in your landscape. Remember cold temperatures,
snow cover, and soil drainage all influence the ornamental grasses'
ability to survive our harsh winters. You may have better or worse
results in the microclimates of your own garden.

Chapter Four

Many of the ornamental grasses are substantial plants, so it's important to allow sufficient space for them to grow and bloom. I have quite a few grasses in my small city lot, but I use single specimens of various species and varieties to add interest, texture, and sound. In larger settings, ornamental grasses make great screens, as well as background or hillside plantings. However, remember your screen will be missing from the late winter, when you trim back the plants, through early summer, when they again reach full size.

Many ornamental grasses come in containers that are 1 gallon or larger. That means you will need a shovel, not a trowel, for planting. Dig the planting hole the same depth and two to three times wider than the rootball. Plant the grass at the same level it was growing in the container. Established grasses rarely need watering or fertilizing except in extreme droughts or where the soil is sandy. Follow soil test recommendations when fertilizing ornamental grasses.

Cut back ornamental grasses in the spring before growth begins. I use hand pruners for my small plantings. A weed whip or electric hedge trimmer will make larger jobs go much faster. This is also a good time to dig, divide, and transplant ornamental grasses that are overgrown, dead in the center, or performing poorly.

Ornamental grasses can make a big impact in the home landscape. With proper selection, you can use ornamental grasses to add low-maintenance, year-round interest to your landscape.

Blue Fescue

Festuca cinerea

Other Names: Gray Fescue, *Festuca glauca, Festuca ovina glauca*
Size: 6 to 10 inches tall by 8 inches wide
Flowers: Blue-green
Fruit/Seed: Beige seedheads
Bloom Period: Midsummer
Zone: 4
Color photograph on page 236.

Light Requirements:

Blue Fescue has long been used in perennial gardens and landscapes. This small grass, 10 to 12 inches tall, is a good fit even in small plots. Blue fescue forms a tuft of narrow, blue-green leaves. Its colorful, fine texture blends well in rock and perennial gardens. Try using this salt-tolerant plant in gardens where winter deicing salts can create problems. I have seen it growing successfully in boulevard plantings, parking lot islands, and groundcover beds next to salted sidewalks.

WHEN TO PLANT

Plant container-grown Blue Fescue during the growing season. I prefer spring and early summer. That allows the grass time to become established before our harsh winter. Divide and transplant Blue Fescue in the spring.

WHERE TO PLANT

Plant Blue Fescue in full sun in well-drained soil. Add organic matter to soil with a heavy clay content to improve drainage. This small grass makes a good edging plant or groundcover. I like to mix Blue Fescue with other plants in my flower gardens. The fine texture is a nice contrast to bolder, coarser-textured plants. Blue Fescue also works well in rock gardens. Use it in areas where its evergreen foliage can be enjoyed throughout the winter—when it's not buried under a blanket of snow!

HOW TO PLANT

Blue Fescue is available in pots from perennial nurseries, garden centers, and catalogs. Plant Blue Fescue at the same level it was growing in the pot. Gently loosen potbound and girdling roots before planting. Space the plants 1 foot apart. You can place the plants a few inches closer together for a denser, groundcover effect.

CARE AND MAINTENANCE
Blue fescue is a relatively low-maintenance plant. Avoid overwatering and overfertilizing, which can lead to poor growth, root rot, and dead plants. Blue Fescue can be short-lived in Minnesota. Try dividing these plants every three or four years to increase vigor. Or replace them with new plants as needed. Although Blue Fescue is an ever-green, parts of the plant turn brown during the winter. You can trim back the older leaves in late winter before growth begins, or just let the new growth mask the old leaves as they fade away. I have done both, and my plants looked fine and remained healthy either way.

ADDITIONAL INFORMATION
The fine-textured, blue-green foliage makes Blue Fescue a nice addition to any garden. Try combining this plant with one of the purple-leaved Coralbells or hardy Geraniums. I have allowed my Moneywort groundcover to creep through the Blue Fescue. The contrasting green leaves and yellow flowers make an attractive display. I saw another gardener do the same thing with a yellow-flowered Creeping Potentilla.

ADDITIONAL SPECIES, CULTIVARS, OR VARIETIES
Check garden centers, perennial nurseries, and catalogs for available cultivars. 'Elijah Blue' is an excellent cultivar available at many garden centers. It grows 8 inches tall and has powdery blue foliage. 'Sea Urchin', sometimes sold as 'Seeigel', is 6 inches tall with sea green foliage. Use 'Blue Glow' ('Blauglut') for dark blue foliage, and 'Blue Fox' ('Blaufuchs') for steel blue foliage. 'Golden Toupe' is a gold-leaved form sometimes available.

Blue Oat Grass

Helictotrichon sempervirens

Other Names: Ornamental Oats,
  Avena sempervirens
Size: 2 to 3 feet tall and wide
Flowers: Pale blue
Fruit/Seed: Brown seedheads
Bloom Period: Early summer
Zone: 4
Color photograph on page 236.

Light Requirements:

B lue Oat Grass is an excellent and dependable plant for Minnesota gardens in Zone 4. It is one of the few ornamental grasses that can tolerate the heavy clay soils. Try including this large tuft of Blue Grass in your perennial garden.

WHEN TO PLANT

Plant container-grown Blue Oat Grass during the growing season. I prefer planting in spring and early summer, which gives the grass time to get established before our harsh winter. Divide and transplant Blue Oat Grass in the spring.

WHERE TO PLANT

Plant Blue Oat Grass in areas with full sun and well-drained soil. It is more tolerant of clay soil than Blue Fescue, but I still add organic matter to soil with a heavy clay content. Blue Oat Grass is larger and slightly coarser than Blue Fescue. Use it as a specimen plant in flower beds. It combines well with bolder, coarse-textured perennials. One of my favorite, quite accidental, combinations is 'Husker Red' Penstemon planted behind Blue Oat Grass. The bronze foliage, white flowers and red seed pods of the Penstemon creates a nice contrast with the Blue Oats.

HOW TO PLANT

Plant container-grown Blue Oat Grass at the same level it was growing in the pot. Gently loosen potbound and girdling roots before planting. Space the plants 24 to 30 inches apart.

CARE AND MAINTENANCE

Blue Oat Grass is a low-maintenance plant. Avoid over-watering and overfertilizing. Too much water and nitrogen can lead to root rot and plant decline. Rust, a fungal disease, can occasionally be a problem during wet, humid weather. Adjust watering if necessary, and remove infected leaves as soon as they appear. The disease usually clears up in drier weather. Blue Oat Grass is evergreen, although the leaves may turn brown during a particularly harsh winter. I find it holds its color better than Blue Fescue. You can trim back the older leaves in late winter before new growth begins, or just let the new growth mask the old leaves as they fade away. I have done both and my plants looked fine and remained healthy either way.

ADDITIONAL INFORMATION

Blue Oat Grass is a more reliable plant than Blue Fescue. It also has better winter interest. Its larger size makes it easier to see through the snow, and the leaves tend to hold their blue color better than Blue Fescue.

ADDITIONAL SPECIES, CULTIVARS, OR VARIETIES

Check perennial nurseries, garden centers, and catalogs for available cultivars. 'Sapphire Fountain' ('Saphirsprudel') was introduced from Germany in 1982. It is more resistant to rust.

Did You Know?

The botanical name, Helictotrichon sempervirens, *is derived from the Greek language.* Helictotrichon *is from the word* helix *meaning spiral and* trichos *meaning hair. The word* sempervirens *means evergreen. This aptly describes the tufts of thin, slightly twisted leaf blades of the evergreen Blue Oat Grass.*

Bluestem

Andropogon scoparius

Other Name: *Schizachyrium scoparium,* Little Bluestem	**Light Requirements:**
Size: 1½ to 3 feet tall and 2 feet wide	
Flowers: Pinkish-white	**Additional Benefits:**
Fruit/Seed: Silvery-white seedhead	
Bloom Period: Fall	
Zones: All	
Color photograph on page 236.	

L ittle Bluestem was a major element in Minnesota's native prairie landscape, and its beauty and year-round interest have helped this ornamental grass find its way into the home landscape as well. This short grass forms loose, upright clumps. Its compact size makes it a practical choice for even the smallest city lot, like mine. Consider adding this native Minnesota resident to your plantings. It will serve as a beautiful reminder of our past.

WHEN TO PLANT

Plant container-grown Little Bluestem during the growing season. I prefer spring and early summer, which gives the grass time to become established before our harsh winter. Divide and transplant Little Bluestem in the spring. Large plantings of Little Bluestem can be seeded in the spring or fall. The seed must be stratified and cold treated to germinate. Little Bluestem and short Prairie Seed mixes are available from several quality Prairie Seed companies. Purchase clean seed that is free of stems, fluff, bracts, and leaves. Although clean seed costs more, you actually get more seed and less debris for the money. Quality companies will provide soil preparation and planting guidelines.

WHERE TO PLANT

Plant Little Bluestem in areas with full sun and well-drained soil. Add organic matter to soil with a heavy clay content to improve drainage. Little bluestem works well in perennial and naturalized gardens. Bluestem plants also help support Asters and other tall plants that would otherwise need staking. A mass planting of Little Bluestem can be quite impressive in a large landscape.

How to Plant

Plant container-grown Bluestem at the same level it was growing in the pot. Gently loosen potbound and girdling roots before planting. Space plants at least 2 feet apart.

Care and Maintenance

When placed in an appropriate spot, Little Bluestem requires very little maintenance. Poor growth will occur in wet, poorly drained soils. Dig up struggling plants in the early spring and move them to a location with better drainage, or add organic matter to the soil to improve drainage before replanting. Avoid overfertilizing. Plants tend to flop over when they receive excessive nitrogen or are grown in nutrient-rich soils. Cut down old stems in the late winter before growth begins.

Additional Information

Little Bluestem can add year-round interest to the garden. The fine-textured green to blue-green foliage fits well in naturalized or perennial gardens. The striking orange-red fall color is guaranteed to brighten up any landscape. The late summer flowers quickly give way to showy silvery-white seedheads. The seedheads are attractive outside in the garden or indoors for flower arrangements. The colorful foliage and seedheads persist into winter.

Additional Species, Cultivars, or Varieties

Big Bluestem, *Andropogon gerardi,* is a larger cousin to Little Bluestem. It was the primary grass of the tall grass prairies. Use this plant, which grows to 4 to 7 feet or more, where it has room to grow. Its heat and salt tolerance as well as attractive seedheads and red-purple fall color make it a good choice for large landscapes.

ORNAMENTAL GRASSES

Feather Reed Grass

Calamagrostis × acutiflora 'Stricta'

Other Names: *Calamagrostis acutiflora*
   'Karl Foerster'
Size: 4 to 5 feet tall and 2 feet wide
Flowers: Pink
Fruit/Seed: Beige seedheads persist;
   wheat-like appearance
Bloom Period: July
Zone: 4
Color photograph on page 237.

Light Requirements:

Additional Benefits:

Feather Reed Grass is one of the best ornamental grasses for use in Minnesota landscapes. The wheat-like seedheads and stiff, upright leaves provide year-round interest. Feather Reed Grass is tall enough to demand attention in a large yard, yet small enough to fit into more limited spaces. This tough plant tolerates a wider range of growing conditions than most grasses. I have seen it used at a custard stand in a narrow planting bed between a wall and the parking lot. It has withstood the salt, winters, clay soil, and reflected heat for several years. If it can grow there, it will thrive in your garden.

WHEN TO PLANT

Plant container-grown Feather Reed Grass during the growing season. I prefer to plant in the spring and early summer, which gives the grass time to get established before our harsh winter. Divide and transplant Feather Reed Grass in the spring.

WHERE TO PLANT

Plant Feather Reed Grass in full sun or lightly shaded locations. It prefers moist, well-drained soil, but will tolerate clay and wet soil with good drainage. Feather Reed is stiffly upright. This makes it a good choice for a background plant or as a vertical accent in the landscape. Use it as a low screen to block the view of a compost pile, neighbor's doghouse, or storage area. Its moisture tolerance makes it suitable for placement alongside a pool or pond. Feather Reed Grass is also salt tolerant. I have seen this plant used effectively near road-ways, walkways, and parking lots that are regularly salted in the winter. Mix Feather Reed Grass with other perennials and shrubs to expand your landscape's seasonal interest.

How to Plant
Plant at the same level it was growing in the pot. Gently loosen potbound and girdling roots before planting. Space plants at least 2 feet apart.

Care and Maintenance
Feather Reed Grass is a low-maintenance plant. It is one of the tougher, more reliably hardy ornamental grasses. It has no serious insect or disease problems. Cut it back to just above ground level in late winter before growth begins.

Additional Information
One of my favorite sites includes this plant. Feather Reed Grass is an island flower that is always attractive despite the winter salts, heavy traffic, and minimal care. The garden includes Feather Reed Grass, Siberian Iris, Black-eyed Susans, 'May Night' Salvia, Daylilies, and Sedum 'Autumn Joy'.

Additional Species, Cultivars, or Varieties

Overdam Feather Reed Grass, *Calamagrostis* × *acutiflora* 'Overdam', is also stiffly upright, but has variegated leaves. The foliage grows up to 24 inches tall, and the plant can be as tall as 36 inches when it's in bloom. Korean Feather Reed Grass, *Calamagrostis arundinacea brachytricha* is a close relative of Feather Reed Grass. It has the same growth habit, but tends to be a little shorter and flowers later in the summer. The more open seedheads and foliage are only effective into early winter. It was selected as the Perennial Plant of the Year for 2001 by the Perennial Plant Association.

Did You Know?
Feather Reed Grass is excellent for fresh and dried flower arangements. Harvest it when the leaves and seedheads are the desired color. Add grass to fresh flower arrangements. Or place the leaves and seedheads in a vase and allow them to air dry.

ORNAMENTAL GRASSES

Fountain Grass

Pennisetum setaceum

Other Name: Annual Fountain Grass
Size: 3 feet tall and 18 to 24 inches wide
Flowers: Pink to purplish-pink
Fruit/Seed: Seedheads
Bloom Period: Midsummer through fall
Zones: Annual
Color photograph on page 237.

Light Requirements:

Additional Benefits:

Fountain Grass is an annual that is bound to brighten up both flower beds and container gardens. It forms an upright clump up to 3 feet tall, but in container gardens the limited root area keeps plants shorter. Fountain Grass has feathery foxtail flowers that extend beyond the leaves. The flowers create colorful motion with the help of a gentle garden breeze. Use the flowers in a vase as a filler for your fresh arrangements. In late fall, the seedheads will shatter and the leaves will brown, but the plant form will remain intact and provide winter interest.

WHEN TO PLANT

Sow seeds indoors in late winter. Keep the starting mix moist and at a temperature of 70 to 80 degrees. The seeds will germinate in 3 to 4 weeks. Plant hardened-off transplants in the spring after all danger of frost is past.

WHERE TO PLANT

Grow Fountain Grass in full sun or partial shade. Excessive shade can result in poor flowering and floppy plants. Fountain Grass prefers moist, well-drained soil but will tolerate a wide range of conditions including clay soil. Include Fountain Grass in containers. It provides vertical interest and is a good substitute for the traditionally used Spike plant. Use Fountain Grass en masse or mixed with annuals and perennials. Its fine texture softens the bold texture of plants such as Cannas and Spider Cleome.

HOW TO PLANT

Fountain grass is difficult to find. Check with the more specialized garden centers in your area. These plants are sold in various-sized containers. Plant container-grown Fountain Grass at the same level it was growing in the pot. Gently loosen potbound and girdling roots before planting. Space plants 1 or 2 feet apart.

CARE AND MAINTENANCE
Fountain Grass is a low-maintenance garden plant, but specimens grown in containers need extra attention. Check the soil moisture in container gardens at least once a day. Water the containers thoroughly, allowing excess water to run out the drainage holes. Fertilize planters frequently throughout the summer.

ADDITIONAL INFORMATION
The feathery flowers and fine leaves of *Pennisetum* create an attractive contrast to the bold texture of Sedum 'Autumn Joy'. The colorful purple leaves and flowers of Red Fountain Grass complement the bronze centers of the yellow-flowered 'Becky Mix' Black-Eyed Susans.

ADDITIONAL SPECIES, CULTIVARS, OR VARIETIES
You may find the red-leafed varieties listed as *Pennisetum setaceum* 'Rubrum', 'Cupreum', or 'Purpureum'. There are several Fountain Grasses that are somewhat hardy in Minnesota. The University of Minnesota has been testing the hardiness of these and other ornamental grasses. They found perennial Fountain Grass (*Pennisetum alopecuroides*) to be marginally hardy in Zone 4a. Oriental Fountain Grass (*Pennisetum orientale*) was slightly less hardy. Both look similar to the annual form. The Oriental Fountain Grass has blue-green leaves and pink flowers.

Did You Know?

Fountain Grass has long been used along city boulevards and in county parks. I am continually asked to identify this attractive grass. Learn this plant and you can wow all your friends and relatives with your plant knowledge.

Hakonechloa

Hakonechloa macra 'Aureola'

Other Name: Golden Variegated
  Hakonechloa
Size: 20 to 24 inches tall and wide
Flowers: Yellow-green
Fruit/Seed: Seedheads
Bloom Period: Late summer
Zone: 4b
Color photograph on page 237.

Light Requirements:

Golden Variegated Hakonechloa makes a good addition to shade gardens. Its variegated foliage forms attractive mounds in the flower garden. The foliage looks like Bamboo, making this grass a good choice for Japanese gardens. Flowers appear in late summer. Though not very showy, I find the light, airy flowers a nice addition to the overall appearance. The flower display is followed by pink color in the fall. This plant is definitely worth a try if you are looking for something different for your shade garden.

WHEN TO PLANT

Plant container-grown Hakonechloa during the growing season. I prefer spring and early summer, which gives the grass time to become established before our harsh winter. Divide and transplant Hakonechloa in the spring.

WHERE TO PLANT

Hakonechloa is one of the few ornamental grasses that will tolerate shade and moist soil. Add organic matter to heavy clay soil to improve drainage and to sandy soil to increase its capacity to hold water. Plant Hakonechloa in a protected location to increase its chances of winter survival. Use it as a specimen plant near the front of a border. Start with just a few plants. If these survive in your garden you can always add more. The variegated leaves brighten up shady areas in the landscape. I like to mix the colorful narrow foliage with the bold leaves of Hosta. Hakonechloa also combines well with Ferns and Astilbe.

How to Plant

Hakonechloa is available in pots from perennial nurseries, garden centers, and catalogs. Plant container-grown hakonechloa at the same level it was growing in the pot. Gently loosen potbound and girdling roots before planting. Space plants 18 to 24 inches apart.

Care and Maintenance

Hakonechloa is a low-maintenance plant. It is slow to get established, so be patient! Leaf scorch or brown-leaf edges can occur on plants grown in full sun or in dry soil. Loss of variegation is common in heavily shaded areas. Extremely cold and fluctuating winter temperatures as well as poor drainage can kill this plant. Use a winter mulch to help it survive the cold. Cover the plants with evergreen boughs, straw, or marsh hay after the ground lightly freezes. Remove the mulch in the spring.

Additional Information

Try growing Hakonechloa in containers, by itself or combined with other plants. The fine-textured, variegated foliage makes this plant a nice filler for container gardens. Check the soil moisture in container gardens at least once a day. Water the containers thoroughly, allowing excess water to run out the drainage holes. Fertilize planters frequently throughout the summer. Use any flowering plant fertilizer, following label directions carefully. Hakonechloa will not survive the winter in a container garden. Sink the pot into the soil for the winter. A protected location will increase its chances of survival. Mulch the sunken container once the ground lightly freezes. Another option is to plant it into the garden or recycle the plant in the compost pile and start over next spring.

Additional Species, Cultivars, or Varieties

Hakone Grass, *Hakonechloa macra,* has bright green foliage and tends to be more vigorous and hardier than the Variegated Hakonechloa. It has a similar growth habit and pink fall color. 'Alba Striata' has white and green drooping leaves.

Miscanthus (Silver Grass)

Miscanthus sinensis species

Other Names: Eulalia, Japanese or Chinese Silver Grass

Size: 3 to 7 feet tall and up to 4 feet wide

Flowers: Pale pink to red

Fruit/Seed: White seedheads

Bloom Period: Fall

Zone: 4

Color photograph on page 237.

Light Requirements:

Additional Benefits:

Miscanthus is one of the most dramatic ornamental grasses for the landscape. This tall plant's attractive seedheads provide fall and winter interest. Gardeners with small yards can include a few specimen plantings and those with large landscapes may want to use this plant en masse.

WHEN TO PLANT

Plant container-grown Miscanthus during the growing season, preferably in spring and early summer so the grass has time to become established before winter. Divide and transplant Miscanthus in the spring.

WHERE TO PLANT

Miscanthus prefers full sun and moist, well-drained soil. It will tolerate clay soil, although I prefer to add organic matter to the soil prior to planting. In shady areas, it tends to flop over and flower poorly. Use these large grasses as screens, hedges, or background plants. Individual plants make good specimens in the landscape, in a flower garden, or near water. Plant miscanthus in an area where you can enjoy the morning or afternoon sun shining through the seedheads. It is quite a spectacular sight. Sunlight and snow add to the beauty of this plant.

HOW TO PLANT

Plant container-grown Miscanthus at the same level it was growing in the pot. Gently loosen potbound and girdling roots before planting. Space plants at least 3 feet apart.

CARE AND MAINTENANCE

Miscanthus is a low-maintenance plant. Lift and divide every four or five years when the center of the plant dies out or becomes floppy. Rust, a fungal disease, can occasionally be a problem during wet, humid weather. Adjust watering if necessary and remove infected leaves as soon as they appear. Cut the plants back in late winter before new growth begins.

ADDITIONAL INFORMATION

Miscanthus plants make great fresh and dried cut flowers. Pick them when leaves and seedheads are the desired color.

ADDITIONAL SPECIES, CULTIVARS, OR VARIETIES

Cultivars vary in height, bloom time, and growing requirements. Match the right cultivar to your landscape situation. Red Flame Miscanthus, *Miscanthus sinensis* var. *purpurascens*, is one of the hardiest (Zone 4). It grows 4 to 5 feet tall, flowers in August, and turns an attractive orange-red in the fall. Maiden Grass, *Miscanthus sinensis* 'Gracillimus', grows 5 to 6 feet tall and should be grown for its fine foliage, not its flowers. The cold weather often arrives before this late-blooming Miscanthus flowers. The slightly twisted foliage is a nice addition to the garden and dried flower arrangements. Variegated Miscanthus, *Miscanthus sinensis* 'Variegatus', is more shade tolerant than the other Miscanthus. It grows 5 to 6 feet tall and is almost hardy to Zone 4a. It has white-striped leaves. *Miscanthus sinensis* 'Zebrinus' (zebra grass) and 'Strictus' (porcupine grass) both grow 6 to 8 feet tall with yellow bands across the leaves. Porcupine Grass is narrower and more stiffly upright than Zebra Grass. Both are marginally hardy in Zone 4a.

Did You Know?

Don't plant Chinese Silver Grass, Miscanthus sacchariflorus. *Though very tolerant of wet areas, it has naturalized in ditches and waste areas throughout the Midwest.*

Moor Grass

Molinia caerulea

Other Name: Purple Moor Grass
Size: 1 to 2 feet tall and wide
Flowers: Purple
Fruit/Seed: Buff seedheads
Bloom Period: Midsummer
Zone: 4
Color photograph on page 237.

Light Requirements:

Additional Benefits:

Use Moor Grass to add motion and color to your perennial garden. This plant forms a tuft of green leaves that easily blends with other plants. The real surprise comes in midsummer when the flowers shoot several feet above the foliage. The purple flowers are open, airy, and blend well with the background. In the fall, the leaves and flowers turn yellow, creating a colorful display. This grass does not have good winter interest, but its other assets more than compensate for that.

WHEN TO PLANT

Plant container-grown Moor Grass during the growing season. I prefer spring and early summer, so the grass has time to get established before our harsh winter. Divide and transplant Moor Grass in the spring.

WHERE TO PLANT

Plant Moor Grass in full sun or partial shade. It prefers moist, well-drained soil. Moor Grass forms dramatic tufts of foliage 1 to 2 feet tall and wide. The flowers shoot several feet above the plant. The fine, airy blooms allow you to see through to the rest of the garden. That feature makes Moor Grass a good choice as a specimen plant or in a small grouping in the perennial garden. Try planting Moor Grass in front of a dark background, like evergreens, to highlight its flower display.

HOW TO PLANT

Moor grass is available in pots from perennial nurseries, garden centers, and catalogs. It is slow to get established, so purchase larger plants for quicker results. Plant container-grown Moor Grass at the same level it was growing in the pot. Gently loosen pot-bound and girdling roots before planting. Space plants 18 to 24 inches apart.

CARE AND MAINTENANCE

Moor Grass is a low-maintenance plant. It is slow to get established. Use larger plants and divisions to get flowers in the first or second year. Moor Grass is self cleaning. The leaves and flower stems drop from the plants in the winter. A little spring cleanup may be all that is needed.

ADDITIONAL INFORMATION

Moor Grass makes great fresh and dried cut flower arrangements. Pick them when the leaves and seedheads are the desired color.

ADDITIONAL SPECIES, CULTIVARS, OR VARIETIES

Check local perennial nurseries, garden centers, or catalogs for available cultivars. Variegated Purple Moor Grass, *Molinia caerulea* 'Variegata', is 18 to 24 inches tall. The flowers rise 6 to 12 inches above the white-striped foliage. This shorter plant makes a nice edging, groundcover, or rock garden plant. Tall moor grass, *Molinia caerulea* subsp. *arundinaceae,* grows 2 to 3 feet tall and is hardy to Zones 4. The flowers are held 3 to 4 feet above the leaves on thin stems. They move with the slightest breeze and appear to be dancing over the flower garden. There are several cultivars of tall Moor Grass you may want to try in your garden. 'Skyracer' is 7 to 8 feet tall when in bloom. It is also more vigorous than the species. 'Transparent' is slightly shorter with a blooming height of 5 to 6 feet. The stems appear almost transparent and should be placed in front of a dark background to display the flowers.

Did You Know?

Moor Grass is native to the wet moorlands of Eurasia. Molinia *was named for the Chilean botanist Juan Ignacio Molina. The name* caerulea *means blue referring to the purplish flowers.*

Spike Grass

Spodiopogon sibiricus

Other Names: Silver Spike Grass, Frost Grass

Size: 4 to 5 feet tall and 24 inches wide

Flowers: Purple turning brown

Fruit/Seed: Seedheads in summer through early winter

Bloom Period: Summer

Zone: 4

Color photograph on page 237.

Light Requirements:

Additional Benefits:

Spike Grass adds form and color to the landscape. Back this plant with a fence, an evergreen, or another plant that will highlight its bamboo-like appearance. Use this medium-sized grass as a specimen, a small summer screen, or as a background plant. Its flowers appear in summer, starting out purple and then turning fuzzy and brown. They are held high over the foliage, giving it a light, airy appearance. Spike Grass flowers look good in the garden or cut and added to fresh arrangements. The leaves turn purplish brown in fall. Winter impact of Spike Grass is limited, since the flower heads shatter and the plants eventually collapse during cold weather, but the outstanding show this hardy plant provides makes it worthy of space in any garden.

WHEN TO PLANT

Plant container-grown Spike Grass during the growing season. I prefer spring and early summer to give the grass time to become established before our harsh winter. Divide and transplant spike grass in the spring.

WHERE TO PLANT

Spike Grass grows best in full sun. It will tolerate some light shade, but the plants will flop over when they are grown in excess shade. Grow this Grass in moist, well-drained soil. Once established, it is somewhat drought tolerant. The leaves on this upright Grass are held perpendicular to the stems. This gives it the look and feel of a tropical plant, such as Bamboo, and makes Spike Grass a perfect choice for Japanese gardens. Try using it as a specimen plant or in groups in the landscape or in a perennial garden.

HOW TO PLANT
Spike Grass is available in pots from perennial nurseries, garden centers, and catalogs. Plant container-grown Spike Grass at the same level it was growing in the pot. Gently loosen potbound and girdling roots before planting. Space plants at least 2 feet apart.

CARE AND MAINTENANCE
Spike Grass is a low-maintenance plant. Provide moisture during extended drought periods. The plants tend to collapse over the winter. A little spring cleanup is usually all that is needed.

ADDITIONAL INFORMATION
One of my favorite plantings at Boerner Botanical Gardens included Spike Grass. They backed this plant with Tamarisk and Tardiva Hydrangea. The bed included Variegated Miscanthus, Sedum 'Autumn Joy', and Japanese Blood Grass. The red and pink hues helped tie together this diverse group of plants. It was a magnificent fall display.

ADDITIONAL SPECIES, CULTIVARS, OR VARIETIES
I am not aware of any Spike Grass cultivars or varieties that are currently available. Keep checking your garden catalogs for new developments.

 Did You Know?

Plant Spike Grass in an area where it can be enjoyed in the fall. Then be sure to check it out on frosty fall mornings. The frost helps to highlight its late season form, flowers, and red fall color. Perhaps that's how it received its other common name: Frost Grass.

Switchgrass

Panicum virgatum

Size: 3 to 8 feet tall by 3 feet wide

Flowers: Pink to red or silver

Fruit/Seed: Brown seedheads

Bloom Period: Midsummer to
late summer

Zones: All

Color photograph on page 237.

Light Requirements:

Additional Benefits:

Bring a little of Minnesota's native prairie into your backyard. Plant some Switchgrass as a backdrop for a flower garden, as a screen, en masse, on a hillside, or as part of a native garden. Use some of the cultivated varieties in your perennial gardens. Switchgrass grows in tall, upright clumps. The colorful flowers look like fireworks exploding 1 to 2 feet above the leaves. This "flowerworks" display is complemented by the beautiful golden-yellow fall color. Be sure to pick a few flowers to enjoy indoors in fresh and dried arrangements. Consider including this year-round pleaser somewhere in your landscape.

WHEN TO PLANT

Plant container-grown Switchgrass during the growing season. I prefer spring and early summer, which gives the grass time to become established before our harsh winter. Divide and transplant Switchgrass in spring. Seed large areas of Switchgrass in the spring or fall. Switchgrass and Prairie Seed mixes are available from several quality Prairie Seed companies in Minnesota. Purchase clean seed that is free of stems, fluff, bracts, and leaves. Though clean seeds cost more, you actually get more seeds and less debris for the money. The quality companies will provide soil preparation and planting guidelines.

WHERE TO PLANT

Plant Switchgrass in full sun or light shade. Shade-grown plants tend to be more open and fall over. Switchgrass prefers moist soil, but will tolerate wet to dry soil. Switchgrass also tolerates salt. Use it near roadsides, paved areas, and walkways that are salted in winter. Switchgrass also works well as a specimen plant, background plant or as a mass planting. It may need a little management to keep it in bounds.

How to Plant

Switchgrass is available in pots from perennial nurseries, garden centers, and catalogs. Plant container-grown Switchgrass at the same level it was grown in the pot. Gently loosen potbound and girdling roots before planting. Space plants 30 to 36 inches apart.

Care and Maintenance

Switchgrass is a low-maintenance plant. The biggest problem is keeping plantings under control. Plants spread by seeds and rhizomes. Weed out strays and dig and divide sprawling clumps to keep them under control. Cultivated varieties are much less aggressive. Rust and fungal leaf spot may occasionally occur. Adjust watering if necessary and remove infected leaves as soon as they appear. Cut the plants back in the late winter before new growth begins.

Additional Information

Try combining Switchgrass with plants you would see it with in nature. The bold textures of Coneflowers, Black-eyed Susans, Sunflowers, and Goldenrod contrast nicely with the light, airy appearance of Switchgrass.

Additional Species, Cultivars, or Varieties

Heavy Metal Switchgrass, *Panicum virgatum* 'Heavy Metal', is a narrow, upright plant that grows 3 to 4 feet tall. It has metallic-blue leaves that turn bright yellow in the fall. Hänse Herms Switchgrass, *Panicum virgatum* 'Hänse Herms', develops red leaves in midsummer that persist until the first frost. The plant is also more compact, reaching a height of 3 to 3 1/2 feet tall.

Did You Know?

Switchgrass provides winter and early spring cover for wildlife. It also provides food for several native butterflies. The larvae of Leonard's skipper (Heperia leonardus) *and tawny edge skipper* (Polites themistochies) *feed on this plant.*

CHAPTER FIVE

Perennials

PERENNIALS HAVE BECOME an important part of Minnesota's landscapes. No longer relegated to a single garden in the back, they are now being used throughout the yard. Many people have eliminated their lawns and replaced them with perennial plantings. Others have ripped out the yews and junipers around the foundation and replaced them with perennials and other ornamental shrubs. Some gardeners have added just a few plants as groundcovers or specimens in their existing landscape. Whether you are adding a few or a few hundred perennials, proper selection, planting, and care are essential to gardening success.

SOIL PREPARATION

Start by evaluating the planting location. Take a soil test to find out how much and what type of fertilizer you need to apply. Your local University of Minnesota Extension Service can provide soil test information. You can incorporate a low-nitrogen, slow-release fertilizer in the soil at planting time. Use 1/2 pound of actual nitrogen per 1,000 square feet if soil test results are not available.

Check the soil drainage. Dig a hole 12 inches deep and fill it with water. Allow the water to drain and fill the hole again. If it takes more than 1 hour to drain the second time, you need to amend the soil. Add several inches of organic matter to the top 6 to 12 inches of garden soil to improve drainage. Sandy soil tends to drain too quickly. Add organic matter such as compost, peat moss, and aged manure to that type of soil. All the preparation will pay off in healthy plants, less maintenance, and years of enjoyment.

DESIGNING THE GARDEN

Most gardeners are looking for perennials that can be planted once, will bloom all season, and require no maintenance. They don't exist.

But selecting the right plant for existing growing conditions will give you a good looking garden with the least amount of work.

Once you have a list of potential plants for the garden, check out their bloom period. You can design your landscape so something is always blooming in every part of the yard. Or you may prefer peak areas of interest that change throughout the season. You may have one garden or a section of a garden that looks great for a short period of time. As it fades another area comes into full bloom and becomes the new focal point. Place the gardens in areas where you will get the most enjoyment when they are at their peak. Design your plantings to fit your lifestyle and needs.

Now look at your design realistically. Most people take on more than they can maintain. I always have bigger plans and more plants than I have time available. Beginning gardeners or those with limited time should start small. Design beds with easy access for planting and maintaining. Try using fewer types but more of each type of perennial in your garden. That type of design will be easier to keep up and will provide a bigger overall effect. Don't forget to plan for some winter interest. Seedpods and evergreen leaves can add impact during our longest season—winter.

PLANTS

Perennials are sold bare root, container grown, and field-potted. Bare-root perennials are plants sold without any growing media on the roots. Store them in a cool, but not freezing, location until you are ready to plant. Keep the roots moist and packed in peat moss, sawdust, or another similar material. Pot up bare-root plants that begin to grow before the weather permits outdoor planting. Plant bare-root perennials outdoors in the spring after the danger of severe weather has passed.

Chapter Five

Container-grown plants are grown and sold in pots. Some are grown outdoors and can be planted as soon as they are purchased. Others are grown in greenhouses and need to be hardened off, or toughened to outdoor conditions, before planting. Store potted perennials in a shaded location until they can be planted in the garden. These small pots need to be watered daily. Water and allow the potted plants to drain prior to planting. Remove container-grown plants from the pot. Slice or loosen potbound roots to encourage root development into the surrounding soil. Plant these at the same level they were growing in the container. Field-potted plants are grown in the field and potted for delivery as they are dug. The freshly potted plants often lack a cohesive rootball. Minimize problems by digging the hole first. Then carefully remove the plant from the container and set it in place. Plant it so the crown is even with the soil level. Check new plantings for soil settling. Perennials often die when the soil settles and their roots are exposed. Fill in low spots and cover exposed roots as needed.

CARE AND MAINTENANCE

Proper soil preparation, plant selection, and planting will help reduce maintenance requirements. Perennials need about an inch of water per week. Water gardens in clay soil once a week during dry weather. Perennials growing in sandy soil need 1/2 to 3/4 inch of water every three or four days in the absence of rainfall. Mulch perennials with a 1- to 2-inch layer of organic material such as cocoa bean shells, twice-shredded bark, shredded leaves, or pine needles. Mulch helps conserve moisture and reduce weed problems. Weeds are a major pest. Pull these invaders as soon as they appear. The perennials will be able to crowd out most weeds by the second or third summer.

Chapter Five

Deadheading and pruning can help control growth, increase flowering, and reduce pest problems. Some plants require a lot of work and others perform fine on their own. Some cultivars require less maintenance and have fewer problems than the species. Select the perennial and its cultivars that best fit your growing conditions and maintenance schedule.

Remove all disease- and insect-infested plant debris in the fall to reduce the source of infection for next year. I like to leave the seedheads and healthy foliage for winter interest. My major cleanup comes in the spring before new growth begins.

Perennials can be divided to improve their health and appearance or to start new plants. Divide perennials that are too big for the location, flower poorly, flop over, or open in the center. In general, lift and divide spring-flowering plants in late summer and fall-flowering plants in the spring.

Winter mulch new plantings and tender perennials. Cover the plants with evergreen branches, straw, or marsh hay after the ground lightly freezes. Remove the mulch in the spring as new growth begins. Winter mulching keeps the soil temperature consistently cold. That eliminates frost heaving caused by the freezing and thawing of soil throughout the winter. Frost heaving damages plant roots and can even push perennials right out of the soil.

Despite the long list of chores, perennial gardening can be relatively low maintenance and worth the effort. The best part, I think, is the seasonal change. It is so exciting to watch the first plants peek through the cold soil in the spring. Through the summer and fall, the garden continues to grow and change. And in winter, the snow-covered seedheads, rustling foliage, and visiting birds will add a new dimension to the season.

Artemisia

Artemisia species

Other Names: White Sage, Wormwood, Silvermound Artemisia

Size: 12 to 36 inches

Flowers: White

Bloom Period: Summer; not effective

Native: *Artemisia ludoviciana*

Zones: All

Color photograph on page 237.

Light Requirements:

Additional Benefits:

The fragrant, silver leaves of Artemisia can brighten any garden. Use it next to dark flowers or plants with glossy green leaves. The contrast makes both plants stand out. Shorter species make nice edging and rock garden plants. The taller ones make a nice backdrop for many other perennials. Add Artemisia to your gardens for season-long interest.

WHEN TO PLANT

Bare-root perennials should be planted in the spring after the danger of severe weather has passed. Hardened-off, container-grown, and field-potted perennials can be planted any time during the growing season.

WHERE TO PLANT

Artemisia must be grown in full sun and well-drained soil. Avoid fertile soils where plants tend to become floppy. Combine Artemisia with blue- and pink-flowering perennials and roses for rich, attractive mixtures. Grow enough plants to dry and use for arrangements and wreaths.

HOW TO PLANT

Prepare the soil prior to planting. Plant Artemisia at the same level it was growing in the nursery or container. Space plants 15 to 24 inches apart. Check new plantings for soil settling. Fill in low spots and cover exposed roots as needed.

CARE AND MAINTENANCE

Proper soil preparation will reduce maintenance and improve growing success. Add organic matter to clay soil to improve drainage.

These plants will rot in poorly drained soil during wet seasons. I visited a trial of these plants at the Chicago Botanic Gardens at the end of a very wet growing season. The field was a mass of brown leaves, not a pretty sight. On the other hand, I saw a beautiful planting of White Sage at a public garden in Denver. The plants were full, upright, and healthy in this sunny, dry location. Avoid excess fertilization. Too much nitrogen makes these plants open up in the center and flop over. Pull weeds as soon as they appear. Established Artemisia will be able to crowd out most weeds by the second or third summer. Divide fast-growing Artemisias every few years, which will also keep the plants healthy.

ADDITIONAL INFORMATION

Artemisias tend to open up in the center and flop over. Prune plantings once or twice a season before flowering, which will encourage shorter, stiffer growth.

ADDITIONAL SPECIES, CULTIVARS, OR VARIETIES

New Artemisias are being bred and introduced. Check catalogs, perennial nurseries, and garden centers for available cultivars. White Sage, *Artemisia ludoviciana;* and Silvermound, *Artemisia schmidtiana,* are two of the more popular Artemisias. White Sage is native to Minnesota and hardy in Zone 4. Like all Artemisias, it needs full sun and well-drained soil. It is 2 to 3 feet tall and can be floppy in moist, fertile soil. You will see this used in wreaths and dried arrangements. Silvermound, *Artemisia schmidtiana* 'Nana', is a shorter member of this group. It forms a neat, tidy mound 12 to 18 inches tall. Clip it back before flowering to prevent open centers. Use this as an edging or rock garden plant. Silvermound is rated hardy throughout Minnesota. 'Oriental Limelight' has clean and crisp green and yellow variegation.

 Did You Know?

The name Wormwood comes from the use of these plants to repel insects such as ants (in cupboards) and moths (in clothing).

Aster

Aster species

Size: 2 to 5 feet tall **Flower:** Purple, white, pink **Bloom Period:** Late summer through fall **Zones:** All *Color photograph on page 237.*	**Light Requirements:** **Additional Benefits:**

Asters can add a last flash of color to the landscape before the snow falls. Small flowers of purple, white, or pink top 2- to 5-foot-tall plants. Asters are at home in both formal and naturalized gardens. Include Asters in your garden design to help attract butterflies, for use as cut flowers, and for a little winter interest.

WHEN TO PLANT

Bare-root perennials should be planted in the spring after the danger of severe weather has passed. Hardened-off, container-grown, and field-potted perennials can be planted any time during the growing season. Plant less hardy species and cultivars early in the season to give them time to get established before winter.

WHERE TO PLANT

Grow Asters in areas with full sun and well-drained soil. They make great additions to perennial and cutflower gardens. Asters look good in formal, informal, and naturalized plantings.

HOW TO PLANT

Prepare the soil before planting. Plant Asters at least 2 feet apart with the crown even with the soil surface. Check new plantings for soil settling. Fill in low spots and cover exposed roots where the soil has settled.

CARE AND MAINTENANCE

New plantings benefit from an inch of water per week. Mulch Asters to conserve moisture and reduce weed problems. Pull weeds as soon as they appear. Pinch back tall Asters to 6 inches throughout June. Cut the stems above a set of leaves. This will help reduce toppling and encourage full, compact growth with lots of flowers. Taller species may still need staking. You can use grow-through stakes, or take your lead from nature and use surrounding plants, just like on the prairie, to support the Aster. Divide Asters every three years or as needed. Overgrown plants open in the center and become floppy. Dividing will help control the growth of taller plants and increase the vigor of smaller species. Less hardy species benefit from winter protection. Cut back asters to 6 inches above ground level in the fall. Cover the flowers with evergreen branches, straw, or marsh hay after the ground freezes. I like to leave my plants standing in the winter garden. I find the seed-heads add subtle interest, plus the stems help catch the snow that makes the best winter mulch.

ADDITIONAL INFORMATION

Asters, like many of our native perennials, were not appreciated until they became popular in Europe. The New England and New York Asters were taken to Europe where they quickly caught on. They returned to the United States as a prized landscape plant.

ADDITIONAL SPECIES, CULTIVARS, OR VARIETIES

There are quite a few Asters on the market. Check catalogs, perennial nurseries, and garden centers for available plants. Select the color and size that best fits your landscape design. The New England Aster, *Aster novae-angliae,* is among the most well-known asters. It is native and grows 4 to 6 feet tall. 'Purple Dome' is a compact cultivar that grows 18 inches tall and can spread to 36 inches wide. 'Alma Potschke' is guaranteed to grab your attention. Its bright pink flowers seem to leap out of the garden. It grows 3 to 4 feet tall and usually needs staking. The New York Aster, *Aster novi-belgii,* grows 3 to 5 feet tall and requires the same basic care as other Asters.

 Did You Know?

Asters have also had practical uses. The Purple Aster has been used to dye wool a greenish-gold color. Aster is the flower for the month of September.

Astilbe

Astilbe species

Other Name: False Spirea
Size: 12 to 48 inches tall
Flowers: White, pink, red, salmon, lavender
Bloom Period: Summer
Zones: All
Color photograph on page 237.

Light Requirements:

Additional Benefits:

ooking for a shade garden alternative to Hostas and Impatiens? Astilbes can add color, attractive foliage, and texture to the shadier side of your landscape. Select a variety of Astilbes with different bloom times to provide summer-long color. Leave seedheads of late bloomers intact. They will persist over winter, adding additional texture and interest.

WHEN TO PLANT

Plant bare-root Astilbe in the spring after the danger of severe weather has passed. Hardened-off potted perennials can be planted any time during the growing season. I like to plant my Astilbes early in the season to give them time to get established before winter. When things don't go as planned, I try to get them in the ground by late August or early September.

WHERE TO PLANT

Grow Astilbe in partial to full shade in moist, well-drained soil. Astilbes tend to burn out in full sun, especially if the soil dries out. No matter where it is planted, Astilbe needs moist, not wet, soil for best results. Use Astilbe for its foliage and flower effect in shade gardens. Shorter cultivars work well in shady rock gardens with moist soil. Try using Astilbes with Ferns and Hostas. The combination of foliage shape, texture, and color make for an attractive display.

HOW TO PLANT

Prepare the soil prior to planting. Add several inches of organic matter to help improve both drainage and the water-holding capacity of the soil. Plant bare-root Astilbe so the crown, the point where the stems and roots join, is even with the soil surface. Plant potted specimens at the same level they were growing in the container.

Check new plantings for soil settling. Fill in low spots and cover exposed roots as needed. Plant small cultivars 12 to 15 inches apart and larger cultivars at least 24 inches apart.

CARE AND MAINTENANCE

Moisture and fertilization are the keys to growing healthy Astilbes. Fertilize them in the spring before growth begins or in the fall as plants are going dormant. Plants do best with an inch of water each week. Mulch them with a 1- or 2-inch layer of organic material to conserve moisture and reduce weed problems. Pull weeds as soon as they appear. Deadheading will not encourage reblooming. I leave the seedheads on the plants to lengthen the season. Regular dividing seems to help revitalize Astilbe. This can be done about every three years in the spring. Lift plants with a shovel or garden fork. Separate the clumps into smaller pieces and replant the divisions in a prepared location.

ADDITIONAL INFORMATION

Astilbes make great cut flowers. They are also grown as a flowering potted plant in some areas. Cut Astilbe when the flowers are halfway open for the maximum vase life.

ADDITIONAL SPECIES, CULTIVARS, OR VARIETIES

There are many Astilbes to choose from. Check with your local garden center, perennial nursery, or catalog for the cultivar that is best suited to your landscape. Dwarf Chinese Astilbe, *Astilbe chinensis* 'Pumila', is the most drought tolerant. This small, 12- to 15-inch-tall plant makes a great groundcover or edge for the perennial garden. It has a rosy-lavender flower in mid- to late summer.

 Did You Know?

Astilbes are native to China and Japan. The name Astilbe comes from the Greek words a (without) and stilbe (brilliance or lustre). Some believe it refers to the small individual flowers that make up the feathery inflorescence. Others say it refers to the lack of shine on some species leaves.

Bellflower

Campanula species

Other Name: Harebells
Size: 6 to 36 inches tall
Flowers: Blue, white, purple
Bloom Period: Late spring to summer
Zones: All
Color photograph on page 237.

Light Requirements:

Additional Benefits:

Bellflowers have long been used in perennial gardens. Their beautiful, blue-and-white, bell-shaped flowers are unmistakable. Use them in formal or informal settings. The stately spikes of flowers on upright forms create a vertical accent in the landscape. The mounded form of Bellflowers makes them easy to blend with other flowers. And don't forget to cut a few—many Bellflowers will continue to share their beauty indoors in a vase.

WHEN TO PLANT

Plant bare-root Bellflowers in the spring after the danger of severe weather has passed. Hardened-off, container-grown, and field-potted perennials can be planted any time during the growing season. I prefer spring and early summer planting to give the Bellflowers time to get established before winter.

WHERE TO PLANT

Grow Bellflowers in full sun or partial shade. They need moist soil with good drainage. Bellflowers have a difficult time surviving the winter with wet feet. Short species and cultivars can be used as edging plants in the perennial garden, or try them in rock gardens where the soil stays moist. Taller species can be used as background plants and in the cutting garden. Some species can be used in informal and more naturalized areas.

HOW TO PLANT

Bellflowers need good drainage. Add several inches of organic matter to the top 12 inches of soil prior to planting. Plant bare-root perennials so the crown, or the point where stems and roots join, is even with the soil surface. Potted plants should be planted at the same level they were growing in the container. Water thoroughly.

Check new plantings for soil settling. Fill in low spots and cover exposed roots as needed.

CARE AND MAINTENANCE

Healthy Bellflowers require minimal care. Mulch the soil to keep the roots cool and moist and to help reduce weed problems. Avoid excess nitrogen fertilizer, which causes many of the taller species to flop over. Some species, like the Clustered Bellflower, may need to be staked even when properly fed. Most Bellflowers benefit from deadheading. Removing the faded flowers will encourage repeat blooming and reduce problems with reseeding. Be careful not to remove the developing buds. Divide Bellflowers when plants become floppy, their centers die out, or they start taking over the garden. Divide in early spring for best results.

ADDITIONAL INFORMATION

The commonly grown Bellflowers are native to Europe and Asia. There are several Bellflowers native to Minnesota. The tall Bellflower *Campanula americana* is native to moist, shady locations. The same goes for Marsh Bellflower, *Campanula aparinoides*, which can be found in swamps and grassy swales throughout the eastern United States. You may find the Common Harebell *Campanula rotundifolia* in cedar glades. The European Bellflower, *Campanula rapunculoides*, is widely naturalized in Minnesota. It is very difficult to eradicate and has serious weed potential. Avoid transplanting this into your garden!

ADDITIONAL SPECIES, CULTIVARS, OR VARIETIES

There are perennial and biennial forms of Bellflowers. Select the species and cultivars that are best suited for your garden design and growing conditions. Canterbury Bell, *Campanula medium*, is a biennial that often reseeds in the garden and thus appears to be perennial. The 'Clips' series of Carpathian Bellflower, *Campanula carpatica*, have become very popular. The 6- to 12-inch plants are covered with white, blue, or dark-blue flowers throughout the summer. Use them in rock gardens or as an edging plant in your perennial garden. Mine look quite nice planted with groundcovers under our Crabapple tree.

Black-Eyed Susan

Rudbeckia species

Other Names: Orange Coneflower, Coneflower
Size: 24 to 36 inches tall
Flowers: Yellow with brown or black centers
Bloom Period: Summer and fall
Zones: All
Color photograph on page 237.

Light Requirements:

Additional Benefits:

B lack-eyed Susans are sure to attract the attention of your neighbors as well as passing butterflies and birds. Their dramatic yellow flowers brighten formal, informal, and naturalized plantings. Of all the unusual plants in my tiny yard, these flowers get the most attention. Don't forget to pick a few for fresh and dried arrangements.

WHEN TO PLANT

Sow seeds in early spring or fall. Plant bare-root Black-eyed Susans in the spring after the danger of severe weather has passed. You can plant hardened-off, container-grown, and field-potted perennials any time during the growing season.

WHERE TO PLANT

Grow Black-eyed Susans in full sun. They tolerate a wide range of soils, including heavy clay soils. Given a choice, they prefer moist well-drained soil. Black-eyed Susans are self-seeding, and can quickly fill in large, bare areas. Combine them with other native plants and grasses for a naturalized or meadow effect.

HOW TO PLANT

Sprinkle seeds on prepared soil, lightly rake, tamp, and water to ensure good seed-soil contact. Plant bare-root perennials so the crown, or the point where the stems and roots join, is even with the soil surface. Plant potted Black-eyed Susans at the same level they were growing in the container. Check new plantings for soil settling. Fill in low spots and cover exposed roots as needed.

CARE AND MAINTENANCE

Black-eyed Susans are low-maintenance plants. They will quickly grow and crowd out weeds with minimal help from you. You may find yourself weeding out more Black-eyed Susans than weeds. I usually pot up the surplus and share with a friend, so it is more of a joy than a chore. Be sure new plantings receive an inch of water each week. Once established, these plants can tolerate dry periods. Mulch them with 1 to 2 inches of organic material to conserve moisture and reduce weed problems. Black-eyed Susans will bloom continuously summer through fall without deadheading. As the flowers fade, the attractive seedheads form. Leave these in place for winter interest. You and the finches will enjoy them all season long. Powdery mildew can be a problem on some species. Plants grown in areas with full sun and good air circulation are less susceptible to this disease. The disease doesn't kill healthy plants; they just look bad. Select mildew-resistant plants to avoid this problem.

ADDITIONAL INFORMATION

The common Black-eyed Susan, *Rudbeckia hirta,* is suscepti-ble to powdery mildew and tends to be a short-lived perennial. It easily reseeds so its presence will be long lived in the garden. Many of the new introductions are being sold as annuals.

ADDITIONAL SPECIES, CULTIVARS, OR VARIETIES

Goldsturm Rudbeckia (*Rudbeckia fulgida* var. *sullivantii* 'Goldsturm') is one of the more popular and easy to find Black-eyed Susans. Its compact size and disease resistance make it a good plant for beginning and busy gardeners. It has glossy green leaves, yellow flowers, and grows 24 inches tall. Orange Coneflower, *Rudbeckia fulgida,* is a larger plant reaching heights of 36 inches. Its bright-yellow flow-ers top glossy green, mildew-resistant leaves. The Great Coneflower, *Rudbeckia maxima,* is gaining popularity in the garden. It has large bluish-green leaves and reaches heights of 5 to 6 feet when in bloom. *Rudbeckia × hirta* 'Chim Chiminee' has unusual, quilted petals circling each bloom.

Bleeding Heart

Dicentra spectabilis

Other Names: Japanese Bleeding Heart, Lyre Flower
Size: 24 to 36 inches tall
Flowers: Rose-red and white
Bloom Period: Spring to early summer
Zones: All
Color photograph on page 238.

Light Requirements:

Additional Benefits:

B leeding Heart is an old-fashioned favorite among gardeners. Many of us include this plant more for sentimental than ornamental reasons. Perhaps your grandmother or a favorite neighbor grew Bleeding Hearts when you were a child. Many others find the folklore attached to this plant appealing. In any case, the beautiful, heart-shaped flowers can add interest and color to shade gardens. Use the flowers for cutting or check with your florist who may sell them as potted blooming plants.

WHEN TO PLANT

Plant bare-root Bleeding Hearts in the spring after the danger of severe weather has passed. Hardened-off, container-grown, and field-potted perennials can be planted whenever plants are available.

WHERE TO PLANT

Grow Bleeding Hearts in partial to full shade. They prefer moist soil. The plants will turn yellow and go dormant earlier when they are grown in full sun and dry soils. These large plants need lots of room. They can grow up to 3 feet tall and 2¹/₂ feet wide. Make plans to cover the bare spot left when these plants die out in midsummer. I like to keep them towards the back of my garden. That way their midsummer departure is not as noticeable.

HOW TO PLANT

Prepare the soil prior to planting. Plant bare-root perennials so the crown, or the point where the stems and roots join, is even with the soil surface. Potted Bleeding Hearts should be planted at the same level they were growing in the container.

CARE AND MAINTENANCE

Bleeding Hearts are relatively low-maintenance plants. Make sure the plants receive an inch of water each week. Mulch Bleeding Hearts with a 1- to 2-inch layer of organic material. This helps conserve moisture and reduce weed problems. Remove faded flowers to encourage a longer bloom period and discourage reseeding. Young seedlings can be moved in early spring to a desired location, or shared with your perennial gardening friends. A nurseryman in Nebraska prunes his plants back halfway after flowering to avoid the summer dormancy. The pruned plants send up new foliage that stays green throughout the season. I usually miss the opportune moment, vowing to try it next year. I'll let you know how this works for me, next year! My Bleeding Heart has been in the same location for over ten years. Plants can be divided in early spring to start new plants or reduce the size of those that have outgrown their location.

ADDITIONAL INFORMATION

The Bleeding Heart is a fun plant for kids of all ages. Take a flower apart to find a dancing lady, slippers, a bath tub, sword, and other items that combine to make great stories. Check children's gardening books for the many stories associated with this plant, or better yet, make up your own.

ADDITIONAL SPECIES, CULTIVARS, OR VARIETIES

'Gold Heart' has foliage that emerges gold and stays brilliant gold all season. Fringed Bleeding Heart, *Dicentra eximia*, is a good plant for the garden and landscape. It grows 12 to 18 inches tall and wide. Its lacy foliage stays green all summer long. These plants are covered with flowers in early summer, but continue producing blooms all season long. Use this Bleeding Heart as an edging plant in the garden or as a groundcover under trees and shrubs.

 Did You Know?

Dutchman's Breeches, Dicentra cucullaria, *is a spring wildflower. The small, white flowers look like white pants hanging on a clothesline to dry.*

Butterfly Weed

Asclepias tuberosa

Size: 18 to 30 inches tall
Flowers: Orange, red, and yellow
Bloom Period: Summer into fall
Zone: 4

Color photograph on page 238.

Light Requirements:

Additional Benefits:

This is no "weed" that needs to be removed from the garden. It is a beautiful plant that deserves a home in most landscapes. The deep orange flowers and the monarchs they attract brighten the landscape from midsummer into fall. Watch for the black, green-and-yellow-striped "Packer" caterpillars (as my daughter used to call them). They feed on the leaves, form cocoons, and soon turn into beautiful adult butterflies. Kids and adults love to watch this amazing process.

WHEN TO PLANT

Purchased seeds can be sown in early spring. Or collect and plant seeds from Butterfly Weed in summer. Hardened-off, container-grown, and field-potted perennials can be planted any time during the growing season.

WHERE TO PLANT

Grow Butterfly Weed in full sun and well-drained soil. Established plants tolerate drought and perform well in poor soil. Use in perennial gardens or naturalized areas. They compete with grass, making them a good addition to meadow and prairie plantings.

HOW TO PLANT

Prepare the soil prior to planting. Butterfly Weed is difficult to transplant, so plant seeds in their permanent location. Sprinkle seeds on prepared soil and lightly rake to cover the seeds. Tamp and water to ensure good seed-soil contact. Thin seedlings as needed. Plant containerized plants at least 24 inches apart and at the same level they were growing in the pot. Check new plantings for soil settling and cover exposed roots as needed.

CARE AND MAINTENANCE

Butterfly Weed is slow to establish. I often find the seedlings that plant themselves do the best. They seem to find the perfect spot and thrive. So I allow them to wander through my garden with very little direction from me. These plants have a large taproot that makes division difficult. Fortunately, they do not need dividing. If you need to move or propagate the plant, transplant and divide Butterfly Weed in early spring. Dig deep to avoid damaging the taproot. Established plants are drought tolerant. New plantings will benefit from an inch of water per week. Mulch young plants to conserve moisture and reduce weed problems. Butterfly Weeds are late to emerge in the spring. Mark their location with plant labels or spring-flowering bulbs. This will reduce the risk of accidentally digging them before they emerge. Remove the first set of flowers as they fade to encourage a second flush of blooms. Remember to let the seed sit on later flowers if you want more plants next year.

ADDITIONAL INFORMATION

My biggest problem has been aphids. The bright orange pests feed in clusters on the new growth. Remember that many of the insecticides that kill these will harm the butterflies you are trying to attract. I wait and let the ladybugs take care of the aphids. If that doesn't work, I spot-spray the pests with insecticidal soap. Do not spray the caterpillars.

ADDITIONAL SPECIES, CULTIVARS, OR VARIETIES

Butterfly Weed plants and seeds are now available from garden centers, perennial nurseries, and catalogs. Most plants have orange flowers, but there are some available with red or yellow blooms. The cultivar 'Gay Butterflies' has all 3 flower colors.

 Did You Know?

This perennial is the food source for monarch caterpillars and one of the nectar sources for the adult butterfly. The toxins in the plant make monarchs distasteful to their predators.

Columbine

Aquilegia hybrids

Size: 12 to 36 inches tall
Flowers: Yellow, red, pink, blue,
  purple, white
Bloom Period: Late spring to early summer
Zones: All
Color photograph on page 238.

Light Requirements:

Additional Benefits:

This delicate beauty will hold its own in your perennial garden. The blue-green leaves make a nice base for the long, flowering stems. The flowers can be single or bi-colored with long or short spurs. You and the hummingbirds will enjoy the flowers from late spring through early to even midsummer. Be sure to include them in gardens where you can sit and watch the hummingbirds feed. Plant extras so you can pick a few to enjoy indoors as well.

WHEN TO PLANT

Plant bare-root perennials in the spring after the danger of severe weather has passed. Hardened-off, container-grown, and field-potted perennials can be planted any time during the growing season.

WHERE TO PLANT

Grow Columbine in full sun or partial shade in moist soil. Plants will deteriorate in dry soil and rot in overly wet conditions. I have had luck growing the plants in fairly heavy shade. They combine well with Ferns, Hostas, and other shade-loving plants. Mix them with other perennials to mask the foliage that tends to deteriorate over the summer.

HOW TO PLANT

Prepare the soil prior to planting. Plant Columbines at the same level they were growing in the nursery or container. Space plants 12 inches apart.

CARE AND MAINTENANCE

Columbines are fairly low-maintenance plants. Make sure the soil stays moist but not wet. Mulch Columbines to help conserve moisture and reduce weed problems. Remove faded flowers to encourage rebloom. Deadheading also prevents reseeding. That is important if you are growing hybrids and do not want your garden overrun by their unpredictable offspring. Columbine seldom needs dividing. Gardeners can carefully divide plants in late summer and preferably by September 1. That will allow the plants to become established before winter. Leaf miners are the biggest pests. These insects feed between the upper and lower leaf surfaces leaving a white, snake-like pattern in the leaves. It doesn't hurt the plant; it just looks bad. Cut severely damaged plants back after flowering to encourage fresh new foliage. Columbine sawfly, which looks like but is not a caterpillar, is a more recent pest problem. It eats the leaves causing the gardeners, not the plants, great stress. Remove the problem insects by hand. If you must use an insecticide be sure to read and follow all label directions carefully.

ADDITIONAL INFORMATION

Wild Columbine, *Aquilegia canadensis,* is native throughout Minnesota and is especially common along the shores of Lake Superior. It has red and yellow nodding flowers. This native is easy to grow. It self-seeds and will quickly fill in shady areas. It is reported to be more resistant to leaf miners.

ADDITIONAL SPECIES, CULTIVARS, OR VARIETIES

There are many Columbine cultivars available from garden centers, perennial nurseries, and catalogs. Select the ones that best fit your landscape design and growing conditions. A few of the popular ones readily available include the 'Biedermeier Strain', 12 inches tall with short, spurred, white, pink, or purple flowers. The popular 'McKana Hybrids' grow 30 inches tall and come in a variety of colors. 'Song Bird' cultivars are 24 to 30 inches tall. They have vibrant colors that brighten up the garden.

 Did You Know?

Columbine is the symbol for folly. If you look closely at the flowers, you may see a jester's cap. Or perhaps you see an eagle's claws. The word Aquilegia *is Latin for eagle.*

Coralbells

Heuchera sanguinea

Other Names: Alum Root
Size: 12 to 20 inches tall
Flowers: Red, pink, white
Bloom Period: Late spring to early summer
Zones: All
Color photograph on page 238.

Light Requirements:

Additional Benefits:

Coralbells are tough plants that provide year-round interest in the landscape. Use them as groundcovers in sun and shade locations. The evergreen foliage looks good throughout most of the year. That fact also makes them a good edging plant for perennial gardens. The small, bell-shaped flowers are held high above the leaves. These light, airy blooms let you see through to the background plants. And don't forget to bring a few indoors to enjoy as cut flowers.

WHEN TO PLANT

Plant bare-root perennials in the spring after the danger of severe weather has passed. Hardened-off, container-grown, and field-potted perennials can be planted any time during the growing season. Plant in the spring and early summer to allow the plants to get established and reduce the risk of frost heaving.

WHERE TO PLANT

Coralbells tolerate full sun to heavy shade but perform best in partial shade. You will get fewer flowers but still have nice foliage in heavy shade. The purple-leafed cultivars tend to scorch in the hot afternoon sun. Keep the soil moist for the best flower display. I have used the straight species of this plant in dry shade with acceptable results. Avoid wet sites where Coralbells suffer winter kill.

HOW TO PLANT

Add several inches of organic matter to improve the soil prior to planting. Coralbells are shallow-rooted plants subject to heaving out of the soil. Make sure the crown, or the point where stems and roots join, is set an inch below the soil surface. Space plants 12 inches apart. Check new plantings for soil settling. Fill in low spots and cover exposed roots as needed.

CARE AND MAINTENANCE

Coralbells perform best in moist soil. Mulch them with a 1- to 2-inch layer of organic material to conserve moisture and reduce weed problems. Mulch after the ground lightly freezes to prevent frost heaving, or when the plants are pushed out of the soil when the ground fluctuates between freezing and thawing. Check Coralbells in the spring and replant frost-heaved plants so the crown is an inch below the soil surface. Spring is also a good time to divide plants. Coralbells need dividing every three years or so when the stems become woody or plants become overgrown. Spring division allows plants time to reestablish before winter. Remove faded and browned leaves in the spring before new growth begins. The green ones can be left in place for the new growth to cover. Deadhead Coralbells to encourage season-long bloom. Use a hand pruner or garden scissors to cut flower stems back to the leaves.

ADDITIONAL INFORMATION

There are over fifty species of Coralbells native to North America. Alum Root, *Heuchera richardsonii*, is native to Minnesota dry prairies and open woods. It has green flowers and coarse textured leaves. The root was used medicinally by the Native Americans.

ADDITIONAL SPECIES, CULTIVARS, OR VARIETIES

There are many different Coralbells available through garden centers, perennial nurseries, and catalogs. Cultivars are available with white, red, and pink flowers. You can also buy plants with green-to-purple, plain, or variegated foliage in a wide range of shapes. 'Velvet Night' is a very dark form with 7-inch almost black/purple leaves. It is especially dramatic when combined with gold-leaved Hosta.

 Did You Know?

Once you see the flowers you will know why this plant is called Coralbells. The botanical name Heuchera *was given in honor of the German botanist Johann Heinrich von Heucher. The species name* sanguinea *means blood-red, referring to the flowers.*

Coreopsis

Coreopsis species

Other Name: Tickseed
Size: 18 to 36 inches tall
Flowers: Yellow
Bloom Period: Late spring to late summer
Zones: All
Color photograph on page 238.

Light Requirements:

Additional Benefits:

Coreopsis is a good choice for sunny, dry gardens. It can be used in formal perennial gardens or incorporated into wildflower and naturalized plantings. The small, daisy-like flowers are great for cutting and attracting butterflies. Beginning gardeners and those who want low-maintenance gardens will like Threadleaf Coreopsis. Its fine-textured foliage is covered most of the season with small, yellow flowers. And the best part—it requires very little care.

WHEN TO PLANT
Plant bare-root Coreopsis in the spring after the danger of severe weather has passed. Hardened-off, container-grown, and field-potted perennials can be planted any time during the growing season.

WHERE TO PLANT
Grow Coreopsis in full sun in well-drained soil. Established plants of most species will tolerate dry conditions. Use Coreopsis in the perennial, wildflower, or naturalized garden. It is a good plant for cutting and attracting butterflies.

HOW TO PLANT
Prepare the soil prior to planting. Plant Coreopsis at the same level it was growing in the nursery or container. Space plants 12 inches apart. Check new plantings for soil settling. Fill in low spots and cover exposed roots as needed.

CARE AND MAINTENANCE
Proper soil preparation, plant selection, and planting will help reduce future maintenance. Keep the soil around new plantings moist, but not wet. Many of the Coreopsis species need deadheading. This encourages a second flush of flowers and reduces problems

with self-seeding. One plant of Mouse Ear Coreopsis has turned into many plants scattered throughout one of my perennial gardens. A little spring weeding and deadheading will keep this plant in check. Divide overgrown and floppy plants in the spring. Dig plants with a shovel or garden fork. Lift clumps, cut them into sections, and replant them in prepared soil. You will probably have plenty to trade with your gardening friends.

ADDITIONAL INFORMATION

There are over 100 species of Coreopsis that are native to the United States (including the Hawaiian Islands) and tropical Africa. *Coreopsis lanceolata,* is very similar to *grandiflora. Coreopsis tripteris* and *Coreopsis palmata,* which are native to Minnesota, can be found in dry prairies.

ADDITIONAL SPECIES, CULTIVARS, OR VARIETIES

Threadleaf Coreopsis, *Coreopsis verticillata,* is a good low-maintenance perennial. Its fine foliage is covered with small, yellow, daisy-like flowers from early summer into fall. This Coreopsis needs no deadheading. Remove faded flowers in summer to encourage a fall bloom. Threadleaf Coreopsis tolerates dry soil and needs no staking. Mouse Ear, *Coreopsis auriculata,* is 18 inches tall and prefers moist, well-drained soil. It can become a weed in the perennial garden. Tickseed, *Coreopsis grandiflora,* grows 2 to 3 feet tall, tolerates dry conditions, and makes a good cut flower. The Annual Golden Coreopsis, *Coreopsis tinctoria,* has fine leaves and yellow, orange, or crimson flowers. Deadhead to keep the plant neat and blooming throughout the first half of summer.

 Did You Know?

The botanical name Coreopsis *comes from the Greek words* koris *meaning a bug and* opsis *for resemblance. The seeds are thought to look like ticks. This is also why the plant is sometimes commonly call Tickseed.*

Daylily

Hemerocallis species and hybrids

Size: 12 to 48 inches tall
Flowers: Most colors
Bloom Period: Summer through fall
Zones: All

Color photograph on page 238.

Light Requirements:

Additional Benefits:

Daylilies are versatile plants that can fit in any garden. The long, grass-like leaves are effective all season. The individual flowers last a day, but the flower display can last up to one month on an individual plant. Use Daylilies as groundcovers, cut flowers, edibles, or in the perennial border.

WHEN TO PLANT
Plant bare-root Daylilies in the spring after the danger of severe weather has passed. Hardened-off, container-grown, and field-potted perennials can be planted any time during the growing season.

WHERE TO PLANT
Grow Daylilies in full sun to partial shade locations. Pastel-colored Daylilies tend to fade in full sun. Poor flowering and floppy growth may occur in heavy shade. Daylilies prefer moist, well-drained soil, but they will tolerate a wide range of conditions including heavy clay.

HOW TO PLANT
Prepare the soil prior to planting. Plant Daylilies with the crown, or the point where the stems and roots join, even with the soil surface.

CARE AND MAINTENANCE
Daylilies are tough plants that are often sold as low maintenance selections. This is misleading for gardeners who like things neat and tidy. Each Daylily flower lasts one day, fades, and then hangs on the stem. That doesn't bother me, but it drives many gardeners out to the garden each day to deadhead their plants. Snap off the faded flower at the base of the blossom. Once all flowers have bloomed, remove the flower stem back to the leaves. Pull out or clip back discolored foliage in mid- to late summer. The newer, fresh leaves will

help mask the old, faded foliage. Most Daylily cultivars grow fast and need little fertilization. Excess nitrogen can cause unattractive growth and poor flowering. Repeat bloomers benefit from regular division and light fertilization in spring. Most garden books say Daylilies are easy to divide. What they mean is that the plants will recover quickly, not necessarily the gardener. Established Daylilies form a tangle of thick fleshy roots that make digging and dividing difficult for the gardener. A friend of mine divides his Daylilies every 3 years to make the job easier on him.

ADDITIONAL INFORMATION

The Orange Daylily (*H. fulva*), often called Ditch Lily, is seen growing wild in drainage ditches and other areas in Minnesota. Deadhead or remove seedpods from garden Daylilies to keep these plants from invading our native grasslands. Daylilies are excellent as cut flowers. Select stems with tight buds for a longer flower display, or remove fresh blossoms and place them on tables around the house for an evening of enjoyment. Animals also love the blossoms. Scare tactics and repellents can be used to discourage these pests. Use a repellent labeled for food crops if you plan on eating the blossoms.

ADDITIONAL SPECIES, CULTIVARS, OR VARIETIES

There are thousands of Daylily cultivars available. Select a variety of Daylilies including early, mid-, and later summer bloomers to have Daylily flowers all season long. Don't forget the new repeat bloomers that will give you several bursts of flowers in 1 season. Hemerocallis 'Kwanzo-variegata' has striped variegation on 24-inch leaves. It has double orange flowers with a red eye zone.

 Did You Know?

Daylily flowers are edible. Use them fresh, in salads, stuffed and cooked, or in soups. One of my students says she never sees the blossoms; her children eat them right off the plants. Don't use pesticides if you plan on eating the flowers.

Delphinium

Delphinium × elatum

Other Name: Larkspur
Size: 4 to 6 feet tall
Flowers: Blue, purple, white, red, pink, yellow
Bloom Period: Early to midsummer
Zones: All
Color photograph on page 238.

Light Requirements:

Additional Benefits:

Stately spikes of blue-and-white Delphinium flowers stir up visions of an English cottage garden. These visions may have enticed you, like many gardeners, to add these high-maintenance plants to your garden. Every time you see a beautiful flowering plant or a bouquet of blossoms you are ready to try again. Join the club.

WHEN TO PLANT

Plant bare-root Delphiniums in the spring after the danger of severe weather has passed. Hardened-off, container-grown, and field-potted perennials can be planted any time during the growing season. Many garden centers sell blooming Delphiniums in early summer. I prefer to plant in the spring and early summer so the Delphiniums have time to get established before winter.

WHERE TO PLANT

Grow Delphiniums in full sun in moist, well-drained soil. Good drainage is essential for winter survival. Place the plants in a protected site with good air circulation. This environment will increase winter survival and reduce wind damage. Good air circulation will help reduce disease problems. These plants make a great backdrop for other perennials, or as a vertical accent or specimen plant.

HOW TO PLANT

Plant Delphiniums at the same level they were growing in the nursery or container. Space plants 24 inches apart.

CARE AND MAINTENANCE

Delphiniums are difficult plants to grow. They do not like the heavy clay or dry sandy soil. Proper soil preparation and watering is

critical to establish and grow healthy Delphiniums. Mulch plants with a 1- to 2-inch layer of organic material to conserve moisture, keep roots cool, and reduce weed problems. Deadhead flowers to encourage a second flush of blossoms. Prune back plants once all the flowers have faded. This encourages new growth and a second flowering later in the season. Stake tall cultivars to prevent flopping and wind damage. Fertilize Delphiniums lightly in the spring as growth begins, and again in the summer, after you clip back the faded foliage. Regular division may help keep this plant vigorous. Divide it in early spring as growth begins. Some gardeners buy flowering plants and treat them as annuals. If they return the following year they consider it a bonus. Check plants frequently for insects and disease problems. They are susceptible to powdery mildew, blight, leaf spot, crown rot, canker, aphids, mites, borers, and leaf miners. Buy healthy transplants and grow them in the right conditions to minimize pest problems.

ADDITIONAL INFORMATION
Seeds and leaves of young plants are poisonous if eaten. The leaves may irritate gardeners with sensitive skin, so wear gloves when working with Delphiniums.

ADDITIONAL SPECIES, CULTIVARS, OR VARIETIES
Belladonna Delphinium, *Delphinium × belladonna,* is a good choice for beginning gardeners, or those who have given up growing Delphiniums. This hybrid is shorter, 3 to 4 feet tall, with more open flower spikes. It tends to perform better in the home garden.

 Did You Know?

Delphinium virescens *is our native Delphinium. It grows 5 feet tall with white flowers and is native to the prairie. The Victorians believed the Delphinium symbolized swiftness and lightness.*

Fern

Athyrium, Matteuccia, Osmunda et al

Other Names: Japanese Painted Fern
Ostrich Fern, Cinnamon Fern
Size: 1 to 3 feet tall
Flowers: Grown for foliage
Bloom Period: Foliage effective all season
Zones: All
Color photograph on page 238.

Light Requirements:

Ferns have always been an integral part of the natural landscape. Many gardeners are now discovering their value for the home landscape. Their wonderful texture, shades of green, and interesting form can add interest to shady gardens.

WHEN TO PLANT
Bare-root perennials should be planted in the spring after the danger of severe weather has passed. Hardened-off, container-grown, and field-potted perennials can be planted any time during the growing season. I like to plant tender Ferns, especially the expensive ones, early in the season. That gives them time to get established before winter.

WHERE TO PLANT
Most Ferns prefer shady locations with moist soil. Use taller ones as background plants in the shade garden. Lower-growing Ferns can be used as groundcovers and edging plants. Ferns combine well with Hosta, Astilbe, Ginger, Daylilies, and other shade lovers.

HOW TO PLANT
Prepare the soil prior to planting. Plant Ferns so the crown, or the point where the stems and roots join, is even with the soil surface. Check new plantings for soil settling. Fill in low spots and cover exposed roots as needed.

CARE AND MAINTENANCE
Proper soil preparation is essential for growing healthy Ferns. Keep the soil moist, but not wet. Mulch Ferns to help conserve moisture and reduce weed problems. Some ferns are fast growing and will

benefit from division. Others are slow growing and seldom need attention. Divide overgrown ferns in the spring as growth begins.

ADDITIONAL INFORMATION

No shade? There may still be a Fern for you. The Hay-Scented Fern, *Dennstaedtia punctilobula;* Interrupted Fern, *Osmunda claytoniana;* and Lady Fern, *athyrium filix-femina,* will all tolerate sun. Shade them from the hot afternoon rays and keep the soil moist for best results.

ADDITIONAL SPECIES, CULTIVARS, OR VARIETIES

You can now find a bigger selection of Ferns and an increasing number of cultivars available at garden centers, perennial nurseries, and through catalogs. Japanese Painted Fern, *Athyrium niponicum* 'Pictum', is a good Fern for beginning and perennial gardeners. This clump-forming Fern works well as a groundcover or edging plant for shady areas. The fronds are gray-green with a maroon stalk and flush to the leaves. 'Silver Falls' has lustrous silvery fronds with contrasting red veins. 'Ursala's Red' has broad silver leaves flushed with wine red. Water during dry periods and remove any solid green growth that appears. This low-maintenance Fern is hardy in Zone 4. Ostrich Fern, *Matteuccia struthiopteris,* is an old-fashioned favorite. These large Ferns can be seen growing along the foundations of many Minnesota homes. The long, lacy fronds stand upright and reach heights of 5 feet. They are fast growers and will quickly fill the space provided. Ostrich Ferns will brown out in the heat and drought of midsummer. Minimize scorch by planting them in a north or east location, mulching, and keeping the soil moist. This Fern is native and hardy throughout Minnesota.

 Did You Know?

Ferns reproduce by spores. To collect spores, shake a fresh spore-covered Fern leaf over paper. Sprinkle the spores on soil and keep it moist. A mass of nondescript green growth will sprout. Divide this into separate pots. Small Fern plants will soon appear.

Gayfeather

Liatris spicata

Other Name: Blazing Star
Size: 2 to 3 feet tall
Flowers: Lavender, rose, white
Bloom Period: Midsummer to fall
Zones: All
Color photograph on page 238.

Light Requirements:

Additional Benefits:

Though native to our prairies, this plant is equally at home in the perennial garden. Gayfeather's whorls of dark green leaves are topped with spikes of purple, rose, or white flowers. These are more than just pretty plants. They attract wildlife to the garden and make long-lasting cut flowers. The flowers are a food source for several kinds of butterflies. Be sure to take a few minutes to sit and enjoy this added benefit. And check out the plants in winter. Birds will stop by to feed on the seeds hidden in the fluffy seedheads.

WHEN TO PLANT

Gayfeather rhizomes can be planted in the spring or fall. Plant hardened-off, container-grown, and field-potted perennials any time during the growing season.

WHERE TO PLANT

Grow Gayfeather in full sun and well-drained soil. These plants will tolerate some light shade, but not wet feet. Mix Gayfeather with other sun-loving perennials. Its upright growth habit makes it a good vertical accent and background plant for the perennial garden. Or combine it with grasses and other native plants to create a naturalized garden.

HOW TO PLANT

Plant the woody corm or rhizome 1 to 2 inches below the soil surface. Containerized plants should be planted at the same depth they were growing in the pot.

CARE AND MAINTENANCE

Gayfeathers are low-maintenance plants. New plantings need about an inch of water per week. Once established, these plants are very drought tolerant. Mulch new plantings to conserve moisture and reduce weed problems. Deadhead plants when most of the flower spike has bloomed. Cut the flower stem back to the first whorl of leaves; this will encourage a second flush of flowers. Let flowers dry and form their fluffy seedheads. I leave these on the plants for the birds and me to enjoy all winter long. The plants will self-seed if the seedheads are left alone. I have supplied Gayfeathers to several friends, a park, and all my gardens from one plant. I simply dig the young plants in the spring and move them to the spot where they are needed. I consider them a gift, not a weed problem. Gayfeather plants seldom need staking. Those grown in rich, moist soil or shade are more likely to topple and need staking. Use commercially available grow-through stakes or surrounding plants to provide support. Divide overgrown gayfeathers in the spring as growth begins.

ADDITIONAL INFORMATION

Several species of Gayfeather are native to Minnesota prairies. The most common include the Tall Blazing Star, *Liatris pycnostachya*, and the Rough Blazing Star, *Liatris aspera.* This native has also been an important crop in the floral industry. It is grown around the world for use as a cut flower. Some are produced right here in Minnesota. Several farmers converted their fields for commercial production of this plant. It may be their Gayfeathers you buy on your next trip to the florist.

ADDITIONAL SPECIES, CULTIVARS, OR VARIETIES

'Kobold' is a compact cultivar. Its smaller size, 18 to 30 inches tall, is easier to blend into most home gardens. The profusion of dark purple flowers will provide enjoyment in the garden and flower vase.

 Did You Know?

Take a close look at Gayfeather the next time it is in bloom. Notice the flowers open at the top first with the bottom flowers opening last. This is just the opposite of most flowers.

Hosta

Hosta species and cultivars

Other Names: Funkia, Plantain-Lily
Size: 2 to 36 inches tall
Flowers: White, lavender
Bloom Period: Summer and fall
Zones: All
Color photograph on page 238.

Light Requirements:

Additional Benefits:

Hostas are low-maintenance, quick-growing, shade-tolerant perennials. These features have helped make Hostas one of the most popular perennials in the landscape. The recent interest has resulted in the introduction of hundreds of new cultivars. The variety of leaf sizes, shapes, colors, and textures adds to its landscape value. Combine Hostas with Ferns and Astilbes for an interesting shade garden. Or use them en masse as a groundcover or edging plant. Grow a few of them in areas where you can enjoy the hummingbirds feeding on the blossoms or winter birds feeding on the seeds.

WHEN TO PLANT
Plant bare-root perennials in the spring after the danger of severe weather has passed. Hardened-off, container-grown, and field-potted perennials can be planted any time during the growing season.

WHERE TO PLANT
Grow Hosta in shady locations with moist, organic soil. Your plants will have the best leaf color in partial shade. Avoid afternoon sun that can cause leaf edges to brown or scorch. Use Hosta alone or in groupings in shade gardens.

HOW TO PLANT
Hostas prefer rich organic soil. Create it by adding several inches of organic matter to the top 6 to 12 inches of garden soil. Plant Hostas so the crown, or the point where the stems and roots join, is even with the soil surface.

CARE AND MAINTENANCE
Hostas are low-maintenance plants. Make sure they receive an inch of water each week. Hosta will scorch in dry soil. Mulch them with a

1- to 2-inch layer of organic material to conserve moisture and reduce weed problems. Early-sprouting Hostas may suffer frost damage. It doesn't hurt the plant; it just looks bad. New growth will help mask some of the browned leaves. You can cover plantings to protect them from late spring frost. Many gardeners deadhead their Hostas to improve their appearance. I like to leave the seedheads for winter interest. The seeds also attract juncos, chickadees, and other seed-eating birds throughout the winter. Some Hostas will reseed. You can easily pull the few unwanted offspring that sprout. Hostas are one of the easiest perennials to divide. You can make divisions any time during the growing season. Mulch fall-divided plants for added winter protection. Slugs and earwigs are the major pests. Beer-baited traps tucked under the Hosta leaves will help capture the slugs. Hostas with thicker and heavier leaves tend to be more resistant to slug damage. Crumpled paper or tubes can be used to trap earwigs. If you use insecticides be sure to read and follow all label directions carefully.

ADDITIONAL INFORMATION

Deer love Hostas. Repellents, scare tactics, and fences around small perennial plantings may help; or you can replace Hosta with Lungwort *Pulmonaria*. It looks similar to Hosta, tolerates shade, and at this point resists deer damage. The International Hosta Registry (where new cultivars are enrolled) and the national display garden of the American Hosta Society are located at the University of Minnesota Landscape Arboretum.

ADDITIONAL SPECIES, CULTIVARS, OR VARIETIES

There are hundreds if not thousands of Hostas on the market. New cultivars are being added every year. Check garden centers, perennial nurseries, and catalogues for available cultivars. Hosta enthusiasts may want to join the American Hosta Society, 338 E. Forestwood Street, Morton, IL 61550. It is a great way to meet other Hosta enthusiasts and learn about this plant.

Mum

Chrysanthemum × morifolium

Other Names: Hardy or Garden Mum
Size: 1 to 3 feet tall
Flowers: Yellow, orange, rust, red, bronze, white, lavender
Bloom Period: Late summer through frost
Zone: 4 (used in all zones as an annual)
Color photograph on page 238.

Light Requirements:

Additional Benefits:

Mums are often called "the last smile of the departing year." It's a good description of their frost-tolerant fall flower display. One plant can provide over a hundred blossoms for cutting and garden use. Consider adding a few Mums to your perennial gardens or annual flower display. A single fall flower show will convince you they are well worth the price.

WHEN TO PLANT

Plant bare-root perennials in the spring after the danger of severe weather has passed. Hardened-off, container-grown, and field-potted perennials are usually available and can be planted in the spring or late summer.

WHERE TO PLANT

Grow Mums in full sun in well-drained soil. Increase winter hardiness by growing them in protected sites. Many botanical gardens, estates, and home gardeners treat Mums as annuals. Use alone for a splash of fall color or en masse for a more formal, breathtaking display. Try planting Mums with your bulbs in the fall. That way you get two seasons of interest from one planting. I like to use Mums in containers. A few plants go a long way in brightening up the landscape.

HOW TO PLANT

Plant Mums at the same level they were growing in the nursery or container. Space plants 2 to 3 feet apart.

CARE AND MAINTENANCE

Mums are not reliably hardy anywhere in Minnesota. Proper soil preparation will give you healthy plants throughout the season and increase the chance of winter survival. Fertilize Mums early in the growing season according to soil test recommendations. Pinch back taller cultivars for compact growth and increased flower production. Start pinching Mums in late May or early June. Cut plants back just above a set of leaves to a height of 6 inches. Stop pinching by late June so blooming will occur prior to snowfall. Winter protection will increase the chance of winter survival. Leave the plants intact for the winter. The stems help capture snow and insulate the plants. I have also had success cutting the plants back halfway and mulching them with evergreen branches.

ADDITIONAL INFORMATION

Garden Mums come in a variety of flower shapes. They can be single or semidouble like the Daisy, Anemone, Brush, or Spoon types. The double-flowering Pompons, Quill, Spider, or Buttons tend to be more rounded with many more petals.

ADDITIONAL SPECIES, CULTIVARS, OR VARIETIES

The University of Minnesota has introduced 76 Garden Mums since the 1930's. 'Rose Blush' is noted for its profusion of early mauve flowers. 'Minngopher' produces crimson red flowers in late September. 'Sesquicentennial Sun' is a golden yellow variety that grows 18 to 24 inches tall and 20 to 23 inches wide. It flowers in early August and was introduced in 2001 to commemorate the 150th aniversery of the University of Minnesota. Select the cultivar with the desired looks, size, and hardiness for your landscape. The related *Chrysanthemum* × *rubellum* tends to be hardier than the Garden Mum. You may want to include some of these cultivars in your perennial garden. 'Clara Curtis' has rosy-pink flowers and grows 2 to 3 feet tall. 'Duchess of Edinburgh' has dull-red flowers on 2-foot-tall plants. 'Mary Stoker' has yellow flowers with a pink blush; this cultivar of *Chrysanthemum* × *rubellum* grows 3 feet tall.

Oriental Poppy

Papaver orientale

Size: 2 to 4 feet **Flowers:** Orange-red, red, pink, white **Bloom Period:** Late spring to early summer **Zones:** All *Color photograph on page 238.*	**Light Requirements:** **Additional Benefits:**

I think I fell in love with Poppies when I saw Georgia O'Keefe's painting, *Red Poppy*. The flowers are just as beautiful in the garden as they are in her picture. They are a little difficult to get started, but your efforts will be rewarded with years of enjoyment.

WHEN TO PLANT

Plant hardened-off, container-grown, and field-potted perennials any time during the growing season. You may have better success planting and dividing Poppies in August and September when the plants are somewhat dormant.

WHERE TO PLANT

Grow Poppies in a sunny location with good drainage. Used en masse, these large flowered plants will steal the show. I have seen them used effectively in naturalized settings and formal gardens. Plan for the void left by these earlier bloomers. By midsummer, the plants dry up and die back to ground level. Plant late-blooming perennials, such as Baby's Breath, nearby to fill the void left by the Poppy.

HOW TO PLANT

Poppies do not respond well to transplanting, making them difficult to establish. However, once established, they are very long lived. Good soil drainage is critical for growing success. Minimize transplanting stress by carefully handling the plants. Plant Poppies at the same depth they were growing in the containers and 2 feet apart.

CARE AND MAINTENANCE

Established Poppies are low-maintenance plants. Winter mulch new plantings with evergreen branches after the ground lightly freezes.

This will help them through their first winter and increase establishment success. Many gardeners, including me, are not successful on their first attempt at planting Poppies. It has taken me several tries to find the best spot to success-fully grow Poppies. Deadheading is not necessary and will not encourage a second flush of flowers. In fact, you may want to leave the large, attractive seedheads for added interest. Some gardeners cut back the plants right after bloom to get a new flush of small leaves. This doesn't always work. I just remove the faded leaves in midsummer and wait for next year's show. A small rosette of leaves may develop in the fall. Leave these in place over the winter. New growth in the spring will cover any of the leaves damaged during cold weather. Pull, don't dig, weeds as soon as they appear. Cultivation can damage the Poppy's roots.

ADDITIONAL INFORMATION

Poppies make great cut flowers. Cut the flowers when the bud is in an upright position. Some floral designers singe the end of the stem, while others feel it is unnecessary and possibly detrimental. See what works best for you. And don't forget to pick the dried seed pods to use in wreaths and dried arrangements.

ADDITIONAL SPECIES, CULTIVARS, OR VARIETIES

Select cultivars propagated from root cuttings to maintain the true characteristics of the plant. Many places start their plants from seed and can't guarantee the quality and growth characteristics of each plant. 'Allegro' has single flowers in dazzling scarlet. 'Beauty of Livermore' has flow-ers in crimson.

 Did You Know?

Poppies have long been grown for beauty, magic, and medicine. The Poppy seeds used in baking come from the Opium Poppy, Papavera somniferum. *The Corn Poppy,* Papaver rhoeas, *is used to commemorate individuals who died in wars. It is the bright red Poppy of Flander's Field.*

Peony

Paeonia hybrids

Other Names: Chinese Peony, Hybrid Peony, Herbaceous Peony
Size: 3 feet tall
Flowers: White, pink, red, salmon
Bloom Period: Late spring to early summer
Zones: All
Color photograph on page 239.

Light Requirements:

Additional Benefits:

Peonies provide a long season of interest in the landscape. The new growth comes up red and soon turns green as the leaves enlarge. The large flowers can be single, semidouble, or double. Many are fragrant and all of them work well as cut flowers. Once the flowers fade, the leaves remain green and attractive throughout the season. In the fall, the leaves turn a nice purple before dying back to the ground.

WHEN TO PLANT

Rhizomes can be planted in the fall before the ground freezes or in the spring after the danger of severe weather has passed. Hardened-off, container-grown, and field-potted perennials can be planted any time during the growing season.

WHERE TO PLANT

Grow Peonies in full sun. They will tolerate light shade, but fail to bloom in excess shade. Peonies will survive in heavy clay soil, but need good drainage. Use them as specimen plants, mixed with shrubs in foundation plantings, or as a background plant for other flowers.

HOW TO PLANT

Plant the rhizomes with the buds (eyes) 2 inches below the soil surface. Planting them deeper may prevent flowering. Plant containerized Peonies at the same level they were growing in the pot. Space Peonies at least 3 feet apart.

CARE AND MAINTENANCE

It takes Peonies several years to become fully established. Once established, the plant can remain in place for many years. A former neighbor has the Peonies her father planted in that yard almost 100 years ago. Some gardeners disbud peonies. Removing the large terminal bud results in many smaller flowers on each stem. These are less subject to flopping. Removing the side buds and leaving just the terminal results in fewer, but larger, blossoms. Many Peony cultivars flop over when they are in full bloom. It doesn't hurt the plants; it just ruins the floral display. Use a Peony cage to provide support without detracting from the beauty of the plant. Peonies do not need regular dividing. September and October are the best times to lift and divide these perennials. Each division should contain 3 to 5 eyes. Mulch fall divided Peonies for added winter protection.

ADDITIONAL INFORMATION

Peonies are subject to several fungal diseases. Mulching not only helps conserve moisture and reduce weeds, it can also help reduce some soil-borne diseases. Remove faded flowers and infected leaves as soon as they appear. This combined with fall cleanup will usually control disease problems. Deadheading will not encourage rebloom, but it will keep the plants looking good. Use some of your Peonies as cut flowers. Harvest them when the buds have started to open.

ADDITIONAL SPECIES, CULTIVARS, OR VARIETIES

Select the Peony cultivar with the color and flower type that is best suited to the landscape. Choose a cultivar with fragrance if this is a desired feature. Some retailers sell unnamed Peonies. This can result in a plant that is not suited to your likes and the landscape design. Check with quality garden centers, perennial nurseries, and catalogs for named cultivars.

  Did You Know?

Peonies fail to bloom the first spring after transplanting when they are planted too deep, if grown in the shade, or when they are overfertilized. Correct the problem to encourage flowering.

Phlox

Phlox paniculata and *Phlox subulata*

Other Names: Garden Phlox,
  Creeping or Moss Phlox
Size: 3 to 48 inches
Flowers: Blue, purple, pink, rose,
  red, white
Bloom Period: Spring and summer to fall
Zones: All
Color photograph on page 239.

Light Requirements:

Additional Benefits:

Use a few creeping Phlox plants to give your spring landscape a little pizzazz. The bright flower display often leads gardeners to convert their front gardens to this plant. But remember, it will just be green the remainder of the season. Use tall garden Phlox for added color in the back of the perennial garden. These stately plants will bloom from summer into early fall.

WHEN TO PLANT

Bare-root perennials should be planted in the spring after the danger of severe weather has passed. Hardened-off, container-grown, and field-potted perennials can be planted any time during the growing season.

WHERE TO PLANT

Grow Phlox in full sun in moist, well-drained soil. Be sure the plants are properly spaced with good air circulation. This will help reduce disease problems.

HOW TO PLANT

Plant bare-root perennials so the crown, or the point where the stems and roots join, is even with the soil surface. Creeping Phlox is often sold as half flats rooted in sand. These can be planted as is or divided into smaller sections. Plant these and containerized plants at the same level they were growing in the flat or container. Check new plantings for soil settling. Fill in low spots and cover exposed roots as needed.

CARE AND MAINTENANCE

Proper soil preparation, plant selection, and siting will help reduce future maintenance. Cut back Creeping Phlox halfway after flowering. This keeps the plants full and attractive and often encourages additional flowers later in the season. Deadhead Garden Phlox to extend the bloom time. This also prevents reseeding. The seedlings won't look like their hybrid parents and can become a weed problem. Powdery mildew is the biggest problem of Garden Phlox. Select mildew-resistant cultivars such as 'David' whenever possible. Remove 1/3 of the stems in the spring to improve air circulation and reduce mildew problems. Remove and discard all infected leaves throughout the season. Fall cleanup will also help reduce mildew problems. Deer love Phlox. Repellents, netting, and fencing can help reduce the damage. Vary control tactics and be persistent.

ADDITIONAL INFORMATION

Several species are native to Minnesota. Wild Blue Phlox, *Phlox divaricata,* tends to creep across the ground. It is 8 to 10 inches tall with blue flowers in the spring. Smooth Phlox, *Phlox glaberrima,* has smooth, shiny leaves. Hairy Phlox, *P. pilosa,* has hairy leaves on 1 1/2-foot-tall plants and is known as Downy Phlox.

ADDITIONAL SPECIES, CULTIVARS, OR VARIETIES

Creeping or Moss Phlox, *Phlox subulata,* grows 3 to 6 inches tall and creeps along the ground. One plant can quickly cover a 2-foot-square area. Its evergreen foliage and early spring bloom make it a popular perennial. Use Creeping Phlox as an edging plant, in rock gardens, or trailing over a wall. Garden Phlox, *Phlox paniculata,* is another popular Phlox. This perennial grows 3 to 4 feet tall. It makes a nice background, cut flower, or specimen plant in the perennial border. Try substituting the more mildew-resistant Wild Sweet William, *Phlox maculata,* for garden phlox. They look very similar but Wild Sweet William is resistant to powdery mildew. All Phlox help attract butterflies to the landscape.

Purple Coneflower

Echinacea purpurea

Other Names: Hedge Coneflower,
   Purple Echinacea
Size: 2 to 4 feet tall
Flowers: Purple, white
Bloom Period: Summer through fall
Zones: All
Color photograph on page 239.

Light Requirements:

Additional Benefits:

Purple Coneflower is as at home in its native environment as it is in the home landscape. A few Coneflowers can create a mass of color in the fall garden or cutflower arrangements. Their large, Daisy-like flowers will help attract butterflies and the seedheads will attract birds to the landscape.

WHEN TO PLANT

Sow seeds outdoors in the fall or early spring. It takes several years for these to flower. Bare-root perennials should be planted in the spring after the danger of severe weather has passed. Hardened-off, container-grown, and field-potted perennials can be planted any time during the growing season.

WHERE TO PLANT

Grow Purple Coneflowers in full sun and well-drained soil. They will tolerate light shade, but excess shade will cause poor growth and flowering. Avoid rich soil and excess fertilizer that can cause the plants to topple and flower poorly. Combine Coneflower with Russian Sage and ornamental or native grasses. The finer textured plants help the Coneflowers blend into the perennial or naturalized garden.

HOW TO PLANT

Spread seeds on prepared soils. Rake the soil to cover the seeds. Tamp the soil and water to ensure good seed-soil contact. Plant Coneflowers at the same level they were growing in the nursery or container.

CARE AND MAINTENANCE

Purple Coneflowers can quickly fill the garden. They will grow and prosper with very little care. Deadheading is not necessary, but will give the plants and garden a neater appearance. Stop dead-heading by early September to allow seedheads to form. These provide good winter interest in the garden and food for the birds. You can cut the plants back halfway in mid-June. Pruning will reduce the plant size and delay flowering. Try pruning just half of your plants to extend the bloom time with pruned and unpruned plants. This gives you more time to enjoy the flowers in the garden or as cut flowers. Established coneflowers are heat and drought tolerant. New plantings benefit from 1 inch of water per week. Mulch the soil to conserve moisture and reduce weed problems. Mulching will help reduce the number of Coneflower seedlings. But don't worry, you will still have plenty of extra plants.

ADDITIONAL INFORMATION

Coneflowers suffer from some leaf spot diseases. I often see stems or individual plants yellow and wilt. Remove the infected stem or plant when these symptoms appear. Surrounding plants will quickly fill in the vacant area. I find sanitation is sufficient to control this problem.

ADDITIONAL SPECIES, CULTIVARS, OR VARIETIES

Echinacea angustifolia is native to the dry prairies of Minnesota. *Echinacea purpurea* 'Magnus' was the 1998 Perennial Plant of the Year. It has large flowers with flat, dark purple petals. 'White Swan' is shorter, 2 to 3 feet tall, with white flowers. It is great as a cut flower and produces fewer seedlings. Check with garden centers, perennial nurseries, and catalogs for available cultivars.

 Did You Know?

Echinacea has long been used for medicinal purposes. Thought to cure colds, scurvy, and snake bites, it was used extensively in the United States. Today you can buy Echinacea tablets at your local pharmacy.

Russian Sage

Perovskia atriplicifolia

Other Name: Azure Sage
Size: 3 to 5 feet tall
Flowers: Blue
Bloom Period: Midsummer through fall
Zone: 4
Color photograph on page 239.

Light Requirements:

Additional Benefits:

Russian Sage was the 1995 Perennial Plant of the Year. Its silvery stems and foliage make a nice backdrop for the perennial garden. This large plant's fine leaves and flowers give it an airy texture, making it a good filler plant. Mix Russian Sage with coarser-textured plants, such as Purple Coneflower and Black-eyed Susan. Russian Sage is a nice addition to the landscape and a good plant for beginning gardeners and those who want low-maintenance plants.

WHEN TO PLANT

Plant bare-root perennials in the spring after the danger of severe weather has passed. Hardened-off, container-grown, and field-potted perennials can be planted any time during the growing season.

WHERE TO PLANT

Grow Russian Sage in full sun and well-drained soil. Good drainage is essential for vigorous growth and winter survival. Use the plants in perennial gardens for year-round interest.

HOW TO PLANT

Add several inches of organic matter to the top 6 to 12 inches of clay soil. Plant Russian Sage at the same level it was growing in the nursery or container. Space the plants 2¹/₂ to 3 feet apart. Check new plantings for soil settling. Fill in low spots and cover exposed roots as needed.

CARE AND MAINTENANCE

Russian Sage is a low-maintenance plant. Once established, it is very drought tolerant. New plantings, however, benefit from an inch of rain or water each week. Russian sage tends to topple as it reaches full size. I usually surround it with other plants to provide some needed support. Pruning the plants early in the season will encourage more compact growth that is less likely to fall over. Cut the plants back halfway when they are 12 inches tall. Or try one of the more compact cultivars that is less likely to flop. Leave the Russian Sage plants standing for winter interest. The silvery stems and some of the foliage will last throughout the winter. You will still get the benefit of its fragrance when you prune it down in spring. Spring pruning is needed to remove the dead stems and encourage sturdy new growth. Prune the stems back to a healthy bud several inches above ground level. Spring pruning is beneficial even when the stems are not killed over the winter. It encourages stronger stems that are less likely to topple. Russian Sage seldom needs dividing, but you can move and divide the plants in early spring if desired.

ADDITIONAL INFORMATION
Russian Sage will occasionally reseed. Seedlings from the straight species can be dug and moved to the desired growing location or shared with a friend. Cultivars do not come true from seed. You may want to weed these out rather than be surprised with a less-than-desirable plant.

ADDITIONAL SPECIES, CULTIVARS, OR VARIETIES
'Login' is narrower and more upright than the species. The leaves are silver, but not as finely divided. Try growing 'Tiligran' for a more compact, 30-inch-tall, and finer-textured plant. Its leaves are more finely divided than the species. 'Blue Spire' Russian Sage produces a profusion of violet-blue flowers. It grows 4 feet tall and 3 feet wide.

 Did You Know?

Try growing Russian Sage in containers alone or mixed with other plants. It will not survive the winter in an above-ground container. You will need to move the plants or sink the containers in the ground for winter.

Salvia

Salvia species

Other Names: Perennial Salvia, Perennial Sage
Size: 2 to 3 feet
Flowers: Blue, violet, rose-pink
Bloom Period: Summer
Zones: All
Color photograph on page 239.

Light Requirements:

Additional Benefits:

Salvia has been a standard plant in perennial gardens for years. The spikes of blue and pink flowers add charm to the garden and color to flower arrangements. Use the taller species as background plants. Plant a few near the window or patio so you can enjoy the butterflies that come to visit.

WHEN TO PLANT

Plant bare-root Salvias in the spring after the danger of severe weather has passed. Hardened-off, container-grown, and field-potted perennials can be planted any time during the growing season.

WHERE TO PLANT

Grow Salvia in full sun in moist soil. Plants tend to flop in excess shade and rich soils. Salvias are nice, long-blooming plants for the perennial garden. Include a few extras for cutting and attracting butterflies.

HOW TO PLANT

Prepare the soil prior to planting. Plant bare-root perennials so the crown, or the point where the stems and roots join, is even with the soil surface. Plant containerized plants at the same level they were growing in the pot. Space plants 18 inches apart.

CARE AND MAINTENANCE

Perennial Salvia performs best in moist, well-drained soil. Once established, the plants will tolerate dry conditions. Just keep in mind they grow better and flower longer in cool temperatures and moist soil. Mulch the soil with a 1- to 2-inch layer of organic material such as cocoa bean shells, twice-shredded bark, shredded leaves, or pine needles. Mulch helps to conserve moisture, keep soil cool, and reduce weed problems. Deadhead Salvia to extend the bloom time. Remove the faded flower stems back to the side buds and stems. Prune Salvia back after flowering. Cutting the plants back to the new growth will reduce the unsightly growth that is common on perennial Salvia. Some Salvia becomes floppy and open in the center during flowering. In that case, skip the deadheading and prune plants back after the first flush of flowers. Keep the soil moist after pruning. Pruned plants will produce a flush of smaller flowers that still look good in the garden and flower arrangements. Leave plants standing for winter to increase hardiness. The stems capture snow for mulch and are less likely than cut stems to collect water and freeze. Divide overgrown Salvia in spring. Regular division will help reduce problems with open centers and leggy growth.

ADDITIONAL INFORMATION

Sage seasoning comes from another perennial Salvia, *Salvia officinalis*. A standard in the herb garden, I often use it in perennial gardens. The colorful leaves and interesting texture make it a nice edging or specimen plant.

ADDITIONAL SPECIES, CULTIVARS, OR VARIETIES

There are several species and hybrids called Perennial Sage. Select a cultivar that holds it shape and is best suited for your landscape. 'May Night' ('Mainacht') was the 1997 Perennial Plant of the Year. It is a long bloomer that stays nice and compact. It produces indigo-blue flowers on 18-inch-tall plants. 'East Friesland' is another compact form that has been around for quite a few years. It is 18 inches tall with dark violet flowers.

 Did You Know?

Salvia is from the Latin word salvus, *meaning safe. This refers to its healing powers. People have used various Salvias to cure problems of the liver, stomach, and heart, as well as fever and plague. It was also believed that women who drank Salvia cooked in wine would never become pregnant.*

Sedum

Sedum species

Sedums have long been known and used for their ability to grow in difficult locations. Many of the newer Sedums are being grown for their impressive flowers and colorful foliage. If you haven't seen some of the new Sedum cultivars, you are in for a pleasant surprise. Chances are you will find a Sedum that fits your landscape.

WHEN TO PLANT

Plant bare-root Sedums in the spring after the danger of severe weather has passed. Hardened-off, container-grown, and field-potted perennials can be planted any time during the growing season.

WHERE TO PLANT

Sedums are tough plants that tolerate a wide range of conditions. They grow best in full sun and well-drained soil. Some Sedums can tolerate light shade, but they will become open and leggy in heavy shade. Sedums will tolerate heavy clay soil as long as they are not kept excessively wet. Use the low-growing Sedums in rock gardens or as groundcovers. The taller Sedums can be used as edging plants or in the perennial garden. Many have decorative foliage, making them good specimen plants.

HOW TO PLANT

Plant bare-root perennials so the crown, or the point where stems and roots join, is even with the soil surface. Containerized plants should be planted so the crown is even with the soil level.

CARE AND MAINTENANCE

Sedums are low-maintenance plants. Established plants are very drought tolerant. Avoid overwatering and overfertilizing that can lead to floppy growth and root rot. Overgrown Sedums can be divided any time during the season. Spring division will allow plants to get established before summer and fall bloom. Dig, divide, and replant by September to give the plants an opportunity to get established before winter.

ADDITIONAL INFORMATION

A couple of Sedum plants go a long way. New plants can easily be started from cuttings or divisions any time.

ADDITIONAL SPECIES, CULTIVARS, OR VARIETIES

Sedum × 'Autumn Joy' is probably the most popular Sedum on the market. It can be used as an edging plant in rose and perennial gardens. Used as a specimen or en masse, it gives an impressive fall flower display. Its thick, fleshy leaves are topped with large, flat-flower clusters in late summer. They start out pale pink, deepen to a rosy red, and then turn a rust color after the first frost. The dried seedheads persist, adding interest to the winter landscape. I know a few railroad enthusiasts that use the seedheads for trees in their miniature railroad landscapes. You can pinch back the plants in early June for more compact growth. Pinch 8-inch-tall stems back to 4 inches. 'Vera Jameson', which has purple stems and purple-pink leaves, has also become popular. The attractive foliage is topped with pink, star-shaped flowers in late summer and early fall. Two-row Stonecrop, *Sedum spurium*, and Orange Stonecrop, *Sedum kamtschaticum*, are low growing and have long been used in rock gardens and as groundcovers.

Did You Know?

Both the common and botanical name reflect Sedum's ability to grow in tough locations. Sedum comes from the Latin word sedo *meaning to sit. This refers to the way the plants attach themselves to rocks and walls. The common name Stonecrop tells us the plant is able to grow on stony ledges.*

Shasta Daisy

Chrysanthemum × superbum

Other Name: *Leucanthemum × superbum*
Size: 1 to 3 feet tall
Flowers: White with yellow center
Bloom Period: Summer until frost
Zone: 4
Color photograph on page 239.

Light Requirements:

Additional Benefits:

Shasta Daisies provide a profusion of white flowers from summer until frost. The large Daisy-like flowers are good for cutting, attracting butterflies, or providing reliable color in the perennial garden.

WHEN TO PLANT

Plant bare-root Shasta Daisies in the spring after the danger of severe weather has passed. Hardened-off, container-grown, and field-potted perennials can be planted in the spring or early summer. That gives the plants time to get established before winter.

WHERE TO PLANT

Grow Shasta Daisies in full sun and moist well-drained soils. Good drainage is important for winter survival. Shasta Daisies provide a long season of bloom. Use them in perennial and cutting gardens. They combine well with perennial Salvia, Veronicas, Yarrow, Coreopsis, Bee Balm, and ornamental grasses.

HOW TO PLANT

Prepare the soil prior to planting. Plant Shasta Daisies at the same level they were grown in the nursery or container. Space plants 2 feet apart.

CARE AND MAINTENANCE

Shasta Daisies tend to be short lived. They seem to do well for several years and then one spring they just don't come back. Regular dividing seems to keep the plants vigorous and prolongs their life in the garden. Divide Shasta Daisies in early spring every two to three years. Staking is often needed for the species and taller cultivars. Spring pruning will help encourage more compact growth that does not need staking. Pinch back tall cultivars to 6 inches in late May or early June. This will delay flowering by one to two weeks, but eliminates the need for staking. Deadheading will prolong blooms. Cut faded flowers back to side buds. Or better yet, pick some fresh flowers to use indoors. This way you have less to deadhead and the added enjoyment of cut flowers. Prune back plants to the new growth once flowering has finished. This will encourage more leaf growth with some sporadic blooms throughout the remainder of the season. Some growers feel this pruning prevents the plants from "blooming themselves to death." Keep Shasta Daisies healthy with a light fertilization in the spring. Keep the soil moist, but not wet, throughout the growing season.

ADDITIONAL INFORMATION

Shasta Daisy has undergone several name changes. Originally named *Chrysanthemum × superbum*, it was one of the many members of the Chrysanthemum group to be renamed. Shasta daisy became *Leucanthemum × superba;* however, the name change was appealed and the plant is once again *Chrysanthemum × superbum*. You may see it listed both ways.

ADDITIONAL SPECIES, CULTIVARS, OR VARIETIES

Northern gardeners should consider 'Alaska' Shasta Daisy. It is an old-time favorite that tends to be longer lived and hardy to Zone 4. Prune back young plants to eliminate the need for staking. 'Becky' and 'Switzerland' are tall cultivars that do not need staking. Try 'Silver Princess' if you want a truly compact plant. It grows 12 inches tall and produces lots of flowers. Divide it every year to prolong its life.

 Did You Know?

Luther Burbank was credited with the introduction of what we now consider the Shasta Daisy. He did a lot of his breeding and research in California near the white peaks of Mount Shasta. Thus the common name, Shasta Daisy.

PERENNIALS

Veronica

Veronica species

Other Name: Speedwell
Size: 4 to 36 inches
Flowers: Blue, red, white
Bloom Period: Late spring to summer
Zones: All
Color photograph on page 239.

Light Requirements:

Additional Benefits:

Veronicas are versatile plants that can fit into many garden situations. The lower growing types are good edging plants and groundcovers. Use the taller ones for cutting and color in the perennial garden. Include a few in your butterfly garden. You will want to be sure to take some time to enjoy both the veronicas and the butterflies.

WHEN TO PLANT

Plant bare-root veronicas in the spring after the danger of severe weather has passed. Hardened-off, container-grown, and field-potted perennials can be planted any time during the growing season.

WHERE TO PLANT

Grow Veronicas in full sun or partial shade. Plants tend to flop open in the center when grown in heavy shade. Most Veronicas prefer well-drained soils. Place the plants in areas where you can sit and watch the butterflies enjoy the Veronica. Don't forget to pick a few flowers to put in a vase indoors.

HOW TO PLANT

Plant Veronicas at the same level they were growing in the nursery or container. Space plants 18 to 24 inches apart. Check new plantings for soil settling. Fill in low spots and cover exposed roots as needed.

CARE AND MAINTENANCE

The upright types of Veronica tend to flop. Select cultivars with sturdier stems that resist flopping. Staking will help keep taller cultivars upright and attractive during blooming. Cut them back by 1/2 after flowering. The new growth will form a mound that is compact and attractive. Deadheading will help extend the flower display. Clip off faded flowers back to side buds or leaves. Pruning should be done after this second flush of flowers. Divide floppy and over-grown Veronicas in the spring. Most cultivars benefit from being divided every two or three years. Mulch to keep the well-drained soil moist and free of weeds. Use an organic material such as cocoa bean shells, twice-shredded bark, shredded leaves, or pine needles.

ADDITIONAL INFORMATION

Veronica is native to Europe and Russia. It was named in honor of Saint Veronica.

ADDITIONAL SPECIES, CULTIVARS, OR VARIETIES

Spike Speedwell, *Veronica spicata,* grows 10 to 36 inches tall and has spikes of white, blue, or red flowers. The 'Red Fox' cultivar flowers for five to six weeks. It grows 15 inches tall and does not need staking. I can't say the same for 'Blue Fox'. The cultivar 'Icicle' produces white flowers most of the summer. This plant is 18 to 24 inches tall and performs well in most gardens. Woolly Speedwell, *Veronica spicata* subsp. *incana,* has blue flowers and gray leaves. This Veronica must be grown in full sun and well-drained soil to avoid disease problems. Prune back poor growth in midsummer. Harebell or Prostrate Speedwell, *Veronica prostata,* is a creeping form. It forms a mat 6 inches high and 16 inches wide. Use this as a groundcover or next to steppers in the perennial garden. *Veronica austriaca* subsp. *teucrium* 'Crater Lake Blue' forms a mat 12 to 15 inches tall and wide that is perfect for the front of the garden. Its beautiful blue flowers appear in early summer.

 Did You Know?

Veronica 'Sunny Border Blue' was the 1993 Perennial Plant of the Year. The plant blooms for most of the summer. It produces spikes of light-blue flowers above dark-green wrinkled leaves. This 18- to 24-inch-tall plant is a good addition to the perennial or cutting garden.

Virginia Bluebell

Mertensia pulmonarioides

Other Names: Bluebell, Cowslip,
  Mertensia virginica
Size: 12 to 24 inches
Flowers: Blue
Bloom Period: Early spring
Zones: All
Color photograph on page 239.

Light Requirements:

Additional Benefit:

The leaves of Virginia Bluebells peek through the cold soil in early spring. The heart-shaped leaves quickly expand as the plant reaches a height of 12 to 24 inches. The pink flower buds open into blue bell-shaped flowers. Virginia Bluebells are one of the early spring bloomers that let us know winter is on its way out.

WHEN TO PLANT

Plant bare-root Virginia Bluebells in spring after the danger of severe weather has passed. Hardened-off, container-grown, and field-potted perennials can be planted any time during the growing season.

WHERE TO PLANT

Grow Virginia Bluebells in shaded locations. They prefer moist, organic soil. Plant them at the edge of a wooded area or naturalized shrub planting. I like to mix them with Daffodils. The yellow Daffodils and Bluebells make a nice color combination. Keep in mind the large leaves of Virginia Bluebells die back soon after flowering and leave empty space in the garden. Mix Virginia Bluebells with later emerging perennials like Hostas and Ferns to fill in these voids.

HOW TO PLANT

Plant bare-root perennials so the crown, or the point where the stems and roots join, is even with the soil surface. Water and allow potted plants to drain prior to planting. Remove container-grown plants from the pot. Slice or loosen potbound roots to encourage root development into the surrounding soil. Plant these at the same level they were growing in the container. Field-potted perennials often lack a cohesive rootball. Minimize problems by digging the hole first. Then carefully remove the plant from the container and set it in place.

Plant it so the crown is even with the soil level. Fill in the hole and water thoroughly. Check new plantings for soil settling. Perennials often die when the soil settles and their roots are exposed. Fill in low spots and cover exposed roots as needed.

CARE AND MAINTENANCE

Virginia Bluebells are low-maintenance plants. They either grow and take over the area or never quite get established. Proper soil preparation and post-transplant care will aid in establishment. Make sure new plantings receive an inch of water each week. Mulch the soil with a 1- to 2-inch-layer of organic material such as cocoa bean shells, twice-shredded bark, shredded leaves, or pine needles. Mulch helps conserve moisture and reduce weed problems. Pull weeds as soon as they appear. Divide Bluebells in early spring as new growth emerges. Regular dividing will prevent the Bluebells from taking over the garden.

ADDITIONAL INFORMATION

Mertensia paniculata is native to the forests of northeast Minnesota, especially along Lake Superior. This relative of Virgina Bluebells can grow up to 3 feet tall. The bell-shaped flowers start out white or pink and turn blue.

ADDITIONAL SPECIES, CULTIVARS, OR VARIETIES

'Alba' is a white-flowered cultivar of Virginia Bluebells. Oyster Plant, *Mertensia maritima*, is low growing, 4 inches tall, and hardy throughout the state. It has blue-green leaves and bright blue flowers in early summer.

 Did You Know?

Once you see the beautiful blue bell-shaped flowers you know where the common name comes from. The botanical name Mertensia *is named for the German botanist Franz Karl* Mertens. Virginica *lets us know it is native to Virginia and the rest of eastern United States.*

Yarrow

Achillea filipendulina and *Achillea millefolium*

Other Names: Fernleaf Yarrow,
  Common Yarrow
Size: 1 to 4 feet tall
Flowers: Yellow, white, cream, pink,
  red, orange, salmon
Bloom Period: Summer
Zones: All
Color photograph on page 239.

Light Requirements:

Additional Benefits:

The golden flowers of Fernleaf Yarrow can be enjoyed in the garden or indoors in fresh and dried flower arrangements. The Fern-like foliage adds interest to the perennial garden from spring through early winter. Cultivars of the Common Yarrow can brighten the landscape with their red, yellow, white, and orange flowers. Use these in the perennial garden or areas where nothing else will grow.

WHEN TO PLANT
Plant bare-root yarrow in the spring after the danger of severe weather has passed. Hardened-off, container-grown, and field-potted perennials can be planted any time during the growing season.

WHERE TO PLANT
Grow Yarrow in full sun in well-drained soil. Yarrow is able to thrive in hot, dry locations where other plants are lucky to survive. These plants will tend to flop when grown in shade and overfertilized gardens. Use Yarrow in perennial and naturalized gardens. The flowers can be cut and used fresh or dried. And don't forget to watch for the butterflies.

HOW TO PLANT
Plant Yarrow at the same level it was growing in the nursery or container. Space plants 2 to 3 feet apart. Check new plantings for soil settling. Fill in low spots and cover exposed roots as needed.

CARE AND MAINTENANCE
Deadhead to encourage a longer blooming period. This will also reduce reseeding problems of the more invasive Yarrow species.

Prune plants back to fresh new growth after the final bloom. The foliage will look attractive into the winter. Fernleaf Yarrow grown in the proper conditions does not need staking. Common Yarrow will become leggy and topple over without pruning. Prune plants back halfway in early June and after the first and second flush of flowers. This will also prevent seeding, which is a major concern with this plant. Divide overgrown, leggy, or poorly flowering plants in the spring. Common Yarrow benefits from division every 2 to 3 years.

ADDITIONAL INFORMATION

Achillea millefolium has naturalized to some of Minnesota's lawns and prairies. It is considered a weed by some when it appears in areas where it is not invited.

ADDITIONAL SPECIES, CULTIVARS, OR VARIETIES

Fernleaf Yarrow, *Achillea filipendulina,* grows 3 to 4 feet tall and seldom needs staking. The yellow flowers are useful fresh and dried. The Fern-like leaves have a gray appearance and give off a spicy odor. 'Coronation Gold' is a shorter cultivar that is very heat tolerant. It makes an excellent dried flower. The hybrid *Achillea* 'Moonbeam' has bright yellow flowers and silvery gray feather-like foliage. This compact plant grows 24 inches tall and works well in perennial gardens. Use Common Yarrow, *Achillea millefolium,* with caution. I am still weeding out plants eight years after removing the original planting. Deadhead plants and select cultivars that are less invasive. Regular pruning will also help reduce seeding and leggy growth.

 Did You Know?

Achillea was named for Achilles, the hero of Homer's Iliad. Achilles supposedly fed Yarrow to his soldiers to help clot the blood from their wounds. Researchers have discovered Yarrow does contains chemicals that help clot blood.

Yucca
Yucca filamentosa

Other Name: Adam's Needle
Size: 2- to 3-foot foliage; up to
  12 feet tall in bloom
Flowers: White
Bloom Period: July
Zones: 4 and 5
Color photograph on page 239.

Light Requirements:

Additional Benefit:

Yucca may bring visions of the desert, and those are the conditions it prefers: hot, dry areas where other plants fail to thrive. Use this evergreen plant as a specimen to show off its bold, narrow foliage. Its strong architectural features may add interest to your perennial gardens, shrub beds, or containers in the landscape.

WHEN TO PLANT
Plant bare-root Yucca in the spring after the danger of severe weather has passed. Hardened-off, container-grown, and field-potted perennials can be planted any time during the growing season. I prefer spring or early summer to give the plants time to get established before winter.

WHERE TO PLANT
Grow Yucca in full sun and well-drained soil. I find Yucca challenging to blend into the landscape. Try using it as a vertical accent in the garden or shrub bed. The tall flower stalk is quite impressive and will temporarily steal attention from the rest of the garden setting. The University of Minnesota Arboretum used these en masse in a rock garden edged with Prickly Pear Cactus. It was quite impressive.

HOW TO PLANT
Improve the drainage of heavy clay soil by adding several inches of organic matter to the top 6 to 12 inches. Plant Yucca at the same level it was growing in the nursery or container. Check new plantings for soil settling. Fill in low spots and cover exposed roots as needed.

CARE AND MAINTENANCE
New plantings benefit from regular watering until the root system becomes established. Once established, plants are very heat and

drought tolerant. Yuccas thrive and put on the best flower display during hot, dry summers. Clip off faded flowers for a neater appearance. I sometimes leave the seedheads in place for added interest. Leave the evergreen leaves in place for winter detail. The new growth in the spring will mask the fading leaves. Older leaves can be removed in the spring. Yucca will occasionally suffer from leaf spot diseases. These are more of a problem in cool, wet seasons. Remove infected leaves to reduce the spread. Sanitation is usually enough to control these diseases. Deer like to eat this plant. Protect the plants if deer are a problem in your landscape.

ADDITIONAL INFORMATION

Start new plants by removing the suckers, or the "pups," that form at the base of the plant. Treat these like cuttings. Root them in moist sand. Once rooted, they can be planted in the garden. New side shoots can also be removed and replanted.

ADDITIONAL SPECIES, CULTIVARS, OR VARIETIES

'Golden Sword' has a yellow stripe down the middle of the green leaves. 'Bright Edge' is just the opposite: the yellow is along the edge of the green leaves. 'Variegata' has blue-green leaves with white margins. These become pink-tinged in the winter.

 Did You Know?

Does your Yucca seem to bloom well for a season and then not the next? That is common. Yucca tends to be a biennial blooming plant, so plant it in areas where either the flowers or foliage can be effective.

"Though an old man, I am

but a young gardener."

—Thomas Jefferson

MINNESOTA
Gardener's Guide

Photographic Gallery
of Featured Plants

Ageratum
Ageratum houstonianum

Alyssum
Lobularia maritima

Annual Pinks
Dianthus chinensis

Begonia
Begonia semperflorens-cultorum

Cleome
Cleome hasslerana

Cockscomb
Celosia argentea

Coleus
Solenostemon scutellarioides

Cosmos
Cosmos

Dusty Miller
Senecio cineraria

Flowering Tobacco
Nicotiana alata

Fuchsia
Fuchsia × hybrida

Geranium
Pelargonium × hortorum

Impatiens
Impatiens wallerana

Lobelia
Lobelia erinus

Madagascar Periwinkle
Catharanthus roseus

Marigold
Tagetes

Moss Rose
Portulaca grandiflora

Nasturtium
Tropaeolum majus

Pansy
Viola × wittrockiana

Petunia
Petunia × hybrida

Salvia
Salvia splendens

Snapdragon
Antirrhinum majus

Spike
Cordyline

Sunflower
Helianthus annuus

233

Verbena
Verbena

Zinnia
Zinnia elegans

Allium
Allium

Caladium
Caladium × bicolor

Calla Lily
Zantedeschia aethiopica

Canna
Canna × generalis

Crocus
Crocus vernus

Daffodil
Narcissus

Dahlia
Dahlia

Gladiolus
Gladiolus × hortulanus

Grape Hyacinth
Muscari armeniacum

Hyacinth
Hyacinthus orientalis

Iris
Iris

Lily
Lilium

Squills
Scilla siberica

Tuberous Begonia
Begonia × *tuberhybrida*

Tulip
Tulipa

Barren Strawberry
Waldsteinia ternata

Barronwort
Epimedium × *rubrum*

Bishop's Weed
Aegopodium podagraria 'Variegatum'

Bugleweed
Ajuga reptans

Deadnettle
Lamium maculatum

Ginger
Asarum canadense

Houttuynia
Houttuynia cordata 'Chameleon'

235

Lily-of-the-Valley
Convallaria majalis

Moneywort
Lysimachia nummularia

Mother of Thyme
Thymus serpyllum

Pachysandra
Pachysandra terminalis

Potentilla
Potentilla

Sweet Woodruff
Galium odoratum

Variegated Yellow Archangel
Lamiastrum galeobdolon 'Variegatum'

Vinca
Vinca minor

Wintercreeper
Euonymus fortunei

Blue Fescue
Festuca cinerea

Blue Oat Grass
Helictotrichon sempervirens

Bluestem
Schizachyrium scoparium

Feather Reed Grass
Calamagrostis × acutiflora 'Stricta'

Fountain Grass
Pennisetum setaceum

Hakonechloa
Hakonechloa macra 'Aureola'

Miscanthus (Silver Grass)
Miscanthus sinensis

Moor Grass
Molinia caerulea

Spike Grass
Spodiopogon sibiricus

Switchgrass
Panicum virgatum

Artemisia
Artemisia

Aster
Aster

Astilbe
Astilbe

Bellflower
Campanula

Black-Eyed Susan
Rudbeckia

Bleeding Heart
Dicentra spectabilis

Butterfly Weed
Asclepias tuberosa

Columbine
Aquilegia

Coralbells
Heuchera sanguinea

Coreopsis
Coreopsis verticillata

Daylily
Hemerocallis

Delphinium
Delphinium x elatum

Fern
Athyrium

Gayfeather
Liatris spicata

Hosta
Hosta

Mum
Chrysanthemum × morifolium

Oriental Poppy
Papaver orientale

Peony
Paeonia

Phlox
Phlox paniculata

Purple Coneflower
Echinacea purpurea

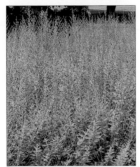

Russian Sage
Perovskia atriplicifolia

Salvia
Salvia × superba

Sedum
Sedum

Shasta Daisy
Chrysanthemum × superbum

Veronica
Veronica

Virginia Bluebell
Mertensia virginica

Yarrow
Achillea filipendulina

Yucca
Yucca filamentosa

Climbing Rose
Rosa

Hybrid Teas
Rosa

Floribunda
Rosa

Grandiflora
Rosa

Miniatures
Rosa

Shrub
Rosa

Alpine Currant
Ribes alpinum

Arborvitae
Thuja occidentalis

Barberry
Berberis thunbergii

Boxwood
Buxus microphylla
var. *koreana* × *Buxus sempervirens*

Burning Bush
Euonymus alatus

Butterfly Bush
Buddleia davidii

Cotoneaster
Cotoneaster

Dogwood
Cornus sericea

Forsythia
Forsythia

Fragrant Sumac
Rhus aromatica

Honeysuckle
Lonicera

Hydrangea
Hydrangea

Juniper
Juniperus

Lilac
Syringa

Mockorange
Philadelphus coronarius

Mugo Pine
Pinus mugo

Potentilla
Potentilla fruticosa

Rhododendron
Rhododendron

Spirea
Spiraea japonica

241

Viburnum
Viburnum dentatum

Weigela
Weigela florida

Witchhazel
Hamamelis virginiana

Yew
Taxus

Alder
Alnus glutinosa

Ash
Fraxinus

Beech
Fagus

Birch
Betula papyrifera

Catalpa
Catalpa speciosa

Crabapple
Malus

Douglasfir
Pseudotsuga menziesii

Elm
Ulmus

242

European Mountain Ash
Sorbus aucuparia

Fir
Abies

Ginkgo
Ginkgo biloba

Hawthorn
Crataegus

Hemlock
Tsuga canadensis

Honey Locust
Gleditsia triacanthos var. *inermis*

Horsechestnut
Aesculus hippocastanum

Ironwood
Ostrya virginiana

Japanese Tree Lilac
Syringa reticulata

Kentucky Coffee Tree
Gymnocladus dioicus

Larch
Larix

Linden
Tilia

243

Magnolia
Magnolia

Maple
Acer

Musclewood
Carpinus caroliniana

Oak
Quercus

Ornamental Plum
Prunus cerasifera 'Newport'

Pine
Pinus

Redbud
Cercis canadensis

Serviceberry
Amelanchier

Spruce
Picea

Bittersweet
Celastrus scandens

Boston Ivy
Parthenocissus tricuspidata

Clematis
Clematis × *jackmanii*

Dropmore Scarlet Honeysuckle
Lonicera × brownii 'Dropmore Scarlet'

Morning Glory
Ipomoea purpurea

Trumpet Vine
Campsis radicans

Wintercreeper
Euonymus fortunei

Wisteria
Wisteria

USDA PLANT
HARDINESS MAP

Minnesota

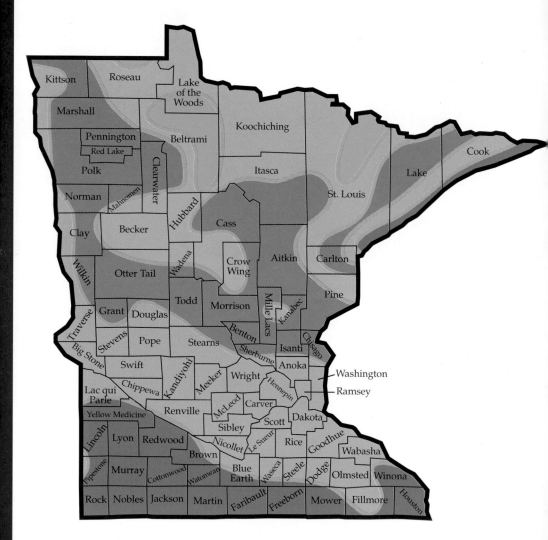

ZONE	Average Minimum Temperature
2B	-40 to -45
3A	-35 to -40
3B	-30 to -35
4A	-25 to -30
4B	-20 to -25

The green thumb gardener is

someone who grows a lot of plants,

kills a few without mentioning

it to others, and keeps

on planting!

CHAPTER SIX

Roses

ROSES ARE BEAUTIFUL PLANTS that provide fragrance and year-round interest to your landscape. There are hundreds of cultivars to choose from in just about every size and color except true blue! And the hybridizers are getting pretty close to that color.

Although roses aren't my favorite plants, it isn't because of the roses themselves as much as it is the frustration they can cause. As a "plant doctor," I have the opportunity to advise many gardeners about what is eating, discoloring, or killing their roses. In addition, many of the popular Hybrid Tea Roses require more care than most gardeners are willing to give.

So why include roses? Because gardeners love them and they can be a valuable addition to any yard. As a matter of fact, I have several rosebushes and am considering adding more. One way to reduce frustration with rose gardening is to keep checking catalogs and garden centers for hardier, more disease-resistant plants.

For best results, roses should be grown in moist, well-drained soil where they receive good air circulation and at least 6 hours of sun per day. Roses need morning sun to dry dew off the leaves and reduce disease problems. Planting roses in a protected location will help them survive cold Minnesota winters.

BUYING ROSES

Roses are available from catalogs, garden centers, and nurseries. The best selection is found in garden catalogs that specialize in roses. Roses are available bare root and in containers. Bare-root roses are often sold according to grades 1, 1^1/$_2$, and 2. Grade 1 plants are the most expensive with three or four heavy canes that are about 18 inches long. Grade 1^1/$_2$ and 2 plants have a smaller root system and fewer canes that are shorter and thinner. Store bare-root plants in a cool, shaded, frost-free location until they can be planted outdoors.

Heel them in or pack the roots in peat moss or sawdust to keep them from drying out.

Planting Roses

Soil preparation is critical to successful rose growing. Spread 2 to 4 inches of organic matter over the soil surface and work it into the top 6 to 12 inches of soil. Plant bare-root roses in the spring while they are still dormant. Soak the roots for 24 hours before planting. Container plants can be planted any time the ground is not frozen. Plant early in the season to allow container-grown plants to get well established before winter.

Many roses are grafted. A bud from the desired plant is attached to a hardy root system. The bud graft is the swollen knob where all the branches are formed. This portion of the plant is very susceptible to winter damage. Plant the graft 2 inches below the soil surface for added winter protection. Nongrafted roses can be planted slightly deeper than the level they were growing in the container. Dig the planting hole at least 2 times larger than the root system. Container roses should be handled with care since they may have been recently potted and lack a cohesive rootball. Minimize root disturbance by cutting away the pot. Cut off the bottom of the container. Set it in the planting hole, making sure the graft will be 2 inches below the soil surface. Now slice the side of the pot and peel it away, leaving the rootball intact. Fill the hole with soil and water. Mulch and keep the soil moist, but not wet, throughout the growing season.

Water and Fertilizing

Roses do best when they receive 1 inch of water per week from rainfall or the hose. Mulch roses with an organic material to conserve moisture, reduce weed problems, and improve the soil.

Test the soil to determine its nutrient content and then fertilize roses according to the test recommendations. In lieu of a test, apply a low-nitrogen fertilizer in spring once new growth is well established, and again 4 to 6 weeks later. Complete fertilizers such as 10-10-10 and 12-12-12 can be used in soils deficient in phosphorus and potassium. Additional fertilizing can be done as needed, but do not fertilize after August 1, since late-season fertilization can contribute to winter damage.

PRUNING AND PICKING ROSES

Pruning requirements vary for each type of rose. (Refer to individual entries for details.) For all roses, remove the suckers that form from the rootstock of grafted roses. Cut them below the soil to discourage resprouting.

Cutting roses for arrangements and deadheading faded flowers is another form of pruning. When properly done, pruning will encourage strong, new growth and repeat blooms. Prune flowering stems back to the first five-leaflet leaf. You can prune back further on established plants, but be sure to always leave at least two five-leaflet leaves behind.

PESTS

Roses are subject to many insect and disease problems. Select the most pest-resistant cultivars available. Black spot, powdery mildew, and rust are the most common disease problems. Remove infected leaves as soon as they appear. Fall cleanup will also help reduce the source of disease for the next growing season. Many gardeners spray disease-susceptible plants with a fungicide on a regular basis. Select a fungicide labeled for this use on roses. Read and follow label directions carefully.

Pests including aphids, mites, leafhoppers, beetles, sawflies, and caterpillars feed on the leaves of rosebushes. Aphids, mites, and leafhoppers suck plant juices, causing leaf discoloration and curling. Several applications of insecticidal soap will control these pests. Handpicking or applying insecticides appropriate for roses will take care of the others. Deer and rabbits are also fond of roses. Using scare tactics, repellents, and fencing may provide relief from these bigger pests.

WINTER PROTECTION

There are as many ways to protect roses from winter weather as there are rose gardeners, but proper timing is the key to the success of each method. We often protect the roses when *we* get cold—not when the roses need it. Rosebushes should not be covered until there is a week of consistently freezing temperatures. Start removing winter protection in the spring when the mercury again starts hovering near freezing. The roses should be pruned only enough to apply winter protection. Save extensive pruning until spring.

For winter protection, try the relatively new and effective Minnesota tip method. Dig a trench next to the rose plant. Tip and bury the rose in the trench. Mulch when the soil freezes.

Or, try the soil mound method. Loosely tie the canes. Many gardeners surround the plants with chicken wire to hold the soil and mulch in place. Cover the bottom 8 to 10 inches of the rose plant with soil. (You may need to raid the compost pile, bring in soil, or dig it from an unfrozen bare spot in your landscape.) Let the soil freeze and then mulch with evergreen branches, marsh hay, or straw.

Climbing Rose

Rosa × hybrida

Size: 6 to 20 feet tall
Flowers: Small; dense clusters
Bloom Period: Summer
Grafted: Some
Zone: 4 (with protection)
Color photograph on page 239.

Light Requirements:

Additional Benefits:

The Climbing Rose is a jack-of-all-trades in Mother Nature's garden. An arbor covered with a colorful and fragrant Climbing Rose can provide a warm welcome to your guests. Another Climbing Rose can provide a discreet and attractive disguise for an unattractive, old chain link fence. The possibilities are endless; use Climbers as vertical accents, flowering specimens, or screens. Select carefully, site properly, and provide proper care to increase success growing climbers in Minnesota.

WHEN TO PLANT

Plant Bare-root Roses in the spring while they are dormant. Container plants can be planted any time the ground is not frozen. Planting early in the season allows the plant time to get established before winter.

WHERE TO PLANT

Roses need full sun and moist, well-drained soil. Good air circulation helps reduce disease problems. Plant Climbers near a fence or trellis.

HOW TO PLANT

Prepare the soil prior to planting. Some Climbing Roses are grafted. Grafted Climbers should be planted with the graft union, or the swollen portion on the stem, 2 inches below the soil surface. Nongrafted Climbers can be planted at the same level as they were grown in the nursery. Dig the planting hole at least 2 times larger than the root system. Handle container Roses with care. Cut away the pot after placing it in the planting hole to minimize root damage. Fill the hole with soil and water. Plant Climbers 8 to 10 feet apart.

CARE AND MAINTENANCE

All Roses benefit from adequate water and fertilization. You will need to train and attach Climbers to their support. Loosely tie the stems to the support with twine. Keep the training simple, since Climbers must be removed and protected from our harsh winter conditions. Only prune dead and damaged wood during the first few years. All Climbers should be pruned after flowering, but plants should not be cut back for winter protection. In the spring, cut any dead stems back to ground level. After blooming you can remove 1/3 of the older canes. Single bloomers can be pruned back by 2/3. Trim side branches of repeat bloomers by 2/3. Prune after flowering throughout the season. Cut the flowering canes on ramblers back to ground level. This improves air circulation and reduces problems with powdery mildew.

ADDITIONAL INFORMATION

After temperatures hover near the freezing mark for about a week, remove Climbers from their support. Tie canes together to make the job more manageable. Bend or tip the Roses over and lay them on the ground. Cover the entire plant with soil. Once the soil freezes, mulch with straw, marsh hay, or evergreen branches.

ADDITIONAL SPECIES, CULTIVARS, OR VARIETIES

Climbing Roses are grouped into two major categories. The ramblers are big, fast-growing, hardy roses. Rambling Roses are an old variety, a kind everyone's grandmother seemed to grow. They bloom profusely with very little care and no winter protection. Rambling Roses grow small, clustered flowers. New disease-resistant and repeat-blooming hybrids are being developed. Ramblers such as 'Lillian Gibson', with its fragrant pink flowers, are good substitutes. These are one-time bloomers. The large-flowered Climbing Roses grow slower. Climbers come from a variety of sources including mutations of Hybrid Teas, Grandifloras, and Multifloras.

Did You Know?

Several of the larger hardy Shrub Roses can be treated like Climbers. Several introductions from Canada, such as repeat-bloomers 'William Baffin' (zone 2), 'John Cabot' (zone 3), and 'Henry Kelsey' (zone 3), can be trained into Climbers and left standing without protection for the winter.

Hybrid Teas

Rosa × hybrida

Size: 4 to 5 feet tall

Flowers: Large; individual or in small groups

Bloom Period: Summer

Grafted: Always

Zones: All (with winter protection)

Color photograph on page 240.

Light Requirements:

Additional Benefits:

When you say roses, Hybrid Teas are the plants most people picture. Their beautiful, large flowers put on quite a show in the garden or in a vase. But there is a price for their beauty. Hybrid Tea Roses require some time and effort on your part. If you are willing to do the work, you will be rewarded with flowers throughout the summer.

WHEN TO PLANT

Plant bare-root Roses in the spring while they are still dormant. Container-grown Roses can be planted any time the ground is not frozen. Planting early in the season allows the Rose time to get established before winter.

WHERE TO PLANT

Roses need full sun and moist, well-drained soil. Good air circulation will help prevent problems with disease. Grow Hybrid Teas in rose gardens, in containers, as specimen plants, or incorporate them into planting beds.

HOW TO PLANT

Prepare the soil prior to planting. Hybrid Teas are grafted and should be planted with the graft union, or the swollen portion on the stem, 2 inches below the soil surface. Dig the planting hole at least 2 times larger than the root system. Handle container Roses with care. Cut away the pot once it is in the planting hole to minimize root damage. Fill the hole with soil and water.

CARE AND MAINTENANCE

All roses thrive on adequate water and fertilization. Prune Roses in the spring as buds swell, but before growth begins. Rose growth begins about the same time the Forsythia bloom. Start by removing

dead and diseased wood. Prune back to healthy, live portions
of the canes where the center of the stem is white. Some
years, the pruning may go to ground level. Prune the Roses
to the desired height, then thin out the center of the plant.
Remove old and crossed canes first. Cut stems back 1/4 inch
above an outward-facing bud. You may want to seal pruning cuts to keep out borers. Deadhead Roses throughout the
season to encourage new blooms and thick, sturdy growth.
Stop deadheading toward the end of the season to slow
down new growth and improve winter hardiness. Roses
need winter protection throughout Minnesota. (See the
page 251 for details.) Some gardeners choose to do nothing
and take their chances that the Roses will survive. The
newest, most effective way to protect non-hardy Roses during the winter is the Minnesota Tip method. Basically, this
involves burying the Rose in a trench dug next to the Rose.

ADDITIONAL INFORMATION

Hybrid Tea Roses are subject to many insect and disease
problems. Black spot, powdery mildew, and rust are the
most common diseases that affect Hybrid Teas. Regular
applications of fungicides will help resolve the problems.
Aphids, mites, leafhoppers, beetles, sawflies, and caterpillars
will also feed on the leaves. Handpicking and insecticidal
soap are environmentally friendly ways to control these pests.

ADDITIONAL SPECIES, CULTIVARS, OR VARIETIES

There are hundreds of Hybrid Teas on the market with
more being added each year. Select the hardiest, most
pest-resistant Hybrid Tea available. They come in a variety
of colors, and some are fragrant. 'Love and Peace' is the
2002 AARS Award Winner. Its golden yellow flowers are
tinged with pink. Check out this introduction from Bailey
Nurseries of St. Paul, Minnesota.

 Did You Know?

*Next time you go rose shopping, check out the All-America Rose
Selections (AARS). These award-winning roses were selected as
the best roses based on flower form, pest resistance, fragrance,
growth habit, and other features. On the web, visit www.rose.org.*

Floribunda

Rosa × hybrida

Size: 3 feet tall
Flowers: Small; in clusters
Bloom Period: Summer
Grafted: Usually
Zones: All (With winter protection)
Color photograph on page 240.

Light Requirements:

Additional Benefits:

Floribundas are hybrids that resulted from crossing Polyantha and Hybrid Tea Roses. The Polyanthas gave these plants increased hardiness, while the Hybrid Teas gave them larger attractive flowers. Both varieties contributed to Floribundas' long blooming season. This Hybrid can be used in mass plantings, hedges, or borders. Floribundas also mix well with other plants and roses.

WHEN TO PLANT
Plant bare-root Roses in spring while they are still dormant. Container plants can be planted any time the ground is not frozen. Planting early in the season allows the Rose time to get established before winter.

WHERE TO PLANT
Roses need full sun and moist well-drained soil. Good air circulation will help reduce disease problems.

HOW TO PLANT
Prepare the soil prior to planting. All grafted Roses should be planted with the graft union, or the swollen portion on the stem, 2 inches below the soil surface. Nongrafted Floribunda can be planted at the same level as they were grown in the nursery. Dig the planting hole at least two times larger than the root system. Handle container Roses with care since some of them may have been recently potted and lack a cohesive rootball. Minimize root disturbance by cutting away the pot once it is in the planting hole. Cut off the bottom of the container and place the plant in the hole with the graft 2 inches below the soil surface. Slice the side of the pot and peel it away, leaving the rootball intact. Fill the hole with soil and water. Mulch and keep the soil moist, but not wet, throughout the growing season.

CARE AND MAINTENANCE

All roses benefit from adequate water and fertilization. Prune Floribunda Roses in the spring as buds swell but before growth begins. In our state that is about the same time the Forsythia bloom. Prune plants back to 10 inches if any above-ground growth survived. Make pruning cuts 1/4 inch above an outward-facing bud. Otherwise, prune plants to ground level. You may want to seal pruning cuts to keep out borers. Deadhead Roses throughout the season to encourage new blooms and thick sturdy growth. Stop deadheading toward the end of the season to slow down new growth and help with winter hardiness. Though hardier than Hybrid Teas, many Floribundas benefit from winter protection. (See the chapter introduction for details.) Some gardeners choose to do nothing. If their Roses make it, great! If not, they replace the plants.

ADDITIONAL INFORMATION

Floribunda Roses, like Hybrid Teas, are subject to many insect and disease problems. Regular applications of fungicides will help control diseases. Many of the insects and mites can be controlled by handpicking or with insecticidal soap. Some avid Rose gardeners use systemic insecticides to control insects.

ADDITIONAL SPECIES, CULTIVARS, OR VARIETIES

There are many Floribundas on the market. More hybridizing is being done to increase the flower size and decrease the number of flowers in the cluster.

 Did You Know?

Roses have long been used for cooking and medicinal purposes. The Romans were the first to eat rose petals. They ate candied rose petals and used petals in wines, puddings, and desserts. But make sure your flowers have not been treated with pesticides before you bite into a rose blossom!

Grandiflora

Rosa × hybrida

Size: 6 feet tall
Flowers: Smaller than Hybrid Teas;
cluster of 5 to 7 flowers
Bloom Period: Summer
Grafted: Always
Zones: All (With winter protection)
Color photograph on page 240.

Light Requirements:

Additional Benefits:

Grandifloras are a relatively recent introduction to the Rose family. They are the result of crossing Hybrid Teas and Floribunda Roses. Their flowers are clustered and larger than Floribundas, but smaller than the Hybrid Teas. Grandifloras tend to bloom more often and more vigorously later in the season. They benefit from winter protection just like the Hybrid Teas.

WHEN TO PLANT

Plant bare-root Roses in the spring while they are still dormant. Container plants can be planted any time the ground is not frozen. I prefer to plant in spring and early summer, which gives the Rose time to get established before winter.

WHERE TO PLANT

Roses need full sun and moist, well-drained soil. Good air circulation will help reduce disease problems. These large plants can be used as background plants in a flower garden or planted with other Roses.

HOW TO PLANT

Prepare the soil prior to planting. Grandifloras are grafted and should be planted with the graft union, or the swollen portion on the stem, 2 inches below the soil surface. Dig the planting hole at least 2 times larger than the root system. Handle container-grown Roses with care. Cut away the pot once it is in the planting hole to minimize root damage. Fill the hole with soil and water.

CARE AND MAINTENANCE

All roses benefit from adequate water and fertilization. Do not fertilize after August 1. Mulch the soil to conserve moisture and control weeds. Prune Roses in the spring as buds swell, but before growth begins, about the same time the Forsythia bloom. Start by removing dead and diseased wood. Prune back to healthy live portions of the canes where the center of the stem is white. This may be to ground level some years. If needed, prune the Roses back to the desired height. Next, thin out the center of the plant. Remove old and crossed canes first. Cut back stems 1/4 inch above an outward-facing bud. You may want to seal pruning cuts to keep borers out. Deadhead Roses throughout the season to encourage new blooms and thick, sturdy growth. Stop deadheading toward the end of the season to slow down new growth and help with winter hardiness. Winter protection is needed statewide. (See chapter introduction for details).

ADDITIONAL INFORMATION

Grandifloras, like many other roses, are subject to insect and disease problems. The susceptibility varies by cultivar. Regular applications of fungicides will help keep diseases under control. Many of the insects and mites can be controlled by handpicking or using insecticidal soap.

ADDITIONAL SPECIES, CULTIVARS, OR VARIETIES

There are many Grandiflora Roses on the market. Decide on a color and then select the variety that is the most pest resistant and cold hardy. The Grandiflora 'Queen Elizabeth' is the second most popular Rose (after 'Peace') of the twentieth century. Nearly thornless, it produces pink flowers through most of the growing season.

 Did You Know?

Avid rose growers, both beginners and experienced hands, may want to contact the American Rose Society (ARS). They provide information and services for backyard rose gardeners. They can be reached at: ARS, P.O. Box 30,000, Shreveport, LA 71130 (http://www.ars.org).

Miniatures

Rosa × hybrida

Size: 3 to 24 inches tall **Flowers:** Miniature **Bloom Period:** Summer **Zones:** All *Color photograph on page 240.*	**Light Requirements:** **Additional Benefits:** 

M iniatures are just that: miniature versions of Hybrid Teas or Floribunda Roses. They are valued for their hardiness, free-flowering nature, and versatility. These small Roses will fit in any landscape. Try using them as an edging plant in the garden or as a specimen in a rock garden. Their small size makes them perfect for window boxes or containers. You will need to move container plantings indoors or to a protected location for the winter. Or you may want to try growing Miniatures as a flowering houseplant in a south window or under artificial lights.

WHEN TO PLANT
Miniatures are almost always sold as container plants. Plant them any time the ground is not frozen. I prefer spring and early summer for planting, which gives the Rose time to get established before winter.

WHERE TO PLANT
Miniatures need full sun and moist, well-drained soil. Good air circulation will help reduce disease problems.

HOW TO PLANT
Prepare the soil prior to planting. Plant Miniatures slightly lower than the level they were grown in the nursery. Dig the planting hole at least 2 times larger than the root system. Handle container Roses with care since some of them have been potted recently and lack a cohesive rootball. Minimize root disturbance by cutting away the pot after setting it in the planting hole. Cut off the bottom of the container and then set it in the hole, making sure the graft is 2 inches below the soil surface. Slice the side of the pot and peel it away, leaving the rootball intact. Fill the hole with soil and water.

CARE AND MAINTENANCE

All roses benefit from adequate water and fertilization. Do not fertilize after August 1. Mulch the soil to conserve moisture and control weeds. Prune Roses in the spring as buds swell, but before growth begins, about the same time the Forsythia bloom. Prune to open the center by removing twiggy growth. Cut the plants back to the desired height. Make cuts 1/4 inch above an outward-facing bud. You may want to seal pruning cuts to keep borers out. Deadhead Roses throughout the season to encourage new blooms and thick sturdy growth. Stop deadheading toward the end of the season to slow down new growth and help with winter hardiness. Even though miniatures are hardier than the Hybrid Teas, many benefit from some winter protection. Some gardeners gamble that their Roses will survive without protection and do nothing.

ADDITIONAL INFORMATION

Miniatures are subject to insect and disease problems. Susceptibility varies with the cultivar. Regular applications of fungicide will help keep diseases under control. Many insects and mites can be controlled by handpicking and using insecticidal soap.

ADDITIONAL SPECIES, CULTIVARS, OR VARIETIES

There are many cultivars of Miniature Roses on the market. Select the hardiest and most pest-resistant Miniature that has the desired flower color and growth habit.

 Did You Know?

The American Rose Society sponsors an award program just for miniatures. It is the American Rose Society Award of Excellence for Miniature Roses (ARSAE). Check out these winners the next time you are shopping for miniature roses.

Shrub

Rosa species and hybrids

Size: 2 feet and taller	**Light Requirements:**
Flowers: Small, single	
Bloom Period: Summer	
Grafted: No	
Zones: All	**Additional Benefits:**
Color photograph on page 240.	

What do you picture when you think of a Shrub Rose? Most Minnesota gardeners think of hardy, pest-resistant Roses with single flowers. Many of the Shrub Roses fit that description, but there is some variety within the group. In general, Shrub Roses have smaller flowers with fewer petals. They tend to be vigorous, low-maintenance Roses: a good choice for my landscape. Some bloom only once, while others repeat one or more times throughout the summer. Use these Roses the same way you use other ornamental shrubs in the landscape.

WHEN TO PLANT

Shrub Roses are usually sold as container plants; however, small plants may be available bare root. Plant bare-root Roses in the spring while they are still dormant. Container plants can be planted any time the ground is not frozen. I prefer to plant in the spring and early summer, which gives the Rose time to get established before winter.

WHERE TO PLANT

Roses need full sun and moist, well-drained soil. Good air circulation will help reduce disease problems. Depending on their size and growth habit, Shrub Roses can be used as short climbers, hedges, specimens, borders, and for winter interest.

HOW TO PLANT

Prepare the soil prior to planting. Plant Shrub Roses slightly lower than the level they were grown in the nursery. Dig the planting hole at least two times larger than the root system. Handle container Roses with care. Cut away the pot once it is in the planting hole to minimize root damage. Fill the hole with soil and water.

CARE AND MAINTENANCE

Shrub Roses require much less care than most other roses. Fertilize as needed in the spring after new growth has developed. Mulch to conserve moisture and reduce weed problems. These Roses also require much less pruning. Remove dead and crowded stems in the spring before growth begins and cut back older stems to keep the growth in bounds. Don't deadhead single blooming Shrub Roses. Stop deadheading repeat bloomers in the late summer. This will allow the plants to form the ornamental fruit called *hips*. Shrub Roses are resistant to insects and disease.

ADDITIONAL INFORMATION

Species Roses are often included with Shrub Roses. The Rugosa Rose, *Rosa rugosa*, is one of the hardiest roses. This species has fragrant pink flowers, blooms all season, and produces attractive hips.

ADDITIONAL SPECIES, CULTIVARS, OR VARIETIES

There are many species and hybrids of Shrub Roses available. Remember, shrub roses can vary in size, so pick one that fits into the space you have available. 'Carefree Wonder' is a free-flowering cultivar with semi-double pink flowers. It is disease resistant and the stems are hardy to 15 degrees below zero. In colder winters it will resprout from the roots. It is a compact plant that produces orange hips for winter display. 'All that Jazz' is another low-maintenance Rose that has become a favorite of landscapers. It is covered with fragrant coral-salmon flowers all season long. 'William Baffin' is a large Shrub used as a climber. It produces deep pink flowers in clusters throughout the season. It is disease resistant and hardy to 20 degrees below zero. 'Starry Night' is the 2002 AARS Award Winner. This medium-sized Shrub produces pure white flowers that resemble a Dogwood flower.

 Did You Know?

Rose hips are high in vitamin C and have long been used for jelly, jam, and tea. Rose hips can also add interest to our winter landscape. Shrub, species, once-blooming, and single flowered roses tend to form attractive rose hips.

CHAPTER SEVEN

Shrubs

S HRUBS, SO WHAT'S THERE TO SAY? You shove a couple of Yews and Spireas up against the foundation of the house and move on to something more interesting, right? Wrong! Along with trees, shrubs form the framework of your landscape. Though they often go unnoticed, shrubs provide structure, background, and seasonal interest when and where other plants can't.

Close your eyes and think of your favorite landscapes. What makes them special? Chances are there are some unusual shrubs or common shrubs used in unique ways that make the settings stand out.

Now picture your landscape. Develop a plan for planting and maintaining the shrubs you are about to invest your time and money in. Select plants that fit the design scheme and add year-round inter-est. The basis for an attractive landscape is putting the right plant in the right location. Make sure the shrubs you choose will fit the space and tolerate the growing conditions in your area.

Once you have determined what plants you want and where they will be placed, do a little preventative maintenance. Call the Gopher State One Call at 1-800-252-1166. Gopher State One Call line is a free utility-locating service. They will mark the location of any underground utilities in the planting area. Give them three working days to complete the task. This is an important step for your safety and pocketbook. Digging into a utility line can be expensive and even deadly.

BUYING THE PLANTS

While waiting for the Gopher State One Call, visit a nursery or garden center to select your plants. You will find a few bare-root shrubs in the spring, but the majority of the shrubs available are balled and burlapped or in containers. The type of plant, place of purchase, and your budget will determine which kind you buy.

PLANTING THE SHRUBS

Store your plants in a cool, shady location until they can be planted. Mulch the roots of bare-root plants and the rootballs of balled-and-burlapped and burlap plants to keep the roots moist. Water these mulched roots and container plants daily.

Plant bare-root shrubs as soon as possible after purchase. Dig a shallow hole wide enough to accommodate the roots. The planting hole should be just deep enough to let you plant the shrub at the same level it was grown in the nursery. Fill the hole with existing soil and water.

Balled-and-burlapped plants should also be planted as soon as possible after purchase. Dig the planting hole the same depth as the rootball, but several feet wider. Set the shrub in the hole, remove the twine, and cut away the burlap. Fill the hole with existing soil and water.

Containerized plants may have been grown in the pot or dug out of the nursery and then potted. Dig a planting hole the same depth and wider than the rootball. Container-grown shrubs should be removed from their pot. Roll the pot on its side or squeeze the container to make it easier to slide the plant out. Loosen or slice through potbound roots. Place the shrub in the hole at the same depth it was grown in the nursery. Fill the hole with existing soil and water. Potted plants usually lack a cohesive rootball. Minimize root damage by cutting the bottom off the pot. Place the shrub, pot and all, in the hole at the same depth it was growing in the nursery. Now cut away the remainder of the container. Fill the hole with soil and water.

Post-Planting Care

New plantings need help to become established. Be sure they receive about an inch of water each week. You may have to water if nature doesn't take care of the job. Established shrubs will need to be watered during drought conditions. Thoroughly water clay soils once a week. Apply the needed water in two applications to sandy soil. Some container-grown shrubs are planted in soilless mixes. The rootball of these shrubs will dry out faster than the surrounding soil. You will need to water the root system more frequently than the surrounding soil to keep both moist, but not wet.

Mulch the soil to conserve moisture and reduce weed problems. Use a 2- to 3-inch layer of wood chips, shredded bark, or other organic materials to help improve the soil. Don't bury the base of the shrub and do not use weed barrier fabrics under these organic mulches. Weeds end up growing into the fabric creating a real mess in several years.

Care and Maintenance

Wait a year to fertilize new shrub plantings. Follow your soil test recommendations for the type and amount of fertilizer to use. If this information is not available, use a high nitrogen fertilizer such as 16-8-8 or 21-0-0 at a rate of 2 pounds per 100 square feet of shrub beds. Young shrubs can be fertilized in late fall after the plants are dormant or in early spring before growth begins. Fertilizing every few years encourages rapid growth on young shrubs. Established shrubs need little if any fertilizer.

Pruning is a regular part of maintenance. Just be sure you have a plan before taking the pruning saw to your plants. Prune shrubs to remove diseased and damaged branches, encourage flowering, improve bark color, control size, and shape the plants. Spring-flowering plants like Lilacs and Forsythia should be pruned right after flowering. Others can be pruned any time during the dormant season. I prefer late winter or early spring. That timetable gives you the opportunity to enjoy the plant's winter interest, and is also better for the plant.

The place you make the cut is also important to the health of the plant. Prune above outward-facing buds, where branches join other branches, or to ground level. These cuts will heal more quickly.

Have you ever noticed shrubs that have leaves at the top of the plant but the stems are bare? Use renewal pruning to avoid this problem. Remove about 1/3 of the older, thicker, canes to ground level. You can also reduce the height of the remaining stems by 1/3. Renovate overgrown shrubs by cutting all the stems back to several inches above the ground. There are some species, however, that will not tolerate this drastic pruning.

Shrubs are often sheared, a process that is easy on the gardener, but hard on the plant. Shearing leaves stubs that make perfect entry-ways for disease and insects. It's better for the plant if you use a hand pruner and selectively remove out-of-bound branches. Hedge plants should be pruned so the top is several inches narrower than the bottom. This allows light to reach all parts of the plants and helps keep leaves on the bottom of the shrub.

With proper selection and care, your shrubs will give you years of enjoyment.

Alpine Currant

Ribes alpinum

Size: 3 to 5 feet tall **Soil:** Well-drained **Zones:** All *Color photograph on page 240.*	**Light Requirements:** **Additional Benefits:**

You will find Alpine Currant hedges in both old and new landscapes. Their small leaves, dense growth habit, and tolerance for shearing make them a popular choice. The flowers are green and not really noticeable. Nurseries typically sell male plants, which are more disease resistant and do not form fruit. I have occasionally seen inedible, red fruit on female Alpine Currant plants. Alpine Currants can be grown unsheared. You may not recognize the Alpine Currant when it is grown in its natural round and spreading shape.

WHEN TO PLANT

Alpine Currants are available from garden centers and local nurseries. They are usually sold as container-grown plants. Alpine Currants can be planted throughout the season.

WHERE TO PLANT

Alpine Currants can be grown in full sun or shade. They will grow in any good soil. Alpine Currants are usually used as sheared hedges.

HOW TO PLANT

Dig a hole the same depth as, but wider than, the rootball. Remove container-grown plants from the pot, gently loosening any potbound roots. Place the plant in the hole, carrying it by the rootball, not the stems. Plant the shrub at the same depth it was growing in the nursery. Fill the hole with the existing soil and water the plants. Plant Alpine Currants three feet apart.

CARE AND MAINTENANCE

New plantings need an inch of water each week. Wait a year to fertilize new plantings. Follow soil test recommendations for fertilizer. Young shrubs can be fertilized in late fall after the plants are dormant, or early spring before new growth begins. Young Alpine Currants can be fertilized every two or three years to encourage rapid growth. Established shrubs need very little, if any, fertilizer. Prune Alpine Currants in the spring before growth begins. Remove the older canes to ground level, which will encourage new growth at the base of the plants. You can also prune back the overgrown shrubs by 1/3. Alpine Currants will tolerate shearing. Shear them so the top of the hedge is narrower than the bottom, which allows light to reach all parts of the hedge. Overgrown plants can be cut back to several inches above ground level. Alpine Currants are susceptible to anthracnose. This is a common problem in cool, wet weather. Rake and destroy infected leaves as they fall. Sanitation and drier weather will help control this disease.

ADDITIONAL INFORMATION

Clove Currant, *Ribes odoratum,* is hardy in Zones 3 and 4. It produces fragrant, yellow flowers on a 6- to 8-foot-tall shrub. Use it in the back of the border for spring color. It is an alternate host for white pine blister rust and should not be grown near White Pine trees.

ADDITIONAL SPECIES, CULTIVARS, OR VARIETIES

'Green Mound' is a dwarf cultivar that grows 2 to 3 feet tall and wide. It has good leaf spot disease resistance and is sometimes listed as 'Nana', 'Pumila', and 'Compacta'.

 Did You Know?

Ribes is from the Arabic word ribas *meaning acid-tasting. This refers to the fruit. The species name* alpinum *is for the Alpine mountains where the Alpine Currant can be found. Odoratum refers to the fragrant flowers of Clove Currant.*

Arborvitae

Thuja occidentalis

Other Name: White Cedar
Size: 3 to 40 feet tall
Soil: Moist
Zones: All

Color photograph on page 240.

Light Requirements:

Additional Benefit:

Arborvitaes are popular evergreen shrubs. The scaly foliage is soft, flattened, and reminds me of fans. This plant is commonly used in long rows as a hedge or screen. Try doing something different by using small clusters of Arborvitae instead of long rows to block views and provide shelter. Mix them with deciduous shrubs for added interest.

WHEN TO PLANT

Arborvitaes are sold as balled-and-burlapped or container-grown plants. Plant balled-and-burlapped Arborvitae as soon as possible after they are purchased. Container-grown plants can be planted throughout the season, but do best if planted by October 1.

WHERE TO PLANT

Grow Arborvitaes in sun or partial shade. Plants grown in heavy shade tend to become loose and open. Avoid open areas and those exposed to drying northwest winter winds. Arborvitaes prefer moist, well-drained soil. Native Arborvitae will grow in both wet and dry soil, but the cultivated plants are not as tolerant of these extremes.

HOW TO PLANT

Dig a hole the same depth as, but wider than, the rootball. Remove container-grown plants from the pot. Make sure to plant the shrub at the same depth it was growing in the nursery. Remove any twine and cut away the burlap on balled-and-burlapped plants once they are set in place. Fill the hole with existing soil and water.

CARE AND MAINTENANCE

New plantings need an inch of water each week. Mulch the soil to help conserve moisture and reduce weed problems. Wait at least 1 year to fertilize new plantings according to soil test recommendations. Once established, Arborvitaes need little, if any, fertilizer.

Arborvitaes need minimal pruning if the right size cultivar is selected for the location. Any pruning should be done in the spring before growth begins, or in midsummer during their semidormant period. You can shear the sides and top of the plants to control their size. Overgrown specimens can be topped, but will be more subject to damage from heavy snow loads. Reshape the topped shrub as new growth fills in. Multistemmed Arborvitaes tend to split apart under the weight of heavy snow. Prevent the problem by loosely tying the upright stems together in the fall using strips of cotton cloth or old nylon stockings. Arborvitae foliage often browns during the winter. Reduce the damage by planting Arborvitaes in protected areas. Water plants thoroughly before the ground freezes. Mulch the soil to help insulate roots and conserve moisture. Arborvitae is a favorite of deer. Use repellents, scare tactics, and fencing to minimize deer damage.

ADDITIONAL INFORMATION

The American Arborvitae tends to turn a yellow-brown color in the winter. Select a cultivar that holds its green color throughout the year.

ADDITIONAL SPECIES, CULTIVARS, OR VARIETIES

Techny Arborvitae, *Thuja occidentalis* 'Techny', is pyramidal, grows 10 to 15 feet tall, and holds its dark green color all year. 'Holmstrup' is a compact, slow-growing, pyramidal Arborvitae. It is 5 feet tall by 2 feet wide and can eventually reach a height of 10 feet. 'Woodwardii' is a globe form that is wider than its 6-foot height. It is bright green in the summer and turns brown in the winter. 'Hetz Midget' is a smaller globe form with bright green foliage. It usually stays under 2 feet tall. 'Wansdyke Silver' is a striking plant with silver-white variegation and loose thread-like foliage.

 Did You Know?

American Arborvitae, Thuja occidentalis, *is native to parts of the upper Midwest. Though not a true Cedar (Cedrus), Arborvitae is often called Cedar or White Cedar.*

Barberry

Berberis thunbergii

Other Name: Japanese Barberry
Size: 3 to 6 feet tall
Soil: Dry
Zones: 3 and 4

Color photograph on page 240.

Light Requirements:

Additional Benefit:

If you have ever walked into a Barberry plant, you understand why they make effective barriers. The fine thorns are guaranteed to keep people out or make the trespassers pay. The plants can also be used as hedges, in groupings, or as a colorful accent. This dense, rounded shrub is covered with bright green leaves that turn a brilliant orange to red in the fall. The yellow flowers aren't showy, but the small, red fruit will put on a show from October through the winter.

WHEN TO PLANT

Container-grown plants transplant easily. They can be planted throughout the season. You will occasionally find larger specimens balled and burlapped. Plant these as soon as possible after they are purchased.

WHERE TO PLANT

Grow Barberries in full sun or light shade. The red- and yellow-leafed forms are not as colorful in the shade. Barberries need well-drained soil. They can tolerate dry soil and urban conditions.

HOW TO PLANT

Dig a hole the same depth as, but wider than, the rootball. Remove container-grown plants from the pot. Plant the shrub at the same depth it was growing in the nursery. Space plants 2$\frac{1}{2}$ to 3 feet apart. Remove any twine and cut away burlap on balled-and-burlapped plants once they are set in place. Fill the hole with existing soil and water the plants.

CARE AND MAINTENANCE

New plantings need an inch of water each week. Established plants are drought tolerant. Wait a year to fertilize new plantings according to soil test recommendations. Young shrubs can be fertilized in late fall after the plants are dormant, or early spring before growth begins. Regular fertilizing encourages rapid growth on young shrubs. Once established, Barberries need little, if any, fertilizer. Barberries can be pruned in late winter or early spring before growth begins. Come prepared with thorn-proof gloves and clothing. Many gardeners shear Barberries to spare themselves the pain. The plants respond and look better if they are hand pruned to their natural shape. Remove 1/5 of the older stems each year. Prune them back to ground level or to a strong shoot low on the plant. Remove dead wood as you find it. The older growth produces the best fall color, so the less pruning, the better the color will be. Barberries are fairly pest free when grown in full sun and well-drained soils. I see quite a few wilt and canker problems on Barberries growing in clay soil. Prune out the diseased and dead branches as soon as they appear.

ADDITIONAL INFORMATION

Ohio State University has been conducting research on compost-amended soil. They are finding fewer disease problems on Barberries grown in that type of soil. Watch for more information.

ADDITIONAL SPECIES, CULTIVARS, OR VARIETIES

The red-leaf Japanese Barberry, *Berberis thunbergii* var. *atropurpurea*, is a full-sized Barberry with reddish-purple leaves. 'Crimson Pygmy' is probably the most popular red-leafed Barberry. This small plant grows 1 1/2 to 2 feet tall and 2 1/2 by 3 feet wide. 'Golden Ring' has reddish purple leaves with a narrow gold margin. 'Roseglow' is an especially nice selection with rose-pink foliage mottled with pink, purple, and cream blotches. 'Helmond Pillar' has dark red-purple foliage and forms a narrow column only 1 foot wide. Check your local nursery for availability of the many new and colorful Barberry cultivars.

 Did You Know?

Seedlings of Japanese Barberries have been found in our native forests. Avoid planting these near native woodland areas.

Boxwood

Buxus microphylla var. *koreana* × *Buxus sempervirens*
cultivars and hybrids

Size: 3 feet tall and wide
Soil: Moist
Zone: 4b

Color photograph on page 240.

Light Requirements:

Additional Benefit:

Boxwood hedges evoke thoughts of English gardens. These broadleaf evergreens have long been used as sheared hedges in the formal landscapes of Europe and the southern United States. If you ever tried growing a large-leafed Boxwood *Buxus sempervirens* you know they are not hardy in Minnesota. Northern gardeners need to select a hardier, small-leafed Boxwood, such as *Buxus microphylla.* These Boxwoods are hardier and more tolerant of Minnesota winters.

WHEN TO PLANT

Plant balled-and-burlapped plants as soon as possible after they are purchased. Container-grown Boxwood can be planted in the spring and early summer, which gives the plants time to get established before winter. Provide winter protection for late plantings.

WHERE TO PLANT

Grow Boxwood in protected locations for best results. These broadleaf evergreens will dry out in the winter sun and wind. Boxwoods thrive in partial shade and moist soil. Use them as a hedge, edging plant, or as part of a formal garden. They are naturally compact, dense growers with a round growth habit. Too often they are sheared beyond recognition and their natural beauty is destroyed.

HOW TO PLANT

Dig a hole the same depth as, but wider than, the rootball. Remove container-grown plants from the pot. Plant the shrub at the same depth it was growing in the nursery. Space plants $2^{1}/_{2}$ to 3 feet apart. Remove any twine and cut away burlap on balled-and-burlapped plants. Fill the hole with existing soil and water the plants.

CARE AND MAINTENANCE

New plantings need an inch of water each week. Mulch the soil with wood chips, shredded bark, or another organic material to keep the roots cool and moist. The mulch will also reduce weed problems. That is important since Boxwoods do not tolerate cultivation near their roots. Wait a year to fertilize new plantings and follow soil test recommendations for the type and amount of fertilizer to use. Fertilize shrubs in late fall after the plants are dormant, or early spring before growth begins. Regular fertilization of young shrubs will encourage rapid growth. Established shrubs need little, if any, fertilizer. Informally maintained, unsheared Boxwoods require very little pruning. Cut overly long branches back to a side branch in midsummer. Remove winter damage and do more severe pruning or shearing in early spring before new growth appears. Sheared hedges should be pruned with the top narrower than the bottom to allow light to reach all parts of the plant.

ADDITIONAL INFORMATION

Winter damage is the biggest concern with Boxwood. Proper plant selection and placement will minimize the damage—and your frustration! Water new and established plants thoroughly in the fall before the ground freezes. Soil mulches help to conserve moisture and insulate the roots. Use burlap or other windbreaks to protect tender cultivars or exposed plants from winter wind and sun.

ADDITIONAL SPECIES, CULTIVARS, OR VARIETIES

'Green Velvet' has been a good choice for southern Minnesota gardens. It has small, dark-green leaves and grows 3 feet tall and wide. 'Chicagoland Green' (*B. × 'Glencoe'*) is a sister to 'Green Velvet' but faster growing. A Chicago Botanic Garden selection, 'Green Mountain' is an extremely hardy hybrid with an upright form.

 Did You Know?

Take a close look at Boxwoods in the spring. They produce small, white flowers which are hard to see. Their lovely fragrance, however, makes a second look worthwhile.

Burning Bush

Euonymus alatus

Other Name: Winged Euonymus
Size: 15 feet tall
Soil: Well-drained
Zones: 4 (Marginally in zone 3)

Color photograph on page 240.

Light Requirements:

Additional Benefit:

Burning Bush is best known for its brilliant fall color. Its bright red leaves are among the first to appear in the autumn landscape. Once the leaves drop, the corky, winged stems are apparent. These stems are even more attractive when they are covered with snow. Euonymus is used in a variety of ways. It makes an excellent hedge, screen, specimen plant, and foundation planting.

WHEN TO PLANT

Burning Bush is available balled and burlapped or in a container. Plant balled-and-burlapped burning bushes as soon as possible after they are purchased. Container-grown plants can be planted throughout the season.

WHERE TO PLANT

Grow Burning Bushes in full sun or shade. They tolerate a wide range of soil conditions, but need good drainage to perform well. Plants will decline in poorly drained soil.

HOW TO PLANT

Dig a hole the same depth as, but wider than, the rootball. Remove container-grown plants from the pot. Place the plant in the hole, making sure the shrub is planted at the same depth it was growing in the nursery. Space the shrubs 4 to 6 feet apart. Remove any twine and cut away the burlap on balled-and-burlapped plants after they are set in place. Fill the hole with existing soil and water the plant.

CARE AND MAINTENANCE

New plantings need about an inch of water each week. Mulch to help conserve water and to reduce weed problems. Wait a year before fertilizing new plantings according to soil test recommendations. Young shrubs can be fertilized in late fall after the plants are dormant, or in early spring before growth begins. Once established, these plants need little, if any, fertilizer. Overfertilization can inhibit fall color. Prune established plants in the spring before growth begins. Burning Bush needs very little pruning. Prune overgrown plants to control their size. Burning Bush grows from a single trunk and should not be pruned back to ground level. Though this shrub has few serious pest problems, euonymus caterpillar has become a problem in the past few years. These worm-like insects build webby nests in the shrubs they feed upon. The web-covered plants look like something you'd find in a haunted house. You can physically remove the webs and insects, or spray the plant with *Bacillus thuringiensis* (Bt). This insecticide kills only true caterpillars and is safe for you, wildlife, and the environment. Yellow leaves and branch dieback occur on plants grown in poorly drained soil. Move the plants to a well-drained location, such as a berm or a planting bed with amended soil.

ADDITIONAL INFORMATION

Rabbits love Euonymus. Extensive feeding will kill the shrub. Fencing is the most effective way to prevent damage, although repellents and scare tactics may also work.

ADDITIONAL SPECIES, CULTIVARS, OR VARIETIES

Compact euonymus, *Euonymus alatus* 'Compactus', is the most frequently used cultivar. Many gardeners are fooled by the name. This compact cultivar is smaller than the species, but still grows 10 feet tall. It is less hardy than the species and frequently suffers winter injury. Select one of the hardier compact cultivars for Minnesota landscapes. The 'Nordine Strain', often sold as 'Koreana', is much hardier and grows only 5 to 8 feet tall. 'Rudy Haag' is a true dwarf selection (4 to 5 feet tall) with consistent red fall color.

 Did You Know?

Burning Bush seedlings have been found in our native forests.
Avoid growing this nonnative euonymus near natural areas.

Butterfly Bush

Buddleia davidii (Buddleja davidii)

Other Name: Summer Lilac
Size: 5 to 8 feet tall
Soil: Well-drained
Zone: Best treated as a herbaeous
   perennial in zone 4
Color photograph on page 240.

Light Requirements:

Additional Benefits:

Picture an arching shrub covered with flowers from July through frost. Now add some flashes of additional color provided by butterflies and hummingbirds. Does this garden dream sound too good to be true? It's not. The Butterfly Bush can give you all this interest and more all year long. In early spring, the new growth bursts from the ground and quickly grows to its mature size. By July, the flowers appear and continue through the remainder of the season. Leave the plants standing to provide winter interest and trap nature's best insulator, the snow.

WHEN TO PLANT

Plant bare-root shrubs in the spring before growth begins. Container-grown plants should be planted in the spring and early summer to give them time to get established before winter.

WHERE TO PLANT

Grow Butterfly Bush in full sun in well-drained soil. This large shrub can be used alone or grouped in shrub beds and perennial gardens.

HOW TO PLANT

Dig a hole the same depth as, but wider than, the rootball. Remove container-grown plants from the pot and loosen potbound roots. Make sure the shrub will be planted at the same depth it was growing in the nursery. Space plants 4 to 5 feet apart. Fill the hole with existing soil and water the shrub.

CARE AND MAINTENANCE

New plantings need an inch of water a week. Many of the container-grown Butterfly Bushes are being grown in soilless mixes. You will need to watch these carefully. Keep the rootball moist, but do not overwater the surrounding soil. Mulch the soil to help conserve water and reduce weed problems. Wait a year to fertilize newly planted Butterfly Bushes. Follow soil test recommendations for the amount and type of fertilizer to use. Young shrubs can be fertilized in late fall after the plants are dormant, or in early spring before growth begins. Butterfly Bush benefits from regular fertilizing. This shrub dies back to ground level every winter in Minnesota. Prune the plants back to several inches above ground level in late winter or early spring. Make your cuts at a slight angle above a bud. You will be amazed at how quickly the plant regains its size and flowers each season. These plants are not long lived in the landscape. They will die out after an extremely harsh winter. But don't give up on them too quickly. Wait until the soil warms before removing the plant. It may be June before the soil warms and the Butterfly Bush sprouts. My first planting lasted five years and my new ones are going strong after three. I feel I get my money's worth each season.

ADDITIONAL INFORMATION

The flowers are 6 to 12 inches or longer and resemble Lilac flowers. They have a light, fruity fragrance and come in purple, white, pink, or yellow. Cut a few to enjoy indoors.

ADDITIONAL SPECIES, CULTIVARS, OR VARIETIES

Many new cultivars are being introduced. The 'Nanho' series grows 4 to 5 feet tall and wide. It comes in purple, white, and blue. 'Pink Delight' grows 5 to 8 feet tall and has large, deep pink flowers. 'Black Knight' has very dark purple flowers and may be hardier than the others.

 Did You Know?

Butterfly Bush is native to China and has been grown and sold as a landscape plant since 1890. The name Buddleja *was given to honor Reverend Adam Buddle.* Davidii *refers to Armand David, a French missionary and plant collector who discovered this plant in China.*

Cotoneaster

Cotoneaster species

Size: Varies **Soil:** Well-drained **Zones:** All *Color photograph on page 240.*	**Light Requirements:** **Additional Benefit:**

Low growing, spreading, weeping, or tall and upright: these terms all describe the popular plant Cotoneaster. With the many sizes and forms available, it can be used in a variety of ways throughout the landscape. Many gardeners call it cotton easter, but it's really pronounced *ko* (long o) *to* (long o) *ne* (long e) *as' ter* (like the flower).

WHEN TO PLANT

Cotoneaster tends to be shallow rooted and does best when it is grown in containers or balled and burlapped. Plant balled-and-burlapped plants as soon as possible after they are purchased. Container-grown plants can be planted throughout the season.

WHERE TO PLANT

Grow Cotoneasters in full sun or light shade. They tolerate a wide range of soil conditions, as long as the soil is well drained. Cotoneasters are tough plants that tolerate dry soil and roadside salt.

HOW TO PLANT

Dig a hole the same depth as, but wider than, the rootball. Remove container-grown plants from the pot. Make sure the Cotoneaster is planted at the same depth it was growing in the nursery. Remove any twine and cut away the burlap on balled-and-burlapped plants once they are set in place. Fill the hole with existing soil and water the shrub.

CARE AND MAINTENANCE

New plantings need an inch of water per week. Wait a year to fertilize new plantings according to soil test recommendations. Established Cotoneasters need little, if any, fertilizer. Established shrubs can be pruned in late winter or early spring before growth begins. Remove old, diseased, and damaged stems at ground level. You can prune back overgrown shrubs by 1/3.

ADDITIONAL INFORMATION

Rabbits live under and will feed on Cotoneaster. Fencing is the best control option, but it is often not practical. A variety of repellents and scare tactics may discourage the rabbits.

ADDITIONAL SPECIES, CULTIVARS, OR VARIETIES

Cranberry Cotoneaster, *Cotoneaster apiculatus*, is hardy in Zone 4. This low grower forms 3-foot-high by 3- to 6-foot-wide mounds of dark green leaves. It is used as a ground-cover, bank cover, trailer over a wall, or edging plant for a shrub bed. The green leaves turn a bronzy-red or purplish color in the fall and persist into November. The pinkish-white flowers appear in late May and early June. Red cranberry-like fruit develops in the fall. Cleanup can be a problem. Fallen leaves and trash are hard to remove from this plant. Hedge Cotoneaster, *Cotoneaster lucidus*, is an upright form. It is hardy throughout Minnesota and grows 6 to 10 feet tall. This plant is usually sheared into a hedge. The green leaves turn yellow, orange, and red in the fall. The flowers are pinkish white and the fruit is black. Spreading *Cotoneaster divaricatus* and Rock Cotoneaster, *Cotoneaster horizontalis*, are medium-sized plants with a spreading growth habit. Many-flowered Cotoneaster, *Cotoneaster multiflorus*, looks like a Weeping Crabapple. It is covered with showy white flowers in May that are replaced with Crabapple-like fruit. The fruit drops with the leaves in the fall.

 Did You Know?

Cotoneasters are native to Siberia, China, and other parts of northern Asia. The name Cotoneaster *comes from the Latin words* cotoneum, *meaning quince, and* aster, *meaning somewhat resembling. This refers to the fact that the leaves of some cotoneasters resemble those of quince.*

Dogwood
Cornus species

Size: 5 to 10 or 15 feet tall	**Light Requirements:**
Soil: Moist	
Zones: All	
	Additional Benefits:
Color photograph on page 241.	

Our Minnesota native Dogwoods have become prominent plants in our landscapes. They can be used in natural settings or formal situations. The flower show may not compare with the Flowering Dogwood of the South, but Minnesota Dogwoods make up for it by providing food and shelter for birds and year-round beauty in the landscape.

WHEN TO PLANT
Different species of Dogwood are available as bare-root, balled-and-burlapped, or container-grown plants. Plant bare-root Dogwoods in the spring before growth begins. Balled-and-burlapped plants should be planted as soon as possible after they are purchased. Container-grown plants can be planted throughout the season.

WHERE TO PLANT
Grow Dogwoods in full sun or shade. Most prefer moist soil, and many tolerate wet sites.

HOW TO PLANT
Dig a hole the same depth as, but wider than, the rootball. Remove container-grown plants from the pot. Make sure to plant the shrub at the same depth it was growing in the nursery. Remove any twine and cut away the burlap on balled-and-burlapped plants once they are set in place. Fill the hole with existing soil and water the shrub.

CARE AND MAINTENANCE
New plantings need an inch of water each week. Mulch to help conserve water and reduce weed problems. Wait a year to fertilize new plantings. Follow soil test recommendations for the amount and type of fertilizer to use. Young shrubs can be fertilized in late fall after the plants are dormant, or in early spring before growth begins. Regular fertilization will encourage rapid growth on young shrubs. Once

established, Dogwoods need little, if any, fertilizer. Established shrubs can be pruned in late winter or early spring. Remove old, diseased, or damaged canes at ground level. The Redosier Dogwood is color coded for pruning. The older stems turn brown. Renewal pruning helps stimulate new brightly colored stems. You can prune back overgrown shrubs by 1/3.

ADDITIONAL INFORMATION

Stressed plants can suffer from scale insects and drought-induced cankers. Proper watering and regular pruning of the discolored, cankered stems will reduce these problems.

ADDITIONAL SPECIES, CULTIVARS, OR VARIETIES

There are many species and cultivars of Dogwood used in the landscape. The following are some of the more popular species that are hardy throughout the state. Redtwig or Redosier Dogwood, *Cornus sericea*, is probably the best known. This native has bright red stems and can be found in natural areas and landscapes. Redosier Dogwoods are spreading shrubs that tolerate moist to wet sites. Use this native as a bank cover or landscape shrub. 'Isanti' is a compact, slower growing selection. It is more tolerant of poorly drained soils. 'Cardinal' was introduced for its vivid red winter twig color. Pagoda Dogwood, *Cornus alternifolia*, is a larger native dogwood with a spreading growth habit. It prefers shade and moist soil. This Dogwood provides year-round interest with its attractive growth habit, cream-colored flowers, blue fruit with persistent red stems, and maroon fall color. Use it as a small tree, specimen plant, or for naturalized areas. Gray Dogwood, *Cornus racemosa*, is another native. It tolerates dry or wet soil and sun or shade. This plant tends to spread, so give it room to grow.

 Did You Know?

Redosier Dogwood, Cornus sericea, *is native throughout most of the United States. It can be found growing in the mountains of the western United States.*

Forsythia

Forsythia hybrids

Size: 1 to 10 feet tall
Soil: Various
Zones: 3b to 4

Color photograph on page 241.

Light Requirements:

Additional Benefit:

The bright yellow flowers of Forsythia signal the start of spring. This tough shrub with its arching branches can be planted in groupings or mixed with other plants. It is best used in shrub plantings, to cover banks, or for massing. Select hardy types for reliable flowering.

WHEN TO PLANT

Forsythias are sold as bare-root, balled-and-burlapped, and container-grown plants. Bare-root Forsythia should be planted in the spring before growth begins. Plant balled-and-burlapped plants as soon as possible after they are purchased. Container-grown plants can be planted throughout the season.

WHERE TO PLANT

Grow Forsythias in full sun for the best flower display. They will tolerate a wide variety of soils, but prefer well-drained soil. Forsythias are tough plants that tolerate whatever pH they are planted in, as well as urban conditions.

HOW TO PLANT

Dig a hole the same depth as, but wider than, the rootball. Remove container-grown plants from the pot. Make sure to plant the shrub at the same depth it was growing in the nursery. Space plants 2$1/2$ to 6 feet apart, depending on species selected. Remove any twine and cut away the burlap on balled-and-burlapped plants once they are set in place. Fill the hole with existing soil and water the Forsythia.

CARE AND MAINTENANCE

New plantings need an inch of water each week. Mulch the soil to help conserve moisture and reduce weed problems. Wait a year to fertilize young plants according to soil test recommendations. Once established, shrubs need little, if any, fertilizer. Established shrubs should be pruned in the spring after flowering. Remove 1/3 of the older stems at ground level. You can cut back overgrown stems by 1/3, or cut all the stems back to several inches above ground level.

ADDITIONAL INFORMATION

Lack of flowers is the major problem on Forsythia. The main cause is damage from cold temperatures. Forsythia plants are hardy in Zone 4, but the flower buds are frequently killed in Minnesota winters. That is why Forsythias usually blossom from the snow line down. The snow-covered flower buds are protected from cold winter temperatures. The best flowering occurs after a mild winter or one with deep and lasting snow. Pruning at the wrong time of year can eliminate flower buds. Only prune Forsythia within a month after flowering. Overfertilization and excess shade can also hinder flowering.

ADDITIONAL SPECIES, CULTIVARS, OR VARIETIES

Select cultivars that have hardy flower buds. Meadowlark Forsythia, *Forsythia* × 'Meadowlark', grows up to nine feet tall and is hardy in Zones 3b through 4. It has bright yellow flowers and an added benefit of purplish fall color. 'Northern Sun' is another large Forsythia reaching heights of 8 to 10 feet. It is hardy in Zone 4. Its flower buds are hardy to -30 degrees. 'Sunrise' is smaller, tolerant of urban conditions, and hardy in Zone 4b. This dense plant grows 5 feet tall and wide.

 Did You Know?

You can force Forsythia branches to bloom indoors in about 2 weeks. Select stems with lots of plump flower buds. Pound the cut ends to ensure water uptake. Now submerge the stems in water overnight. The next morning, place them in a bucket of water and store at 60 to 70 degrees.

Fragrant Sumac

Rhus aromatica

Size: 2½ to 5 feet tall
Soil: Well-drained
Zones: 3 through 4

Light Requirements:

Additional Benefits:

Color photograph on page 241.

Fragrant Sumac is a tough plant that will provide lots of interest in the garden. In spring, it produces small, yellow flowers before the leaves emerge. The glossy green leaves have 3 parts and are up to 3 inches long. They make a nice backdrop for the red berries that develop in the summer and persist into winter. Sumac's fall color is a spectacular orange to maroon. And the fragrance? Well, crush a leaf and take a whiff. I think *Rhus odiferous* is a more fitting name!

WHEN TO PLANT

Fragrant Sumacs are usually sold as container plants. They can be planted throughout the growing season.

WHERE TO PLANT

Grow Fragrant Sumac in full sun or light shade. It tolerates a wide range of soil conditions, but prefers well-drained to dry soil. Use this fast grower en masse, to cover banks, and for erosion control. The low-growing cultivars can also be used as a groundcover.

HOW TO PLANT

Dig a hole the same depth as, but wider than, the rootball. Remove container-grown plants from the pot. Loosen potbound roots. Place the plant in the hole, making sure to plant the shrub at the same depth it was growing in the nursery. Space plants 3 feet apart. Fill the hole with existing soil and water the shrub.

CARE AND MAINTENANCE

New plantings need an inch of water each week. Once established, these plants are drought tolerant and can survive with normal rainfall. Mulch the soil to help conserve moisture and reduce weed problems. Wait a year to fertilize new plantings. Follow soil test recommendations for the type and amount of fertilizer to use. Once established, Fragrant Sumac needs little, if any, fertilizer. Established shrubs can be pruned in early spring before growth begins. Remove the older canes to ground level. Overgrown plantings can be pruned back to several inches above ground level.

ADDITIONAL INFORMATION

Fragrant Sumac is late to leaf out. Don't be alarmed if all the other shrubs are showing green before the Sumac's buds even swell.

ADDITIONAL SPECIES, CULTIVARS, OR VARIETIES

'Gro-Low' Fragrant Sumac has become a popular landscape plant in the Midwest. It grows 2 feet tall and up to 6 feet wide. This low grower is good as a groundcover, bank cover, or trailer over a wall. The flowers are yellow, it has hairy red berries, and the fall color is an impressive orange to maroon. Staghorn Sumac, *Rhus typhina,* is the plant everyone passes driving down the freeway. It has large, ferny leaves that are the first to turn bright red in the fall. This large Minnesota native grows 15 feet or taller, and is hardy in Zones 3b through 4. Staghorn Sumac is a fast-growing, aggressive plant that should only be used where it has lots of room to grow. Otherwise, you may spend more time and effort eliminating it rather than maintaining it. The cut leaf cultivars *Rhus typhina* 'Laciniata' and 'Dissecta' have finer, more Fern-like leaves. They also tolerate full sun and dry soil. You will see them growing along the freeway with the Staghorn Sumacs. The fine leaves and orange fall color make these cultivars stand out from the rest.

 Did You Know?

The fruits of Sumac are clusters of small, red, hairy berries that persist throughout the winter. Native Americans used them to make pink sumacade (lemonade). The berries were bruised and soaked in hot water for 15 minutes, cooled, and strained.

Honeysuckle

Lonicera species

Size: 3 to 12 feet
Soil: Moist; well-drained
Zones: All

Light Requirements:

Additional Benefits:

Color photograph on page 241.

Honeysuckles were once thought to be the answer to all our landscaping problems. This low-maintenance plant was promoted for its fragrant flowers, pest free nature, and tolerance of tough growing conditions. Does it sound too good to be true? It was. An insect pest and the invasive nature of the plant have reduced its value in the landscape. Use European Fly Honeysuckle cultivars or our native Bush Honeysuckle, *Diervilla lonicera,* to avoid these problems.

WHEN TO PLANT
Honeysuckles are easily transplanted and are available as bare-root and container plants. Bare-root plants should be planted in the spring before growth begins. Container-grown plants can be planted throughout the season.

WHERE TO PLANT
Grow Honeysuckle in full sun or partial shade. It prefers moist, well-drained soil, but will grow in a variety of conditions. Avoid wet soils.

HOW TO PLANT
Dig a hole the same depth as, but wider than, the rootball. Remove container-grown plants from the pot. Make sure to plant the shrub at the same depth it was growing in the nursery. Space plants 3 to 5 feet apart, depending on the species and cultivar selected. Fill the hole with existing soil and water the planting.

CARE AND MAINTENANCE
New plantings need an inch of water each week. Established plants are more drought tolerant. Minimal fertilizer is needed for these fast-growing shrubs. Once established, Honeysuckles need little, if any, fertilizer. Established shrubs can be pruned in early spring before growth begins, or prune right after flowering so you can enjoy the

fragrant blooms. Remove the older canes to ground level to encourage new growth at the base of the plant. You can prune back any remaining stems by 1/3. Honeysuckles will also tolerate severe pruning. Cut the entire plant back to several inches above ground level. Honeysuckles were once thought to be low-maintenance plants. Then the Honeysuckle leaf folding aphid came to Minnesota. This aphid feeds on Honeysuckle leaves from late April until frost, causing fine, twiggy growth, or brooms, to form on the ends of branches. Established plants will tolerate the damage. Remove and destroy the aphid-filled brooms. Systemic insecticides can be used to control this pest. To be honest, many people were happy to see this insect. They were hoping it would reduce the overpopulation of Honeysuckle in the landscape and slow down its invasion into our forests.

ADDITIONAL INFORMATION

Honeysuckles have fragrant flowers that are attractive to kids, butterflies, and hummingbirds.

ADDITIONAL SPECIES, CULTIVARS, OR VARIETIES

Clavey's Dwarf Honeysuckle, *Lonicera* × *xylosteoides* 'Clavey's Dwarf', is resistant to the leaf folding aphid. This compact form grows 5 feet tall and 3 feet wide. It works well as a hedge. 'Miniglobe' is another cultivar. It forms a dense globe 2 feet tall and wide. Both are hardy in Zone 4. *Lonicera* × 'Honey Rose' has showy pink flowers in late May and is a good choice for tough sites in southwestern Minnesota. *Lonicera* hybrid 'Freedom' is a University of Minnesota introduction resistant to witches broom and is recommended for windbreaks.

🌿 Did You Know?

Many of the Honeysuckles are invading our natural areas and should not be planted. Amur (Lonicera maackii), *Tatarian* (Lonicera tatarica), *Morrow's* (L. morrowii), *and Belle's* (L. × bella) *Honeysuckles have invaded our natural areas and are crowding out the native plants.*

Hydrangea

Hydrangea paniculata and *Hydrangea arborescens*

Size: 3 to 15 feet tall **Soil:** Moist; well-drained **Zones:** All *Color photograph on page 241.*	**Light Requirements:** **Additional Benefits:**

Hydrangea is an old-fashioned favorite. The large, white flowers remind many of us of our childhoods, and perhaps visits to grandma's house. Hydrangeas are among the few shrubs that can put on a dramatic floral display even in the shade. The white flowers dry to beige and persist on the plants through winter. I like to leave the flowers and plants intact for added winter interest.

WHEN TO PLANT

Hydrangeas are sold at nurseries and garden centers as balled-and-burlapped or container plants. Balled-and-burlapped hydrangeas should be planted as soon as possible after they are purchased. Container-grown plants can be planted throughout the season.

WHERE TO PLANT

Grow Hydrangeas in partial shade for best results. They will tolerate full sun as long as the soil is kept moist. Hydrangeas tolerate a wide range of growing conditions, but prefer moist, well-drained soil. The plants do become ratty in drought conditions.

HOW TO PLANT

Dig a hole the same depth as, but wider than, the rootball. Remove container-grown plants from the pot. Loosen potbound roots. Place the Hydrangea in the planting hole at the same depth it was growing in the nursery. Remove any twine and cut away the burlap on balled-and-burlapped plants once they are set in place. Fill the hole with existing soil and water the shrub.

CARE AND MAINTENANCE

New plantings need an inch of water each week. You will need to water established plants during dry periods. Mulch the soil to help conserve moisture and reduce weed problems. Wait a year to fertilize new plantings. Hydrangeas benefit from a light fertilization in the spring before growth begins. That is also the best time to prune Hydrangeas. Cut back the snowball-type Hydrangeas to ground level. This should be done every year. PeeGee Hydrangea requires very little pruning. Cut back stems to maintain the desired size and shape. Improve flowering on these Hydrangeas by pruning them back to their woody framework annually.

ADDITIONAL INFORMATION

Hydrangeas are good as fresh cut and dried flowers. Flowers for drying should be cut as the blooms begin to fade. Cut them at the base of the stem, remove the leaves, and hang the flowers upside down to dry.

ADDITIONAL SPECIES, CULTIVARS, OR VARIETIES

Snowhill Hydrangea, *Hydrangea arborescens* 'Snowhill', is one of the more popular Hydrangeas in Minnesota. This shrub grows up to 5 feet tall, and is covered with large, white snowball-type flowers in the summer. 'Annabelle' is another popular cultivar of this species. It has larger flowers and denser growth than 'Snowhill'. Both tolerate shade and moist soils. PeeGee Hydrangea, *Hydrangea paniculata* 'Grandiflora', is a larger and hardier plant. It is usually grown in a tree form. Its large, white, cone-shaped flowers develop a hint of pink color as they pass their peak. The dried flowers provide nice winter interest. 'Tardiva' is a later-blooming cultivar. 'Pink Diamond' has pink buds that open white, then quickly turn pink. 'Kyushu' has large lacy white flower heads that start in July and last well into winter. 'Pee Wee' is a semi-dwarf variety with lacy blooms that eventually turn pink. 'Limelight' is a new variety with bright lime green flowers unlike any other. 'The Swan' has pure white florets that are as large as the palm of your hand!

 Did You Know?

Soil pH influences the flower color of Bigleaf Hydrangea, which is not hardy in Minnesota. You cannot change white Hydrangeas to pink or blue without the use of floral dyes or spray paint!

Juniper

Juniperus species

Other Name: Red Cedar
Size: Up to 20 feet tall
Soil: Well-drained
Zones: All

Color photograph on page 241.

Light Requirements:

Additional Benefit:

Its wide variety of sizes, shapes, and foliage colors make Juniper a valuable landscape plant. These tough evergreens can be used as windbreaks, groundcovers, screens, hedges, or rock garden plants. Use them alone as specimens or in groups for a mass display.

WHEN TO PLANT

Plant balled-and-burlapped plants as soon as possible after they are purchased. Container-grown plants can be planted spring through September. Planting by October 1 gives the plants time to put down roots before winter.

WHERE TO PLANT

Grow Junipers in full sun and well-drained soil. They tolerate a variety of soil conditions from sandy to clay. These tough plants grow in urban areas, dry soil, and windy locations. Some species are salt tolerant, but none of them tolerate wet soil.

HOW TO PLANT

Dig a hole the same depth as, but wider than, the rootball. Remove container-grown plants from the pot. Plant the Juniper at the same depth it was growing in the nursery. Remove any twine and cut away the burlap on balled-and-burlapped plants after setting them in place. Fill the hole with existing soil and water the plant.

CARE AND MAINTENANCE

New plantings need an inch of water each week. Established plantings can tolerate dry soil. Wait a year to fertilize new plantings according to soil test recommendations. Once established, Junipers need little, if any, fertilizer. Water Junipers and other evergreens in the fall before the ground freezes. This, combined with mulching, will reduce winter damage. Prune Junipers in the spring before growth begins, or in midsummer during their semi-dormant period. Be sure to wear long sleeves and gloves; otherwise you may proudly wear the Juniper rash for several days. When properly sited and spaced, Junipers need little pruning. You can clip back the sides and tops of upright Junipers to maintain the desired size. Overgrown Junipers can be topped and reshaped. Prune spreading and creeping Junipers by selectively removing the longest branches. Cut these back to a side branch or main stem. Multi-stemmed upright Junipers are subject to splitting under heavy snow. Loosely tie the stems in the fall, using strips of cotton or old nylon stockings.

ADDITIONAL INFORMATION

Phomopsis blight is a fungal disease that causes tip dieback on many Junipers. Prune out infected branches back to healthy side shoots. Avoid problems by selecting resistant cultivars. Cedar rust is a common problem on Red Cedar, *Juniperus virginiana.* This fungal disease spends half its life on this Juniper and the other half on Apples, Crabapples, or Hawthorns. It won't kill the plant, but it looks bad when the galls sprout their slimy, orange tendrils. Juniper may experience some browning after extremely cold winters. Prune out the damaged foliage.

ADDITIONAL SPECIES, CULTIVARS, OR VARIETIES

There are hundreds of Juniper species and cultivars available. They come in upright forms, spreading types, and low-growing ground huggers. Select the form that best fits your landscape design. Many Junipers can spread to 20 feet wide. Save yourself a lot of work and frustration by selecting the Juniper that fits the space available. Use the hardiest, most disease-resistant cultivars available.

 Did You Know?

Junipers produce an attractive blueberry-like cone. This can add ornamental value to the plant, and flavor to your gin: oil of Juniper is used to flavor gin.

Lilac

Syringa species and cultivars

Size: 4 to 15 feet tall	**Light Requirements:**
Soil: Well-drained	
Zones: All	
	Additional Benefits:
Color photograph on page 241.	

M any Lilacs end up in the landscape thanks to the fond memories they elicit. Other gardeners are lured by the sweet fragrance. For those who don't like the smell, less fragrant cultivars are available. That way everyone can enjoy a bouquet of freshly cut lilacs.

WHEN TO PLANT

Lilacs are sold at garden centers and nurseries as balled-and-burlapped or container-grown plants. Balled-and-burlapped Lilacs should be planted as soon as possible after they are purchased. Container-grown plants can be planted throughout the season.

WHERE TO PLANT

Grow Lilacs in full sun and well-drained soil. They can be used as hedges, screens, or as a backdrop for other plantings. Be sure to plant them where you can enjoy both the flowers and the fragrance.

HOW TO PLANT

Dig a hole the same depth as, but wider than, the rootball. Remove container-grown plants from the pot. Loosen potbound roots. Be sure the Lilac is planted at the same depth it was growing in the container. Remove any twine and cut away the burlap on balled-and-burlapped plants once they have been set in place. Fill the hole with existing soil and water the plants.

CARE AND MAINTENANCE

New plantings need an inch of water each week. Mulch the soil to help conserve moisture and reduce weed problems. Wait a year to fertilize new plantings. Follow soil test recommendations for the amount and type of fertilizer to use. Avoid high-nitrogen fertilizers that can prevent flowering. Established Lilacs need little, if any, fertilizer. Remove old flower heads to encourage good flowering the following season. Lilacs bloom on the previous season's growth. Prune established Lilacs after flowering so you can enjoy this year's flowers and not interfere with next year's blooms. Remove the older canes to ground level. You can also prune back overgrown stems by 1/3. Regular pruning will reduce pest problems and control plant growth, while improving the overall appearance.

ADDITIONAL INFORMATION

Common Lilacs are subject to a variety of insect and disease problems. Powdery mildew is the most common disease. When a plant is affected, it looks like someone sprinkled baby powder on the leaves. Grow Lilacs in full sun with good air circulation to reduce this problem. Proper pruning allows air and light to reach all parts of the plants, reducing mildew problems. The disease won't kill the Lilac; it just makes the plants look bad. Bacterial blight and scale insects are easily controlled with proper pruning. These pests attack older, stressed stems. Regular pruning removes the susceptible stems and infected growth.

ADDITIONAL SPECIES, CULTIVARS, OR VARIETIES

There are hundreds of common Lilacs, *Syringa vulgaris*, on the market. They grow up to 15 feet tall with white, blue, purple, pink, or magenta flowers. *Syringa vulgaris* 'Dappled Dawn' is a striking variegated Lilac with cream-mottled leathery leaves. Palabin Lilac, *Syringa meyeri* 'Palabin', is a smaller plant, growing 4 to 5 feet tall and up to 7 feet wide. The smaller leaves and flowers give this Lilac a finer texture in the landscape. This easy-to-grow Lilac is disease resistant. Miss Kim Lilac, *Syringa patula* 'Miss Kim', grows up to 6 feet tall and 4 feet wide. It produces fragrant, icy-blue flowers and has purple fall color. It is disease resistant and hardy to Zone 3b.

 Did You Know?

Lilacs are grown for their lovely, fragrant flowers, and we're not the only ones enjoying them: Keep an eye out for fly-by visitors. Several butterflies feed on the nectar of Lilacs.

Mockorange

Philadelphus coronarius

Other Name: Sweet Mockorange
Size: Up to 10 feet tall
Soil: Moist; well-drained
Zone: 4

Color photograph on page 241.

Light Requirements:

Additional Benefits:

The sweet, citrus fragrance of Mockorange is the feature that won this plant a place in the landscape. Select cultivars carefully. Many are subject to winter injury, eliminating the spring flower display. Other cultivars lack fragrance, which is the main reason gardeners grow this plant. The attractive blossoms are a wonderful addition to the spring landscape. Its appearance the rest of the year is less desirable.

WHEN TO PLANT

Mockorange is sold as a container plant in nurseries and garden centers. Plant container-grown plants throughout the season.

WHERE TO PLANT

Grow Mockoranges in full sun or partial shade. They prefer moist, well-drained soil. Mockorange is an old-time favorite. It has traditionally been used as a hedge, or for the spring color and fragrance it provides in shrub beds. Plant it in a location where it can be enjoyed if it blooms, but not waste prime gardening space if it doesn't.

HOW TO PLANT

Dig a hole the same depth as, but wider than, the rootball. Remove container-grown plants from the pot and loosen potbound roots. Be sure to plant the shrub at the same depth it was growing in the container. Space plants 3 to 6 feet apart. Fill the hole with existing soil and water the Mockorange.

CARE AND MAINTENANCE

New plantings need an inch of water each week. Mulch with wood chips, shredded bark, or another organic material to help conserve moisture and reduce weed problems. Wait a year to fertilize new plantings. Follow soil test recommendations for the type and amount of fertilizer to use. Young shrubs can be fertilized in late fall after the plants are dormant, or early spring before growth begins. Avoid high-nitrogen fertilizers that can prevent flowering. Established shrubs need little, if any, fertilizer. Prune established Mockorange shrubs in the spring after flowering. Remove the older canes to ground level. You can prune back overgrown stems by 1/3. All the stems or overgrown plants can be cut to ground level.

ADDITIONAL INFORMATION

Mockorange, like the Forsythia and Lilac, blooms on the previous season's growth. The flower buds, and even the above-ground growth, may be killed over the winter, eliminating the spring flowers. Without these, it's just another green plant. You may want to limit the number of plants used, since they have such narrow landscape interest.

ADDITIONAL SPECIES, CULTIVARS, OR VARIETIES

The first three Mockoranges included in this listing are cultivars of *Philadelphus × virginalis* and are hardier than the common Mockorange and more suitable to Minnesota landscapes. 'Minnesota Snowflake' Mockorange has double, fragrant white flowers and is rated hardy throughout the state. This upright plant grows 8 feet tall. It produces very fragrant, double-white flowers in midsummer. 'Dwarf Minnesota Snowflake' grows 3 to 4 in. tall and gives a good display even in poor soils. Glacier Mockorange is hardy to Zone 4b. The fragrant, double blossoms appear in midsummer. The smaller, 5-foot-tall plant is a better size for most landscapes. Several variegated Mockoranges will survive in Minnesota. *Philadelphus × lemoine* 'Innocence' is an old French variety dating back to the early 1900s. Its leaves are splashed with creamy yellow. *Philadelphus coronarius* 'Variegatus' has leaves with an irregular border of creamy white. It provides a dramatic foliage display but the white flowers are almost hidden by the bold foliage.

 Did You Know?

The botanical name is Greek. Coronarius *refers to the fact that this plant was once used in garlands.*

Mugo Pine

Pinus mugo

Other Name: Swiss Mountain Pine

Size: Up to 15 feet

Soil: Well-drained

Zones: All

Color photograph on page 241.

Light Requirements:

M ugo Pine was once the only shrubby pine for the landscape. It has been a popular foundation plant for years. An increase in the number of cultivars has resulted in more uses for this durable plant.

WHEN TO PLANT

Mugo Pines are available as balled-and-burlapped or container-grown plants. Balled-and-burlapped plants should be planted as soon as possible after purchase. Container-grown plants can be planted spring through September. Planting Mugo Pines by October 1 will give them time to root before winter.

WHERE TO PLANT

Grow Mugo Pines in full sun, although they will tolerate light shade. Mugo Pines prefer moist, well-drained soil, but grow fine in well-drained to dry soil. Cultivars of Mugo Pines are used as foundation plantings, rock garden plants, and en masse.

HOW TO PLANT

Dig a hole the same depth as, but wider than, the rootball. Remove container-grown plants from the pot. Plant the shrub at the same depth it was growing in the container. Remove any twine and cut away the burlap on balled-and-burlapped plants after they are set in place. Fill the hole with existing soil and water the planting.

CARE AND MAINTENANCE

New plantings need an inch of water each week. Established Mugo Pines are drought tolerant. Mulch the soil to help conserve moisture and reduce weed problems. Wait a year before fertilizing new plantings. Follow soil test recommendations for the type and amount of fertilizer to use. Avoid excess fertilization that can stimulate more growth and bigger plants than you want. Established shrubs need little, if any, fertilizer. Water Mugo and other Pines in the fall before the ground freezes. Mulching will also help conserve moisture, insulate the roots, and help reduce winter injury. Prune Mugo Pines in the spring as the buds elongate into soft, new growth called candles. Remove 1/2 to 2/3 of each candle. Prune Mugo Pines yearly to control growth. Once the plant is overgrown, it is usually impossible to greatly reduce its size.

ADDITIONAL INFORMATION

Pine needle scale is the major pest of Mugo Pine. It looks like flecks of white paint spilled on the needles. Proper timing is critical to control this pest. Treat with insecticidal soap or an insecticide when the shell-less immature scales are present. This is the same time the Vanhoutte (Bridal Wreath) Spirea are blooming. Repeat this treatment when the Snowhill Hydrangeas bloom. European pine sawfly will also damage Mugo Pines by feeding on the needles. Physically smash the sawflies or prune off and destroy the infested branch.

ADDITIONAL SPECIES, CULTIVARS, OR VARIETIES

The straight Mugo species is seldom grown in the landscape. There are quite a few cultivars and varieties that have been selected for their superior form or smaller size. Dwarf Mugo Pine, *Pinus mugo mugo,* is a lower-growing variety. Don't be fooled by its name-this dwarf is smaller than the species but can grow up to 8 feet tall. The variety *pumilio* is a creeping form with shorter needles. This slow grower can eventually grow to 10 feet wide. 'Aurea' is an outstanding golden yellow form. 'Sunshine' has bright gold variegation in bands that break up the green. A number of very fine dwarf forms are available for the rock garden.

 Did You Know?

Mugo Pine is native to the mountains of central and southern Europe, thus the common name Swiss Mountain Pine. The name Mugo *is an old Tyrolese name. Tyrol is a mountainous region in western Austria and northern Italy where the Mugo Pine is native.*

Potentilla

Potentilla fruticosa

Size: 1 to 4 feet tall **Soil:** Dry **Zones:** All *Color photograph on page 241.*	**Light Requirements:** **Additional Benefit:**

Potentilla's bright yellow blossoms add color to the summer landscape. Its color, as well as its dense growth habit and pest-free nature, make it a popular landscape plant. And just like any tough plant, we gardeners push it beyond its limits. Gardeners started putting Potentillas in shady, wet locations, resulting in poor growth. The poor growth, plus improper pruning, have resulted in some less than desirable landscape specimens. Proper cultivar and site selection and correct pruning will keep Potentillas looking good in the landscape.

WHEN TO PLANT

Potentillas are usually sold as container-grown plants at nurseries and garden centers. Plant them any time during the growing season.

WHERE TO PLANT

Grow Potentillas in full sun in well-drained soil. These shrubs are used in a shrub border, for mass plantings, mixed with perennials, or as a low hedge.

HOW TO PLANT

Dig a hole the same depth as, but wider than, the rootball. Remove container-grown plants from the pot. Loosen potbound roots. Place the Potentilla in the planting hole at the same depth it was growing in the nursery. Space plants 2½ to 3 feet apart. Fill the hole with existing soil and water the plants.

CARE AND MAINTENANCE

New plantings need an inch of water each week. Established Potentillas can tolerate dry conditions. Mulch the soil to help conserve moisture and reduce weed problems. Wait a year to fertilize new plantings. Follow soil test recommendations for the type and amount of fertilizer to use. Young shrubs can be fertilized in late fall after the plants are dormant, or early spring before growth begins. Avoid high-nitrogen fertilizers that can prevent flowering. Established shrubs need little, if any, fertilizer. Potentilla needs regular pruning to maintain an attractive appearance. Prune overgrown and floppy Potentillas in the spring before growth begins. Cut the plants back halfway to the ground. Remove about 1/3 to 1/2 of the stems to ground level, or prune all the stems back to just above ground level. This rejuvenation pruning can be done every second or third year as needed.

ADDITIONAL INFORMATION

Several red-flowering Potentillas have been introduced to the United States from Europe. Don't be fooled by the catalogue pictures and descriptions. Most of these cultivars prefer the cool European summers and their red flowers quickly fade to yellow in our hot landscapes.

ADDITIONAL SPECIES, CULTIVARS, OR VARIETIES

Contact your local nursery or garden center to find out which Potentilla cultivars are available in your area. Select the cultivar with the flower color, bloom time, and plant size that best suits the location. Among the more readily available cultivars is 'Abbotswood', with blue-green foliage and outstanding white flowers. It grows 3 feet tall. Others include 'McKay's White', developed in Wisconsin at McKay Nursery. It has more of a creamy-white flower with yellow-green leaves. 'Goldfinger' has large, bright yellow flowers that last into fall. This compact cultivar grows 3 to 4 feet tall and has dark green leaves.

 Did You Know?

Potentilla is one of the few woody plants native throughout the Northern Hemisphere. You can find plants in Washington, Minnesota, Great Britain, Europe, and China. The botanical name Potentilla *is Latin. It comes from the word* potens *meaning powerful. That refers to its medicinal properties. The name* fruticosa *means shrubby.*

Rhododendron

Rhododendron species

Other Name: Azalea
Size: Up to 5 feet tall
Soil: Moist; well-drained
Zones: 3b through 4

Color photograph on page 241.

Light Requirements:

Additional Benefits:

Rhododendrons like cool, moist, acidic soil and milder winters than we usually have. So why are so many Minnesota gardeners trying to grow them? The large, beautiful, and often fragrant flowers cannot be duplicated by another plant. Their unique beauty has driven gardeners to amend soil and winter protect plantings. The gardeners' interest has encouraged plant breeders to develop more northern-hardy cultivars.

WHEN TO PLANT

Balled-and-burlapped plants should be planted as soon as possible after they are purchased. Container-grown plants should be planted in the spring or early summer to allow them to get established before winter.

WHERE TO PLANT

Grow rhododendrons in moist, acidic soil. Rhododendrons prefer full sun if the soil is kept moist. They will also grow fine in dappled shade. Avoid planting these shrubs where the leaves will be subject to drying by winter wind and sun.

HOW TO PLANT

Add several inches of organic matter to the top 12 inches of soil prior to planting to improve the drainage in heavy clay soil and the water-holding capacity of sandy soil. Dig a hole the same depth as, but wider than, the rootball. Remove container-grown plants from the pot. Place the shrub in the planting hole at the same depth it was growing in the container. Remove any twine and cut away the burlap on balled-and-burlapped plants. Fill the hole with soil and water the plantings.

CARE AND MAINTENANCE

New plantings need an inch of water each week.
Established Rhododendrons prefer moist soil, so you may
need to water during dry periods. Mulch the soil to conserve moisture and reduce weed problems. Those with
alkaline soil may want to incorporate granular sulfur or
some other acidifying material into the soil prior to planting. Wait a year to fertilize new plantings. Follow soil test
recommendations for the amount and type of fertilizer to
use. Rhododendrons require little pruning. Remove any
winter damage and thin out overcrowded branches in the
spring after flowering, or when they should have flowered.

ADDITIONAL INFORMATION

Winter injury is the biggest problem facing Rhododendrons.
Water them thoroughly in the fall before the ground freezes.
Mulching helps conserve moisture and insulates the roots.
Winter protection will help these tender plants through our
harsh winters. A burlap windbreak or evergreen branch
mulch will prevent drying caused by winter wind and sun.

ADDITIONAL SPECIES, CULTIVARS, OR VARIETIES

There are over 900 species of Rhododendrons and many
more cultivars of these. Northern Lights Azaleas and PJM
Rhododendrons are the most reliable Rhododendrons for
Minnesota. The Northern Lights Azaleas are hardy to Zone
3b. These compact plants grow up to 5 feet tall and have
fragrant pink, orange, yellow, or white flowers. PJM
Rhododendron is evergreen and hardy in Zone 4. The large
leaves turn purple in the fall. PJM produces many laven-
der-pink flowers in early spring.

 Did You Know?

Azaleas and Rhododendrons are all part of the genus
Rhododendron. *There is no clear distinction between them.
In general, Rhododendrons are evergreen and Azaleas are
deciduous. Azalea flowers have 5 stamens (male flower parts)
and Rhododendrons have 10 or more. Azaleas have funnel-form
flowers, while Rhododendrons are more bell shaped.*

Spirea

Spiraea species

Size: 2 to 8 feet tall
Soil: Wide range
Zones: All

Color photograph on page 241.

Light Requirements:

Additional Benefits:

Spireas are tough, colorful plants that have been used extensively in the landscape. With its arching branches and white flowers, the traditional Bridal Wreath Spirea conjures up memories of childhood landscapes and grandma's house. The summer-blooming Spireas have become more prominent in recent years. These colorful shrubs require little maintenance and tolerate the stresses of urban landscapes.

WHEN TO PLANT

Spireas are usually sold as container-grown plants. A few large specimens of certain species may be sold balled and burlapped. Plant balled-and-burlapped shrubs as soon as possible after they are purchased. Container-grown plants can be planted throughout the season.

WHERE TO PLANT

Grow Spireas in full sun for best results. They will tolerate a wide range of soils, except for wet sites. Spireas can be used in mass plantings, as filler plants, and as bank cover.

HOW TO PLANT

Dig a hole the same depth as, but wider than, the rootball. Remove container-grown plants from the pot. Be sure to plant the shrub at the same depth it was growing in the nursery. Remove any twine and cut away the burlap on balled-and-burlapped plants. Fill the hole with existing soil and water the plantings.

CARE AND MAINTENANCE

New plantings need about an inch of water each week. Established plants are drought tolerant. Mulch to conserve moisture and reduce weed problems. Wait at least a year to fertilize new plantings. Follow soil test recommendations for the amount and type of fertilizer to use. Spireas are fast growers and need minimal fertilizer when young, and very little, if any, once they are established. Spring-blooming Spireas flower on the previous season's growth. Prune them just after flowering. Pruning at any other time will eliminate the flowers. Summer-blooming Spireas flower on new growth. They can be pruned in early spring before growth begins. Prune overgrown and floppy Spireas back halfway to the ground. Remove about 1/3 to 1/2 of the stems to ground level.

ADDITIONAL INFORMATION

Rejuvenation pruning can be done yearly to summer blooming, and as needed to spring flowering Spireas. Prune all the stems back to ground level. I find this is the easiest way to keep the plants full and attractive. Lightly shear summer-blooming Spireas as the flowers fade to encourage a second flush of flowers.

ADDITIONAL SPECIES, CULTIVARS, OR VARIETIES

There are too many species and cultivars to cover in this limited space. *Spiraea × vanhouttei* is the spring bloomer now used as Bridal Wreath Spirea. It is a large, arching shrub with bluish-green leaves. The long branches are covered with white flowers in the spring. *Spiraea thunbergii* 'Mt. Fuji' is a striking new cultivar with thin willowy stems and narrow white and green variegated leaves on a delicate looking shrub, and airy white flowers in spring. It is rated as hardy to zone 5 but well worth experimenting with. Cultivars of the Japanese Spirea are among the most popular of the summer-blooming Spireas. They all produce pink, rose, or white flowers in the summer. The leaves of 'Goldflame' emerge orange-red, fade to yellow, and eventually turn green for the summer. The spring colors are repeated in the fall. 'Goldmound' is low growing with yellow leaves in the spring that turn yellow-green for the remainder of the season. 'Anthony Waterer' and 'Froebelii' are popular green-leafed forms of summer-blooming Spireas.

Did You Know?

Leave the seedheads and shiny brown stems in place for added winter interest in a snow-covered landscape.

Viburnum

Viburnum species

Other Names: Cranberrybush Viburnum, Nannyberry, Blackhaw

Size: 2 to 15 feet tall

Soil: Moist; well-drained

Zones: All

Color photograph on page 242.

Light Requirements:

Additional Benefits:

Viburnums are excellent landscape plants. Their white, sometimes pink-tinged, flowers provide spring interest. The leaves can be glossy and green, or slightly hairy, giving the plant a softer look. The red, blue, or black berries help attract birds to your landscape. Some Viburnums have spectacular red or purple fall color. These ornamental features, combined with the diversity of sizes and shapes, make Viburnums good additions to any landscape.

WHEN TO PLANT

Garden centers and nurseries sell Viburnums balled and burlapped or in containers. Plant balled-and-burlapped plants as soon as possible after they are purchased. Container-grown plants can be planted throughout the season. Plant tender Viburnums in spring or early summer to give them time to get established before winter.

WHERE TO PLANT

Viburnum species vary slightly in their light and soil requirements. Most tolerate full sun to partial shade. They all prefer moist soil, but some species are drought tolerant. Use Viburnums as screens, hedges, backdrops, specimen plants, and wildlife plants.

HOW TO PLANT

Dig a hole the same depth as, but wider than, the rootball. Remove container-grown plants from the pot. Loosen potbound roots. Place the shrub in the planting hole at the same depth it was growing in the container. Remove any twine and cut away the burlap on balled-and-burlapped plants after they are set in place. Fill the hole with existing soil and water the plants.

CARE AND MAINTENANCE

New plantings need about an inch of water each week. Established Viburnum species that require moist soil should be watered during dry periods. Mulch the soil to conserve moisture and reduce weeds. Wait a year to fertilize new plantings. Follow soil test recommendations for the type and amount of fertilizer to use. Established shrubs need little fertilizer. Slow-growing Viburnums need very little pruning. Prune out old wood to ground level in the spring after flowering. You can prune back the remaining stems by 1/3.

ADDITIONAL INFORMATION

Viburnums are great wildlife plants. The flowers will help attract butterflies to the landscape. And be sure to watch for the birds feeding on the berries of many of these plants.

ADDITIONAL SPECIES, CULTIVARS, OR VARIETIES

American Cranberrybush Viburnum, *Viburnum trilobum,* is a large shrub that prefers moist soil. It has white flowers in the spring, persistent red berries, red fall color, and is hardy statewide. The berries are edible, with limited appeal. Arrowwood Viburnum, *Viburnum dentatum,* also prefers moist soil but is only hardy in Zone 4. This multistemmed shrub has long, straight stems that were once used to make arrows. The spring flowers are white, and the blue fruit is a favorite of the birds. 'Blue Muffin' has loads of white spring flowers, and an impressive display of rich blue berries. Koreanspice Viburnum, *Viburnum carlesii,* is used as a specimen plant and produces fragrant pink-to-white flowers. Its blue-black fruit and red fall color provide additional interest and is hardy to Zone 4b. 'Emerald Triumph' is an exciting new hybrid from the University of Minnesota Landscape Arboretum with emerald green disease resistant leaves, creamy-white flowers, and red and black fruit.

 Did You Know?

*Wayfaring Viburnum,*Viburnum lantana, *and European Cranberrybush Viburnum,* Viburnum opulus, *are nonnatives that are starting to invade our forests. Avoid planting these if you live near natural sites.*

Weigela

Weigela florida

Other Name: Old-Fashioned Weigela
Size: Up to 6 feet tall
Soil: Well-drained
Zone: 4b

Color photograph on page 242.

Light Requirements:

Additional Benefits:

Weigela is an old-time landscape plant that gardeners either love or hate. The coarse texture and spreading growth habit remind me of a plant you would find on an old farmstead. Others consider it unkempt and not desirable for the home landscape. Some of the compact cultivars have a tidier appearance.

WHEN TO PLANT

Weigelas are sold as bare-root and container-grown plants. Plant bare-root Weigela in the spring before growth begins. Container-grown plants can be planted throughout the season. Planting in the spring or early summer gives the plants time to get established before winter.

WHERE TO PLANT

Grow Weigela in full sun in well-drained soil. It works best when used for massing, in the shrub border, or combined with other plants.

HOW TO PLANT

Dig a hole the same depth as, but wider than, the rootball. Remove container-grown plants from the pot. Loosen potbound roots. Place the shrub in the planting hole at the same depth it was growing in the container. Space plants 3 to 4 feet apart. Fill the hole with existing soil and water.

CARE AND MAINTENANCE

New plantings need an inch of water each week. Established plants may need to be watered during dry periods. Mulch the soil to help conserve moisture and reduce weed problems. Wait a year before fertilizing new plantings. Follow soil test recommendations for the type and amount of fertilizer to use. Established shrubs need little, if any, fertilizer. Young Weigelas need very little pruning. Remove any dead wood as it is discovered. Prune established shrubs in early summer after the first flush of flowers. Reduce the overall shrub size by cutting back long flowering stems to older upright growth. Remove several older stems to ground level each season. Overgrown Weigela can be pruned back to ground level. Weigelas frequently suffer winter injury. Extensive damage will require major pruning. The plants will survive but you will lose the first and largest flush of flowers.

ADDITIONAL INFORMATION

The tube-shaped flowers come in pink, red, white, or purplish-red. The first flush of flowers appears about the time the Lilacs bloom. They will continue to flower sporadically throughout the summer. The flowers are perfect for hummingbirds. Include them in your wildlife garden.

ADDITIONAL SPECIES, CULTIVARS, OR VARIETIES

The cultivar 'Red Prince' is hardier than the species. It will survive in Zone 4b. The 6-foot-tall plant has red flowers that do not fade with age and it reblooms in late summer. 'Minuet' is a dwarf form that grows to 30 inches tall. The purple-tinged leaves make a nice backdrop for the fragrant, ruby red flowers. It has shown good hardiness. 'Java Red' has purplish leaves with red buds opening into pink flowers. It grows 4 feet tall. 'Bristol Snowflake' is a white-flowering cultivar. 'Variegata' has green leaves with pale yellow-to-white edges. This compact plant grows 4 feet tall and has deep rose flowers. A new popular cultivar, 'Wine and Roses', grows 4 to 5 feet tall and has hot rose-pink flowers and burgundy leaves.

Did You Know?

Weigela florida *is native to China. It was first brought to England in 1845. The botanical name* Weigela *was given in honor of the German botanist Christian Ehrenfried von Weigel.* Florida *doesn't refer to the state. It means flowering.*

Witchhazel

Hamamelis virginiana

Other Name: Common Witchhazel
Size: 10 to 15 feet tall
Soil: Moist
Zones: 3b to 4

Color photograph on page 242.

Light Requirements:

Additional Benefit:

Witchhazel is occasionally found growing in shaded areas along the banks of streams in southeast Minnesota forests. In the landscape, it can tolerate a wider range of conditions. Its fragrant, yellow flowers are the last of the season. They open in mid-October or November as the leaves turn yellow and drop from the plant. Use this native in natural plantings or more traditional home landscapes. Be sure to give Witchhazel plenty of room since it can eventually grow up to 15 feet tall and wide.

WHEN TO PLANT

Nurseries and garden centers sell Witchhazels balled and burlapped or in containers. Plant balled-and-burlapped shrubs as soon as possible after they are purchased. Container-grown plants can be planted throughout the season. Plant Witchhazels in spring or early summer to give them time to get established before winter.

WHERE TO PLANT

Grow Witchhazel in full sun or shade. It performs best in moist soil but will tolerate some extremes. Avoid growing Witchhazel in very alkaline soil. This large shrub is excellent for naturalizing large areas. It can also be included in shrub borders or near large buildings.

HOW TO PLANT

Dig a hole the same depth as, but wider than, the rootball. Remove container-grown plants from the pot. Place the shrub in the hole at the same depth it was growing in the container. Remove any twine and cut away the burlap on balled-and-burlapped plants once they are set in place. Fill the hole with existing soil and water the shrubs.

CARE AND MAINTENANCE

New plantings need an inch of water per week. Established plants are more tolerant of dry soil. Mulch the soil to help conserve moisture and reduce weed problems. Wait at least a year before fertilizing new plantings. Follow soil test recommendations for the type and amount of fertilizer to use. Avoid high-nitrogen fertilizers that may inhibit flowering. Established shrubs need little, if any, fertilizer. Keep pruning to a minimum with Witchhazels. They are slow growing and respond slowly to pruning. Remove dead, damaged, or wayward branches in the spring. Prune them back to young healthy growth. Witchhazel leaves may yellow in alkaline soil. Use acidifying fertilizers, such as ammonium sulfate and organic mulches, to try to minimize the problem. You may need to replace Witchhazel growing in high pH soils with a more alkaline-tolerant plant. Rabbits feed on the trunks of Witchhazel over the winter. Extensive feeding will kill the plant. Fencing is the most effective way to protect these plants, although scare tactics and repellents may provide some protection.

ADDITIONAL INFORMATION

Witchhazel fruits are dried capsules that form in November or December and persist for a year. The seeds ripen in twelve months and are literally shot out of the capsule. It is fun to listen to this unique seed-planting technique.

ADDITIONAL SPECIES, CULTIVARS, OR VARIETIES

Vernal Witchhazel, *Hamamelis vernalis,* blooms in late winter instead of fall. The flowers are yellow to red and appear in late February or March. These winter blossoms are often killed by our cold winter temperatures.

 Did You Know?

Witchhazel plants have an interesting and useful history. Divining rods made out of Witchhazel were used to locate water. The witchhazel extract you buy at the pharmacy is made from distilled bark of young Witchhazel stems and shoots.

Yew

Taxus species

Size: Up to 20 feet	**Light Requirements:**
Soil: Moist; well-drained	
Zones: All	
	Additional Benefit:
Color photograph on page 242.	

Evergreen Yews can be found in most Midwest landscapes. The wide variety of shapes and sizes available, along with the Yew's ability to grow in sun or shade, make it adaptable to many landscape situations. Yews are used as foundation plants, screens, and hedges. The soft, dark-green needles add texture to the landscape while the red fruit and bark provide additional interest. Combine Yews with deciduous shrubs for added beauty.

WHEN TO PLANT

Yews transplant best as balled-and-burlapped plants, and should be planted as soon as possible after purchase. Some nurseries and garden centers dig Yews and place them in pots for easy handling. Plant Yews by October 1 to give them time to get established before winter.

WHERE TO PLANT

Grow Yews in sun or shade. Avoid areas with drying winter winds. Good drainage is essential to grow attractive healthy Yews. Plants grown in poorly drained soils will eventually die. Grow Yews in raised beds in areas where the soil is not well drained.

HOW TO PLANT

Dig a hole the same depth as, but wider than, the rootball. Potted plants are not always well rooted. Cut off the bottom of the container and place the plant, pot and all, in the hole. Be sure the planting depth is correct. Cut away the container. Remove any twine and cut away the burlap on balled-and-burlapped plants after they are set in place. Fill the hole with existing soil and water the plantings.

CARE AND MAINTENANCE

New plantings need about an inch of water each week. Established plants prefer moist soil and may need to be watered during dry weather. Old and new plantings should be watered well in the fall before the ground freezes. Mulch the soil to help conserve moisture, insulate the roots, and reduce weed problems. Wait at least a year to fertilize new plantings. Established Yews need little, if any, fertilizer. Most landscape cultivars require very little pruning if the right-sized plant is selected for the location. Prune Yews in the spring before growth begins or midsummer when they are semi-dormant. They are traditionally sheared into formal shapes, but are quite attractive when grown in their natural form. Maintain the Yew's natural form by pruning branches back to a healthy bud, where the branch joins another branch, or back to the main trunk. Yews will also tolerate severe pruning, but be patient—it takes time for the plants to recover. Browning caused by winter damage or disease can be pruned out to improve the plant's appearance and control the spread of disease.

ADDITIONAL INFORMATION

Canadian Yew, *Taxus canadensis,* is native to Minnesota and hardy to Zone 2. It is the hardiest of all the Yews, but is not well suited to most landscape situations. It is sometimes used as a groundcover in shade in naturalized situations.

CAUTION: The fruit of the Yew, which consists of a single oval seed covered by a thick, fleshy red cup, is sweetish, but unpleasant to the taste. The fruit is often eaten by children, and the foul-tasting "berry" is usually spit out before it is swallowed. Although the fleshy, red, berry-like cone is not poisonous; the foliage, bark, and seeds of Yew, whether eaten fresh or dried, are toxic to animals and people.

ADDITIONAL SPECIES, CULTIVARS, OR VARIETIES

There are hundreds of cultivars of Yews on the market. Select one of the hardy Japanese *Taxus cuspidata* or Anglojap *Taxus × media* cultivars for your landscape. Look for the cultivar with the best size and shape for your landscape.

CHAPTER EIGHT

Trees

TREES GIVE STRUCTURE TO OUR LANDSCAPE, providing form and year-round interest. They perform a variety of functions—offering privacy and shelter, serving as a habitat for wildlife, and providing a focal point for outdoor plantings. With proper selection, planting, and care, these plants can be an integral part of the Minnesota gardener's landscape for years to come.

TREE SELECTION

Planting the right tree in the right spot is a vital first step toward keeping it healthy throughout its life. Select the tree that is best suited to the soil, moisture, temperature, and other growing conditions of its location. Then choose a tree that will fit the available space, making sure the roots and crown will have enough room when they reach full size. Remember to check for overhead and underground utility lines.

With the choices narrowed down, the final consideration is picking a tree appropriate for your landscape's design and function. Trees are available in upright, spreading, weeping, and irregular forms. Use the species and form bested suited to your needs. Locate the planting site and call Gopher State One Call at 1-800-252-1166. It is a FREE utility locating service. They will mark the location of any underground utility in the planting area within three working days. Making that call is important for your safety and your pocketbook. Digging into a utility line can be deadly and expensive.

PURCHASING THE TREE

Now it's time to go shopping. Purchase your trees from a quality nursery or garden center. Trees are available bare root, balled and burlapped, or container grown. Bare-root plants are cheaper, but should only be planted in the spring before growth begins. Balled-and-burlapped trees are dug in the spring and fall. They are more expensive and are available for a longer period than bare-root trees. Container-grown trees are planted and grown in pots. They can be purchased and planted throughout the season.

Choose a tree with a straight trunk, good structure, and no signs of insect or disease problems. Smaller trees are easier to handle and recover more quickly from transplanting. A 2^1/$_2$-inch-diameter transplanted tree will soon surpass a 6-inch-diameter transplanted tree—plus you get the joy of watching it grow.

TRANSPORTING

Give your tree a safe ride home. Transporting the tree in a pickup truck or trailer is easier for you and better for the tree—or you can have it delivered. It is worth the extra effort to get your investment home safely.

Use a tarp to cover the top of the tree and prevent wind damage to leaves on the trip home. Cover the roots of bare-root trees to prevent drying. Wrap the trunk where it will rest on the vehicle with a towel. And always move the tree by the rootball, NOT the trunk, to prevent damage to the roots.

Plant your new trees as soon as possible. Keep them in a cool, shaded location until planting. Mulch bare-root and balled-and-burlapped trees with wood chips to keep their roots moist. Check these and container-grown trees daily and water as needed.

PLANTING

Locate the tree's root flare, the bell-shaped area, where the roots angle away from the trunk. Plant the tree with the root flare at or slightly above the soil line. Dig a shallow planting hole the same depth as and three to five times wider than the root system.

Roughen the sides of the planting hole to make it easier for the roots to enter the surrounding soil. Remove container-grown plants from the pot. Loosen or slice potbound and girdling roots. Place the tree in the planting hole. Be sure the tree is straight, moving it by the root-ball, not the trunk, to minimize root damage. Remove the tags, twine, and metal baskets and cut away the burlap on balled-and-burlapped trees. Fill the hole with existing soil. Do not amend the backfill. The tree roots need to adjust to their new environment, and amended soils encourage roots to stay in the planting hole instead of moving out into the landscape. Water to settle the soil; mulch. Remove trunk wraps and tags.

Do not stake balled-and-burlapped or container-grown trees unless they have a large canopy and a small root system or are subject to high winds and vandalism. Stake bare-root plants. Install the stakes in undisturbed soil outside the planting hole. Use a soft strap rather than wire around the tree trunk. Remove the stakes one or two years after planting.

CARE FOR NEWLY PLANTED TREES

Do not prune newly planted trees. Research shows that the more leaves a tree has, the more energy it can produce, and the quicker it develops new roots and recovers from transplant shock. Do remove broken and damaged branches at planting time. Structural pruning will start in the next few years once the tree has adjusted to its new home.

Water the area near the trunk to beyond the planting hole. The key to success with watering is to water thoroughly, but infrequently. Check the soil moisture before watering. It's time to break out the sprinkler when the top 6 to 8 inches of soil start to dry. Apply enough water to wet the top 12 inches of soil. A thorough watering once every 7 to 10 days is enough for clay soils. Water quick-drying sandy soils twice a week.

Mulch the soil to conserve moisture, reduce competition from grass, and prevent weeds. Apply a 3-inch layer of wood chips or shredded bark on the soil surface. Keep the mulch an inch or so away from the tree trunk.

Ongoing Care

Do not fertilize newly planted trees. Wait until the following spring to apply fertilizer. Use the amount recommended by soil test results or read and follow label directions on the fertilizer packet. Established trees do not need routine fertilization. They get plenty of nutrients from the fertilizers applied to lawns and gardens.

Prune young trees to establish a strong framework, keeping the plant's growth habit in mind. Remove crossed, rubbing, and parallel branches. Select branches with wide crotch angles, the angle between the trunk and branch, to form the framework. Prune out competing central leaders. Pruning young trees results in smaller wounds that heal faster. Do not apply pruning paint; it can trap in problems instead of keeping them out.

Despite your best efforts, pest problems may arise. Get a proper diagnosis and control recommendation from the local County Extension Office or a certified arborist (tree care professional). Many problems that look bad to us are not really detrimental to healthy trees. If treatment is needed, select an effective method that is the safest for you, the tree, and the environment.

Your efforts will be rewarded with years of enjoyment.

Alder

Alnus glutinosa

Other Names: European Alder,
   Black Alder
Size: 40 feet tall by 20 to 30 feet wide
Soil: Moist
Zones: 3 to 4
Color photograph on page 242.

Light Requirements:

Alders are tough trees that can survive in difficult growing situations. They tolerate a wide range of conditions commonly found in the landscape. This fast grower has a pyramidal shape when it is young that tends to open up and become more rounded with age. Multistemmed plants are also available and are quite attractive. In spring, long, yellow-green catkin flowers appear. The fruit is a small, woody, egg-shaped strobile that resembles a small pinecone. It is often dipped in gold or silver to make pendants and earrings. Fruits stay on the tree, providing winter interest.

WHEN TO PLANT

Alders adapt well to transplanting. Balled-and-burlapped trees should be planted as soon as possible after they are purchased. Container-grown plants can be planted throughout the growing season.

WHERE TO PLANT

Plant Alders in a location with full sun or partial shade. They prefer moist soil, but tolerate both wet or dry and acidic or slightly alkaline soil conditions. Use Alders in areas subject to temporary flooding. The Alder is a good substitute for the Willow Tree in wet locations. It isn't messy like the Willow, nor does it create problems with invasive roots. The Alder tree can be used alone as a specimen or planted in a group for mass effect. It looks nice growing in a backyard or next to a pond.

HOW TO PLANT

Locate the tree's root flare. Plant the tree with the root flare at, or slightly above, the soil line. Dig a shallow planting hole the same depth and three to five times wider than the root system. Place the tree in the planting hole. Remove the container, twine, and the metal baskets. Cut away the burlap. Fill the planting hole with existing soil, water to settle the soil, and mulch.

CARE AND MAINTENANCE

Alder is a fairly low-maintenance tree. Like most fast growers, it can be short lived. Use the Alder for quick impact in the landscape. Tent caterpillar, leaf miner, and woolly aphids can feed on this specimen. Prune out tent caterpillar nests to control this pest. Tolerate the damage of the leaf miner; the tree does. Woolly aphids can create an unsightly mess. These aphids are covered with white fibers. As they feed, they secrete a clear, sticky substance called honeydew. A black, sooty mold can grow on the honeydew, creating sticky globs. Small populations are not a problem. Control large populations of woolly aphid with insecticidal soap.

ADDITIONAL INFORMATION

The Alder is native to Europe, western Asia, and northern Africa. It has been used as a landscape plant for many years. Here in the United States, the alder has escaped cultivation and has even established some pure stands along waterways.

ADDITIONAL SPECIES, CULTIVARS, OR VARIETIES

'Pyramidalis' is an upright, columnar form growing 40 to 50 feet tall. 'Laciniata' is a large form growing 50 to 70 feet with deeply lobed and cut leaves. Speckled Alder, *Alnus rugosa*, is native to the northern half of Minnesota in moist habitats. It is a small tree, 15 to 20 feet tall. Like the European Alder, it tolerates moist to wet soil, making it a good choice for wet sites along ponds and waterways. The white flecks, or lenticels, on the stem give it the name Speckled Alder.

 Did You Know?

Alder wood is very durable. It resists rot and decay caused by water and weather. For this reason, it was used to make bridges, sluice gates, and even wooden shoes in the Netherlands.

Ash

Fraxinus species

Other Names: White Ash, Green Ash **Size:** 50 or more feet tall by 25 or 　　more feet wide **Soil:** Moist; well-drained **Zones:** All *Color photograph on page 242.*	**Light Requirements:** **Additional Benefits:**

A sh trees are commonly seen in nature and in landscapes. The yellow flowers create a subtle display in early spring. The green leaves that follow provide shade for home and land alike. In the fall, the leaves turn an attractive yellow or purple.

WHEN TO PLANT

Ash trees adapt well to transplanting. Balled-and-burlapped trees should be planted as soon as possible after they are purchased. Container-grown plants can be planted throughout the growing season.

WHERE TO PLANT

Ash trees tolerate a wide range of growing conditions. They prefer full sun with moist, well-drained soil. The Green Ash is tougher than the White Ash. It will tolerate wet to dry soil. Both trees make good medium- to fast-growing shade trees.

HOW TO PLANT

Locate the tree's root flare. Plant the tree with the root flare at or slightly above the soil line. Dig a shallow planting hole the same depth as and three to five times wider than the root system. Place the tree in the planting hole. Remove the container, twine, and the metal baskets. Cut away the burlap and fill the planting hole with existing soil. Water to settle the soil and mulch it.

CARE AND MAINTENANCE

When we find a tough landscape plant, we tend to overuse it and plant it in areas it really can't tolerate. Problems often develop as a result. That's the case with the Green Ash. It suffers from ash plant bug, borers, and Verticillium wilt. It also can yellow and decline if planted in an inappropriate spot. The best defense is to plant this tree in the right location. Keep it healthy by mulching, watering during extreme droughts, and fertilizing as needed. Call a certified arborist (a tree care professional) when problems develop. You will need an expert with the proper equipment to manage problems with these large trees.

ADDITIONAL INFORMATION

Green Ash can cause a few problems in the landscape. The trees produce lots of seeds, creating a weed problem in gardens and hedges. Select a male clone to avoid this problem. Ash flower gall is the other chief concern. It doesn't harm the plant, but it can be a nuisance in the landscape. Mites feed on the emerging male flowers in the spring. This causes small brown growths to form on the branches. The galls eventually drop, creating a litter problem on walks and patios. Sweep them up, or avoid planting the trees where this will create a problem.

ADDITIONAL SPECIES, CULTIVARS, OR VARIETIES

White Ash, *Fraxinus americana*, is native to south eastern Minnesota. This large tree has a wonderful reddish-purple fall color. Use it as a specimen in large landscapes. 'Autumn Applause' and 'Autumn Purple' are seedless white ash cultivars with reliable fall color. Green Ash, *Fraxinus pennsylvanica*, is native throughout Minnesota. It is much more tolerant of difficult sites, but twiggy and often irregularly shaped. Their leaves turn yellow in the fall. 'Marshall's Seedless' and 'Patmore' have a better growth habit and are seedless. Some of the seedless cultivars have been known to start producing seeds.

 Did You Know?

White Ash wood is very strong. It is often used to make sports equipment, such as bats, paddles, and oars, or the handles of garden tools, such as shovels or hoes.

Beech

Fagus species

Other Names: American Beech, European Beech

Size: 50 or more feet tall by 35 or more feet wide

Soil: Moist, well-drained

Zone: 4b

Color photograph on page 242.

Light Requirements:

Additional Benefit:

The Beech tree is one of the majestic trees of the woods and land-scape. These slow-growing trees carefully build a strong framework that lasts for many years. The smooth gray bark provides beauty and interest in all four seasons. Watch with great anticipation as the bronze leaves unfurl in the spring. Soon, they turn green for the summer and develop a rich brown hue in the fall. Some of the leaves will persist on the tree through the winter, providing contrast to the snow. Don't forget to stop and listen: the winter wind rustling through the dried leaves can add another dimension to your enjoyment of the Beech.

WHEN TO PLANT

Transplant young trees in early spring. European Beeches adapt better to transplanting and are more readily available.

WHERE TO PLANT

Beech trees prefer full sun, but will tolerate some shade. They must have moist, well-drained soil. The European Beech tends to be a little more tolerant of varied conditions. Use American Beeches as specimen plants or for naturalizing. The European Beech also makes a nice specimen plant. It can be trimmed into a hedge, although it is difficult for many gardeners, including me, to severely prune such a lovely, sometimes hard-to-find, and expensive tree! Both the American and European Beech trees will eventually grow into large shade trees.

HOW TO PLANT

Locate the tree's root flare. Plant the tree with the root flare at or slightly above the soil line. Dig a shallow planting hole the same depth as and three to five times wider than the root system. Place the tree in the planting hole. Remove the container, twine, and metal baskets. Cut away the burlap and fill the hole with existing soil. Water to settle the soil and mulch it.

CARE AND MAINTENANCE

If planted in the proper location, Beech trees are low maintenance and have no real problems. Patience is the only thing gardeners will need for this slow-growing plant.

ADDITIONAL INFORMATION

The Beech tree is shallow rooted, making it nearly impossible to grow grass beneath its canopy. Mulch the area under the tree. It is better for the Beech, and it will reduce your frustration trying to grow and maintain grass where it just won't grow. Or, better yet, leave the Beech branched to the ground. This is an attractive way to grow this large tree.

ADDITIONAL SPECIES, CULTIVARS, OR VARIETIES

The American beech, *Fagus grandifolia*, is hardy in Zone 4b. Although it used to be nearly impossible to find this tree in nurseries, with the increased interest in native plants it is becoming more readily available. European Beeches, *Fagus sylvatica*, and their cultivars are more available from nurseries. 'Atropunicea' ('Purpurea') is the most common of the purple-leaf forms. 'Roseomarginata' ('Purpurea Tricolor') is another attention grabber. It has purple leaves with pinkish white and rose-colored leaf margins. Cutleaf and weeping forms are also available.

 Did You Know?

Beechnuts used to be fed to pigs, and are still a favorite food for many birds. The botanical name Fagus *means "to eat." The words Beech and book are from the same root, which refers to the ancient practice of using Beech wood for writing boards. Unfortunately, lovers and graffiti artists have used trunks of the Beech for writing boards as well.*

Birch

Betula species

Other Names: Paper Birch, Canoe Birch **Size:** 40 to 50 feet or more tall and 20 to 25 feet wide **Soil:** Moist; well-drained **Zones:** All *Color photograph on page 242.*	**Light Requirements:** **Additional Benefits:**

Paper Birch is a very popular tree in Minnesota and Wisconsin. When I moved north 20 years ago, I was amazed to see white Birches in front of so many homes. I knew of the problems common to the Birch, and I couldn't imagine why so many people grew them. Then I went "up north," and realized that everyone wanted a piece of the north woods in their home landscape.

WHEN TO PLANT
Transplant Birch trees in the spring for best results.

WHERE TO PLANT
Take your lead from nature on how to use and where to plant these trees. They prefer woodland-type settings. Grow Birches in full sun or partial shade, with moist, well-drained soil. These growing conditions are especially important in southern Minnesota, where the summers can be too warm for this plant. Use Birches as specimen or shade plants. Plant them en masse to create a northern woodland in your backyard or include Birches in planting beds. The beds provide an attractive setting and healthy environment for the Birch trees. Plant the tree where you can enjoy the attractive bark year-round. Place it in front of an evergreen for an even better show.

HOW TO PLANT
Locate the tree's root flare. Plant the tree with the root flare at or slightly above the soil line. Dig a shallow planting hole the same depth as and three to five times wider than the root system. Place the tree in the planting hole. Remove the container, twine, and metal baskets. Cut away the burlap. Fill the hole with existing soil. Water to settle the soil and mulch.

CARE AND MAINTENANCE

Birches need cool, moist soil. Mulch or plant groundcovers under the trees to create this environment. Water trees weekly during drought periods. Water thoroughly, wetting the top 12 inches of soil. Leaf miners and borers are the most common pests of the Birch. The leaf miner feeds between the upper and lower leaf surface, causing the leaves to brown. Treat leaf miner to reduce plant stress and borer problems. Bronze birch borer is deadly. Plant species resistant to this pest or minimize plant stress to prevent problems. Infected trees can be treated by a certified arborist or tree care professional. Timing is critical for effective control. Birch trees will "bleed" when pruned in the spring. It won't hurt the plant; it just makes the job messy.

ADDITIONAL INFORMATION

'Whitespire' Birch is a University of Wisconsin introduction. This white-barked tree is supposed to be resistant to bronze birch borer. There have been some problems with seeded trees becoming infested. Purchase 'Whitespire Senior' for borer resistance. It is a vegetatively reproduced (made from tissue culture) plant.

ADDITIONAL SPECIES, CULTIVARS, OR VARIETIES

Paper birch, *Betula papyrifera*, is native to our north woods. It is a medium to fast grower with outstanding white exfoliating bark. River Birch, *Betula nigra*, is also native to Minnesota and is resistant to bronze birch borer. The bark on this Birch is multicolored with gray, cinnamon, or reddish brown exfoliating bark. I have seen problems with chlorosis, or yellowing leaves, on plants grown in the high pH soils.

 Did You Know?

Paper Birch has been used by many cultures in the past. Native Americans made canoes, baskets, utensils, and wigwam covers from it.

Catalpa

Catalpa speciosa

Other Names: Northern Catalpa,
  Cigartree, Indian-Bean
Size: 40 to 60 feet tall and 20 to
  40 feet wide
Soil: Various
Zone: 4
Color photograph on page 242.

Light Requirements:

Additional Benefits:

Catalpa is a tree you either love or hate. Its large size and coarse texture limit its use in home landscapes. The attractive cone-shaped flowers stand out against the large, heart-shaped leaves. The rough, furrowed bark and persistent bean-like fruit stand out in the winter. There are quite a few of these trees planted in urban lots. This is not a tree for my small city lot, but it is definitely on my list of trees to plant when I buy those five or maybe ten acres to grow all my favorites.

WHEN TO PLANT

Plant small balled-and-burlapped trees in the spring. Container-grown plants can be planted throughout the growing season.

WHERE TO PLANT

Grow Catalpas in full sun or partially shaded locations. They prefer moist, fertile soil, but will tolerate a variety of soils including wet and dry. That makes them a good choice for difficult conditions in large areas. Their size and coarse texture can be overwhelming in a small setting. Place Catalpas in areas where the dropping twigs and falling flowers don't create a cleanup nightmare. There are several Catalpas on the route between my house and the botanical gardens. I always look forward to their June flower display. After that, they are forgotten until winter arrives and their coarse texture and persistent cigar-like fruit add interest to my winter drive.

HOW TO PLANT

Locate the tree's root flare. Plant the tree with the root flare at or slightly above the soil line. Dig a shallow planting hole the same depth as and three to five times wider than the root system. Place the tree in the planting hole. Remove the container, twine, and metal

baskets. Cut away the burlap. Fill the hole with existing soil, water to settle the soil, and mulch.

CARE AND MAINTENANCE

Catalpas do require some cleanup. The trees will lose small branches in wind and ice storms. A post-storm cleanup will take care of this problem. The falling flowers have been known to drive meticulous gardeners to distraction. Proper placement will allow you to enjoy the flowers without worrying about the mess. Catalpas are subject to Verticillium wilt. This fungal disease blocks the flow of water and nutrients between the roots and leaves, causing branch dieback. Contact a certified arborist for positive diagnosis. Do not plant Catalpas in locations where other plants have died from this disease.

ADDITIONAL INFORMATION

The beauty of the individual Catalpa flower is often missed on the large tree. I will never forget the first time I had a close-up look at a Catalpa flower. The individual Catalpa blooms remind me of orchids. Each flower is white with a purple blotch in the center. The ends of the bell-shaped flowers are frilled. These blooms combine to form the cone-shaped flowers that are impressive at a distance.

ADDITIONAL SPECIES, CULTIVARS, OR VARIETIES

None hardy to Minnesota.

 Did You Know?

Catalpas are often called Cigartree or Indian-bean for their long bean-like fruits. The name Catalpa *is the North American Indian name for this tree.* Speciosa *means showy. Though brittle, Catalpa wood will resist rot. That is why it was once used for railroad ties.*

Crabapple

Malus hybrids

Other Name: Flowering Crabapple
Size: Up to 25 feet tall and wide
Soil: Moist; well-drained
Zones: All

Color photograph on page 242.

Light Requirements:

Additional Benefits:

top! Don't turn the page! If you have an old Crabapple tree, you may be wondering what ever possessed me to recommend this plant. Many of you may have suffered through the mess of summer leaf drop and fallen fruit. Fortunately, there are many new disease-resistant Crabapples with small, persistent fruit, eliminating the litter problem. Select Crabapples for their year-round features. The colorful white, pink, or red flowers provide several weeks of beauty in the spring. The fruit, however, will give you months of enjoyment. Look for persistent fruit in many shades of yellow, orange, and red. The trees can be small and mounded, spreading, weeping, or upright. I'm sure there is a Crabapple out there for every gardener!

WHEN TO PLANT

Crabapples respond best to spring transplanting. Plant balled-and-burlapped trees as soon as possible after they are purchased. Container-grown plants can be planted throughout the growing season.

WHERE TO PLANT

Grow Crabapples in full sun with moist, well-drained soil. Use them as specimen plants or in small groupings. The weeping cultivars complement water features, and the spreading types blend well in Japanese gardens. Include some of the smaller types in your perennial gardens. They can provide structure and year-round interest in large flower gardens.

HOW TO PLANT

Locate the tree's root flare. Plant the tree with the root flare at or slightly above the soil line. Dig a shallow planting hole the same depth as and three to five times wider than the root system. Place the tree in the planting hole, remove the container or twine, and the metal baskets. Cut away the burlap. Fill the hole with existing soil; water and mulch.

CARE AND MAINTENANCE

Prune only to establish and maintain the tree's structural framework. Excessive pruning will encourage water sprouts. Prune Crabapple trees in late winter for quick healing and to reduce the risk of disease. Select disease-resistant cultivars to avoid major problems. Fireblight is a bacterial disease that can eventually kill the tree. Prune out infected branches 12 inches beneath the canker, or sunken area, to control the disease. Disinfect tools with alcohol or a bleach and water solution between cuts. Apple scab causes leaf spotting and dropping. Rake and destroy fallen leaves to reduce the source of infection. Several applications of a fungicide in early spring will help control this disease. Be sure to read and follow label directions carefully. Or replace it with a scab-resistant plant. Crabapples are a favorite food for tent caterpillars. Physically remove the caterpillar-filled tent to control this pest.

ADDITIONAL INFORMATION

Get some added benefits from late winter pruning. Force the removed Crabapple branches into bloom for indoor enjoyment. Recut the stems and place them in warm water.

ADDITIONAL SPECIES, CULTIVARS, OR VARIETIES

There are over 600 Crabapples in cultivation with new ones being introduced each season. Contact your local nursery to find the Crabapple with the flower, fruit, and growth habit that best suits your needs. Remember to select a disease-resistant cultivar with persistent fruit.

 Did You Know?

Crabapples are useful, as well as ornamental, plants. They are living bird feeders. Select a cultivar that produces fruit the birds prefer. In the past, Crabapple wood was used to make saw handles, wood mallet heads, and wedges for splitting wood.

Douglasfir

Pseudotsuga menziesii

Other Names: Douglas Fir, *Pseudotsuga douglasii* and *P. taxifolia*
Size: 70 feet tall by 20 feet wide
Soil: Moist; well-drained
Zones: 3b to 4
Color photograph on page 242.

Light Requirements:

Additional Benefit:

Douglasfir's majestic appearance is striking. Its needles can be green to bluish green and have a camphor smell when crushed. It grows at a medium rate, adding twelve to fifteen feet over a ten-year period. Consider using this tree where a large vertical accent is needed. Like the Colorado Blue Spruce, this tree will outgrow most small city lots. You will then face the tough decision of cutting down the overgrown tree, limbing it up and ruining its appearance, or crawling under it to get to your front door.

WHEN TO PLANT

Douglasfir adapts well after transplanting when it is balled and burlapped. Plant the balled-and-burlapped tree as soon as possible after it is purchased. Container-grown trees can be planted throughout the growing season. Plant evergreens before October 1 for best results.

WHERE TO PLANT

Grow Douglasfir in full sun or partial shade. They need moist, well-drained soil. Douglasfir will not tolerate high winds or dry, rocky soil. Don't use these trees as windbreaks. Take advantage of their form and stature by planting them as a specimen tree or en masse. Give this Douglasfir plenty of room to grow and show off its beauty.

HOW TO PLANT

Locate the tree's root flare. That is the bell-shaped area where the roots angle away from the trunk. Plant the tree with the root flare at or slightly above the soil line. Dig a shallow planting hole at the same depth as and 3 to 5 times wider than the root system. Place the tree in the planting hole. Be sure the tree is straight, but move it by the rootball, not the trunk, to minimize root damage. Remove the container, twine, and metal baskets. Cut away the burlap. Fill the hole with existing soil, water to settle the soil, then mulch.

CARE AND MAINTENANCE

Douglasfir needs very little care if it is planted in the proper location. Water it during periods of drought. Water the whole area under the tree thoroughly, wetting the top twelve inches of the soil. Mulching will also help keep the roots cool and moist. Monitor the plants for insect problems and fungal diseases. Contact your local County Extension office or certified arborist for proper identification and recommended treatment.

ADDITIONAL INFORMATION

Douglasfir was once the most important lumber tree in the United States. Its strong wood was used for railroad ties, poles for telegraph and telephone lines, and plywood. Its persistent needles make it one of the best short-needled Christmas trees.

ADDITIONAL SPECIES, CULTIVARS, OR VARIETIES

Douglasfir is native to the Rocky Mountains and the Pacific Coast. Plants from the Rocky Mountains tend to be shorter, tougher plants that do not live as long as those on the coast. They are the best choice for our area. The Coastal Douglasfir grows taller, lives longer, and is pickier about its growing conditions. *Pseudotsuga menziesu glauca* has reliably blue-green needles. It is more compact than the species. 'Anguina' has long, snake-like branches. 'Fastigiata' is a dense, pyramidal form. 'Pendula' has long, drooping branchlets.

 Did You Know?

Douglasfir is named for the Scottish botanist David Douglas. He was sent to the United States by the Royal Horticultural Society to collect plants. He discovered the Douglasfir on one of his journeys in 1825.

Elm

Ulmus species and hybrids

Other Name: American Elm
Size: 30 to 80 feet tall and up to
   40 feet wide
Soil: Moist
Zones: All
Color photograph on page 242.

Light Requirements:

Additional Benefits:

Everyone has seen or heard about the magnificent Elm-lined city streets. Or perhaps you had a favorite American Elm in your yard or nearby park. The advent of Dutch Elm Disease (DED) and the overuse of this tree changed the urban forest forever. In the 1960s, the air was filled with the sound of dropping Elms. Tree care professionals scrambled to find large quantities of trees to replace them. Now researchers are trying to develop DED-resistant hybrids and cultivars that look like the vase-shaped American Elm so many people loved.

WHEN TO PLANT

Elms adapt well to transplanting. Plant balled-and-burlapped trees as soon as possible after they are purchased. Container-grown plants can be planted throughout the growing season.

WHERE TO PLANT

Grow Elms in full-sun locations. They prefer moist soil, but many will tolerate wet soil and even temporary flooding. Large Elms make good shade trees. Some species have been sheared into hedges.

HOW TO PLANT

Locate the tree's root flare. Plant the tree with the root flare at or slightly above the soil line. Dig a shallow planting hole the same depth as and three to five times wider than the root system. Place the tree in the planting hole. Remove the container, twine, and metal baskets. Cut away the burlap. Fill the hole with existing soil; water and mulch.

CARE AND MAINTENANCE

Elms tend to be fast growers and weak wooded. Proper pruning throughout the tree's life will help reduce storm damage. American and Red Elms are susceptible to Dutch Elm Disease (DED). Plant resistant species and hybrids to avoid this disease. Use a preventative fungicide treatment to protect valuable trees. Even lightly infected (5% or less) trees have been successfully treated. Contact a certified arborist for proper diagnosis and more details on treatment.

ADDITIONAL INFORMATION

The University of Wisconsin has developed and introduced several DED-resistant elms. Each cultivar has its own unique characteristic, but it doesn't quite look like the American Elm. 'New Horizon' and 'Regal' are two DED-resistant hybrids that are hardy in Zones 4 and 5. The 'American Liberty' Elm is the result of crossing six different American Elm clones. These DED-resistant trees are being distributed by the Elm Research Institute in cooperation with the Boy Scouts of America. Watch for updates on the success of this effort.

ADDITIONAL SPECIES, CULTIVARS, OR VARIETIES

The Chinese or Lacebark Elm, *Ulmus parvifolia*, is a superior plant. It is a tough tree that can tolerate a wide range of conditions. It is resistant to DED, as well as both Elm leaf and Japanese beetle. The small leaves and beautiful bark make this an attractive and useful shade tree. Be sure you are getting the right tree when buying a Chinese Elm. The Siberian Elm, *Ulmus pumila*, is often sold as Chinese Elm. The Siberian Elm is messy, weak wooded, and not suited for the landscape.

 Did You Know?

Another native Elm is the Red or Slippery Elm, Ulmus rubra. *It is named slippery for its moist and slimy inner bark. Pioneers used to chew on the inner bark to quench their thirst. You can still buy throat lozenges containing Slippery Elm in some drugstores today.*

European Mountain Ash

Sorbus aucuparia

Other Name: Mountain Ash
Size: 30 feet tall by 20 feet wide
Soil: Cool; well-drained
Zones: All

Color photograph on page 243.

Light Requirements:

Additional Benefit:

Mountain Ash has long been a favorite tree for Minnesota gardens. It has white flowers in the spring, followed by showy, orange-red fruit in the fall. The fruit attracts birds to the landscape, adding color and motion. Mountain Ash can put on a good show in its short life. Planted in appropriate growing conditions, it will grow to 25 or 30 feet in about twenty years.

WHEN TO PLANT

Plant balled-and-burlapped trees as soon as possible after they are purchased. Container-grown trees can be planted throughout the growing season.

WHERE TO PLANT

European Mountain Ash must have good growing conditions to thrive. Plant it in areas with full sun and cool, moist, but well-drained soil. It will not tolerate heat, drought, pollution, or compacted soil. Keep specimens away from heat-reflecting structures and pavement. Try planting them on the east, north, or cool side of your home in a spot where they can be enjoyed. The flower show is good, but not spectacular, and just a bit smelly. You may want to keep this tree away from open windows. The fruit display is excellent and attractive to birds. Every December, the cedar waxwings join my students for their final exam. They fill the Mountain Ash tree and eat the fruit as the students identify the plant.

HOW TO PLANT

Locate the tree's root flare. Plant the tree with the root flare at or slightly above the soil line. Dig a shallow planting hole the same depth as and three to five times wider than the root system. Place the tree in the planting hole. Remove the container, twine, and metal

baskets. Cut away the burlap. Fill the planting hole with existing soil; water and mulch.

CARE AND MAINTENANCE

Plant Mountain Ash in the right location to minimize maintenance. Mulch the roots with wood chips or another organic material to keep them cool and moist. Water Mountain Ash thoroughly during drought periods. Soak the top 12 inches of soil once every seven to ten days in clay soil and every three to five days in sandy soil to get trees through the dry spell. Avoid using high-nitrogen fertilizers that can increase the risk of fireblight and interfere with flowering. Mountain Ash trees are susceptible to quite a few disease and insect problems. The shiny, smooth bark is susceptible to sunscald and frost cracking. We saw great decline in Mountain Ash trees after the drought of 1988 and the heat wave of 1995.

ADDITIONAL INFORMATION

American Mountain Ash, *Sorbus americana,* is native to Minnesota. It is considered a small tree or large shrub between 15 and 30 feet tall. It is hardy throughout the state and can grow in swampy areas. This short-lived plant has white flowers and orange-red fruit. The Showy Mountain Ash, *Sorbus decora,* is native to the north shore of Lake Superior and is hardy to Zone 2. It has white flowers, red fruit with leaflets about three times as long as broad and somewhat whitened beneath

ADDITIONAL SPECIES, CULTIVARS, OR VARIETIES

Korean Mountain Ash, *Sorbus alnifolia,* puts on a better flower and fruit display than the European Mountain Ash. It tends to bloom heavily one year and lighter the next. This tree is considered the best of the Mountain Ash trees.

 Did You Know?

The botanical name is Latin. Sorbus *means service tree.* Aucuparia *comes from the words* avis *for bird and* capere *meaning "to catch." This tree certainly catches the birds with its tasty fruit. I think it even catches a few homeowners who plant this tree after seeing a bird-filled, fruit-laden plant.*

Fir

Abies species

Other Names: White Fir (*Abies concolor*), Balsam Fir (*Abies balsamea*)
Size: 70 feet tall and 30 feet wide
Soil: Moist; well-drained
Zones: All
Color photograph on page 243.

Light Requirements:

Additional Benefit:

If you like the look of a Blue Spruce but are tired of fighting the pest problems, I have the perfect tree for you. The White Fir, *Abies concolor,* has blue-green needles and a pyramidal shape similar to the Colorado Blue Spruce. The broader, flat needles and growth habit of White Fir give it a softer appearance than the Spruce. This feature makes the White Fir easier to blend with other plants. The Balsam Fir is a beautiful part of our native landscape. Unfortunately, that is where it prefers to stay. Balsam Firs, like most Firs, must have proper growing conditions to thrive. You will be better off planting a White Fir in your landscape and visiting the Balsam Fir in its native woodlands.

WHEN TO PLANT

For best results, plant balled-and-burlapped trees in the spring. Container-grown plants do best if they are planted early in the season. Plant before October 1 so plants will root before the harsh winter.

WHERE TO PLANT

Grow Firs in full sun or light shade. They prefer moist, well-drained soil in cool, humid locations. Firs do not tolerate hot, dry conditions. The White Fir is the most tolerant of dry soil and city conditions. Use the White Fir individually as a specimen plant or in small groupings. These large trees need big landscapes to show off their beauty.

HOW TO PLANT

Locate the tree's root flare. Plant the tree with the root flare at or slightly above the soil line. Dig a shallow planting hole the same depth as and three to five times wider than the root system. Place the tree in the planting hole. Remove the container, twine, and metal

baskets. Cut away the burlap. Fill the planting hole with existing soil, water to settle the soil, and mulch.

CARE AND MAINTENANCE

Proper site selection is critical for growing success. A well-placed Fir will require little maintenance. Use the heat- and drought-tolerant White Fir for landscapes. Healthy Fir trees suffer few pest problems and require very little pruning. Mulch the soil with wood chips or another organic material to keep the roots cool and moist. Soak the top 12 inches of soil every seven to ten days in heavy clay soil or every three to five days in sandy soil during dry periods.

ADDITIONAL INFORMATION

Balsam Fir, *Abies balsamea,* is native to Minnesota. This short-needled evergreen can be found in the woods of central and northern Minnesota. It is a favorite Christmas tree even though it tends to lose its needles quickly indoors. The wonderful fragrance signals the start of the holiday season for many of us.

ADDITIONAL SPECIES, CULTIVARS, OR VARIETIES

White Fir, *Abies concolor,* is the best Fir for home landscape situations. It prefers ideal growing conditions, but is more tolerant of heat, drought, and urban conditions than other Firs. This large tree resembles a Blue Spruce in shape and needle color. Its name, *concolor,* means same color, referring to the needles that are blue-green on both the upper and lower surfaces. 'Candicans' is a narrow cultivar with bright silvery blue needles.

 Did You Know?

The Fraser Fir has become a very popular Christmas tree in the last few years. It has the look of a Balsam Fir but is much fuller and holds its needles longer. Like all Firs, it requires cool, moist growing conditions. Enjoy it for the holidays, but don't count on it for your landscape.

Ginkgo

Ginkgo biloba

Other Name: Maidenhair Tree

Size: 50 or more feet tall and
30 or more feet wide

Soil: Well-drained

Zone: 4

Color photograph on page 243.

Light Requirements:

Additional Benefit:

Ginkgo is a beautiful tree that deserves consideration. The attractive, fan-shaped leaves add to the overall uniqueness of this plant. Its irregular shape and open appearance can make it difficult to blend in small landscapes. Mature specimens are breathtaking, especially in the fall. The leaves turn a clear yellow and, best of all, they all drop from the tree at the same time, making cleanup easier.

WHEN TO PLANT

Ginkgo trees adapt easily to transplanting. Plant balled-and-burlapped trees as soon as possible after they are purchased. Container-grown plants can be planted throughout the growing season.

WHERE TO PLANT

Ginkgo is a tough tree that seems to thrive where it is planted. It prefers full sun and slightly moist, well-drained soil. It is very tolerant of salt, pollution, and other urban conditions. I am always amazed to see how well the Ginkgo performs in the hostile environment of sidewalk plantings in downtown areas. Remember, this slow grower will eventually get big, so leave it room. Ginkgo trees have an open growth habit making them very picturesque in the landscape. Plant them where their fall color can be appreciated.

HOW TO PLANT

Locate the tree's root flare. Plant the tree with the root flare at or slightly above the soil line. Dig a shallow planting hole the same depth as and three to five times wider than the root system. Place the tree in the planting hole. Remove the container, twine, and metal baskets, and cut away the burlap. Fill the planting hole with existing soil, water to settle the soil, and mulch.

CARE AND MAINTENANCE

Ginkgo trees have no real pest problems and tolerate a wide range of growing conditions. The open growth habit eliminates the need for regular pruning. They do require patience, adding about 10 to 15 feet of growth in ten to twelve years. You can speed things up by providing adequate, not too much, water and fertilizer. Female Ginkgo trees produce smelly, messy fruit. I remember walking to the library on the Ohio State University campus thinking the dog owners should clean up their mess. Once enrolled in horticulture classes, I learned it was the female Ginkgo trees, not the dogs, that needed curbing. Plant male clones to avoid the problem. Otherwise, rake and compost the fruit.

ADDITIONAL INFORMATION

Ginkgoes are often called living fossils. They have been growing on the earth for over 150 million years. The Ginkgo was thought to be extinct until it was discovered in China. Though its place of origin is listed as China, it was once found in many parts of the world, including North America.

ADDITIONAL SPECIES, CULTIVARS, OR VARIETIES

Purchase named male clones to avoid the messy fruit. Ginkgo Biloba 'Fastigiata' and 'Princeton Sentry' are upright forms of Ginkgo. 'Pendula' has strong, horizontal branching. Sold as a weeper, it actually spreads horizontally, creating an interesting look. 'Jade Butterflies' is a striking introduction from New Zealand with small jade-green leaves that clump close together forming a compact tree. 'Tschi-Tschi' develops a multitude of strange protuberances along the bark as the tree matures. 'Tubiformis' has very unusual leaves which form narrow, upward-facing funnels when they unfurl in spring. They hold water drops in light rains for an outstanding display.

 Did You Know?

The ginkgo seeds, hidden within the smelly covering, are edible. The seeds have long been used in Oriental cooking and ritual. Called silver apricots, they are tasty and still eaten today.

Hawthorn

Crataegus species

Other Name: Thornapple
Size: 20 to 30 feet tall and wide
Soil: Well-drained
Zones: All

Color photograph on page 243.

Light Requirements:

Additional Benefits:

Hawthorns are nice, small trees that can provide year-round interest in both small and large settings. Their white flowers are effective for up to two weeks in May. But don't plant them next to your window unless you're sure you like the smell. The fruit is orange-red and usually quite showy fall through winter. Whether flowering, fruiting, or bare, the horizontal habit is quite attractive. Select a native or introduced species that is best suited to your landscape.

WHEN TO PLANT

Plant small balled-and-burlapped trees in the spring. Container-grown plants can be planted throughout the growing season.

WHERE TO PLANT

Grow Hawthorns in full-sun locations. They will tolerate a variety of soils as long as they are well-drained. Hawthorns are tough trees that will withstand city conditions. Use them as specimen plants where their floral and fruit display can be enjoyed. Their strong, horizontal branching helps anchor large buildings to the landscape. I have seen Hawthorns used for screening, hedging, and as barrier plants. One gentleman used native Hawthorns in a short-grass prairie planting to create a small scale Oak savanna. Just remember the thorns can be a liability. Avoid using these plants next to entrances and walkways where people may be injured.

HOW TO PLANT

Locate the tree's root flare. Plant the tree with the root flare at or slightly above the soil line. Dig a shallow planting hole the same depth as and three to five times wider than the root system. Place the tree in the planting hole. Remove the container, twine, and metal baskets. Cut away the burlap. Fill the hole with existing soil, water, and mulch.

CARE AND MAINTENANCE

The amount of maintenance required depends on the species and cultivar used. Falling fruit from the large fruited Hawthorns can create a mess. Grow groundcovers under these trees. As the fruit drops, it will compost out of sight in the groundcover. Avoid the area until the fruit rots and the German yellow jackets are done feeding. Or plant a Hawthorn with smaller, persistent fruit. Prune Hawthorns to establish and maintain the tree's structural framework. Late winter pruning cuts will heal quickly and minimize the risk of disease.

ADDITIONAL INFORMATION

Hawthorns are susceptible to several major diseases including fireblight, scab (see Crabapples), and rust. Select the least susceptible species whenever possible. Rust is the most common disease. It causes leaves and fruit to develop orange spots and drop prematurely. This usually doesn't hurt the tree; it just looks bad. Rake and destroy fallen leaves. Avoid planting Red Cedar (*Juniperus virginiana*), the alternate host for this disease, in the same area.

ADDITIONAL SPECIES, CULTIVARS, OR VARIETIES

Cockspur hawthorn, *Crataegus crusgalli,* has glossy green leaves, 1-inch red fruit, and long, sharp thorns. The variety 'Inermis' is thornless. Washington and Winter King Hawthorns are finer textured with smaller fruit. Both are quite effective in winter. Heavy snow loads may cause damage.

 Did You Know?

Many Hawthorns hold their fruit through the winter. The small, red, apple-like fruit looks even prettier when capped with fresh fallen snow. As the fruit softens over winter, the hungry birds will start feeding on them. It is quite entertaining to watch the birds feed on the fermented fruit.

Hemlock

Tsuga canadensis

Other Name: Canadian or Eastern Hemlock **Size:** 75 feet or more tall by 25 or more feet wide **Soil:** Moist; well-drained **Zones:** 3b to 4 *Color photograph on page 243.*	**Light Requirements:** **Additional Benefit:**

Hemlock is a graceful beauty that is often overlooked for landscape use. This native evergreen tree is pyramidal when it is young. With age, Hemlock maintains its pyramidal shape but the branches begin to weep, giving it a soft, graceful silhouette. The straight species is large and best suited for sizable landscapes. Many dwarf and uniquely shaped cultivars have recently been introduced, making Hemlock an option for those with small yards.

WHEN TO PLANT

Plant balled-and-burlapped trees as soon as possible after they are purchased. Container-grown trees can be planted throughout the growing season. Install by October 1 to allow root establishment before winter.

WHERE TO PLANT

Hemlocks are particular about their growing location. They are one of the few evergreens that prefer shade. Plants grown in full sun need moist, well-drained soil and must be protected from drying winds. Grow Hemlocks in a sheltered location out of wind, drought, pollution, and water-logged soil. Hemlocks are attractive grown individually or in small groups. Dwarf cultivars are nice additions to small landscapes and perennial gardens. They provide structure and year-round interest to the garden. Use them as specimens, accents, screens, or transition plants on the woodland's edge. Their light, airy texture can soften surrounding plants and landscape structures. Hemlocks tolerate pruning and can be used as a hedge. Before you reach for the shears, take a look at its beautiful shape. Maybe an informal hedge will work just as well.

How to Plant

Plant the tree with the root flare at or slightly above the soil line. Dig a shallow planting hole the same depth as and three to five times wider than the root system. Place the tree in the planting hole. Remove the container, twine, and metal baskets. Cut away the burlap. Fill the hole with existing soil, water to settle the soil, and mulch.

Care and Maintenance

Water during dry periods. Mulch the roots to keep the soil cool and moist. Stressed trees are susceptible to quite a few pests. Brown needles and branch dieback can occur when the plants are exposed to temperatures over 95 degrees, drying winter winds or drought. Prune out damaged branches. Eliminate the stress or move the plants to a better location.

Additional Information

This is not poison hemlock. That plant, *Conium maculatum*, is herbaceous and looks more like Queen Anne's Lace. All parts of that plant are poisonous.

Additional Species, Cultivars, or Varieties

The increased interest in dwarf cultivars has resulted in the introduction of quite a few compact and uniquely shaped hemlocks. 'Cole's Prostrate' (sometimes listed as 'Cole'), is a ground-hugging plant that grows 8 inches tall and up to 7 feet wide. It works well as a ground cover or rock garden plant in protected locations. There are several interesting weeping forms including 'Sargentii', 'Pendula', and 'Kelsey's Weeping'. These all make interesting specimens in the landscape and can be trained to take on all kinds of shapes.

 Did You Know?

The botanical name Tsuga *is Japanese for tree-mother. The common name is based on the descriptive name used by native Americans in what is now New York.*

343

Honey Locust

Gleditsia triacanthos var. *inermis*

Other Name: Thornless Honey Locust
Size: 40 feet tall and up to 30 feet wide
Soil: Moist; well-drained
Zone: 3

Color photograph on page 243.

Light Requirements:

Additional Benefit:

Honey Locust is a popular tree in the home landscape. This fast-growing tree provides fine texture and interesting form in both summer and winter. The small green leaves (actually leaflets) provide shade while allowing the sun to reach the grass below. The leaves turn a nice yellow in the fall. The flowers aren't showy, but they do provide a pleasant fragrance in early June. If you have a honey locust, take good care of it and keep it healthy. Mature specimens are quite impressive.

WHEN TO PLANT

Plant balled-and-burlapped trees as soon as possible after they are purchased. Container-grown plants can be planted throughout the growing season.

WHERE TO PLANT

Grow Honey Locust in full sun with moist, well-drained soil. It is a tough plant that tolerates a wide range of conditions including drought, salt, and high pH. Honey Locusts are frequently used near roadways and in other difficult growing spots. You will see it used near patios and decks for shade. The Honey Locust is commonly used in lawn areas. Its filtered shade is cooling, but not detrimental to the grass.

HOW TO PLANT

Plant the tree with the root flare at or slightly above the soil line. Dig a shallow planting hole the same depth as and three to five times wider than the root system. Place the tree in the planting hole. Remove the container, twine, and metal baskets. Cut away the burlap. Fill the hole with existing soil, water to settle the soil, and mulch.

CARE AND MAINTENANCE

Honey Locusts suffer from a variety of insect and disease problems. If you ever sat under a Honey Locust, you have probably experienced a few of the pests firsthand. In the spring, Honey Locusts are often attacked by plant bugs and leafhoppers. These insects often drop from the tree onto the innocent bystanders below. The insects won't kill the tree, but heavy populations can delay leaf development and cause twig dieback. The biggest problem is canker. Fungal diseases can cause sunken and discolored areas to develop on the branches and trunk. The area above the canker eventually dies. Prevention is the only treatment for this disease. Select healthy, disease-free trees and avoid injuries to the trunk and branches during transplanting and maintenance. These wounds serve as entryways for the disease. Keep lawn mowers and weed whips away from the trunk. Prune during the dormant season whenever possible. Honey Locusts also produce lots of sprouts off the main trunk. Remove these during the dormant season or dry weather to maintain the tree's structure and appearance.

ADDITIONAL INFORMATION

The Honey Locust's fruit is a long brown pod. Some gardeners think they are ugly, but I think they can be ornamental in the winter. There is no debate about the mess they create when they fall. Many podless cultivars have been introduced to alleviate this problem.

ADDITIONAL SPECIES, CULTIVARS, OR VARIETIES

Select cultivars with the desired growth habit. Remember, podless cultivars are available for those who don't want the mess.

 Did You Know?

The Honey Locust, Gleditsia triacanthos, *has long, thin thorns. During the Civil War, soldiers used the thorns as pins to fasten their coats. In the landscape, these thorns can create a nuisance to the people using and maintaining the tree.*

Horsechestnut

Aesculus hippocastanum

Size: 50 or more feet tall and 40 feet wide
Soil: Moist; well-drained
Zone: 4

Color photograph on page 243.

Light Requirements:

Additional Benefit:

Flowering Horsechestnuts steal the show in late spring in the landscape. Their large, cone-shaped blossoms make them a popular choice for gardeners. After they bloom in late spring, Horsechestnuts become just another shade tree for the rest of the year. The Horsechestnut's coarse texture, attractive platy bark, and large size make it a good fit in park-like settings.

WHEN TO PLANT

Horsechestnuts respond best to spring transplanting. Plant balled-and-burlapped trees as soon possible after they are purchased. Container-grown plants can be planted throughout the growing season.

WHERE TO PLANT

Plant Horsechestnut trees in full sun or lightly shaded locations. They prefer moist, well-drained soil, although I have seen them growing in clay soil. Horsechestnuts are massive trees that need room to showcase their beauty. Place them where their late spring bloom can be enjoyed. Use them as a shade or large specimen tree in expansive lawn areas or on a woodland edge.

HOW TO PLANT

Locate the tree's root flare. That is the bell-shaped area where the roots angle away from the trunk. Plant the tree with the root flare at or slightly above the soil line. Dig a shallow planting hole the same depth as and three to five times wider than the root system. Place the tree in the planting hole. Make sure the tree is straight, moving it by the rootball, not the trunk, to minimize root damage. Remove the container, twine, and metal baskets. Cut away the burlap. Fill the hole with existing soil, water to settle the soil, and mulch.

CARE AND MAINTENANCE

Leaf blotch, anthracnose, and powdery mildew can all cause leaves to discolor and drop prematurely. Rake and destroy infected leaves as soon as they fall from the tree. This reduces the source for future infection. Healthy trees can tolerate these diseases. It's too late to treat the disease once symptoms appear. Water the Horsechestnut during extended dry periods.

ADDITIONAL INFORMATION

Horsechestnut trees produce light brown, spiny fruits that look like the spiked metal head of a mace. Inside are dark brown nuts with a light blotch. The falling fruit and seeds can create a mess. Squirrels will take care of the nuts by planting them throughout the neighborhood. I still haven't found the Horsechestnut or the squirrel responsible for the seedlings that appear in my garden each year.

ADDITIONAL SPECIES, CULTIVARS, OR VARIETIES

'Baumannii' is a fruitless variety that produces long-lasting double flowers. They are hard to find and slow to establish, but they are still a good choice for home owners. Ohio Buckeye, *Aesculus glabra,* is a shorter cousin to the Horsechestnut. It grows to 30 to 40 feet tall, making it a better fit for most home landscapes. The tree starts off the season with yellow-green flowers that are attractive, but less impressive than the Horsechestnut. The real show comes in the fall when the leaves turn a brilliant orange. The common name is descriptive of the seed. Like the Horsechestnut's, it is glossy brown with a white scar, and looks like a buck's eye.

 Did You Know?

These are NOT the holiday chestnuts that are roasted on an open fire. Those edible chestnuts come from the American Chestnut tree, Castanea dentata. *The nuts and twigs of Horsechestnuts are poisonous.*

Ironwood

Ostrya virginiana

Other Name: Hophornbeam **Size:** 30 feet tall and 20 or more feet wide **Soil:** Moist; well-drained **Zones:** 3b to 5 *Color photograph on page 243.*	**Light Requirements:** **Additional Benefit:**

Ironwood is an underutilized native tree. It is a slow grower, adding 10 to 15 feet of height in fifteen years. The slow growth rate and shade tolerance make it an appropriate tree for small settings and city lots. It is somewhat pyramidal when young, becoming more rounded (like many of us!) with age. The fine, horizontal branches and finely shredded bark ensure year-round interest.

WHEN TO PLANT
Plant balled-and-burlapped or container-grown trees in the early spring. Ironwood takes time to recover from transplanting.

WHERE TO PLANT
Plant Ironwood trees in full sun or partial shade. They prefer moist, well-drained soil, but can tolerate dry, gravelly soils and sandy soils. These small trees are a good fit in small landscapes. Plant them in groupings for a bigger impact in larger settings. Ironwood's graceful growth habit helps soften vertical elements in the landscape. Take advantage of Ironwood's shade tolerance. Use them in woodland gardens or as understory plants for your larger shade trees. This native tree is at home in both natural and manicured landscapes.

HOW TO PLANT
Locate the tree's root flare. That is the bell-shaped area where the roots angle away from the trunk. Plant the tree with the root flare at or slightly above the soil line. Dig a shallow planting hole the same depth as and three to five times wider than the root system. Place the tree in the planting hole. Make sure the tree is straight, but move it by the rootball, not the trunk, to minimize root damage. Remove the container, twine, and metal baskets. Cut away the burlap. Fill the hole with existing soil, water to settle the soil, and mulch.

CARE AND MAINTENANCE

Ironwood has no serious pests. It tolerates dry soil, but should be watered during extended drought periods. I observed quite a bit of damage on trees that were not watered during the drought of 1988. Once established, this tree will grow a bit faster.

ADDITIONAL INFORMATION

Ironwood is native to Minnesota. It flowers in the early spring. It produces a subtle show providing a glimpse of other spring blooms yet to come. The long, narrow flowers (catkins) droop from the fine branches. These later develop into small, hop-like fruit; thus the other common name, Hophornbeam.

ADDITIONAL SPECIES, CULTIVARS, OR VARIETIES

Ironwood may be a little difficult to find. Start by checking with nurseries and garden centers that specialize in native plants. Hornbeam or Blue Beech (*Carpinus caroliniana*), also called Ironwood, is similar in common name and appearance. The bark of Ironwood (Ostrya) is finely shredded, while the bark of *Carpinus* is smooth, gray, and looks like flexed muscles. The other common names for *Carpinus* are Musclewood and Blue Beech, after its appearance. (See Musclewood for more information on this plant.)

 Did You Know?

Ironwood may be small, but it is very strong. The wood is hard and durable. That helps the plant resist wind and ice damage. The strong wood has been used for wedges, levers, and other tools. Ironwood's small size has limited its use as a lumber tree.

TREES

Japanese Tree Lilac

Syringa reticulata

Size: 25 feet tall by 15 feet wide	**Light Requirements:**
Soil: Well-drained	
Zones: All	
	Additional Benefit:
Color photograph on page 243.	

Would you like large, white, fragrant, Lilac blossoms in mid-June? You will have them once you plant a Japanese Tree Lilac in your landscape. The massive blossoms look just like common Lilac, only bigger. They are fragrant, but the fragrance gets mixed reviews from gardeners. You'll have to let your nose make the call. Japanese Tree Lilac offers more than just pretty flowers. The bark is smooth and shiny like a Cherry tree, becoming gray and rough with age. The attractive bark adds year-round interest to the tree. It's a small beauty that fits into most garden locations.

WHEN TO PLANT

Japanese Tree Lilacs recover quickly from transplanting. Plant balled-and-burlapped trees as soon as possible after purchase. Container-grown trees can be planted throughout the growing season.

WHERE TO PLANT

Grow Japanese Tree Lilacs in full sun and well-drained soil. In a good location, Japanese Tree Lilacs will add about 9 to 12 feet of growth in six to eight years. These small, flowering trees make nice specimen plants in both small and large settings. Plant them in small groups for greater impact. Use Japanese Tree Lilacs near large homes and buildings to soften and blend these structures into the landscape.

HOW TO PLANT

Plant the tree with the root flare at or slightly above the soil line. Dig a shallow planting hole the same depth as and three to five times wider than the root system. Place the tree in the planting hole. Remove the container, twine, and metal baskets. Cut away the burlap. Fill the hole with existing soil, water, and mulch.

CARE AND MAINTENANCE

Japanese Tree Lilacs are the easiest Lilacs to grow. Once the framework is established, minimal pruning is needed to remove dead wood and maintain the shape. They tend to bloom heavily one year and light the next. Prevent this variation by removing spent flowers right away. The plant will then put its energy into producing next year's flower buds instead of setting seed. You may need a pole pruner to reach the flowers on top. Japanese Tree Lilacs are fairly trouble free in our state. They do not suffer from borer, mildew, and scale like the common Lilacs. I have seen some herbicide damage on these plants. Be sure to keep weed killers, including weed and feed products, away from this and other ornamental plants.

ADDITIONAL INFORMATION

Japanese Tree Lilacs may compete with surrounding grass and groundcovers. Mulch the soil to eliminate weeds and keep the roots cool and moist. Or use groundcovers suited for dry shade that can compete with the shallow roots of the Japanese Tree Lilac.

ADDITIONAL SPECIES, CULTIVARS, OR VARIETIES

Plants are available single or multistemmed. Select the one that best fits your landscape design. 'Ivory Silk' is the most readily available cultivar. It is a more compact plant with a rounded crown. 'Ivory Silk' starts flowering at an earlier age and produces more flowers than the species. Pekin Lilac, *Syringa pekinensis*, is similar to Japanese Tree Lilac. This smaller plant has beautiful amber bark, but a less impressive flower display.

 Did You Know?

Wisconsin's largest Japanese Tree Lilac is located on E. Division Street in Shawano. It measures 35 feet tall with branches spreading out 27 feet wide. The circumference of the trunk measured at 4½ feet above the ground is 70 inches. It might be worth a weekend trip. It must look spectacular in bloom!

Kentucky Coffee Tree

Gymnocladus dioicus

Size: 75 feet tall and 40 feet wide
Soil: Moist; well-drained
Zones: 3b to 4

Color photograph on page 243.

Light Requirements:

Additional Benefit:

Kentucky Coffee Tree is a southern Minnesota native that makes an excellent landscape plant. It is a close relative of the Honey Locust. Both are in the Pea family, although it is hard to believe these big trees are related to the Pea plants in your garden. If you take a close look at the fragrant flowers in early June, you will see the similarity. Use the large Kentucky Coffee Tree to provide shade in the summer and an interesting silhouette in winter. Give it time and space to grow. The Kentucky Coffee Tree grows at a rate of about 10 to 14 feet in ten years. This versatile plant tolerates a wide range of conditions while blending into formal and informal landscape designs.

WHEN TO PLANT

Kentucky Coffee Tree responds best to spring transplanting. Plant balled-and-burlapped trees as soon as possible after they are purchased. Container-grown trees can be planted throughout the growing season.

WHERE TO PLANT

Grow Kentucky Coffee Trees in full sun. They prefer moist, well-drained soil, but will tolerate wet and dry locations. This tough tree is a great choice for windy sites and urban areas. Use Kentucky Coffee Trees as specimen plants. Their large compound leaves can reach 36 inches in length and 24 inches in width. They are made up of many small blue-green leaflets that are only 1½ to 3 inches long. The feathery leaves help soften the coarse features of this plant. Once the leaves drop, the brown pods, scaly bark, and thick, stark branches stand out against the winter sky.

TREES

How to Plant
Plant the tree with the root flare at or slightly above the soil line. Dig a shallow planting hole the same depth as and three to five times wider than the root system. Place the tree in the planting hole. Remove the container, twine, and metal baskets. Cut away the burlap. Fill the hole with existing soil, water to settle the soil, and mulch.

Care and Maintenance
Kentucky Coffee Tree is a low-maintenance plant. There are no serious pests. The fruit and leaves, however, can be messy. Fall leaves tend to drop over a long period of time. The small leaflets can easily be chopped with the mower. The long leaf stem (rachis) is what causes the mess. Meticulous gardeners may be annoyed by this extended fall cleanup.

Additional Information

The toxic seeds of Kentucky Coffee Tree contain low levels of alkaloid materials that can cause nausea. Early Kentucky settlers used the seeds as a coffee substitute. It is thought that the roasting helped eliminate the toxic properties. I hear the taste isn't that great—I think I'll stick to the real thing.

Additional Species, Cultivars, or Varieties
Kentucky Coffee Tree may be hard to locate, so pick up the phone before you hop in the car. 'Espresso' is a fruitless (male) cultivar. It is smaller with an Elm-like growth habit.

 Did You Know?

The botanical name for Kentucky Coffee Tree is from the Greek language. Gymnos *stands for naked and* klados *means a branch, referring to the fact that the tree is deciduous.* Dioica *tells us the plant is dioecious, which means there are male and female plants.*

Larch

Larix species

Other Name: Tamarack **Size:** Up to 80 feet tall and 25 feet wide **Soil:** Moist; well-drained **Zones:** All *Color photograph on page 243.*	**Light Requirements:**  **Additional Benefit:**

Driving through northern Minnesota, you are bound to pass a grove of our native Larch trees. These tall, pyramidal plants are most noticeable in the fall when their needles turn a beautiful golden yellow. Look for them in wet, soggy locations. In the landscape, you are more likely to see the European or Japanese Larch. These beautiful trees are less tolerant of wet soil, but more adapted to transplanting than our American Larch. Consider using one of these graceful plants near a pond or water feature in large landscapes.

WHEN TO PLANT

Plant balled-and-burlapped trees in the spring when the plants are dormant. Container-grown plants can be planted throughout the growing season.

WHERE TO PLANT

Plant Larches in full sun in moist, well-drained soil. Though our native Larch tolerates wet, soggy soils in the wild, it performs best in landscapes with moist, well-drained soil. Avoid dry soil and polluted locations. Larches are good plants for large landscapes. The European and Japanese Larches make attractive specimen plants. Plant individually or en masse. Groupings of Larch make effective screens. Use the American Larch for moist areas. Create a grove using a grouping of these plants.

HOW TO PLANT

Locate the tree's root flare. That is the bell-shaped area where the roots angle away from the trunk. Plant the tree with the root flare at or slightly above the soil line. Dig a shallow planting hole the same depth as and three to five times wider than the root system. Place the tree in the planting hole. Remove the container, twine, and metal baskets. Cut away the burlap. Fill the hole with existing soil, water to settle the soil, and mulch.

CARE AND MAINTENANCE

Properly placed Larch trees need little maintenance. They suffer from just a few insect and disease problems. Healthy plants usually resist and tolerate the damage. Mulch to keep the roots cool and moist. Water plants during dry periods.

ADDITIONAL INFORMATION

Larches are deciduous conifers. The needles turn golden yellow in the fall before falling to the ground. The tree silhouette is quite effective in the winter landscape. I have heard several stories of new home owners and uninformed ground managers cutting down their Larch tree because this evergreen lost all its needles in the fall. I am glad I didn't have to deliver the news that the felling of the tree wasn't needed.

ADDITIONAL SPECIES, CULTIVARS, OR VARIETIES

The American Larch, *Larix laricina*, is also called Tamarack. It is native to Minnesota, and grows in wet, boggy conditions. Although it is a nice plant, it is the least tolerant of transplanting. Look for this plant at nurseries specializing in native plants. The Japanese Larch, *Larix kaempferi*, is the most ornamental, but needs lots of space to grow and show off its beauty. Both the Japanese and European Larch are more adaptable to transplanting than the American Larch. The European Larch, *Larix decidua*, is a good screening or specimen plant for large areas.

 Did You Know?

Tamarack is very rot-resistant wood. It was once used for water pipes. Parts of the tree were hollowed out and individual pieces were connected. Sections of an old system were discovered during a construction project in downtown Milwaukee. Many pieces were still intact.

Linden

Tilia species

Other Name: Basswood
Size: Up to 75 feet tall and 40 feet wide
Soil: Moist; well-drained
Zones: All

Color photograph on page 243.

Light Requirements:

Additional Benefits:

Lindens are a useful group of plants. The large American Linden can be found in our native landscapes, and its European relatives have become important landscape plants here. The Lindens provide several seasons of interest. The fragrant yellow flowers are quite effective in late June and early July. The fall color is usually a good yellow. All Lindens have attractive forms, adding year-round interest.

WHEN TO PLANT

Lindens adapt well to transplanting. Plant balled-and-burlapped trees as soon as possible after they are purchased. Container-grown plants can be planted throughout the growing season.

WHERE TO PLANT

Plant Lindens in full sun with moist, well-drained soil. Most of the Lindens tolerate the heavy clay soil. All of the Lindens make good shade trees. The American Linden is good for naturalized settings or woodland areas. The Littleleaf Linden is the most frequently used in the landscape. It is an excellent choice for street trees, planters, and planting beds. The strong, pyramidal shape, and glossy, green leaves make this an attractive choice for most situations. Use Littleleaf Lindens to line a driveway or a wide walkway. Littleleaf Lindens can also be trimmed into a large hedge.

HOW TO PLANT

Locate the tree's root flare. That is the bell-shaped area where the roots angle away from the trunk. Plant the tree with the root flare at or slightly above the soil line. Dig a shallow planting hole the same depth as and three to five times wider than the root system. Place the tree in the planting hole and remove the container, twine, and metal baskets. Cut away the burlap. Fill the hole with existing soil, water to settle the soil, and mulch.

CARE AND MAINTENANCE

Lindens require minimal maintenance. Prune young trees to establish their structure. Little Leaf Linden tends to have poor branch structure. They produce lots of side branches very close together. These will need to be thinned out to prevent future problems with rubbing branches. There are a few diseases and insects that attack Lindens. It is not unusual to find a few holes chewed in their leaves. Before you panic, step back and take a look at the whole tree. The damage is usually minimal and does not require treatment.

ADDITIONAL INFORMATION

Lindens have fragrant yellow flowers. Watch for them in late June or early July. You will probably smell them before you see them. Bees love the flowers. In fact, the honey they make from these flowers is supposed to be some of best.

ADDITIONAL SPECIES, CULTIVARS, OR VARIETIES

American Linden, *Tilia americana,* is a large, irregularly shaped, upright tree with large leaves. It's a good plant for large, informal yards and naturalized landscapes. Use the 'Redmond' cultivar for urban situations. Littleleaf Linden, *Tilia cordata,* has small, glossy, heart-shaped leaves. Its smaller size and pyramidal shape make it suitable for landscapes. This tough tree is also very tolerant of pollution and city conditions.

 Did You Know?

The name Tilia *is Latin for lime. In Europe, they often call these Lime Trees.* Cordata *means heart shaped, referring to the leaves. This is sometimes called Small-leaved Lime Tree. The wood has been used for cabinets, excelsior, and pulp.*

Magnolia

Magnolia species

Size: 15 to 40 feet tall and up to 30 feet wide

Soil: Moist

Zone: 4

Color photograph on page 244.

Light Requirements:

Additional Benefit:

When you hear the word Magnolia, you may think of the South and its trees with large, fragrant flowers and huge, glossy, green leaves. Many northern gardeners would also like to enjoy these beautiful plants. We can't enjoy the same species as our southern friends, but we can enjoy Magnolias. Select a Magnolia hardy to your landscape. Plant it in the right location and keep your fingers crossed that Mother Nature cooperates. Once you have seen a blooming Magnolia, you will understand why gardeners grow this tree. The smooth, gray bark is beautiful year-round. The form of this plant makes it suitable for most landscapes. And when the blooms appear, they are spectacular.

WHEN TO PLANT

Magnolias do not respond well to transplanting. Plant balled-and-burlapped and container-grown plants in the early spring.

WHERE TO PLANT

Plant Magnolias in full sun or light shade. They must have moist, well-drained soil. These trees will not tolerate wet or dry conditions. Small Magnolias can be used as an accent, a flowering specimen, or as a mass display in small or large yards. Save the larger Magnolias for bigger settings.

HOW TO PLANT

Locate the tree's root flare. Plant the tree with the root flare at or slightly above the soil line. Dig a shallow planting hole the same depth as and three to five times wider than the root system. Place the tree in the planting hole and remove the container, twine, and metal baskets. Cut away the burlap. Fill the hole with existing soil, water to settle the soil, and mulch.

CARE AND MAINTENANCE

Magnolias have no serious pest problems. Water trees during drought. Mulch the soil with wood chips or another organic material to keep the roots cool and moist. Magnolias are subject to snow and ice damage. Reduce the risk with proper training and pruning. Very little pruning is needed once the framework is established on young trees. Prune Magnolias after flowering. Finish the job by early summer so you don't interfere with the next season's bloom.

ADDITIONAL INFORMATION

Magnolias will occasionally develop fruit shaped like a small cucumber. It is pink and splits to reveal orange seeds.

ADDITIONAL SPECIES, CULTIVARS, OR VARIETIES

The small Star Magnolia, *Magnolia stellata,* is hardy in Zone 4b. This Magnolia can be used as a large shrub or a small tree. It has white, 3- to 4-inch-wide flowers. Both the Star and Saucer Magnolias are earlier bloomers. Their blossoms are often damaged by early spring cold snaps. Reduce the risk with proper plant placement. Do not plant Magnolias on the south side of your home where the warmer temperatures will encourage earlier bloom. The Saucer Magnolia, *Magnolia × soulangiana,* is a small tree that is only reliably hardy in Zone 5 but is often tried in Zone 4. It produces large, pink flowers before the leaves. The Cucumber Magnolia, *Magnolia acuminata,* is the hardiest (Zone 4). This large Magnolia is pyramidal when young, but becomes wide and spreading with age. The flower display is less effective on this magnolia, but it is still an attention grabber. I think the large, glossy leaves remind people of Southern Magnolias.

 Did You Know?

Fossils have been uncovered showing the Magnolia was around long before modern man. The Chinese were the first to grow this plant. They used the buds for flavoring rice and medicine. The bark of the Cucumber Magnolia was used as a substitute for quinine in the treatment of malaria.

Maple

Acer species

Size: Up to 75 feet tall and 40 feet wide **Soil:** Moist; well-drained **Zones:** All *Color photograph on page 244.*	**Light Requirements:** **Additional Benefits:**

The familiar Maple is one of the most widely used landscape plants. I'm sure you remember throwing Maple seeds (we called them helicopters or whirlybirds) in the air as a child. Select the species and cultivars that best fit your growing conditions and landscape design.

WHEN TO PLANT
Maples can be transplanted in the spring or fall. Move larger plants of Red Maple, *Acer rubrum,* in the spring. Plant balled-and-burlapped trees as soon as possible after they are purchased. Container-grown plants can be planted throughout the growing season.

WHERE TO PLANT
Maples prefer full sun and moist well-drained soil. Some species are more tolerant of wet, dry, or other difficult conditions.

HOW TO PLANT
Plant the tree with the root flare at or slightly above the soil line. Dig a shallow hole the same depth as and three to five times wider than the root system. Remove the container, twine, and metal baskets and cut away the burlap. Fill the hole with existing soil, water, and mulch.

CARE AND MAINTENANCE
Prune young trees to establish a central leader and sturdy framework. Maple trees will bleed when pruned in the spring. It won't hurt the plant. Verticillium wilt can be deadly. Do not replace Verticillium wilt-killed trees with other susceptible plants. Anthracnose, petiole borer, cottony maple scale, aphids, and galls are a few of the problems Maples are susceptible to. Healthy trees will tolerate all these pests. Rake and destroy the spotted anthracnose-infected leaves. Tolerate the galls. They are just benign bumps on leaves caused by insects.

Additional Information

Maples are shallow-rooted trees that make it difficult to grow and maintain grass. Eliminate this frustration by mulching the roots or growing shade-tolerant groundcovers under the tree. Do NOT cut or bury the roots. This can eventually kill the tree.

Additional Species, Cultivars, or Varieties

Sugar Maples, *Acer saccharum,* are native trees that grow best in moist, rich soil. They do not tolerate heat, drought, or salt. Use them as shade trees in lawn areas and other park-like settings. The Norway Maple, *Acer platanoides*, is a tough Maple tolerant of urban conditions in Zone 4b. It has been overused as a street and shade tree. The large leaves cast heavy shade making it difficult to grow grass. The red-leafed forms are often incorrectly called Red Maple. Norway Maple has become a weed problem in our natural areas. The true Red Maple, *Acer rubrum,* gets its common name from its brilliant red fall color. Red Maples will tolerate wet conditions, but must have acid soil. The leaves yellow and the trees struggle in the high pH soils. Silver Maple, *Acer saccharinum*, is a fast-growing, weak-wooded native plant that tolerates wet soil. It tends to fall apart in storms. Proper pruning can help extend the life of this tree. The Freeman Maple, *Acer × freemanii*, is a naturally occurring hybrid of Silver and Red Maples. It has the stronger wood and often the fall color of the Red Maple. It gets its increased tolerance to alkaline soils from the Silver Maple. 'Autumn Blaze' is a seedless cultivar with good red fall color. Amur Maple, *Acer ginnala*, is the little cousin of this group. This small multistemmed tree grows 15 to 20 feet tall. Use it as a small specimen, screen, accent, or container plant. It has fragrant white flowers, red fruit and a wonderful orange-red fall color.

 Did You Know?

It takes about forty gallons of Sugar Maple sap to make one gallon of maple syrup.

Musclewood

Carpinus caroliniana

Other Names: American Hornbeam,
   Blue Beech, Ironwood
Size: Up to 30 feet tall and wide
Soil: Moist
Zones: 3b to 4
Color photograph on page 244.

Light Requirements:

Musclewood is a beautiful element in nature that is often overlooked for use in the home landscape. It tolerates moist soil, even
temporary flooding, and shade. That is quite unusual for specimen-
quality shade trees. The fine texture and smooth, gray bark give this
tree year-round appeal. The Elm-like leaves turn yellow, orange, or red
in the fall. The flowers are not very effective, but the papery fruit can
persist and add winter interest.

WHEN TO PLANT

Musclewood trees do not respond well to transplanting. Plant
balled-and-burlapped and container-grown trees in the spring.

WHERE TO PLANT

Musclewood is native to the forests of Minnesota. The trees are often
found growing along streams and swamps. They prefer partial shade
and moist soil in the landscape, but will tolerate heavy shade and
temporary flooding. Musclewood works equally well in a naturalized area or a more formal landscape. Their shade tolerance makes
them a good choice for an understory tree in woodland settings. The
attractive bark, fine texture, and growth habit make them specimen-
quality plants. Or you can use multistemmed forms of this wide
plant to provide screening.

HOW TO PLANT

Locate the tree's root flare. That is the bell-shaped area where the
roots angle away from the trunk. Plant the tree with the root flare at
or slightly above the soil line. Dig a shallow planting hole the same
depth as and three to five times wider than the root system. Place the
tree in the planting hole, making sure the tree is straight moving it
by the rootball, not the trunk, to minimize root damage. Remove the

container, twine, and metal baskets. Cut away the burlap. Fill the hole with existing soil, water to settle the soil, and mulch.

CARE AND MAINTENANCE

Patience is the key to care. New trees take time to adjust to their new location. The slow-growing Musclewood averages less than a foot of growth each year. Once established, Musclewood requires very little maintenance. Although trees are subject to damage from ice storms, properly trained trees will be less susceptible. Prune young trees to establish a structurally sound framework. Minimal pruning should be done after this. Mulch the roots to keep the soil cool and moist.

ADDITIONAL INFORMATION

Musclewood goes by several common names. The slate gray, fluted bark looks like flexed muscles. That's how it got the name Musclewood. The bark also resembles that of a Beech; thus Blue or Water Beech. And like the other Ironwood, *Ostrya virginiana* has very hard and durable wood.

ADDITIONAL SPECIES, CULTIVARS, OR VARIETIES

Musclewood may take a little effort to locate. They are sold as single or multistemmed plants. Call your local nursery or garden center about available plants. I know of a nursery that is working on cultivars with reliable fall color. Hopefully, we will see some introductions soon.

 Did You Know?

One of the largest, if not the biggest, Musclewood trees is in Ulster County, New York. It measured 95 inches in circumference and 69 feet tall with a spread of 56 feet.

Oak

Quercus species

Size: 50 to 80 feet tall and wide **Soil:** Moist; well-drained **Zones:** All *Color photograph on page 244.*	**Light Requirements:** **Additional Benefit:**

Oaks are the majestic trees of nature, and they bring the same feel-ing of majesty to large landscapes. Oak trees are becoming more readily available thanks in part to an increased interest in native plants and greater transplanting success. These large trees are slow growing, but can still be enjoyed in our lifetime. Plus they are a great gift to leave to our children.

WHEN TO PLANT
Most Oaks are difficult to transplant. Plant balled-and-burlapped trees in the spring as soon after purchase as possible.

WHERE TO PLANT
In general, Oaks prefer full sun and moist, well-drained soil. Plant these trees for future shade and specimen plants. Give them plenty of room; they will eventually need it.

HOW TO PLANT
Plant the tree with the root flare at or slightly above the soil line. Dig a shallow planting hole the same depth as and three to five times wider than the root system. Place the tree in the hole. Remove the twine, metal baskets, and cut away the burlap. Fill the hole with existing soil, water the soil, and mulch it.

CARE AND MAINTENANCE
Prune Oaks during the dormant season to minimize the risk of Oak wilt infection. Oak wilt is a deadly disease that enters through wounds, such as pruning cuts. The upper leaves wilt, then turn brown and drop from Oak wilt-infected trees. Apply pruning paint to Oaks pruned during the growing season. This is the only time you should use a pruning paint. Consult your local Extension Office or certified arborist immediately if you suspect Oak wilt. The fungal

disease anthracnose causes leaves to brown and drop. Rake and destroy the fallen leaves. Bumps and strange-looking growths on stems and leaves are common, but not harmful. The growths, called galls, are caused by insects feeding on the plant. Several Oaks are very intolerant of alkaline (high pH) soil. They develop chlorosis, a yellowing of leaves, due to a lack of iron and manganese. Avoid planting acid-loving oaks in alkaline soils.

ADDITIONAL INFORMATION

Oaks tend to hold some of their brown leaves over the winter. That can add subtle interest and sound in the winter landscape.

ADDITIONAL SPECIES, CULTIVARS, OR VARIETIES

White Oak, *Quercus alba,* is a native tree with beautiful, red fall color. It is hardy to Zone 4b. It prefers moist, well-drained soil, but will tolerate dry soil. It is difficult to transplant and intolerant of high pH soil. The native Swamp White Oak, *Quercus bicolor,* tolerates moist, even wet, soil conditions. It is a good choice for urban areas and the exfoliating bark is an added ornamental feature. This Oak is hardy in Zones 4 and 5. Bur Oak, *Quercus macrocarpa,* will tolerate wet to dry soil. It has no real fall color and is difficult to transplant, but the coarse texture and furrowed bark provide year-round interest in the landscape. The Red Oak, *Quercus rubra,* is a good choice for urban areas. This native Oak is faster growing than other Oaks and is hardy statewide. It needs well-drained soil. Pin Oak, *Quercus palustris,* is also faster growing. It tolerates moist soil and is hardy in Zone 4b. This tree will develop chlorosis when grown in alkaline soils. Both the Pin and Red Oak have red fall color.

 Did You Know?

The Bur Oak is the oak of the Oak savannas. These are grassy areas with a few Bur Oaks scattered throughout. The thick, corky bark of the Bur Oak protected it from the fires that traversed the savannas.

Ornamental Plums and Cherries

Prunus species

Other Names: Flowering Almond, Cherry, Newport Plum, Purple Leaf Sand Cherry
Size: Up to 30 feet tall and wide
Soil: Well-drained
Zones: All
Color photograph on page 244.

Light Requirements:

Additional Benefits:

Ornamental Plums and Cherries are grown for their impressive flowers or decorative foliage. These small trees can add early spring interest to both large and small landscapes. Many have decorative bark, fruit for the wildlife, and interesting form. The native Cherries and Plums are often considered less ornamental, but are more suited to our climate. Some of the fruit is attractive to birds. Check with nurseries and garden centers that specialize in native plants.

WHEN TO PLANT

The Ornamental Plums and Cherries respond best to spring transplanting. Plant bare-root, balled-and-burlapped, and container-grown trees in the spring.

WHERE TO PLANT

The Ornamental Plums and Cherries tend to be short lived in our area. Proper siting is important with all these trees. They need well-drained soil and have difficulty growing in heavy clay soil. Grow them in a protected site or on the east side of your home in full sun. That will reduce the risk of winter injury and flower damage from a late spring frost. Use these ornamental trees as a temporary (10 to 20 years) specimen or accent plant. They work well in patio and Japanese gardens.

HOW TO PLANT

Plant the tree with the root flare at or slightly above the soil line. Dig a shallow planting hole the same depth as and three to five times wider than the root system. Remove the container, twine, and metal cage, and cut away the burlap. Fill the hole with existing soil, water, and mulch.

Care and Maintenance

These ornamental plants have many insect and disease problems. Healthy plants are the best defense against these problems. Plant trees in protected areas with well-drained soil. Mulch the roots to keep them cool. Reduce problems by avoiding injuries caused by mowers, weed whips, or other items. Prune these trees during dry weather to avoid the spread of disease. Despite your best efforts, these trees tend to be short lived.

Additional Information

These plants also tend to sucker freely. You will discover little trees throughout your lawn. Cut them off below ground level to discourage resprouting. Do not treat the sprouts with chemicals unless you want to kill the parent tree, too.

Additional Species, Cultivars, or Varieties

Newport Plum, *Prunus cerasifera* 'Newport', is probably one of the most popular purple-leaved plums. Consider *Prunus virginiana* 'Schubert' or its branch sport 'Canada Red'. They have green leaves that turn reddish purple for the season. Both are hardy throughout the state. Purple-leaf Sand Cherry, *Prunus × cistena*, is more of a shrub than a tree. It is hardy throughout Minnesota. Renewal pruning will reduce pest problems and maintain the plant's form and leaf color. Amur Chokecherry, *Prunus maackii*, is a reliable bloomer and hardy throughout Minnesota. It flowers after the leaves making the display a little less effective. The real feature is the shiny, amber-colored exfoliating bark. The Double-Flowering Plum, *Prunus triloba*, is hardy to Zone 4. It has double pink flowers and does not produce fruit.

 Did You Know?

The Black Cherry, Prunus serotina, *is native to Minnesota forests. It has distinct scaly bark that looks like someone glued burnt potato chips to the trunk. It has hard, tight-grained red wood. It finishes well and has long been used for making furniture and cabinets.*

Pine

Pinus

Size: Up to 75 feet tall and 40 feet wide **Soil:** Well-drained **Zones:** All *Color photograph on page 244.*	**Light Requirements:** **Additional Benefit:**

Pines are an important evergreen in the landscape. They have long been used as windbreaks, screens, and wildlife habitats. Don't overlook them as specimen plants, and they also create a nice backdrop for deciduous plants. The dark green needles make the colorful bark of Birches, Dogwoods, and Red Maples stand out. Most Pines are pyramidal when young. As they age, they open up, becoming more picturesque. Planted in the right location with sufficient space, Pines can provide years of beauty.

WHEN TO PLANT
Plant balled-and-burlapped trees in the spring or fall as soon as possible after they are purchased. Container-grown plants can be planted throughout the growing season. Plant by October 1 to allow the plants to get established before winter.

WHERE TO PLANT
Pines prefer full-sun locations with moist, well-drained soil. Most Pines can tolerate dry conditions. Use these evergreens for windbreaks, screens, specimen plants, and winter color. Select the Pine that is best suited for the job. Give them room to grow. Remember, these nice, small "Christmas" trees will grow into large, spreading trees sooner than you think.

HOW TO PLANT
Plant the tree with the root flare at or slightly above the soil line. Dig a shallow planting hole the same depth as and three to five times wider than the root system. Place the tree in the planting hole. Remove the container, twine, and metal baskets, and cut away the burlap. Fill the hole with existing soil, water, and mulch.

CARE AND MAINTENANCE

Pines need minimal pruning. Prune out dead and damaged branches and maintain a central leader. Watch for insects and disease problems. There are several fungal diseases and insect problems that can be damaging. Contact your local University of Minnesota Extension Office or certified arborist for diagnosis and treatment recommendations.

ADDITIONAL INFORMATION

Pines can be pruned to limit growth. This is done in the spring as the new growth elongates. This tight, new growth is called a candle. Cut off $1/2$ or $2/3$ of the candles to shorten and thicken the new growth.

ADDITIONAL SPECIES, CULTIVARS, OR VARIETIES

White Pine, *Pinus strobus,* is native to Minnesota. This beautiful tree becomes picturesque with age. The soft green needles gently rustle in the wind, adding another element to the landscape. It is hardy statewide, but it will not tolerate salt, pollution, and alkaline soils. Austrian Pine, *Pinus nigra,* was once the workhorse of the landscape. Hardy to Zone 4, it tolerated the tough urban conditions found in most home settings. Unfortunately, it has been besieged by pest problems. The blue-green needles of Scotch Pine, *Pinus sylvestris,* provide an attractive contrast to the orange bark. This tough tree will tolerate a variety of soils, as long as they are well drained. The Minnesota State Tree, Red Pine, *Pinus resinosa,* is a tough native that is frequently used for windbreaks. It has red bark and green needles that turn yellow-green over the winter.

 Did You Know?

White Pine has been an important lumber tree throughout the history of the United States. Carpenters like the wood because it is easy to work with and finishes nicely.

Redbud

Cercis canadensis

Other Name: Eastern Redbud
Size: 30 feet tall and wide
Soil: Moist; well-drained
Zone: 4

Color photograph on page 244.

Light Requirements:

Additional Benefits:

The Redbud is one of the most beautiful trees when it is in bud and bloom. The dark branches and trunk are covered with reddish-purple buds in early spring. The buds open into rosy pink flowers and put on quite a show. Once the flowers are gone, the tree is covered with green heart-shaped leaves that turn a pretty yellow in the fall. After the leaves fall, a graceful silhouette is left to adorn the winter landscape.

WHEN TO PLANT

Redbuds respond best to spring transplanting. That allows them to get established before our tough winters.

WHERE TO PLANT

Grow Redbuds in a protected location. They can tolerate full sun or partial shade, but do best in moist, well-drained soil. Redbuds often grow more wide than tall, so give them plenty of room to show off their attractive form. They are often used as specimen plants, along a woodland edge, or in a naturalized setting. Their strong, horizontal branching and flower display make them a good addition to a Japanese garden.

HOW TO PLANT

Locate the tree's root flare. That is the bell-shaped area where the roots angle away from the trunk. Plant the tree with the root flare at or slightly above the soil line. Dig a shallow planting hole the same depth as and three to five times wider than the root system. Place the tree in the planting hole. Make sure it is straight, moving it by the rootball, not the trunk, to minimize root damage. Remove the container, twine, and metal baskets, and cut away the burlap. Fill the hole with existing soil, water to settle the soil, and mulch.

CARE AND MAINTENANCE

Growing a hardier strain of Redbuds in a protected location will reduce maintenance needs. Mulch the soil to keep the roots cool and moist. Water plants during drought to minimize stress.

ADDITIONAL INFORMATION

The Redbud, like Kentucky Coffee Tree and Honey Locust, is a member of the Pea family. All 3 trees produce pod-type fruits. The Redbud fruit is much smaller than that of the other trees. It is about 2 to 3 inches long and 1/2 inch wide. Redbuds can thrive in Minnesota, given the proper location and growing conditions.

ADDITIONAL SPECIES, CULTIVARS, OR VARIETIES

Redbuds are available as single or multistemmed plants. Select a plant from the 'Minnesota Strain'. These plants were propagated from hardy Redbuds in the Minnesota Landscape Arboretum. They display an attractive dark pink to purple flower in early May. Growing 12 feet, the small trees are open-spreading with multi-stems and are suitable for protected sites in southern Minnesota. They were introduced in 1992.

Did You Know?

Redbud flowers are edible as well as ornamental. They can be used raw in salads or fried for an appetizer. Folk healers used the bark of this tree to treat diarrhea.

Serviceberry

Amelanchier species

Other Names: Juneberry, Shadblow
Size: Up to 40 feet tall and 30 feet wide
Soil: Moist; well-drained
Zones: All

Color photograph on page 244.

Light Requirements:

Additional Benefits:

The Minnesota native Serviceberry is among my favorite small trees. It provides four seasons of interest in any landscape. The white flowers open in spring. Once done, they are followed by small berries. The fruit starts out pink and then turns purple-black. Don't worry about the mess; the birds will clean up the fruit before it hits the ground. I have robins lined up on my fence every June waiting for the fruit to ripen. Next comes the colorful fall display when the leaves turn a brilliant yellow, orange, or red.

WHEN TO PLANT
Plant balled-and-burlapped trees as soon as possible after purchase. Container-grown plants can be planted throughout the growing season. Serviceberries take time to establish after transplanting.

WHERE TO PLANT
Serviceberries grow in full sun or partial shade and prefer moist, well-drained soil. Serviceberries are native to woodland edges, stream banks, fence rows, and hillsides. This adaptability helps them tolerate a wide range of landscape conditions. Use the shrub forms of Serviceberry in groupings, as screens, or as an unsheared hedge. The small trees make good specimen plants near water features, in planting beds, or small landscapes. Larger trees can provide shade and ornamental value in larger settings.

HOW TO PLANT
Plant the tree with the root flare at or slightly above the soil line. Dig a shallow planting hole the same depth as and three to five times wider than the root system. Place the tree in the planting hole. Remove the container, twine, and metal baskets, and cut away the burlap. Fill the hole with existing soil, water to settle the soil, and mulch.

CARE AND MAINTENANCE

Serviceberries often take time to adjust to a new location. Water newly planted trees and the soil beyond the planting hole when the top 6 inches of soil starts to dry. Mulch the soil to conserve moisture, eliminate grass competition, and keep the roots cool. Serviceberries are susceptible to some insects and diseases, but none of them are serious problems.

ADDITIONAL INFORMATION

Serviceberries are edible. They have a nutty, Blueberry flavor. The only trick is beating the birds to the fruit. We eat them right from the tree for a tasty treat while weeding the garden. One year, we were fortunate to gather enough berries for a pie. It was delicious!

ADDITIONAL SPECIES, CULTIVARS, OR VARIETIES

There are many species and cultivars available from local garden centers and nurseries. Select the one that best fits your landscape design. Downy Serviceberry, *Amelanchier arborea,* is an upright, small tree. This slow grower can eventually reach heights of 30 feet. It is hardy to Zone 3b and is more tolerant of dry soil. Apple Serviceberry, *Amelanchier × grandiflora,* is another slow-growing tree. It tolerates partial shade and is hardy to Zone 3. Allegheny Serviceberry, *Amelanchier laevis,* is hardy to Zone 4. This upright, small tree is good for moist soils. Its larger fruit makes it an excellent choice for wildlife. There are several shrub forms available.

 Did You Know?

Serviceberry has several descriptive common names. The name Shadblow relates to the fact these trees bloom at the same time the shad fish swim up the rivers of New England to spawn. The fruit ripens in June as indicated by the name Juneberry.

Spruce

Picea

Size: Up to 60 feet tall and
30 feet wide
Soil: Moist; well-drained
Zones: All

Color photograph on page 244.

Light Requirements:

Additional Benefit:

Spruce trees start out and end up about the same shape: just bigger. These large trees provide a strong, pyramidal silhouette in the garden. Use them as screens, windbreaks, and specimens. Remember, these trees will get huge. Too many gardeners have planted a cute little Spruce by their front entrance only to have it consume the whole yard!

WHEN TO PLANT

Plant balled-and-burlapped trees in the spring as soon as possible after they are purchased. Container-grown trees can be planted throughout the growing season. Plant by October 1 for greater chances of winter survival.

WHERE TO PLANT

Grow Spruces in full sun with moist, well-drained soil. These large, pyramidal trees are difficult to use in small landscapes. Dwarf cultivars are more suitable for small yards and use in perennial and rock gardens.

HOW TO PLANT

Plant the tree with the root flare at or slightly above the soil line. Dig a shallow planting hole the same depth as and three to five times wider than the root system. Place the tree in the planting hole. Remove the container, twine, metal baskets, and cut away the burlap. Fill the hole with existing soil, water the soil, and mulch.

CARE AND MAINTENANCE

Spruce need very little pruning. Touch-up pruning can be done in the spring before growth begins. Make cuts on branch tips above a healthy bud. Spruces are subject to many disease and insect problems. Plants growing in optimum conditions are less susceptible to damage.

Mites can be a problem in hot dry weather. Spray the plants once a week with a strong blast of water from the garden hose.

ADDITIONAL INFORMATION

You do not have to prune off the lower branches of these trees unless you want to grow grass under the tree or open up a view. Limbing up the tree is for the gardener's benefit, not the plant's.

ADDITIONAL SPECIES, CULTIVARS, OR VARIETIES

The most popular Spruce for the home landscape is probably the Colorado Blue Spruce, *Picea pungens f. glauca.* It can reach a height of 60 feet and is hardy throughout Minnesota. It will tolerate dry soil and urban conditions. Its stiff, pyramidal shape and blue needles make it hard to blend with the rest of the landscape. It is susceptible to cytospora canker and spruce galls. *Pices abies* can also be found in many Minnesota landscapes. It is hardy throughout Minnesota and grows to 75 feet tall. This Spruce needs moist soil. The dark green needles held on pendulous branches make this a graceful specimen. White Spruce, *Picea glauca*, is native and hardy throughout Minnesota. It has light green needles and can grow up to 50 feet tall. Be sure to grow it in moist soil and full sun. Black Hills Spruce is a shorter (20 feet), slower-growing cultivar of White Spruce. Dwarf Alberta Spruce, *Picea glauca* 'Conica', appears to be a naturally sheared Spruce. This extremely slow-growing plant has fine needles. Use it in rock gardens, dwarf evergreen collections, and small landscapes. Protect it from winter sun. Gardeners in Zone 4b looking for something different and attractive should try the Serbian Spruce, *Picea omorika.* It has a narrow, pyramidal shape and grows to 50 feet tall. Its pendulous branches make a graceful statement in the landscape.

 Did You Know?

White Spruce, Picea glauca, *has also been called Skunk Spruce. Crush the needles and you will find out why when you smell their bad odor.*

CHAPTER NINE

Turfgrass

N O MATTER HOW MUCH EFFORT and money you invest in grass seed or sod, your lawn will be only as good as the soil it is grown in. Taking the time to plan carefully before the first seed is sown or the sod is laid will help ensure a healthy, attractive lawn you can be proud of. After the soil is properly prepared, selecting the right grass for growing conditions in your area will also improve chances for a lush, green, outdoor carpet. Once the grass is established, mowing, watering, and fertilizing regularly are the three keys to maintaining a first-class lawn.

LAWN ESTABLISHMENT

Start by taking a close look at the earth beneath your feet. If your yard does not have at least 4 to 6 inches of topsoil, you will need to add blended topsoil or amend the existing soil by adding organic matter. Add 2 to 3 cubic yards per 1,000 square feet of peat moss, compost, aged manure, or another organic material to the existing soil. A good topsoil is able to hold moisture and nutrients, but also has adequate drainage. Do not add sand. Mixing sand into clay soil can result in poor growing conditions. Allow the soil to settle and rake it smooth, leveling high areas and filling in low areas. Next take a soil test to determine how much and what type of fertilizer your lawn needs. Spread no more than the recommended lime, phosphorus, and potassium combination over the soil surface and till it into the top 6 inches of the soil. If soil test recommendations are not available, spread 10 pounds of a 10-10-10 or 12-12-12 fertilizer per 1,000 square feet on the soil surface just before seeding. Lightly rake the fertilizer into the soil.

With healthy soil in place, the next step is choosing the right grass for your yard. Cool-weather grasses, such as Bluegrass, Fine Fescue, and turf-type Perennial Ryegrass, do best in Minnesota. Select a mix containing a variety of disease-resistant cultivars. Zoysia, a warm-weather grass, is better for southern states where the summers are long and hot. The best time to seed is August 15 through September 20. May is the second best time to seed. Apply half the seed over the entire lawn, moving in a north-south direction. The remaining seed should be applied in an east-west direction to ensure good coverage. Rake the seed and then roll the yard with an empty lawn roller, which will help guarantee good contact with the soil. Mulch with straw, marsh hay, or one of the season-extending fabrics. Keep the surface of the soil moist until the grass seeds germinate, then water thoroughly but less frequently.

Soil preparation is just as important for sodded lawns. Sod can be laid any time it is available and the ground is not frozen. Start by laying the first roll of sod next to a walk or driveway. Butt the ends of the sod pieces together, overlapping them slightly to compensate for shrinkage. Stagger the joints for a nice finished look. Water frequently to keep the soil beneath the sod moist. Reduce watering once the sod roots into the soil and resists a light tug.

Lawn Maintenance

A healthy lawn is the best defense against weeds and disease. Mowing, watering, and fertilizing on a regular basis will keep your yard green and hearty. Keep Bluegrass lawns cut to a height of 2$1/2$ to 3$1/2$ inches. The taller grass will be more drought tolerant and better able to compete with weeds. No more than $1/3$ of the total height should be cut at each mowing. Clippings should be left on the lawn to decompose, adding moisture and nutrients to the soil. Ideally, lawns should receive 1 inch of water per week. Use a sprinkler, if needed, to supplement rainfall. Lawns in clay soils should be watered once a week. Yards in sandy soil should receive needed water in two applications per week. Fertilizer is the third component of a healthy yard. Minnesota lawns generally need 3 to 4 pounds of nitrogen per

1,000 square feet a year. One of my friends uses annual holidays to remind him of the fertilization schedule: a light fertilization on Memorial Day, a heavier fertilization on Labor Day, and the final, heaviest application of fertilizer on Halloween.

WEED CONTROL

When weeds appear, it's a sure sign that the grass isn't vigorous or healthy enough to keep them at bay. Do some detective work to determine why weeds have invaded your lawn. Is the area too shady? Is the soil compact, or is the grass not receiving needed water and nutrients? Correct the conditions for long-term weed control. You may decide instead to live with a few weeds rather than using chemicals or adjusting your yard-maintenance efforts in some other way. It's up to you to determine how good a lawn you want and the time and effort you are willing to invest. If you do decide to use an herbicide be sure to read and follow all label directions carefully. These really are plantkillers. They can't tell the difference between a dandelion and a geranium, so use them carefully to minimize the risk to you, the landscape, and the environment. Timing is critical for successful treatment. Fall applications are most effective against perennial weeds like plantain and dandelions. Treat that bothersome creeping Charlie in spring when it is in full bloom or in fall after a hard frost. All those chemicals you previously used unsuccessfully will work if applied at the right time. Reduce your exposure by spot treating problem areas. You do not need to treat the entire lawn and should not be treating it every year. Yearly applications indicate poor grass-growing conditions that need to be fixed.

Gardeners looking for a safer option may want to try a new weed killer made of corn gluten meal. It interferes with the germination of many lawn weeds. It won't kill existing weeds but prevents weed seeds from germinating. This is an appealing alternative for many lawn owners whose children and pets play on the grass.

THATCH CONTROL

Thatch is a problem on highly managed lawns. Lots of fertilizer and water encourage thick, dense growth. As the old grass plants die, they have no way to reach the soil surface to decompose. The old grass stems, leaf coverings, and roots-not grass clippings-form the thatch layer. Remove thatch when it becomes 1/2 inch or thicker. Topdress the lawn with 1/4 inch of soil to help compost the thatch in place. This is good for the lawn, but hard on your back! Core aeration is another method to control thatch. The core-aerating machine removes plugs from the soil. It opens the lawn, allowing the thatch to decompose. Dethatching machines and verti-cut mowers physically remove the thatch. Be prepared—the lawn will look awful when you finish! But a couple of weeks later, you will be amazed at its recovery. Core aeration and dethatching should be done in the spring or fall when the lawn is actively growing.

PEST CONTROL

Disease and insects can invade Minnesota lawns, although keeping grass in good shape will help avert these problems. Contact your local county office of the University of Minnesota Extension for proper diagnosis and control options.

Kentucky Bluegrass

Poa pratensis

Soil: Moist, well-drained
Zones: All

Light Requirements:

Kentucky Bluegrass is the most popular lawn grass in Minnesota. This cool-weather grass is well suited to our climate. It is green most of the year when the ground isn't frozen or covered with snow. Bluegrass may go dormant during hot, dry periods in July and August, but as soon as the weather cools, the grass turns green and begins to grow. Grass is a unifying element and functional part of any landscape design. Grassy areas provide walkways, play areas, and as my husband says, "something to keep your feet from getting muddy when it rains."

WHEN TO PLANT

The best time to seed Bluegrass is between August 15 and September 20. The next best time is May. Sod can be laid any time the ground is workable and sod is available.

WHERE TO PLANT

Grow Bluegrass in full sun in moist, well-drained soil. It does not perform well in extremely wet or dry locations. Bluegrass lawns will thin and eventually fail in heavily shaded areas.

HOW TO PLANT

Bluegrass is available as seed or sod, and soil preparation is critical to the success of either one. Once the soil is prepared and leveled, you are ready to plant. Sow pure Bluegrass seed at a rate of 2 pounds per 1,000 square feet. Sunny grass mixes (65 percent Bluegrass, 20 percent Fine Fescue, and 15 percent Perennial Rye) are seeded at a rate of 3 to 4 pounds per 1,000 square feet. Shady grass mixes (15 percent Bluegrass, 70 percent Fine Fescue, and 15 percent Perennial Rye) are seeded at a rate of 4 to 5 pounds per 1,000 square feet. Rake the soil surface to lightly cover the seed. Mulch to conserve moisture and increase seeding success. Keep the soil surface moist until the seeds germinate. Once the grass appears, water thoroughly but less frequently. If you are laying sod, place it on well-prepared soil. Butt the ends together, overlapping slightly to compensate for shrinkage.

Alternate joints where the sod pieces come together for a nicer finished look. Water daily until the sod knits into the soil below. Then water thoroughly but less frequently.

CARE AND MAINTENANCE
Mowing, watering, and fertilizing are essential for maintaining a healthy and attractive lawn. Keep Bluegrass lawns at a height of 2$\frac{1}{2}$ to 3$\frac{1}{2}$ inches. Remove no more than $\frac{1}{3}$ of the total height of the grass at each cutting. Leave the clippings on the lawn to decompose, which will add moisture and nutrients to the soil. Bluegrass awns perform best when they receive an inch of water per week. Supplement rainfall with the sprinkler as eeded. To remain vigorous, Bluegrass lawns generally need 3 to 4 pounds of nitrogen per 1,000 square feet a year. Fertilize lightly on Memorial Day, follow with a heavier fertilization on Labor Day, and apply the last and heaviest dose of fertilizer on Halloween.

ADDITIONAL INFORMATION
Highly managed lawns are more susceptible to thatch. Thatch is a layer of partially decomposed grass stems, leaf covers, and roots. See the introduction to this chapter for details on controlling thatch.

ADDITIONAL SPECIES, CULTIVARS, OR VARIETIES
Use a blend of three to five cultivars to provide greater resistance to disease. Adelphi, Baron, Glade, Nassau, and Parade are a few of the readily available disease-resistant Bluegrasses.

Did You Know?

Short grasses were popular during the Middle Ages. Without modern lawn mowers, people beat and trampled the grass to keep it short. Later scythes were used to achieve a more even cut.

Fine Fescue

Festuca species

Soil: Well-drained	
Zones: All	**Light Requirements:**

I ts low maintenance requirements and its tolerance to drought and shade have made Fine Fescue the second most popular lawn grass in Minnesota. You will find a large percentage of Fine Fescue in shade-tolerant lawn seed mixes.

WHEN TO PLANT

The best time to seed Fine Fescue is between August 15 and September 20. The next best time is May.

WHERE TO PLANT

Fine Fescues prefer partial shade and well-drained soil. Although Fescue will tolerate full sun, it needs cool soil temperatures for best results. The fescues are more tolerant of full-sun locations in northern Minnesota. They are much more tolerant of shade, drought, and acid and infertile soils than Bluegrass.

HOW TO PLANT

Fine Fescues are available as seed. Soil preparation is critical to establishing and growing healthy grass. Once the soil is prepared and leveled, you are ready to plant. Sow seeds at a rate of 4 pounds per 1,000 square feet. Shade grass mixes are seeded at a rate of 4 to 5 pounds per 1,000 square feet. Rake the soil surface to lightly cover the seed. Mulch and keep the soil surface moist until the seeds germinate. Once the grass appears, continue to water thoroughly but less frequently.

CARE AND MAINTENANCE

Keep Fescue lawns at a height of at least 2 1/2 inches. Remove no more than 1/3 of the total height of the grass at each cutting. Fine Fescue lawns are more drought tolerant than Bluegrass. Water often enough to prevent wilting. Disease problems can result from over-watering. Have your soil tested to find out how much and what type of fertilizer is needed. Fescues require much less fertilizer than

Bluegrass lawns. Overfertilization can lead to leaf spot and other fungal diseases. Fertilize pure stands of Fescue growing in the shade only when the leaves are pale or the plants stop growing. One-half pound of actual nitrogen per 1,000 square feet applied in the fall often is enough for fine fescue lawns. Grass seed mixes containing Bluegrass and Perennial Rye will need 2 to 4 pounds of actual nitrogen per 1,000 square feet annually. The percentage of each grass in the mixture will determine the amount of fertilizer needed.

ADDITIONAL INFORMATION
Many of the Fescues grow in clumps and, as a result, do not fill in damaged areas as quickly as creeping grasses. Much research and breeding is being done to develop heat-tolerant and disease-resistant Fescues that will spread more aggressively.

ADDITIONAL SPECIES, CULTIVARS, OR VARIETIES
The Creeping Red, *Fetuca rubra rubra,* is the most commonly used Fine Fescue. It blends well with Kentucky Bluegrass. Creeping Red spreads slowly by rhizomes so it is sluggish when recovering from injury. This Fescue will tolerate drought and shade, but not heat. Once established, it can be left unmowed for a meadow-like effect. Chewing Fescue, *Festuca rubra commutata,* is a bunch-type Fescue that has the same growth requirements as Creeping Red. Its bunching habit makes it more difficult to create an even stand. Hard Fescue, *Festuca ovina duriuscula,* are often combined with Sheep Fescue, *Festuca ovina,* for low-maintenance lawns. Both are bunch-type grasses and the lower-growing varieties require less frequent mowing.

 Did You Know?

Grasses have been around for a long time. Our lawn grasses are descendants of prairie and meadow grasses that were heavily grazed by animals. The grasses that survived had low growing points and were able to tolerate the heavy grazing—an early form of mowing.

TURFGRASS

Perennial Ryegrass

Lolium perenne

Soil: Moist; well-drained
Zones: All, but subject to winter kill

Light Requirements:

Turf-type Perennial Ryegrass is an important part of lawn seed mixes in Minnesota. It germinates quickly and aids in the establishment of seeded lawns. Although it is not a grass that should be used on its own, it is an important part of both sun and shade lawn mixes used throughout our state.

WHEN TO PLANT

Seed turf-type Perennial Ryegrass from August 15 through September 20 for best results. The next best time to seed is May.

WHERE TO PLANT

Use this Ryegrass as a filler mixed with Bluegrass and Fine Fescue. The mixture should contain no more than 10 to 15 percent Perennial Rye. It is a very aggressive grass that is not reliably hardy. Using more Ryegrass will interfere with the establishment of a strong, healthy lawn. Perennial Ryegrass lawns are not practical since this grass is subject to winter kill.

HOW TO PLANT

Turf-type Perennial Ryegrass is available as seed. It is usually sold as part of a premixed lawn seed. Some garden centers sell individual grasses so you can create your own blend. Remember to use only 10 to 15 percent Perennial Ryegrass in the mixture. Properly prepare the soil prior to seeding. Sow sunny lawn mixes at a rate of 3 to 4 pounds per 1,000 square feet and shady mixes at a rate of 4 to 5 pounds per 1,000 square feet. Rake to cover the seed lightly. Mulch and keep the soil surface moist until the seeds germinate. Once the grass appears, water thoroughly but less frequently.

CARE AND MAINTENANCE

Mowing, watering, and fertilizing are the three keys to maintaining a healthy and attractive lawn. Keep lawns 2½ to 3½ inches tall. Remove no more than ⅓ of the total height of the grass at each

cutting. Leave the clippings on the lawn to decompose quickly, adding moisture and nutrients to the soil. Lawns perform best when they receive an inch of water per week. You may need to supplement natural rainfall with the sprinkler. Lawns generally need 3 to 4 pounds of nitrogen per 1,000 square feet a year. Lightly fertilize on Memorial Day, follow with a heavier fertilization on Labor Day, and finish the year with the heaviest fertilization on Halloween. Perennial Ryegrass is subject to red thread and rust disease. Select disease-resistant cultivars whenever possible. Proper care will also help reduce disease problems. Perennial Ryegrass leaves can be tough. Be sure your mower blade is sharp. This will make your job easier and the newly cut lawn will look better.

ADDITIONAL INFORMATION

Perennial Turf-type Ryegrasses are an improvement on common Ryegrass. They were bred to be easier to cut and more heat and cold tolerant.

ADDITIONAL SPECIES, CULTIVARS, OR VARIETIES

Many new Turf-type Perennial Ryegrasses are being evaluated. Select the hardiest and most disease-resistant cultivars available. Annual Ryegrass, *Lolium multiflorum*, is the quick-start grass of old mixtures. It is an annual that dies within the first year. Its coarse texture blends poorly with other grasses. Quick-fix miracle grasses contain a large percentage of this grass. They provide a quick-growing, short-lived lawn.

 Did You Know?

Have you ever walked through a newly seeded lawn in late summer or early fall and ended up with orange feet? The culprit was a fungus called rust. It can attack all types of grasses, but Perennial Ryegrass is the most susceptible. Freshly seeded lawns with a high percentage of Ryegrass are frequently infected.

CHAPTER TEN

Vines

ARE YOU RUNNING OUT OF SPACE in your garden? Do you need to mask a bad view? Try using some of the many annual and perennial vines that are available through catalogues, nurseries, and garden centers. Vines don't need much—just a little soil, and a wall, fence, or other vertical support. Select vines that will tolerate the growing conditions, give the look you want, serve your needs, and climb on the type of support provided.

Vines attach themselves to structures in different ways. Some, like Bittersweet and Clematis, have twining stems and work well on chain-link fences, arbors, and trellises. Don't grow twining vines up tree trunks. They can encircle the trunk and kill the tree. Other vines have holdfasts. Boston Ivy and other clinging vines have stick tight tendrils, aerial rootlets, or adhesive pads for attaching to masonry or wood structures. Grow these vines on brick or stone walls, and wooden trellises, arbors, or pergolas. Do not grow these vines on wood-sided homes. They can damage the siding and must be removed every time your home needs painting or repair.

Use your imagination when selecting a support structure suitable for the vines you have chosen. I have seen twining vines climb up mailbox posts, lampposts, and downspouts. Some gardeners use attractive antique grates, door frames, or discarded play structures. Others attach a sheet of plastic or wire mesh to a wall or fence, to give the twining vines something to attach to. It also makes mainte-nance much easier. You can carefully remove the support from the wall, lay it on the ground, and make needed repairs to the fence or wall. When the work is complete, reattach the support, vine and all, to the structure. Very handy gardeners use hinged trellises, which have lockable hinges at the soil surface. The hinges make it possible to carefully bend the vine-clad trellis out of the way when repairing the wall or fence. Do all of those choices sound like too much work?

Chapter Ten

Don't worry, garden centers and catalogs are full of standard or unusual attractive, preassembled trellises.

No matter what type of support you select, make sure it is well anchored. Vine-covered structures can act like a sail and take off in a strong wind. The structure also must be strong enough to support the weight of the vine. Bittersweet, Trumpet Vine, and Wisteria can become quite massive and heavy. These plants will need a strong, well-anchored structure for support.

Once the support is in place, it's time to select the best vine for the landscape design and maintenance. Rampant growers like Boston Ivy may not be as showy as a Clematis, but they can quickly cover an ugly wall or hide a bad view. They will need regular pruning to keep them in line. Dropmore Scarlet Honeysuckle is a beautiful flowering plant that needs very little pruning, but it may need occasional aphid control.

For added interest, mix several vines together on one support structure. Two Clematis planted on the same trellis or several different vine species planted in an arbor can increase bloom time and have a dramatic visual effect. Add an annual vine to a perennial planting for a temporary quick fill while the perennial vine gets established. Select vines that are equally aggressive, or the stronger plant will engulf the weaker one, giving you a single-plant display.

Vines can also be used as groundcovers. Allow them to crawl unrestrained through the garden to create attractive and unexpected plant combinations. Monitor and prune vines to make sure they don't overrun or choke out their neighbors.

Take a look around your landscape. I bet you can find a little vertical space just begging for a vine.

Bittersweet

Celastrus scandens

Other Names: American Bittersweet
Size: 20 to 30 feet or more
Flowers: Yellow-white; not effective
Fruit/Seed: Yellow and orange seed
  capsule
Bloom Period: May to June
Attachment: Twining
Zones: All
Color photograph on page 244.

Light Requirements:

Additional Benefits:

Bittersweet is the perfect vine for tough places. It is a fast-growing plant that will quickly cover a fence or trellis and mask a bad view. This ornamental native can add year-round interest to your landscape. Bittersweet's yellow fall color can be effective, and the decorative fruit not only adds winter interest, but can be used in dried arrangements. Birds also enjoy feeding on the seeds throughout the winter.

WHEN TO PLANT

Plant bare-root plants in early spring before growth begins. Container-grown plants can be planted any time during the growing season.

WHERE TO PLANT

Bittersweet thrives in full sun and well-drained soil. It will tolerate partial shade, but produces a poor fruit display in heavy shade. If Bittersweet receives lots of moisture and fertilizer it will grow bigger and faster, with lots of leaves but no fruit. The plant can be trained on a large pergola or arbor, allowed to crawl over a rock pile or used to cover a fence. Just remember it grows quickly and needs a strong support and regular pruning to keep it under control.

HOW TO PLANT

Bittersweet is available as a bare-root plant from mail-order catalogs and as a container-grown plant from your local nursery and garden center. You will need both a male and a female plant to produce fruit. Since you can tell the sex of the plants only by the flowers, you will have to depend on the nursery to label the plants correctly. Plant bare-root Bittersweet with the crown, where the roots join the stem, even with the soil surface. Water thoroughly and mulch to help keep the roots cool and moist. Bare-root plants need moist soil to establish new roots. Plant container-grown bittersweet at the same level it was growing in the pot. Gently loosen potbound roots. Place the plant in a hole that is as deep as the rootball and two to three times wider. Water thoroughly and mulch. Allow the soil to dry slightly before watering again. Train new growth to the support after planting.

CARE AND MAINTENANCE

Bittersweet needs regular pruning to keep it under control. Prune in the late winter or early spring before growth begins. Prune dead, damaged, or out-of-place stems back to where they join another stem. Long side shoots can be pruned back to within three or four buds of the main stem. Just prune enough to control growth. Overpruning can lead to excessive growth and poor fruit production.

ADDITIONAL INFORMATION

Bittersweet fruit has a yellow capsule that splits and opens to expose an orange-red seed. The fruit is frequently used in dried arrangements, wreaths, or swags. Harvest the mature seed capsules in the fall and hang them upside down to dry.

ADDITIONAL SPECIES, CULTIVARS, OR VARIETIES

Chinese Bittersweet, *Celastrus orbiculatus*, is very similar to American Bittersweet. It is a little less vigorous and can be sheared into hedges or grown on arbors, fences, and pergolas. Although Chinese Bittersweet is versatile, it should be avoided. It has become an invasive weed in Minnesota.

 Did You Know?

Although Bittersweet is a vigorous native plant, it is illegal to collect fruit from plants growing on public property. Ask permission of private property owners before collecting fruit from their plants. Better yet, grow your own.

Boston Ivy
Parthenocissus tricuspidata

Other Name: Japanese Creeper
Size: 50 to 60 feet
Flowers: Greenish-white; not effective
Fruit/Seed: Blue-black berries
Bloom Period: June and July
Attachment: Clinging tendrils with
   adhesive disks and tendrils
Zone: 4
Color photograph on page 244.

Light Requirements:

Additional Benefit:

You are probably looking at Boston Ivy when you see a vine-covered cottage or an old university building in Minnesota. Though not a true ivy, this tough, fast-growing plant gives you the same look. It is an excellent vine for covering large areas quickly. Boston Ivy is one of the first plants to brighten up the landscape with its bright red fall color. The blue, grape-like fruit is apparent and decorative after the leaves drop. Planting Boston Ivy will bring birds into your landscape. They love to sit in the vines and feed on the fruit.

WHEN TO PLANT
Plant container-grown Boston Ivy any time during the growing season.

WHERE TO PLANT
Boston Ivy is a good plant to use in difficult growing conditions. It will tolerate full sun to full shade. Boston Ivy prefers well-drained soil, but can take just about any type of soil. It can survive tough urban situations such as pollution, road salt, and wind. This fast-growing plant can be trained on stone and brick buildings, walls, or other structures. It attaches with suction cup-like pads and needs no additional support.

HOW TO PLANT
Dig a planting hole the same depth as the rootball and 2 to 3 times wider. Plant container-grown Boston Ivy at the same level it was growing in the pot. Gently loosen potbound roots. Water thoroughly and mulch.

CARE AND MAINTENANCE

Pruning is the only regular maintenance established plants need. They can grow as much as 6 to 10 feet in a year. Prune vines away from windows, eaves, and gutters. Remove stems that are no longer attached to the structure. Older overgrown plants can be renovated. Prune them back to 3 feet.

ADDITIONAL INFORMATION

Boston Ivy is difficult to remove from buildings and other structures. You can pull the vines off a wall, but the hold-fast suction cups will remain attached. There is no easy way to remove them. Rubbing them off the structure with leather glove-clad hands seems to be one of the most effective methods. Or you can wait until they eventually dry up and fall off, but that will take quite a while.

ADDITIONAL SPECIES, CULTIVARS, OR VARIETIES

The Boston Ivy cultivar 'Veitchii' is less aggressive and finer textured. The leaves are purple when young, green for the summer, and red in fall. This cultivar is a better choice than the species for most landscape situations. A close relative is the Virginia Creeper, *Parthenocissus quinquefolia*. It is native to Minnesota and hardy throughout the state. It has five-part leaves, grape-like fruits, and good red fall color. Like Boston Ivy, it tolerates full sun to full shade and most soil types. Use this plant where it has plenty of room to grow. Engelmann Virginia Creeper, *Parthenocissus quinquefolia* 'Engelmannii', has smaller leaves, making it more finely textured than Virginia Creeper.

 Did You Know?

The fruit from Boston Ivy may look like grapes, but do not eat it. It will give you an upset stomach. Leave the fruit for the birds. They will feed on the berries from fall through winter.

Clematis

Clematis × jackmanii

Size: 5 to 18 feet
Flowers: White, purple, pink, or red
Fruit/Seed: Fluffy seeds
Bloom Period: Summer
Attachment: Twining tendrils
Zones: All
Color photograph on page 244.

Light Requirements:

Additional Benefit:

Most gardeners can't resist Clematis once they have seen it in full bloom. This small plant provides lots of summer color, even in very small spaces.

WHEN TO PLANT

Plant container-grown Clematis in the spring and early summer. Small, dormant plants are often sold with their roots packed in peat moss-filled plastic bags. These plants often break dormancy and begin to grow on the shelves of garden centers. Plant the growing Clematis in containers and keep it indoors or in a cold frame outside. These plants can be moved outdoors after all danger of frost is past. If growth has not begun, the plant is still dormant. Keep it in a cool, frost-free location. Plant dormant Clematis outdoors as soon as the soil is workable.

WHERE TO PLANT

The old saying *Clematis like their face in the sun and feet in the shade* is true. Plant Clematis in full sun or light shade. Mulch the soil to keep the roots cool and moist. Grow Clematis in moist, well-drained, alkaline soil. Gardeners with alkaline soil do not need to adjust the soil pH. Gardeners with acid soil will need to add lime. Consult soil test information for specific application rates. Use Jackman Clematis to brighten up any vertical space. The Jackman vines grow well on trellises, mailboxes, and lampposts. Because of the Jackman's growth habit, it is a better choice for ornamental interest than for a screen.

HOW TO PLANT

Plant Clematis next to the support structure. Plant dormant Clematis at the same depth as it was growing in the nursery. You will be able to see the soil line when you remove the packing material. Many container-grown Clematis plants come with a stake in the pot. This can be cumbersome and may even damage the plant during transplanting. Remove the plant carefully to avoid stem damage. Plant in a hole the same depth and at least two to three times as wide as the rootball. The plant should end up at the same level it was growing in the container. Pinch off the growing tips of newly planted Clematis. Carefully attach the young stems to the trellis or support.

CARE AND MAINTENANCE

Jackman Clematis plants need minimal care. They will flourish and bloom if they like their location. Sometimes moving an unhappy plant to a new location, even just a few feet away, can turn it around. Mulch the soil around the Clematis after planting. Keep the soil moist, but not wet, throughout the growing season. Clematis is fairly pest free. Avoid damage to the stems. Although yellow leaves are a common sight during cool Minnesota springs, as temperatures warm, the plants will green up and start to flourish. Stem cankers can cause stems to wilt and turn brown. Avoid piling mulch over the stems. Prune out infected stems to ground level.

ADDITIONAL INFORMATION

Jackman Clematis blooms on new growth. Prune Clematis in late winter or early spring before growth begins. Most gardeners prune heavily each year to maintain a small flowering plant. Prune stems above a set of healthy buds 6 to 12 inches above the soil. Remove any dead stems to ground level to encourage new growth.

ADDITIONAL SPECIES, CULTIVARS, OR VARIETIES

Sweet Autumn Clematis, *Clematis terniflora,* is probably the easiest and fastest growing Clematis in Zone 4. It is covered with small, white, fragrant flowers in the fall. Minnesota has two native species which can be used in a wild garden. Virgin's Bower, *Clematis virginiana,* blooms in the fall and has clusters of small white flowers. These are followed by beardlike tufts of seeds. It can be grown on a fence, trellis or used as a groundcover. The Purple Virgin's Bower, *Clematis verticillaris,* grows in rocky, wooded places. It has large blue/purple flowers more like those of the garden Clematis.

Dropmore Scarlet Honeysuckle

Lonicera × *brownii* 'Dropmore Scarlet'

Size: 12 feet
Flowers: Red
Fruit/Seed: Red berries
Bloom Period: June through October
Attachment: Twining
Zones: All
Color photograph on page 245.

Light Requirements:

Additional Benefits:

Here's a vine that will work in every Minnesota garden. Dropmore Scarlet Honeysuckle is hardy throughout the state and puts on a great show in full sun and partial shade. Single plants can be trained on an arbor creating lots of color in a small yard. Larger plantings can be used to create a fence full of blossoms in a bigger landscape.

WHEN TO PLANT

Dropmore Scarlet Honeysuckle does best if it is planted in the spring. Container-grown vines can be planted any time during the growing season. Be careful not to injure the roots, especially on late-season transplants.

WHERE TO PLANT

Plant Dropmore Scarlet Honeysuckle in full-sun or shady locations. Mine flowers in the shade, but it is more susceptible to powdery mildew. This plant thrives in moist, well-drained soil. Use it on a fence, arbor, or other upright structure. Plant it in an area where you can enjoy the fragrant flowers and the hummingbirds that come to visit.

HOW TO PLANT

Plant container-grown Dropmore Scarlet Honeysuckle at the same depth it was growing in the container. Minimize root disturbance on late-season plantings by cutting away the pot at transplant time. Cut off the bottom of the container. Set it in a planting hole that is the same depth and at least two to three times wider than the rootball. Slice the side of the pot and peel it away, leaving the rootball intact. Fill the hole with soil and water. Mulch and keep the soil moist, but not wet, throughout the growing season. Prune damaged shoots at planting time. Tie young shoots to a support. They will soon attach to the structure on their own.

CARE AND MAINTENANCE

Dropmore Scarlet Honeysuckle is a low-maintenance vine. I have done nothing to my plant for the last six years except enjoy the flowers from late May through October. The vines may have problems with aphids, however. The plants survive the pests, but an infestation can ruin many of the blossoms. Nature may take care of this pest for you. Heavy rains knock the aphids off the plant and lady bee-tles eat them. I have only had to use insecticidal soap once to keep them under control. Systemic insecticides can be used on severe infestations. Be sure to carefully read and follow all label directions. Powdery mildew can also be a problem, especially on the vines grown in the shade. Thinning the vines will help improve air circulation and reduce disease problems.

ADDITIONAL INFORMATION

These vines require very little pruning. Prune back over-grown plants to fit the available space. Trim back to where the branch joins another branch or above a healthy bud. Prune older stems back to ground level.

ADDITIONAL SPECIES, CULTIVARS, OR VARIETIES

Trumpet Honeysuckle, *Lonicera sempervirens,* is one of the parents of Dropmore Scarlet. This fast-growing vine can quickly reach a mature size of 10 to 20 feet. It produces colorful flowers from spring through summer. It has very attractive foliage and variable flowers of red-orange to orange on the outside and yellow to orange- yellow on the inside. *Lonicera pericyclemenum* 'Harlequin' is an irregularly variegated form with foliage splashed in cream, pink and dark green. The tubular flowers are wonderfully scented and come in a pale rose-purple with a white to yellow lip from May to July. It grows 8-10 feet. *Lonicera tatarica* 'Honey Rose' is a new hybrid from the University of Minnesota Landscape Arboretum. It flowers in clusters of deep rosy red with deep blue-green foliage that is resistant to Honeysuckle witches broom aphid.

Morning Glory

Ipomoea purpurea

Size: 8 to 10 feet
Flowers: Purple, blue, pink, white
Fruit/Seed: Not effective
Bloom Period: Summer
Attachment: Twining
Zones: All; Annual
Color photograph on page 245.

Light Requirements:

Additional Benefits:

Morning Glory is an old-fashioned favorite that is still popular in modern landscapes. Whether it is shading a porch, covering a trellis, or hiding an unsightly view, this fast grower provides summer-long beauty with very little care. The heart-shaped green leaves provide a nice backdrop to the funnel-shaped flowers.

When to Plant

Morning Glory vines can be started from seeds indoors or outdoors in the garden. Nick the seed or soak it in warm water for 24 hours before planting. Start seeds indoors four to six weeks prior to the last spring frost. The seeds need moist, warm temperatures, 70 to 85 degrees, to germinate in five to seven days. Plant the seeds outdoors after all danger of frost is past. Hardened-off transplants can be planted outdoors after the last spring frost.

Where to Plant

Plant Morning Glories in areas with full sun and well-drained soil. Use fast-growing annual vines like morning glories to provide temporary screening or shade until your permanent trees and shrubs grow big enough to do the job. Grow morning glory vines in areas you will see early in the day since the flowers tend to close in the low light of afternoon and on cloudy days.

How to Plant

Nick the seeds or soak them overnight before planting them outdoors in the garden. Plant seeds 6 inches apart and 1 inch deep. Thin 3-inch tall plants to 12 inches apart. Plant hardened-off transplants 12 inches apart and at the same depth they were growing in a container. Guide young plants onto a support structure. But once they reach the support, stand back! They will take off on their own! Morning Glory will reseed. My neighbor has had Morning Glories growing on both sides of her wooden fence for over eight years. They came with the house and return every year.

CARE AND MAINTENANCE

Each flower opens in the morning and lasts only one day. But it is replaced the next day with new blossoms. The plants will remain in bloom all season long. The less care Morning Glories receive, the better. Excess water and fertilizer will result in lots of leaves, but no flowers.

ADDITIONAL INFORMATION

Annual vines are becoming more readily available. Try growing them on small trellises in large containers. They make great vertical accents and mix well with other plants. Or grow them on some of the attractive garden structures that are available in garden centers and catalogs. Annual vines provide lots of flowering in very little space—and very little space is what I have in my city lot. They also give me the flexibility to try something new in that spot next year.

ADDITIONAL SPECIES, CULTIVARS, OR VARIETIES

Moonflower, *Ipomoea alba,* aptly describes this climber. It has white flowers that open at dusk. The Sweet Potato Vines, *Ipomoea batatas,* have become very popular. Though not as big as the Morning Glory, they make nice trailing foliage plants for containers. New cultivars of this plant are being added yearly.

 Did You Know?

The Morning Glory is similar to Bindweed (Convolvulus). This is the noxious weed many people call Wild Morning Glory. It can choke out garden plants and is very difficult to kill. Morning Glory is also considered a noxious weed in some states.

Trumpet Vine

Campsis radicans

Size: Rampant grower
Flowers: Orange and yellow
Fruit/Seed: Sausage-like pods
Bloom Period: July
Attachment: Clinging rootlets
Zone: 4
Color photograph on page 245.

Light Requirements:

Additional Benefits:

Trumpet Vine's beautiful flowers and its appeal to hummingbirds make it a good addition to any landscape. The vine produces clusters of large, orange, trumpet-shaped flowers often featured in artwork, on book covers, and with articles on hummingbirds and nectar plants. Its aggressive nature means you will need to get out the pruners every year. But once the pruning is finished, so is the yearly maintenance for the Trumpet Vine. Just sit back, relax, and enjoy the show.

WHEN TO PLANT

Plant bare-root Trumpet Vines in the early spring before growth begins. Container-grown plants can be planted any time during the growing season.

WHERE TO PLANT

Trumpet Vines are excellent choices for large, difficult locations. These rampant growers will overtake anything in their path. Grow them in full sun in moist, well-drained to dry soil, although the vines are tolerant of most growing situations. Trumpet Vines need strong structures for support. They are great on fences in the landscape or on more unusual supports. One family let the Trumpet Vine wind around their childrens' old play structure. The vine had the support it needed and the family got to keep their memories neatly tucked away under this plant. A nearby bakery has trained their Trumpet Vine into a small tree.

HOW TO PLANT

Trumpet Vines are available as bare-root plants through mail order catalogs and as container-grown plants from your local nursery and garden center. Plant bare-root Trumpet Vines with the crown, the place where the roots join the stem, even with the soil surface. Water thoroughly and mulch to help keep the roots cool and moist. Plant container-grown Trumpet Vines at the same level they were growing in the pot. Gently loosen potbound roots. Water thoroughly and mulch. Train new growth to the support after planting. Once aerial rootlets form, it will attach itself. You may need to provide additional help to keep this fast-growing plant attached to its support structure.

CARE AND MAINTENANCE

Yearly pruning is necessary to keep this plant under control. The best time to prune is late winter through early spring. Prune young plants to fit the support structure. This will be the plant's basic framework and your basis for future pruning. Cut back the side shoots on established plants each year. Prune back to within three or four buds of the main framework. Remove overcrowded shoots as needed.

ADDITIONAL INFORMATION

Poor flowering is the biggest complaint I hear about the Trumpet Vine. Excessive shade and nitrogen can prevent flowering. Trumpet Vines are luxury feeders. They will take in all available nutrients. This results in lots of leaves and stems, but no flowers. Avoid high-nitrogen fertilizers. Keep Trumpet Vines away from highly fertilized areas.

ADDITIONAL SPECIES, CULTIVARS, OR VARIETIES

Yellow Trumpet Vine, *Campsis radicans* 'Flava', is readily available through garden centers and catalogs. It produces yellow flowers on a plant similar otherwise to the Trumpet Vine. 'Crimson Trumpet', has red flowers.

 Did You Know?

Trumpet Vine is also a rampant grower underground. It develops suckers by sending runners under the surface of the soil. New plants can sprout quite a distance from the parent plant. Use a sharp shovel to prune out suckers below ground level.

Wintercreeper

Euonymus fortunei vegeta

Other Names: Wintercreeper Euonymus, Evergreen Bittersweet

Size: 40 feet

Flowers: Greenish-white; not effective

Fruit/Seed: Split red capsule with exposed orange seed on a few species

Bloom Period: June or July; not effective

Attachment: Clinging rootlets

Zone: 4

Color photograph on page 245.

Light Requirements:

Additional Benefit:

Wintercreeper can be grown as a groundcover, as a small shrub, or as a vine trained to a wall or structure. Vining types of Wintercreeper can soften a brick wall or a garden structure. If it is put in an appropriate spot, this vine will provide year-round interest.

WHEN TO PLANT

Container-grown plants can be planted any time during the growing season. Spring planting will result in established plants with the greatest chance for winter survival.

WHERE TO PLANT

Plant Wintercreeper in areas with full or partial shade, and moist, well-drained soil. They will tolerate full sun in the summer, but can be damaged by winter sun and wind. Protect plants from winter winds.

HOW TO PLANT

Plant container-grown Wintercreeper at the same level it was growing in the pot. Gently loosen potbound roots. Water thoroughly and mulch. Wintercreeper will crawl along the ground until it finds something to attach to. Some can be trained into small shrubs if they are left unattached. Gently guide the plant to the support structure. Once clinging rootlets form, Wintercreeper will support itself.

CARE AND MAINTENANCE

Proper cultivar selection and plant placement are the best ways to reduce maintenance and keep Wintercreeper healthy. Select cultivars and varieties that are hardy for your location. Prevent winter injury by growing this plant in a protected site or east exposure where it will be safe from winter wind and sun. Scale insects and crown galls are the worst pest problems. Treat the immature scale insects with an insecticide when the Japanese Tree Lilacs are just starting to bloom. Repeat two times at intervals of ten to twelve days. Read and follow all label directions carefully. Crown gall is caused by a bacteria. Infected plants develop golf ball-like nodules on the roots and stems. Remove and destroy badly infected plants. Light infections can be controlled with sanitation. Prune out and destroy gall-infested stems. Disinfect tools with denatured alcohol between cuts.

ADDITIONAL INFORMATION

Prune Wintercreeper in the early spring. This will allow you to remove any winter damage while doing routine pruning. Train Wintercreeper vines to a wall or trellis. Loosely tie the main stem and side branches of young plants to the support. Prune back any stems that are growing directly away from or into the support. Prune off the top few buds on long, bare branches. This will encourage branching to fill in vacant areas. Prune established vines to keep them healthy and growing within the available space. Remove weak, damaged, dead, and winter-injured branches back to a healthy branch. Shorten stems that are outgrowing the structure.

ADDITIONAL SPECIES, CULTIVARS, OR VARIETIES

Big Leaf Wintercreeper, *Euonymus fortunei* 'Vegetus', is considered one of the hardiest (Zone 4b) of the Wintercreepers. It can be grown as a shrub or trained to cling to a structure. The variegated forms are not reliably hardy in Zone 4.

 Did You Know?

Wintercreeper is starting to appear in wild areas around the state. Fruitless types, though less ornamental, are less of a threat to our native areas. Watch for stray plants. People living near natural areas may want to avoid this plant.

Wisteria

Wisteria species

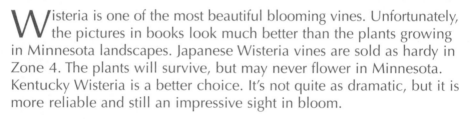

Other Names: Japanese Wisteria,
   Chinese Wisteria, Kentucky Wisteria

Size: 30 feet or more

Flowers: Purple to violet

Fruit/Seed: Pea-like pods into fall

Bloom Period: Late spring or summer; varies with species

Attachment: Twining

Zone: 4

Color photograph on page 245.

Light Requirements:

Wisteria is one of the most beautiful blooming vines. Unfortunately, the pictures in books look much better than the plants growing in Minnesota landscapes. Japanese Wisteria vines are sold as hardy in Zone 4. The plants will survive, but may never flower in Minnesota. Kentucky Wisteria is a better choice. It's not quite as dramatic, but it is more reliable and still an impressive sight in bloom.

WHEN TO PLANT

Plant container-grown Wisteria in the spring. Some gardeners find this plant slow to respond after transplanting. Spring planting will give Wisteria more time to become established before winter.

WHERE TO PLANT

Plant Wisteria in full sun or in lightly shaded areas. The plants grow best in moist, well-drained soil. Espalier Wisteria vines on a wall, grow them on a pergola, or train them into a small tree. Use sturdy supports. These fast growers can cause weak structures to collapse.

HOW TO PLANT

Plant container-grown Wisteria plants at the same level they were growing in the container. Handle Wisteria with care to reduce transplant shock. Mulch and keep the soil moist, but not wet, throughout the growing season.

CARE AND MAINTENANCE

The Japanese Wisteria flower buds are usually killed by our cold winters. Every few years, after a mild winter, you may be fortunate enough to see one of their breathtaking flower displays. Kentucky Wisteria is plant and flower hardy to Zone 4, with reports of plants surviving and even blooming in Zone 3. Avoid overfertilizing Wisteria. Excess nitrogen prevents flowering and encourages too much growth that can overtake the landscape. Pruning is the only real maintenance needed. Prune established Japanese Wisteria in the early summer after they normally would flower. Kentucky Wisteria can be pruned in late winter before growth begins. Wisteria may not bloom for the first seven years.

ADDITIONAL INFORMATION

Wisteria can also be trained into a tree. Train the main stem to a stake. After several years of pruning back the main stem and side shoots, you can develop a tree-form Wisteria. Prune yearly to maintain the desired size and shape.

ADDITIONAL SPECIES, CULTIVARS, OR VARIETIES

The Kentucky Wisteria, *Wisteria macrostachya,* is the best choice for Minnesota landscapes, but it is difficult to find. It produces beautiful 12-inch purple flowers in the summer after the leaves emerge. 'Blue Moon' is a fast blooming variety. It is hardy and blooms three times a year. The Japanese Wisterias seldom bloom in Minnesota. Japanese Wisteria, *Wisteria floribunda,* is sold for its extremely long, 12- to 20-inch, fragrant, purple flowers.

 Did You Know?

The American Medical Association reports that all parts of the Wisteria plant are toxic. Some older gardening books talk about how the Chinese harvested, steamed, and ate the mature blossoms of the Chinese Wisteria. I'm going with the AMA on this one!

Sources

Gardening Resources

Maps

Things I Have Learned

Bibliography

Botanical Gardens and Arboreta

Botanical gardens and arboreta are the best places to find out which plants are hardy and suitable for your growing conditions. Pictures in books and catalogs often look very different from the actual plants that grow in Minnesota's challenging environment. I have a small yard, but I take home great ideas on plant combinations or unique plantings from botanical gardens. Visit often for landscaping ideas; plants change throughout the season.

August Schell Brewery
1860 Schell Rd.
New Ulm, MN 56073
Phone: (507) 354-5528

Carleton College's Cowling
   Arboretum
Carleton College
One North College Street
Northfield, Minnesota, USA 55057
Phone: (507) 646-4000

Como Conservatory
1325 Aida Place
St. Paul, MN 55103-1054
Phone: (651) 487-8201,
   (651) 487-8250

Eastern Nature Center,
Elm Creek Park Reserve
13351 Elm Creek Rd.
Osseo, MN 55369-9344
Phone: (763) 420-4300

Eloise Butler Wildflower Gardens
4125 E. Lake Harriot Parkway
Minneapolis, Minnesota
Phone: (612) 370-4900

Enger Olson Observation Tower
   and Gardens
Sky Line Drive
Duluth, MN 55800
Phone: (218) 723-3300-
   Duluth City Hall

Historic Mayowood Mansion
   Gardens
1195 W. Circle Dr. SW
Rochester, MN 55902
Phone: (507) 282-9447

The Japanese Garden at
   Normandale
9700 France Avenue South
Bloomington, MN 55431
Phone: (952) 487-8200

Linnaeus Arboretum
Gustavus Adolphus College
St. Peter, MN 56082
Phone: (507) 933-7003,
   (507) 933-6181

Loring Park Garden of the
   Seasons
1382 Willow Street
Minneapolis, Minnesota
Phone: (612) 661-4800

Minneapolis Sculpture Garden
726 Vineland Place
Minneapolis, Minnesota
Phone: (612) 370-3996

Minnesota Landscape Arboretum
PO Box 39
3675 Arboretum Dr.
Chanhassen, MN 55317-0039
Phone: (952) 443-1400

Munsinger Gardens & Clemens Gardens
1339 Killian Blvd.
St. Cloud, MN 56301
Phone: (320) 650-1050

Nokomis Naturescape Gardens
2401 E. Minnehaha Ave.
Minneapolis, Minnesota
Phone: (612) 370-4900

Northland Arboretum
NW 7th St.
Brainerd, MN 56401
Phone: (218) 829-8770

Peace (Rock) and Rose Gardens
4125 E. Lake Harriet Parkway
Minneapolis, Minnesota
Phone: (612) 370-4900

Pergola Garden
4801 Minnehaha Ave. South
Minneapolis, Minnesota
Phone: (612) 661-4800

River Bend Nature Center Inc.
1000 Rustad Rd.
PO Box 186
Fairbault, MN 55021-0186
Phone: (507) 332-8151

The Rose Garden at Leif Erikson Park
13th Avenue East and
London Road
Duluth, MN 55805
Phone: (218) 723-3300-
Duluth City Hall

Roseville Community Arboretum
Harriet Alexander Nature Center
2520 N. Dale St.
Roseville, MN 55113-1701
Phone: (651) 415-2161

All-America Selections Display Gardens

Minnesota Landscape Arboretum
3675 Arboretum Drive
Chanhassen, MN 55317

North Central Experiment Station
1861 Hwy. 169 East
Grand Rapids, MN 55744

Lyndale Park Gardens
4125 E. Lake Harriet Parkway
Minneapolis, MN 55407

West Central Experiment Station
PO Box 471, State Hwy. 329
Morris, MN 56267

University of Minnesota, St. Paul
1970 Folwell Avenue
St. Paul, MN 55108

Gardening Resources

Department of Natural Resources
Urban and Community Forestry Program

The Minnesota Department of Natural Resources has helped communities build and care for their urban trees. They can provide tree care information to you and your community. Contact your regional office for more information:

DNR Information Center
500 Lafayette Road
St. Paul, MN 55155-4040
Phone: (651) 296-6157 or 888-MINNDNR
TTY: (651) 296-5484 or 800-657-3929
E-Mail: info@dnr.state.mn.us

Metro Region Forestry Headquarters
1200 Warner Road
St. Paul, MN 55106
Phone:(651) 772-7925
Fax:(651) 772-7599

Bemidji Region Forestry Headquarters
6603 Bemidji Avenue North
Bemidji, MN 56601-8669
Phone:(218) 755-2891
Fax:(218) 755-4063
Forestry Area Offices:
Bemidji-2220 Bemidji Avenue, 56601-3896; (218) 755-2890
Bagley-Highway 92 North, Route 4, Box 186, 56621-9801; (218)694-2146
Blackduck-HC3 Box 95B, 56630; (218) 835-6684
Warroad-1101 Lake Street Northeast, 56763; (218)386-1304
Wannaska- - 16945 Highway 89, 56761-9721; (218) 425-7793
Baudette-206 Main Street East, 56623; (218) 634-2172
Park Rapids-Box 113, 607 West 1st Street, 56470-1311; (218) 732-3309

Alexandria-2605 Aga Drive, Unit 6, 56308; (320) 762-7812
Detroit Lakes-14583 County Hwy 19, 56501; (218) 847-1596

Brainerd Region Forestry Headquarters
1601 Minnesota Drive, Suite 2
Brainerd, MN 56401-3971
Phone:(218) 828-2616
Fax:(218) 828-2432
Forestry Area Offices:
Brainerd-1601 Minnesota Drive Suite 2, 56401; (218) 828-2565
Little Falls-16543 Haven Road, 56345-6401; (320) 616-2450
Backus-P.O. Box 6, 56435-0006; (218) 947-3232
Pequot Lakes-P.O. Box 27, 56472; (218) 568-4566
Hill City-P.O. Box 9, 454 Highway 169, 55748; (218) 697-2476
Aitkin-P.O. Box 138, Minnesota Avenue South, 56431-0138; (218) 927-4040
Moose Lake-Route 2, 701 South Kenwood Avenue, 55767; (218) 485-5400

Gardening Resources

Hinckley-312 Fire Monument Road, 55037; (320) 384-6146
Cambridge-800 Oak Savanna Lane Southwest, 55008; (763) 689-7100
Sauk Rapids-940 Industrial Drive Suite #103, 56379; (320) 255-4279

Grand Rapids Region Forestry Headquarters
1201 East Highway 2
Grand Rapids, MN 55744-3296
Phone:(218) 327- 4418
Forestry Area Offices:
Deer River-P.O. Box 157, 56636-0157; (218) 246-8343
Effie-P.O. Box 95, 56639; (218) 743-3694
Hibbing-1208 East Howard Street, 55746; (218) 262-6760
Orr-P.O. Box 306, 4656 Highway 53, 55771-0306; (218) 757-3274
Tower-P.O. Box 432, 609 North 2nd Street, 55790; (218) 753-4500
Cloquet-1604 South Highway 33, 55720; (218) 879-0880
Two Harbors-1568 Highway 2, 55616; (218) 834-6600
Grand Marais-Box 156, 55604; (218) 387-3037
Littlefork-421 Third Avenue, Box 65, 56653-0538; (218) 278-6651

Rochester Region Forestry Headquarters
2300 Silver Creek Road Northeast
Rochester, MN 55906
Phone:(507) 285-7428
Fax:(507) 285-7144

Forestry Area Offices:
Lewiston-Box 279, 55952-0279; (507) 523-2183
Caledonia-603 North Sprague Street, 55921; (507) 724-5264
Preston-912 Houston Street Northwest, 55965; (507) 765-2740; fax (507) 765-2740
Lake City-1801 South Oak, 55041; (651) 345-3216
Rochester-2300 Silver Creek Road Northeast, 55906; (507) 285-7428
Mankato-1230 South Victory Drive, 56001; (507) 389-6713
New Ulm-P.O. Box 607, 56073-0607; (507) 359-6057
Willmar-4566 Highway 71 North, Suite 1, 56201; (320) 231-5164
Faribault-1810 Northwest 30th Street, 55021; (507) 333-2012

Gopher State One Call
Gopher State One Call is a free utility-locating service. They will mark the location of any underground utilities in the planting area. Give them three working days to complete the task. This is important for your safety and pocketbook. Digging into a utility line can be expensive and even deadly.

1-800-252-1166 throughout Minnesota

Minnesota Garden Clubs and Plant Societies

The Minnesota State Horticultural Society is the place to go for information on Minnesota chapters of national plant societies and garden clubs. For those with access to the Internet, you may want to start at: www.northerngardener.org

Garden clubs and plant societies are a great way to learn more about gardening and plants. Members trade knowledge, resources, and often plants. In many cases you will need to contact the national organization to find the club nearest you. For those with access to the Internet, you may want to start at: www.globalgardens.com. This web site will help you access several different plant societies.

VARIOUS PLANT SOCIETIES

African Violets
African Violet Society of America, Inc.
2375 North Street
Beaumont, TX 77702-1722

Bonsai
American Bonsai Society
P.O. Box 1136
Puyallup, WA 98371-1136
http://www.paonline.com/abs

Conifers
American Conifer Society
P.O. Box 360
Keswick, VA 22947-0360
Cactus and Succulents
Cactus and Succulent Society of America
P.O. Box 2615
Pahrump, NV 89041-2615
http://www.cactus-mall.com/cssa/

Dahlia
American Dahlia Society
1 Rock Falls Court
Rockville, MD 20854

Daylily
American Hemerocallis Society
Dept WWW, P.O. Box 10
Dexter, GA 31019
http://www.daylilies.org/ahs

Hosta
American Hosta Society
338 E. Forestwood Street
Morton, IL 61550
http://www.hosta.org

Iris
American Iris Society
P.O. Box 55
Freedom, CA 95019
http://www.isomedia.com/homes/ais/

Rose
American Rose Society
P.O. Box 30,000
Shreveport, LA 71130
http://www.ars.org.

Water Lily
International Water Lily Society
Suite 328-G12, 1401 Johnson
    Ferry Road
Marietta, GA 30062-8115
http://h20lily.rain.com

INSTITUTIONS OFFERING HORTICULTURE PROGRAMS

Anoka-Hennepin Technical College
Phone: (763) 427-1880

Central Lakes Community College
Phone: (218) 828-2525

Dakota County Technical College
Phone: (651) 423-8301

Hennepin Technical College
Phone: (763) 550-2115

North Dakota State University
Phone: (701) 237-8162

Rochester Community & Technical
    College
Phone: (507) 285-7219

South Dakota State University
Phone: (605) 688-5136

Southeast Technical Institute
Phone: (605) 367-7826

University of Minnesota at St. Paul
Phone: (612) 624-4242

University of Minnesota at
    Crookston
Phone: (218) 281-6510

University of Wisconsin at
    River Falls
Phone: (715) 425-3911

University of Minnesota Extension Service

The University of Minnesota Extension Service is a great resource for gardeners. They bring research-based information to you through classes, workshops, newspaper articles, and the master gardeners. Their printed publications are the best resource for gardeners and landscape professionals. The information and recommendations are based on the soils and climates of Minnesota. Contact your local county office, from the following list, for a list of publications and other resources available in your county.

Aitkin County
Aitkin County Courthouse
209 2nd Street NW
Aitkin, MN 56431-1257
Phone: (218) 927-7321
Fax: (218) 927-7372
e-mail: aitkin@extension.umn.edu

Anoka County
Anoka County Activities Center
550 Bunker Lake Boulevard NW
Andover, MN 55304-4199
Phone: (763) 755-1280
Fax: (763) 755-6950
e-mail: anoka@extension.umn.edu

Becker County
Ag Service Center
809 8th Street SE
Detroit Lakes, MN 56501-2842
Phone: (218) 847-3141
Fax: (218) 847-6969
e-mail: becker@extension.
   umn.edu

Beltrami County
815 15th Street NW
Bemidji, MN 56601-2501
Phone: (218) 759-0038
Fax: (218) 759-0243
e-mail: beltrami@extension.
   umn.edu

Benton County
Courthouse
531 Dewey St, P.O. Box 650
Foley, MN 56329-0650
Phone: (320) 968-5077
Fax: (320) 968-5319
e-mail: benton@extension.umn.edu

Big Stone County
Courthouse
20 SE 2nd Street
Ortonville, MN 56278-1544
Phone: (320) 839-2518
Fax: (320) 839-3571
e-mail: bigstone@extension.
   umn.edu

The Blue Earth County Extension
   Service
P.O. Box 8608, 410 South 5th Street
Mankato, MN 56002-8608
Phone:(507) 389-8325
Fax: (507) 389-8812
e-mail:blueearth@extension.
   umn.edu

Brown County
300 2nd Avenue SW
Sleepy Eye, MN 56085-1402
Phone: (507) 794-7993
Fax: (507) 794-5290
e-mail: brown@extension.umn.edu

Gardening Resources

Carlton County
310 Chestnut Street
P.O. Box 307
Carlton, MN 55718-0307
Phone: (218) 384-3511
Fax: (218) 384-3512
e-mail: carlton@extension.
    umn.edu

Carver County
609 West First Street
Waconia, MN 55387-1204
Phone: (952) 442-4496
Fax: (952) 442-4497
e-mail: carver@extension.
    umn.edu

Cass County
Courthouse
P.O. Box 3000
Walker, MN 56484-3000
Phone: (218) 547-7392
Fax: (218) 547-7397
e-mail: cass@extension.umn.edu

Chippewa County
Courthouse
629 North 11th Street
Montevideo, MN 56265-1685
Phone: (320) 269-6521
Fax: (320) 269-5223
e-mail: chippewa@extension.
    umn.edu

Chisago County
38694 Tanger Drive
North Branch, MN 55056-9500
Phone: (651) 674-4417
Fax: (651) 674-0310
e-mail: chisago@extension.
    umn.edu

Clay County
919 8th Avenue North
P.O. Box 280
Moorhead, MN 56561-0280
Phone: (218) 299-5020
Fax: (218) 299-7533
e-mail: clay@extension.umn.edu

Clearwater County
Clearwater County Building
113 7th Street NE, Box B
Bagley, MN 56621-9103
Phone: (218) 694-6151
Fax: (218) 694-3875
e-mail: clearwater@extension.
    umn.edu

Cook County
Community Center Building
P.O. Box 1150
317 West 5th
Grand Marais, MN 55604-1150
Phone: (218) 387-3015
Fax: (218) 387-3016
e-mail: cook@extension.umn.edu

Cottonwood County
235 9th Street
Windom, MN 56101-1642
Phone: (507) 831-4022
Fax: (507) 831-4024
e-mail: cottonwood@extension.
    umn.edu

Crow Wing County
Courthouse
326 Laurel Street
Brainerd, MN 56401-3578
Phone: (218) 824-1065
Fax: (218) 824-1066
e-mail: crowwing@extension.
    umn.edu

Gardening Resources

Dakota County Extension and
   Conservation Center
4100 220th Street West, Suite 101
Farmington, MN 55024-9539
Phone: (651) 480-7700
Fax: (651) 463-8002

Dodge County
42 East Main Street
P.O. Box 159
Dodge Center, MN 55927-0159
Phone: (507) 374-6435
Fax: (507) 374-2954
e-mail: dodge@extension.
   umn.edu

Douglas County
720 Filmore, Suite B090
Alexandria, MN 56308-1763
Phone: (320) 762-3890
Fax: (320) 762-3871
e-mail: douglas@extension.
   umn.edu

Fillmore County
902 Houston Street NW #3
Preston, MN 55965-1080
Phone: (507) 765-3896
Fax: (507) 765-4512
e-mail: fillmore@extension.
   umn.edu

Freeborn County
Courthouse Room 222
411 South Broadway
Albert Lea, MN 56007-1147
Phone: (507) 377-5660
Fax: (507) 377-5272
e-mail: freeborn@extension.
   umn.edu

Goodhue County
Government Center Room 105
509 5th Street
West Red Wing, MN 55066
Phone: (651) 385-3100 or
   (800) 385-3101
Fax: 651-385-3089
e-mail: goodhue@extension.
   umn.edu

Grant County
411 First Street SE, P.O. Box 1099
Elbow Lake, MN 56531-1099
Phone: (218) 685-4820
Fax: (218) 685-4817
e-mail: grant@extension.umn.edu

Hennepin County
1525 Glenwood Avenue
Minneapolis, MN 55405-1264
Phone: (612) 374-8400
Fax: (612) 374-8417
e-mail: hennepin@extension.
   umn.edu

Houston County
620 North Highway 44/76
P.O. Box 228
Caledonia, MN 55921-0228
Phone: (507) 725-5807
Fax: (507) 724-2832
e-mail: houston@extension.
   umn.edu

Hubbard County
201 Fair Avenue
Park Rapids, MN 56470-1483
Phone: (218) 732-3391
Fax: (218) 732-8173
e-mail: hubbard@extension.
   umn.edu

Gardening Resources

Isanti County
555 18th Avenue SW
Cambridge, MN 55008-9386
Phone: (763) 689-1810 or
    (800) 621-7973
Fax: (763) 689-8257
e-mail: isanti@extension.umn.edu

Itasca County
1861 Highway 169 E
Grand Rapids, MN 55744-3396
Phone: (218) 327-4177
Fax: (218) 327-4219
e-mail: itasca@extension.umn.edu

Jackson County
419 Main St
P.O. Box 309
Lakefield, MN 56150-0309
Phone: (507) 662-5293
Fax: (507) 662-5016
e-mail: jackson@extension.umn.edu

Kanabec County
905 East Forest Avenue #140
Mora, MN 55051-1617
Phone: (320) 679-6340
Fax: (320) 679-6344
e-mail: kanabec@extension.
    umn.edu

Kandiyohi County
Health\Human Services Building
2200 23rd Street NE #2090
Willmar, MN 56201-9423
Phone: (320) 231-7890
Fax: (320) 231-6535
e-mail: kandiyohi@extension.
    umn.edu

Kittson County
Courthouse
410 South 5th Street, P.O. Box 369
Hallock, MN 56728-0369
Phone: (218) 843-3674
Fax: (218) 843-2580
e-mail: kittson@extension.umn.edu

Koochiching County
Courthouse Complex
718 5th Street
Intl Falls, MN 56649-2486
Phone: (218) 283-1182
Fax: (218) 283-1183
e-mail: koochiching@extension.
    umn.edu

Lac Qui Parle County
Courthouse
600 6th Street
Madison, MN 56256-1295
Phone: (320) 598-3325
Fax: (320) 598-3305
e-mail: lacquiparle@extension
    umn.edu

Lake County
Courthouse, 601 3rd Avenue
Two Harbors, MN 55616-1517
Phone: (218) 834-8377
Fax: (218) 834-8365
e-mail: lake@extension.umn.edu

Lake of the Woods County
    Extension
Courthouse
206 SE Eighth Avenue
P.O. Box 598
Baudette, MN 56623-0598
Phone: (218) 634-1511 or
    (800) 493-1511
Fax: (218)634-2509

Gardening Resources

Le Sueur County
88 South Park
LeCenter, MN 56057-1620
Phone: (507) 357-2251 or
    (800) 445-7543
Fax: (507) 357-6375
e-mail: lesueur@extension.umn.edu

Lincoln County
402 North Harold
P.O. Box 130
Ivanhoe, MN 56142-0130
Phone: (507) 694-1470
Fax: (507) 694-1290
e-mail: lincoln@extension.umn.edu

Lyon County
Courthouse
607 West Main
Marshall, MN 56258-3099
Phone: (507) 537-6702
Fax: (507) 537-6576
e-mail: lyon@extension.umn.edu

Mahnomen County
Courthouse
311 Main
P.O. Box 477
Mahnomen, MN 56557-0477
Phone: (218) 935-2226
Fax: (218) 935-5412
e-mail: mahnomen@extension.
    umn.edu

Marshall County
Courthouse
208 East Colvin Avenue
Warren, MN 56762-1698
Phone: (218) 745-5232
Fax: (218) 745-8801
e-mail: marshall@extension.
    umn.edu

Martin County
104 Courthouse
201 Lake Avenue
Fairmont, MN 56031-1845
Phone: (507) 235-3341
Fax: (507) 235-5772
e-mail: martin@extension.umn.edu

McLeod County
840 Century Avenue, Suite B
Hutchinson, MN 55350-3754
Phone: (320) 587-0770 or
    (800) 587-0770
Fax: (320) 234-4310
e-mail: mcleod@extension.umn.edu

Meeker County
Family Services Center
114 North Holcombe Avenue #260
Litchfield, MN 55355-2274
Phone: (320) 693-5275
Fax: (320) 693-5289
e-mail: meeker@extension.umn.edu

Mille Lacs County
620 Central Avenue North
Milaca, MN 56353-1788
Phone: (320) 983-8317 or
    (888) 680-8317
Fax: (320) 983-8367
e-mail: millelacs@extension.
    umn.edu

Morrison County
Government Center
213 First Avenue SE
Little Falls, MN 56345-3100
Phone: (320) 632-0161
Fax: (320) 632-0166
e-mail: morrison@extension.
    umn.edu

Gardening Resources

Mower County
Courthouse
201 NE 1st Street
Austin, MN 55912-3475
Phone: (507) 437-9552
Fax: (507) 437-9471
e-mail: mower@extension.
  umn.edu

Murray County
2848 Broadway Avenue
P.O. Box 57
Slayton, MN 56172-0057
Phone: (507) 836-6927
Fax: (507) 836-6019
e-mail: murray@extension.
  umn.edu

Nicollet County
Courthouse
501 South Minnesota Avenue
St. Peter, MN 56082-2533
Phone: (507) 931-6800
Fax: (507) 931-9220
e-mail: nicollet@extension.
  umn.edu

Norman County
101 West Third Avenue
Ada, MN 56510-1200
Phone: (218) 784-7183
Fax: (218) 784-2473
e-mail: norman@extension.
  umn.edu

Olmsted County
1421 SE 3rd Avenue
Rochester, MN 55904-7947
Phone: (507) 285-8250
Fax: (507) 285-8401
e-mail: olmsted@extension.
  umn.edu

Otter Tail, East County
118 North Main
P.O. Box 250
New York Mills, MN 56567-0250
Phone: (218) 385-3000
Fax: (218) 385-3001
e-mail: eottertail@extension.
  umn.edu

Pennington County
Courthouse, P.O. Box 616
Thief River Falls, MN 56701-0616
Phone: (218) 683-7030
Fax: (218) 683-7033
e-mail: pennington@extension.
  umn.edu

Pine County
105 Fire Monument Road
P.O. Box 370
Hinckley, MN 55037-0370
Phone: (320) 384-6156 or
  (800) 657-3813
Fax: (320) 384-7299
e-mail: pine@extension.umn.edu

Pipestone County
Municipal Building
119 SW 2nd Avenue Suite 2
Pipestone, MN 56164-1684
Phone: (507) 825-6715
Fax: (507) 825-6719
e-mail: pipestone@extension.
  umn.edu

Polk, East County
Municipal Building
P.O. Box 69
McIntosh, MN 56556-0069
Phone: (218) 563-2465
Fax: (218) 563-4750
e-mail: epolk@extension.umn.edu

Polk, West County
University Teaching & Outreach
  Center
P.O. Box 556
Crookston, MN 56716-0556
Phone: (218) 281-8696
Fax: (218) 281-8694
e-mail: wpolk@extension.umn.edu

Pope County
Courthouse
130 Minnesota Avenue East
Glenwood, MN 56334-1628
Phone: (320) 634-5735
Fax: (320) 634-5736
e-mail: pope@extension.umn.edu

Ramsey County
Historic Ramsey County Barn
2020 White Bear Avenue
Saint Paul, MN 55109
Phone: (651) 704-2080
Fax: (651) 704-2081

Red Lake County
Courthouse
P.O. Box 279
Red Lake Falls, MN 56750-0279
Phone: (218) 253-2895
Fax: (218) 253-2656
e-mail: redlake@extension.umn.edu

Redwood County
Courthouse
P.O. Box 130
Redwood Falls, MN 56283-0130
Phone: (507) 637-4025 or
  (800) 310-8323
Fax: (507) 637-4017
e-mail: redwood@extension.
  umn.edu

Renville County
Renville County Office Building
410 East DePue Avenue, Room 320
Olivia, MN 56277-1483
Phone: (320) 523-3713 or
  (800) 450-2522
Fax: (320) 523-3755
e-mail: renville@extension.umn.edu

Rice County
Government Services Building
320 NW Third Street, Suite 7
Faribault, MN 55021-6143
Phone: (507) 332-6109
Fax: (507) 332-5999
e-mail: rice@extension.umn.edu

Rock County
311 West Gabrielson #2
P.O. Box 898
Luverne, MN 56156-0898
Phone: (507) 283-8685
Fax: (507) 283-5006
e-mail: rock@extension.umn.edu

Roseau County
606 5th Avenue SW, Room 130
Roseau, MN 56751-1477
Phone: (218) 463-1052
Fax: (218) 463-3252
e-mail: roseau@extension.umn.edu

Scott County
7151 190th Street West
Suite 100
Jordan, MN 55352-2104
Phone: (952) 492-5410
Fax: (952) 492-5405
e-mail: scott@extension.umn.edu

Sherburne County
Sherburne County Government
   Center
13880 Highway 10
Elk River, MN 55330-4601
Phone: (763) 241-2720 or
   (800) 433-5236
Fax: (763) 241-2727
e-mail: sherburne@extension.
   umn.edu

Sibley County
Courthouse
P.O. Box 207
Gaylord, MN 55334-0207
Phone: (507) 237-4100
Fax: (507) 237-4099
e-mail: sibley@extension.umn.edu

Stearns County
Midtown Office Buildings
3400 First Street North, Suite 400
Saint Cloud, MN 56303-4000
Phone: (320) 255-6169
Fax: (320) 255-6167
e-mail: stearns@extension.umn.edu

Steele County
635 Florence Avenue
P.O. Box 890
Owatonna, MN 55060-0890
Phone: (507) 444-7685
Fax: (507) 444-7682
e-mail: steele@extension.umn.edu

Stevens County
Colonial Square
208 Atlantic Avenue
Morris, MN 56267-1321
Phone: (320) 589-7423
Fax: (320) 589-7440
e-mail: stevens@extension.umn.edu

Swift County
Courthouse
301 14th Street North, P.O. Box 305
Benson, MN 56215-0305
Phone: (320) 843-3796
Fax: (320) 843-4850
e-mail: swift@extension.umn.edu

Todd County
Courthouse Annex
119 3rd Street South
Long Prairie, MN 56347-1354
Phone: (320) 732-4435
Fax: (320) 732-6233
e-mail: todd@extension.umn.edu

Traverse County
Courthouse
702 2nd Avenue North
P.O. Box 457
Wheaton, MN 56296-0457
Phone: (320) 563-4515
Fax: (320) 563-4424
e-mail: traverse@extension.
   umn.edu

Wabasha County
611 Broadway Avenue #40
Wabasha, MN 55981-1613
Phone: (651) 565-2662
Fax: (651) 565-2664
e-mail: wabasha@extension.
   umn.edu

Wadena County
Courthouse
415 South Jefferson Street
Wadena, MN 56482-1594
Phone: (218) 631-7623
Fax: (218) 631-7625
e-mail: wadena@extension.
   umn.edu

Gardening Resources

Waseca County
300 North State Street, Suite #1
Waseca, MN 56093-2933
Phone: 507-835-0600

Washington County
Suite 202
1825 Curve Crest Boulevard
Stillwater, MN 55082-6054
Phone: (651) 430-6800
Fax: (651) 430-6801
e-mail: washington@extension.
    umn.edu

Watonwan County
Courthouse
P.O. Box 68
St. James, MN 56081-0068
Phone: (507) 375-1275 or
    (800) 204-1295
Fax: (507) 375-1260
e-mail: watonwan@extension.
    umn.edu

Wilkin County
P.O. Box 199
Breckenridge, MN 56520-0199
Phone: (218) 643-5481
Fax: (218) 643-1434
e-mail: wilkin@extension.umn.edu

Winona County
202 West 3rd Street
Winona, MN 55987-3115
Phone: (507) 457-6440
Fax: (507) 454-9362
e-mail: winona@extension.umn.edu

Wright County
Room 130
10 2nd Street NW
Buffalo, MN 55313-1186
Phone: (763) 682-7394 or
    (800) 362-3667
Fax: (763) 682-6178
e-mail: wright@extension.umn.edu

Yellow Medicine County
1004 10th Avenue
P.O. Box 128
Clarkfield, MN 56223-0128
Phone: (320) 669-4471
Fax: (320) 669-7525
e-mail: yellowmedicine@extension.
    umn.edu

TOTAL PRECIPITATION
IN INCHES

January 1 to December 31
Averaged from 1961 to 1990

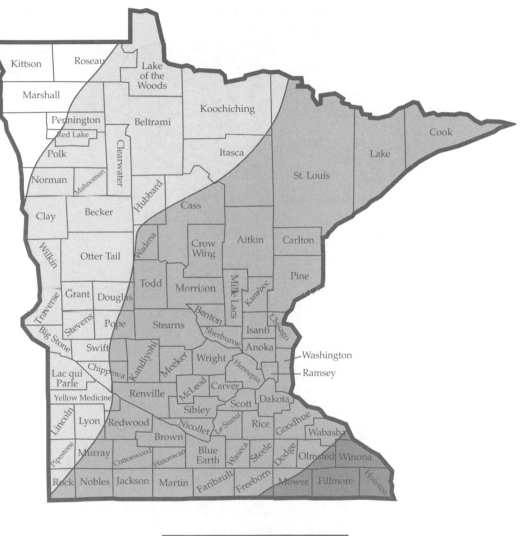

under 25   25   30   35   40

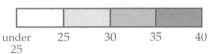

421

LAST SPRING FREEZE

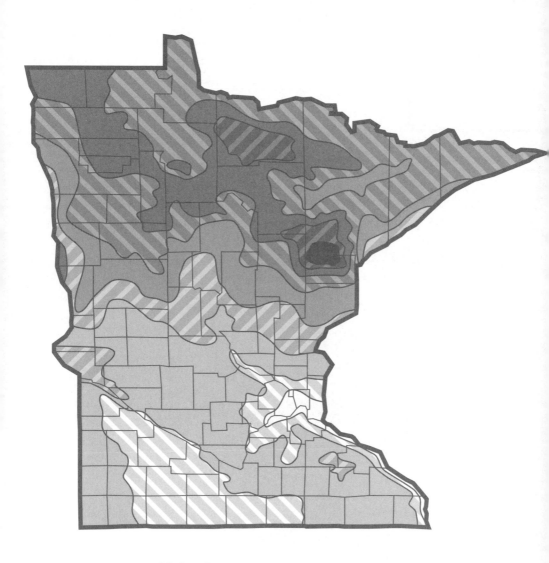

Median Dates

	Jun. 11 - 7
	Jun. 6 - 2
	Jun. 1 - May 28
	May 27 - 23
	May 22 - 18

Median Dates

	May 17 - 13
	May 12 - 8
	May 7 - 3
	May 2 - 6

FIRST FALL FREEZE

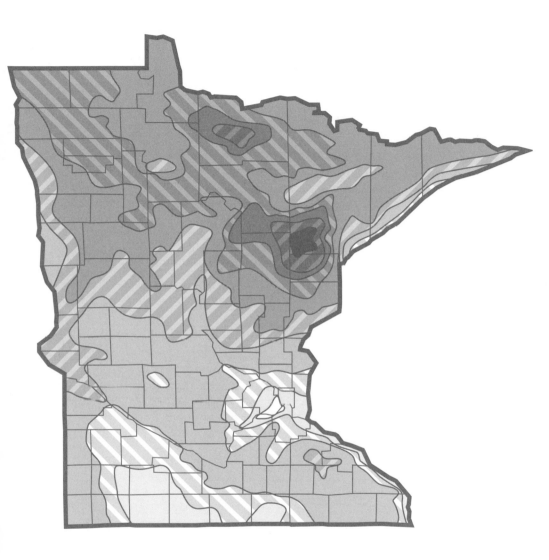

Median Dates		Median Dates
Aug. 27 - 31		Sep. 21 - 25
Sep. 1 - 5		Sep. 26 - 30
Sep. 6 - 10		Oct. 1 - 5
Sep. 11 - 15		Oct. 6 - 10
Sep. 16 - 20		Oct. 11 - 15

THINGS I HAVE LEARNED

Great gardening successes are often planned, but I find many of mine result from lucky combinations, observations of the successes of others, and ideas shared by fellow gardeners. A Master Gardener, Lowell Kendall, once compared the value of sharing ideas and money with others. He said, "If I had a dollar and you had a dollar and we decided to share with each other, we would still only each have a dollar. But if I had an idea and you had an idea, and we decided to share—we would each have 2 ideas." Sharing ideas with other gardeners helps all of us improve the beauty and fun we experience. Use these pages to write down some of those ideas you discover, shared, or want to try.

_____

_____

_____

_____

_____

_____

_____

_____

_____

_____

_____

_____

_____

_____

_____

_____

_____

 Annuals

Mix common and uncommon annuals to liven up containers and flower beds. I get many of my ideas from botanical gardens. Look for simple plant combinations that can be replicated in your own garden. Interplant Blue Heliotrope with Rosey Red Geraniums. You may not even recognize the Geraniums and the added fragrance is nice.

Things I Have Learned

 Bulbs

Mix Daffodils and Daylilies. Once the Daffodils are done blooming the Daylily foliage starts to grow and masks the daffodil leaves that seem to last forever in the garden. Hostas are a nice cover up for declining Virginia Bluebell foliage.

Things I Have Learned

Fruits

Espalier and train dwarf fruit trees into an attractive wall dressing or fence. Yearly pruning and training can give you a fruit in very small places. I think I need to talk to my neighbor—she has a bare wall that is just begging for an espaliered Apple tree.

Things I Have Learned

Herbs and Vegetables

Mix herbs and vegetables with ornamental plants. Asparagus is a favorite of mine, but I have limited growing space. I have three pots waiting for the perfect spot. They will either get planted with my Hardy Roses as a feathery filler or as a background in my perennial garden.

Things I Have Learned

 Houseplants

I move my Hibiscus, Jasmine, and a few other annuals from outdoors in the summer to my basement window in the laundry room. I visit that room often so it is easy to remember to water the plants as needed. Plus, the Hibiscus flowers make laundry more bearable.

Things I Have Learned

Lawns

Plant a pot of Ryegrass for a little green relief. Place cut flowers in water picks to add a little color. Mowing the lawn with scissors and running your fingers through the small lawn can add a little laughter and chase away the winter blahs.

Things I Have Learned

Perennials

One of my students, Linda Wenthur says, "Things are dead longer than they are alive." Some flowers age gracefully while others must be maintained to keep their appearance acceptable. Plant to mask the undesirable features of old age or remove them from the garden if you don't have time to give them the needed attention.

Things I Have Learned

 Roses

Consider using hardy Roses as a decorative screen or barrier planting. It took me two years but I finally found a spot for the large hardy William Baffin Rose. It fills a corner of my alley garden. It provides beautiful flowers for me and my neighbors— while keeping the curious children off my neighbor's roof.

Things I Have Learned

 Shrubs

My small city lot is filled with ornamental plants instead of lawn. I am always on the lookout for small ornamental shrubs to add year-round structure. I have added several Dwarf Conifers (I still have a few more on the list to buy!), as well as Winterberry, Clethra, and several other small scale shrubs with good fall color, flowering, and fruit effect.

Things I Have Learned

 Trees

My small yard does not allow for all my favorite trees. I plan my errands and work route to include a pass by my favorite trees in their peak display. A drive through the arboretum for peak Crabapple bloom, a pass by the Performing Art Center when the Horsechestnut bosco (a mass of trees) is at its peak, and a visit to the Sugar Maple near the shopping mall to see its colorful fall display.

Things I Have Learned

 Vines

Try using low growing groundcovers around Hosta and other larger shade loving plants. The light colors help brighten the shade and fill in the vacant space in the shade garden. Yellow Moneywort makes a nice backdrop for Hosta. Colorful Ajuga makes an attractive contrast and out competes weeds as Hostas grow and spread.

BIBLIOGRAPHY

Brickell, Christopher and Judith D. Zuk, ed. *The American Horticultural Society: A-Z Encyclopedia of Garden Plants.* DK Publishing, Inc., New York, NY, 1997.

Brickell, Christopher, and David Joyce. *The American Horticultural Society: Pruning and Training.* DK Publishing, Inc., New York, NY, 1996.

Browne, Jim, William Radler, and Nelson Sterner, ed. *Rose Gardening.* Pantheon Books, New York, 1995.

Coombes, Allen J. *Dictionary of Plant Names.* Timber Press, Portland, OR, 1993.

Curtis, John T. *The Vegetation of Wisconsin.* The University of Wisconsin Press, 1978.

Dirr, Michael A. *Manual of Woody Landscape Plants, 4th edition.* Stipes Publishing Co., Urbana, IL, 1990.

DiSabato-Aust, Tracy. *The Well-Tended Perennial Garden.* Timber Press, Portland, OR, 1998.

Fell, Derek. *Annuals.* HP Books, Los Angeles, CA, 1983.

Johnson, Eric. *A Growing History.* Minnesota State Horticultural Society. Falcon Heights, MN, 2001.

Martin, Laura. *The Folklore of Trees and Shrubs.* The Globe Pequot Press, Chester, CT, 1992.

Meyer, M.H. *150 Years of Hardy Plants.* University of Minnesota Agriculture Experiment Station, 2000.

Reilly, Ann. *Park's Success with Seeds.* Geo. W. Park Seed Co., Inc., Greenwood, SC, 1978.

Schneider, Donald. *Park's Success with Bulbs.* Geo. W. Park Seed Co., Inc., Greenwood, SC, 1981.

Still, Steven M. *Manual of Herbaceous Plants, 4th Edition.* Stipes Publishing Company, Urbana, IL, 1994.

Tryon, Rolla. *Ferns of Minnesota.* University of Minnesota Press, Minneapolis, MN, 1980.

Wyman, Donald. *Wyman's Gardening Encyclopedia.* McMillan Publishing Co., Inc., New York, 1977.

INDEX

Abies balsamea, 336, 337
Abies concolor, 336, 337
Abies species, 336
Acer × freemanii, 361
Acer ginnala, 361
Acer platanoides, 361
Acer rubrum, 360, 361
Acer saccharinum, 361
Acer saccharum, 361
Acer species, 360
Achillea
  filipendulina, 226, 227
Achillea millefolium, 226, 227
Achillea
  'Moonbeam', 227
Aconite, Winter, 109
Adam's Needle, 228
Aegopodium podagraria, 121
  'Variegatum', 120
Aesculus glabra, 347
Aesculus hippocastanum, 346
African Marigold, 60
Ageratum, 30
  'Blue Danube', 31
  'Hawaii' Series', 31
  'Leilani Blue', 31
  'Swing Pink', 31
Ageratum
  houstonianum, 30
Ajuga, 122
Ajuga reptans, 122
  'Alba', 123
Alder, 318
  'Laciniata', 319
  'Pyramidalis', 319
Alder
  Black, 318
  European, 318, 319
  Speckled, 319
Allegheny
  Serviceberry, 373
  Spurge, 137
Allium, 84
Allium giganteum, 84, 85
Allium montanum glaucum, 85
Allium seneceus glaucum, 85
Allium spaerocephalon, 85
Allium species, 84
Almond, Flowering, 366
Alnus glutinosa, 318
Alnus rugosa, 319
Alpine Currant, 268
  'Compacta', 269
  'Green Mound', 269
  'Nana', 269
  'Pumila', 269
Alum Root, 190, 191

Alyssum, 32, 74
  'Easter Bonnet', 33
  'New Carpet of Snow', 33
  'Rosie O'Day', 33
  'Snow Crystals', 33
Alyssum, Sweet, 32
Amelanchier arborea, 373
Amelanchier × grandiflora, 373
Amelanchier laevis, 373
Amelanchier species, 372
American
  Arborvitae, 271
  Beech, 322, 323
  Bittersweet, 388, 389
  Chestnut, 347
  Cranberrybush
    Viburnum, 307
  Elm, 332
    'New Horizon', 333
    'Regal', 333
  Hornbeam, 362
  Larch, 354, 355
  Linden, 356, 357
    'Redmond', 357
  Marigold, 60
  Mountain Ash, 335
Amur
  Chokecherry, 367
  Honeysuckle, 289
  Maple, 361
Andropogon gerardi, 155
Andropogon scoparius, 154
Angel Wings, 86
Anglojap Yew, 313
Annual
  Carnation, 35
    'Scarlet Luminette', 35
  Fountain Grass, 158
  Golden Coreopsis, 193
  Pinks, 34
    'Carpet' Series, 35
    'Parfait' Series, 35
    'Telstar' Series, 35
  Ryegrass, 385
Annuals, 26
Antirrhinum majus, 72
Apple Serviceberry, 373
Apple, 293
Aquilegia canadensis, 189
Aquilegia hybrids, 188
Arborvitae, 270
  'Hetz Midget', 271
  'Holmstrup', 271
  'Wansdyke Silver', 271
  'Woodwardii', 271
Arborvitae
  American, 271

  Techny, 271
Archangel
  Herman's Pride, 143
  Variegated
    Yellow, 125, 142
  Yellow, 142
Armenian Grape
  Hyacinth, 101
Arrowroot, Queensland, 91
Arrowwood
  Viburnum, 307
Artemisia ludoviciana, 175
Artemisia, 174
  'Oriental Limelight', 175
Artemisia schmidtiana, 175
  'Nana', 175
Artemisia,
  Silvermound, 174, 175
Artemisia species, 174
Arum Lily, 88
Asarum arifolium, 127
Asarum canadense, 126, 127
Asarum europaeum, 126, 127
Asarum naniflorum
  'Eco Dècor', 127
Asarum speciosum
  'Buxom Beauty', 127
Asclepias tuberosa, 186
Ash, 320
  American Mountain, 335
  European Mountain, 334
  Green, 320, 321
  Korean Mountain, 335
  Mountain, 334
  Showy Mountain, 335
  White, 320, 321
Asperula, 141
Asperula odorata, 141
Aster, 154, 176
  New England, 177
  New York, 177
Aster novae-angliae, 177
Aster novi-belgii, 177
Aster species, 176
Astilbe, 13, 126, 160, 178,
  198, 202
  Dwarf Chinese, 179
Astilbe chinensis
  'Pumila', 179
Astilbe species, 178
Athyrium, 198
Athyrium filix-femina, 199
Athyrium niponicum
  'Pictum', 199
Austrian Pine, 369
Autumn Crocus, 93
Avena sempervirens, 152

Index

Azalea, 302, 303
  Northern Lights, 303
Aztec Marigold, 60
Azure Sage, 214
Baby's Breath, 98, 206
Balsam Fir, 336, 337
Bamboo, 160
Barberry, 272
  'Crimson Pygmy', 273
  'Golden Ring', 273
  'Helmond Pillar', 273
  'Roseglow', 273
Barberry,
  Japanese, 272, 273
Barren Strawberry, 116
Barrenwort, 118
  Sulphur Bicolor, 119
Basil
  'Purple Ruffle', 27, 61
Basswood, 356
Bearded Iris, 104, 105
  Miniature Dwarf, 105
  Standard Dwarf, 105
  Tall, 105
Bedding
  Begonia, 36
  Geranium, 52
Bedstraw, 141
Bee Balm, 220
Beech, 322, 363
  American, 322, 323
  Blue, 349, 362, 363
  European, 322
  Water, 363
Begonia, 36
  Bedding, 36
  Fibrous-rooted, 36
  Tuberous, 110
  Wax, 36
Begonia
  'Cocktail' Series, 37
Begonia semperflorens-
  cultorum, 36
Begonia × tuberhybrida, 110
Belladonna
  Delphinium, 197
Belle's Honeysuckle, 289
Bellflower, 180
  Carpathian, 181
  Clustered, 181
  European, 181
  Marsh, 181
Berberis thunbergii, 272
Berberis thunbergii var.
  atropurpurea, 273
Betula nigra, 325
Betula papyrifera, 325

Betula species, 324
Big Bluestem, 155
Big Leaf Wintercreeper, 401
Bigleaf Hydrangea, 291
Bindweed, 397
Birch, 324, 368
  Canoe, 324
  Paper, 324, 325
  River, 325
Birch
  'Whitespire', 325
  'Whitespire Senior', 325
Bishop's
  Hat, 118
  Weed, 120
    Variegated, 120
Bittersweet, 386, 387, 388
  American, 388, 389
  Chinese, 389
  Evergreen, 400
Black
  Alder, 318
  Cherry, 367
Black-eyed Susan, 157, 169,
  182, 214
  'Becky Mix', 159
Blackhaw, 306
Blazing Star, 200
  Rough, 201
  Tall, 201
Bleeding Heart, 184
  Fringed, 185
  Japanese, 184
Bleeding Heart
  'Gold Heart', 185
Blood Grass, Japanese, 167
Blue
  Beech, 349, 362, 363
  Fescue, 148, 150, 152, 153
    'Blaufuchs', 151
    'Blauglut', 151
    'Blue Fox', 151
    'Blue Glow', 151
    'Elijah Blue', 151
    'Golden Toupe', 151
    'Sea Urchin', 151
    'Seeigel', 151
  Flag, 105
  Oat Grass, 152
    'Saphirsprudel', 153
    'Sapphire
      Fountain', 153
  Salvia, 61
  Spruce, 336, 337
  Squill, 108
Bluebell, 224
  Virginia, 224

Blueberry, 293, 373
Bluegrass, 376, 380, 381, 382,
  383, 384
  Kentucky, 380, 383
Bluestem, 154
  Big, 155
  Little, 154
Boston Ivy, 386, 387, 390
  'Veitchii', 391
Boxwood, 274
  'Chicagoland Green', 275
  'Green Mountain', 275
  'Green Velvet', 275
Brazilian Verbena, 79
Bridal Wreath
  Spirea, 299, 304, 305
Bronze Fennel, 75
Buckeye, Ohio, 347
Buddleia davidii, 278
Buddleja davidii, 278
Bugleweed, 122
  'Burgundy Glow', 123
  'Catlin's Giant', 123
  'Chocolate Chip', 123
Bulbs, 82
Bur Oak, 365
Burning Bush, 276
  'Koreana', 277
  'Nordine Strain', 277
  'Rudy Haag', 277
Bush Honeysuckle, 288
Busy Lizzie, 54
Butterfly Bush, 278
  'Black Knight', 279
  'Nanho' Series, 279
  'Pink Delight', 279
Butterfly Weed, 186
  'Gay Butterflies', 187
Buxus × 'Glencoe', 275
Buxus microphylla, 274
Buxus microphylla var.
  koreana × Buxus
  sempervirens, 274
Buxus sempervirens cultivars
  and hybrids, 274
Cactus, 41
  Prickly Pear, 228
Cactus-flowered Zinnia, 80
Caladium, 86
  'Pink Beauty', 86
  'White Christmas', 86
Caladium × bicolor, 86
Caladium × hortulanum, 86
Caladium,
  Fancy-leaved, 86
Calamagrostis acutiflora
  'Karl Foerster', 156

Index

Calamagrostis arundinacea brachytricha, 157
Calamagrostis × *acutiflora*
  'Overdam', 157
  'Stricta', 156
Calibrachoa
  'Million Bells', 69
Calla, Garden, 88
Calla Lily, 88
  'Crowborough',89
  'Green Goddess', 89
  'Little Gem', 89
Campanula americana, 181
Campanula aparinoides, 181
Campanula carpatica, 181
Campanula medium, 181
Campanula rapunculoides, 181
Campanula rotundifolia, 181
Campanula species, 180
Campsis radicans, 398
  'Flava', 399
Canada Ginger, 126
Canadian
  Hemlock, 342
  Yew, 313
Canna, 90, 158
  'Cleopatera', 91
  'Phasion', 91
  'President', 91
  'Pretoria', 91
  'Stuttgart', 91
  'Tropical Rose', 91
  'Tropicana', 91
Canna edulis, 91
Canna × *generalis*, 90
Canna Lily, 90
Canna, Water, 91
Canoe Birch, 324
Canterbury Bell, 181
Cardinal Flower, 57
Carnation, Annual, 35
Carpathian Bellflower, 181
Carpinus, 349
Carpinus caroliniana, 349, 362
Castanea dentata, 347
Catalpa, 137, 326
  Northern, 326
Catalpa speciosa, 326
Catharanthus roseus, 58
Cedar, 271
  Red, 292, 293, 341
  White, 270, 271
Cedrus, 271
Celastrus orbiculatus, 389
Celastrus scandens, 388
Celosia, 41
Celosia argentea, 40

Celosia cristata, 40
Celosia spicata, 41
Cercis canadensis, 370
Cherry, 350, 366
  Black, 367
  Ornamental, 366
  Purpleleaf Sand, 366, 367
Chestnut, American, 347
Chewing Fescue, 383
Chinese
  Bittersweet, 389
  Elm, 333
  Peony, 208
  Silver Grass, 162, 163
  Wisteria, 402
Chionodoxa luciliae, 109
Chives, Drumstick, 85
Chokecherry, Amur, 367
Chrysanthemum × *morifolium*, 204
Chrysanthemum × *rubellum*, 205
Chrysanthemum × *superbum*, 220, 221
Cigartree, 326
Cineraria maritima, 46
Cinnamon Fern, 198
Cinquefoil, 138
  Spring, 139
  Three-toothed, 138
  Wineleaf, 139
Clavey's Dwarf
  Honeysuckle, 289
Clematis
  Jackman, 392, 393
  Sweet Autumn, 393
Clematis × *jackmanii*, 392
Clematis terniflora, 393
Clematis verticillaris, 393
Clematis virginiana, 393
Clematis, 386, 387, 392
Cleome, 38
  'Helen Campbell' Series, 39
  'Queen' Series, 39
  'Sparkler Blush', 39
Cleome hasslerana, 38
Cleome, Spider, 38, 158
Cleome spinosa, 39
Climbing
  Rose, 252
    'Lillian Gibson', 252
Clove Currant, 269
Clustered Bellflower, 181
Cockscomb, 40
  'Apricot Brandy' Series, 41

'Castles' Series, 41
'Flamingo Feather', 41
'Jewel Box', 41
'Pink Candle', 41
'Prestige Scarlet', 41
Cockspur Hawthorn, 341
  'Inermis', 341
Colchicum, 93
Coleus, 42
  'Cranberry Salad', 43
  'Fiji' Series, 43
  'Hurricane' Series, 43
  'India Frills', 43
  'Palisandra', 43
  'Saber' Series, 43
  'Solar Sunrise', 43
  'Wizard' Series, 43
Coleus × *hybridus*, 42
Colocasia, 87
Colorado Blue Spruce, 330, 336, 375
Columbine, 188
  'Biedermeier Strain', 189
  'McKana Hybrids', 189
  'Song Bird', 189
Columbine, Wild, 189
Common
  Grape Hyacinth, 100
  Harebell, 181
  Hyacinth, 102
  Snapdragon, 72
  Sunflower, 76
  Witchhazel, 310
  Yarrow, 226, 227
Coneflower, 13, 169, 182
  Great, 183
  Hedge, 212
  Orange, 182, 183
  Purple, 212, 214
Conium maculatum, 343
Convallaria majalis, 130
Convolvulus, 397
Coralbells, 151, 190
  'Velvet Night', 191
Cordyline, 75
Cordyline indivisia, 74
Coreopsis, 192, 220
  Annual Golden, 193
  Mouse Ear, 193
  Threadleaf, 84, 98, 192
Coreopsis auriculata, 193
Coreopsis grandiflora, 193
Coreopsis lanceolata, 193
Coreopsis palmata, 193
Coreopsis species, 192
Coreopsis tinctoria, 193

Index

Coreopsis tripteris, 193
Coreopsis verticillata, 193
Corn Poppy, 207
Cornus alternifolia, 283
Cornus racemosa, 283
Cornus sericea, 283
Cornus species, 282
Cortaderia selloana, 148
Cosmos bipinnatus, 44
   'Sea Shells', 45
Cosmos, 44, 98
   'Sonata' Series, 45
Cosmos species, 44
Cosmos sulphureus, 44
   'Ladybird' Series, 45
   'Sunny Delight', 45
Cotoneaster, 280
   Cranberry, 281
   Hedge, 281
   Rock, 281
Cotoneaster apiculatus, 281
Cotoneaster divaricatus, 281
Cotoneaster horizontalis, 281
Cotoneaster lucidus, 281
Cotoneaster
   multiflorus, 281
Cotoneaster species, 280
Cowslip, 224
Crabapple, 181, 293, 328, 341
   Flowering, 328
   Weeping, 281
Cranberry Cotoneaster, 281
Cranberrybush
   Viburnum, 306
Crataegus crusgalli, 341
Crataegus species, 340
Creeping
   Jenny, 132
   Phlox, 210, 211
   Potentilla, 151
   Red, 383
   Thyme, 134, 135
Crocus, 92, 106
   Autumn, 93
   Dutch, 92
   Golden, 93
   Saffron, 93
   Showy, 93
Crocus chrysanthus, 93
Crocus sativus, 93
Crocus speciosum, 93
Crocus vernus, 92
Cucumber, 44, 359
   Magnolia, 359
Currant
   Alpine, 268
   Clove, 269

Daffodil, 82, 94, 100, 106, 224
Dahlia, 77, 96
   Garden, 96
   Water Lily, 97
Dahlia-flowered Zinnia, 80
Dahlia hybrids, 96
Daisy, Shasta, 220
Daylily, 157, 194, 198
   Orange, 195
Deadnettle, 124, 143
   'Beacon Silver', 125
   'Silbergroschen', 125
   'White Nancy', 125
Deadnettle, Spotted, 124, 125
Delphinium, 196
   Belladonna, 197
Delphinium × belladonna, 197
Delphinium × elatum, 196
Delphinium virescens, 197
Dennstaedtia punctilobula, 199
Dianthus caryophyllus, 35
Dianthus chinensis, 34
Dicentra cucullaria, 185
Dicentra eximia, 185
Dicentra spectabilis, 184
Diervilla lonicera, 288
Ditch Lily, 195
Dogwood, 263, 282, 368
   Flowering, 282
   Gray, 283
   Pagoda, 283
   Redosier, 283
   Redtwig, 283
Dogwood
   'Cardinal', 283
   'Isanti', 283
Double-Flowering Plum, 367
Douglas Fir, 330
Douglasfir, 330
   'Anguina', 331
   'Fastigiata', 331
   'Pendula', 331
Downy
   Phlox, 211
   Serviceberry, 373
Dracaena, 74, 75
Dropmore Scarlet
   Honeysuckle, 387, 394
Drumstick Chives, 85
Dry Strawberry, 116
Duchesnea indica, 117
Dusty Miller, 30, 46, 57, 59,
   71, 74
   'Cirrus', 47
   'Silver Dust', 47
   'Silver Lace', 47
   'Silver Queen', 47

Dutch
   Crocus, 92
   Hyacinth, 102
Dutchman's Breeches, 185
Dwarf
   Alberta Spruce, 375
   Chinese Astilbe, 179
   French Marigold, 60
   Minnesota
      Snowflake, 297
   Mugo Pine, 299
   Sunflower, 77
Easter Lily, 107
Eastern
   Hemlock, 342
   Redbud, 370
Echinacea angustifolia, 213
Echinacea purpurea, 212, 213
Edging Lobelia, 56
Elephant's Ear, 86
Elm, 332, 353, 362
   American, 332
   Chinese, 333
   Lacebark, 333
   Red, 333
   Siberian, 333
   Slippery, 333
Elm
   'American Libery', 333
Engelmann Virginia
   Creeper, 391
Epimedium, 119
Epimedium × rubrum, 118
Epimedium × versicolor
   'Sulphureum', 119
Eranthis hyemalis, 109
Eulalia, 162
Euonymus, 146, 147, 277
   Winged, 276
   Wintercreeper, 146, 400
Euonymus alatus, 276
   'Compactus', 277
Euonymus fortunei var.
   coloratus, 147
Euonymus fortunei
   vegeta, 400
Euonymus fortunei, 146
   'Vegetus', 401
European
   Alder, 318, 319
   Beech, 322
      'Atropunicea', 323
      'Purpurea
         tricolor', 323
      'Purpurea', 323
      'Roseomarginata', 323
   Bellflower, 181

Index

Cranberrybush
Viburnum, 307
  Fly Honeysuckle, 288
  Ginger, 126, 127
  Larch, 354, 355
  Mountain Ash, 334
Evergreen Bittersweet, 400
Fagus grandifolia, 323
Fagus species, 322
Fagus sylvatica, 323
False
  Spirea, 178
  Strawberry, 117
Fancy-leaved Caladium, 86
Feather Reed Grass, 156
  Korean, 157
  Overdam, 157
Fennel, Bronze, 75
Fern, 54, 126, 160, 178, 188,
  198, 202, 224
  Cinnamon, 198
  Hay-Scented, 199
  Interrupted, 199
  Japanese Painted, 198, 199
  Lady, 199
  Ostrich, 198, 199
Fern
  'Silver Falls', 199
  'Ursala's Red', 199
Fernleaf Yarrow, 226, 227
Fescue
  Blue, 150, 152, 153
  Chewing, 383
  Fine, 376, 380, 382, 384
  Gray, 150
  Hard, 383
  Sheep, 383
Festuca cinerea, 150
Festuca glauca, 150
Festuca ovina duriuscula, 383
Festuca ovina, 383
Festuca ovina glauca, 150
Festuca rubra commutata, 383
Festuca species, 382
Fetuca rubra rubra, 383
Fibrous-rooted Begonia, 36
Fine Fescue, 376, 380,
  382, 384
Fir, 336
  Balsam, 336, 337
  Douglas, 330
  Fraser, 337
  White, 336, 337
Firecracker Plant, 70
Flag, Blue, 105
Floribunda Rose, 256,
  258, 260

Flossflower, 30
Flowering
  Almond, 366
  Crabapple, 328
  Dogwood, 282
  Onion, 84
  Tobacco, 48
    'Domino' Series, 49
    'Nikki' Series, 49
Forsythia, 254, 257, 267,
  284, 297
  Meadowlark, 285
Forsythia
  'Northern Sun', 285
  'Sunrise', 285
Forsythia hybrids, 284
Forsythia ×
  'Meadowlark', 285
Fountain Grass, 158
  Annual, 158
  Oriental, 159
  Perennial, 159
Fragrant Sumac, 286
  'Gro-Low', 287
Fraser Fir, 337
Fraxinus americana, 321
Fraxinus pennsylvanica, 321
Fraxinus species, 320
Freeman Maple, 361
  'Autumn Blaze', 361
Fringed Bleeding
  Heart, 185
Frost Grass, 166
Fuchsia, 50
  'Firecracker', 51
  'Golden Marinka', 51
  'Thalia', 51
Fuchsia × *hybrida*, 50
Funkia, 202
Galanthus nivalis, 109
Galeobdolon luteum, 143
Galium, 141
Galium odorata, 141
Galium odoratum, 140
Garden
  Calla, 88
  Dahlia, 96
  Hyacinth, 102
  Impatiens, 55
  Lily, 106
  Lobelia, 57
  Mum, 204
  Phlox, 210, 211
  Pinks, 34
  Sage, 71
  Snapdragon, 72
  Verbena, 78

Gayfeather, 200
  'Kobold', 201
Geranium, 28, 30, 48, 51, 52,
  55, 57, 59, 74, 151
  Bedding, 52
  Ivy, 53
  Scented, 53
  Zonal, 52
German Iris, 104
Giant Onion, 84, 85
Ginger, 126, 198
  Canada, 126
  European, 126, 127
  Shiny-Leaf, 126
  Wild, 126, 127
Ginkgo, 338
  'Jade Butterflies', 339
  'Pendula', 339
  'Tschi-Tschi', 339
  'Tubiformis', 339
Ginkgo biloba, 338, 339
  'Fastigiata', 339
  'Princeton Sentry', 339
Glacier Mockorange, 297
Gladiola, 98
Gladiolus, 98
Gladiolus × *hortulanus*, 98
Gleditsia triacanthos, 345
Gleditsia triacanthos var.
  inermis, 344
Glory-of-the-Snow, 109
Golden
  Crocus, 93
  Variegated
    Hakonechloa, 160
Goldenrod, 169
Goldsturm Rudbeckia, 183
Goutweed, 120, 121
  Silveredge, 120
Grandiflora Rose, 253, 258
  'Peace', 259
  'Queen Elizabeth', 259
Grape Hyacinth, 100
  Armenian, 101
Gray
  Dogwood, 283
  Fescue, 150
Great Coneflower, 183
Green Ash, 320, 321
  'Marshall's Seedless', 321
  'Patmore', 321
Groundcovers, 114
Gymnocladus dioicus, 352
Hänse Herms
  Switchgrass, 169
Hairy Phlox, 211
Hakone Grass, 161

Index

Hakonechloa macra, 161
  'Aureola', 160
Hakonechloa, 148, 160
  Golden Variegated, 160
  Variegated, 161
Hakonechloa,
  'Alba Striata', 161
Hamamelis vernalis, 311
Hamamelis virginiana, 310
Hard Fescue, 383
Hardy
  Lily, 106
  Mum, 204
Harebell, 180, 223
  Common, 181
Hawthorn, 293, 340
  Cockspur, 341
  Washington, 341
  Winter King, 341
Hay-Scented Fern, 199
Heavy Metal
  Switchgrass, 169
Hedge
  Coneflower, 212
  Cotoneaster, 281
Helianthus annuus, 76
Helichrysum, 78
Helictotrichon
  sempervirens, 152, 153
Heliotrope, 52
Hemerocallis
  'Kwanzo-variegata', 195
Hemerocallis fulva, 195
Hemerocallis species and
  hybrids, 194
Hemlock, 342
  Canadian, 342
  Eastern, 342
Hemlock
  'Cole', 343
  'Cole's Prostrate', 343
  'Kelsey's Weeping', 343
  'Pendula', 343
  'Sargentii', 343
Herbaceous Peony, 208
Herman's Pride
  Archangel, 143
Heuchera richardsonii, 191
Heuchera sanguinea, 190
Honey Locust, 344, 371
  Thornless, 344
Honeysuckle, 288
  'Freedom', 289
  'Honey Rose', 289
  'Miniglobe', 289
Honeysuckle
  Amur, 289

Belle's, 289
Bush, 288
Clavey's Dwarf, 289
Dropmore
  Scarlet, 387, 394
European Fly, 288
Morrow's, 289
Tatarian, 289
Trumpet, 395
Hophornbeam, 348, 349
Hornbeam, 349
  American, 362
Horsechestnut, 346
  'Baumannii', 347
Hosta, 13, 54, 126, 160, 178,
  188, 191, 198, 202, 224
Hosta species and
  cultivars, 202
Houttuynia cordata, 129
  'Chameleon', 128
  'Tricolor', 128
Houttuynia, 128
  'Plena', 129
Hyacinth, 102
  Armenian Grape, 101
  Common, 102
  Common Grape, 100
  Dutch, 102
  Garden, 102
  Grape, 100
Hyacinthus, 103
Hyacinthus orientalis, 102
Hybrid
  Peony, 208
  Tea Rose, 248, 253, 254,
    256, 257, 258, 260
    'Love and Peace', 255
Hydrangea, 290
  Bigleaf, 291
  PeeGee, 291
  Snowhill, 291, 299
  Tamarisk, 167
  Tardiva, 167
Hydrangea
  'Annabelle', 291
  'Kyushu', 291
  'Limelight', 291
  'Pink Diamond', 291
  'Tardiva', 291
  'The Swan', 291
Hydrangea arborescens, 290
  'Snowhill', 291
Hydrangea paniculata, 290
  'Grandiflora', 291
Impatiens, 54, 178
  Garden, 55
  Sun, 55

Impatiens
  'Accent' Series, 55
  'Blitz', 55
  'New Guinea', 55
Impatiens balfourii, 55
Impatiens capensis, 55
Impatiens pallida, 55
Impatiens wallerana, 54
Indian
  Cress, 64
  Pinks, 34
  Shot, 90
Indian-Bean, 326
Intermediate Iris, 105
Interrupted Fern, 199
Ipomoea alba, 397
Ipomoea batatas, 397
Ipomoea purpurea, 396
Iris florentina, 105
Iris hybrids, 104
Iris sibirica, 105
Iris versicolor, 105
Iris, 104
  Bearded, 104, 105
  German, 104
  Intermediate, 105
  Miniature Dwarf
    Bearded, 105
  Siberian, 105, 157
  Standard Dwarf
    Bearded, 105
  Tall Bearded , 105
Ironwood, 348, 362, 363
Ivy Geranium, 53
Ivy, Boston, 386, 390
Jackman Clematis, 392, 393
Japanese
  Spirea, 305
  Barberry, 272, 273
  Bleeding Heart, 184
  Blood Grass, 167
  Creeper, 390
  Larch, 354, 355
  Pachysandra, 137
  Painted Fern, 198, 199
  Silver Grass, 162
  Spurge, 136
  Tree Lilac, 137, 147,
    350, 401
    'Ivory Silk', 351
  Wisteria, 402, 403
Jewelweed, 55
Johnny-jump-up, 67
Jonquil, 94, 95
Juneberry, 372, 373
Juniper, 292
Juniperus species, 292

Index

Juniperus virginiana, 293, 341
Kentucky Bluegrass, 380, 383
  Adelphi, 381
  Baron, 381
  Glade, 381
  Nassau, 381
  Parade, 381
Kentucky Coffee
  Tree, 352, 371
  'Espresso', 353
Kentucky Wisteria, 402, 403
  'Blue Moon', 403
Korean
  Feather Reed Grass, 157
  Mountain Ash, 335
Koreanspice Viburnum, 307
Lacebark Elm, 333
Lady Fern, 199
Lady's-Eardrops, 50
Lamiastrum galeobdolon, 143
  'Herman's Pride', 143
  'Variegatum', 142, 143
Lamiastrum, 143
Lamium, 125
Lamium, 143
Lamium galeobdolon, 143
  'Variegatum', 142, 143
Lamium maculatum, 124
Larch, 354
  American, 354, 355
  European, 354, 355
  Japanese, 354, 355
Larix decidua, 355
Larix kaempferi, 355
Larix laricina, 355
Larix species, 354
Larkspur, 196
Lavender, 71
Leucanthemum × superba, 221
Leucanthemum ×
  superbum, 220
Liatris aspera, 201
Liatris pycnostachya, 201
Liatris spicata, 200
Licorice Vine, 78
Lilac, 267, 279, 294, 295, 297,
  309, 350, 351
  Japanese Tree, 137, 147,
    350, 401
  Miss Kim, 295
  Palabin, 295
  Pekin, 351
  Summer, 278
Lilium lancifolium, 107
Lilium species, 106
Lilium tigrinum, 107
Lily-flowered Tulip, 113

Lily of the Nile, 88
Lily, 41, 106
  Arum, 88
  Calla, 88
  Canna, 90
  Ditch, 195
  Easter, 107
  Garden, 106
  Hardy, 106
  Tiger, 107
  Trumpet, 88
  Water, 97
Lily-of-the-Valley, 130
  'Albostriata', 131
  'Aureovariegata', 131
  'Flore Pleno', 131
  'Fortin's Giant', 131
  'Variegata', 131
Linden, 356
  American, 356, 357
  Littleleaf, 356, 357
Little Bluestem, 154
Littleleaf
  Linden, 356, 357
  Mockorange, 297
Lobelia, 56
  Edging, 56
  Garden, 57
Lobelia
  'Blue Moon', 57
  'Cascade' Series, 57
  'Crystal Palace', 57
  'Fountain' Series, 57
  'Rosamund', 57
  'Sapphire', 57
Lobelia cardinalis, 57
Lobelia erinus, 56
Lobularia maritima, 32
Locust, Honey, 344, 371
  Thornless Honey, 344
Lolium multiflorum, 385
Lolium perenne, 384
Lonicera
  'Honey Rose', 395
Lonicera × bella, 289
Lonicera × brownii
  'Dropmore Scarlet', 394
Lonicera maackii, 289
Lonicera morrowii, 289
Lonicera pericyclemenum
  'Harlequin', 395
Lonicera sempervirens, 395
Lonicera species, 288
Lonicera tatarica, 289
Lonicera × xylosteoides
  'Clavey's Dwarf', 289
Lotus Vine, 78

Lungwort, 203
Lyre Flower, 184
Lysimachia nummularia, 132
  'Aurea', 133
Madagascar Periwinkle, 58
  'Cooler' Series, 59
  'Jaio Scarlet Eye', 59
  'Parasol', 59
  'Pretty in Pink', 59
  'Pretty in Rose', 59
  'Pretty' Series, 59
Magnolia acuminata, 359
Magnolia × soulangiana, 359
Magnolia species, 358
Magnolia stellata, 359
Magnolia, 358
  Cucumber, 359
  Saucer, 359
  Star, 359
Maiden Grass, 163
Maidenhair Tree, 338
Malus hybrids, 328
Maple, 360
  Amur, 361
  Freeman, 361
  Norway, 120, 361
  Red, 18, 360, 361, 368
  Silver, 361
  Sugar, 361
Marigold, 28, 30, 60
  African, 60
  American, 60
  Aztec, 60
  Dwarf French, 60
  Signet, 60, 61
Marsh Bellflower, 181
Matteuccia, 198
Matteuccia struthiopteris, 199
Meadowlark Forsythia, 285
Mealycup Sage, 71
Melon, 44
Mertensia maritima, 225
Mertensia paniculata, 225
Mertensia pulmonarioides, 224
Mertensia virginica, 224
Miniature
  Dwarf Bearded Iris, 105
  Rose, 260
Miscanthus sacchariflorus, 163
Miscanthus, 162
  Red Flame, 163
  Variegated, 167
Miscanthus sinensis
  'Gracillimus', 163
  'Strictus', 163
  'Variegatus', 163
  'Zebrinus', 163

Miscanthus sinensis
  species, 162
Miscanthus sinensis var.
  purpurascens, 163
Miss Kim Lilac, 295
Mockorange, 296
  Glacier, 297
  Littleleaf, 297
  Sweet, 296
Mockorange
  'Dwarf Minnesota
    Snowflake', 297
  'Innocence', 297
  'Minnesota
    Snowflake', 297
  'Variegatus', 297
Molinia caerulea subsp.
  arundinaceae, 165
Molinia, 165
Molinia caerulea, 164
  'Variegata', 165
Moneywort, 132
Moonflower, 397
Moor Grass, 148, 164
  Purple, 164
  Variegated Purple , 165
Moor Grass
  'Skyracer', 165
  'Transparent', 165
Morning Glory, 77, 396
Morrow's
  Honeysuckle, 289
Moss
  Phlox, 210, 211
  Rose, 62
    'Afternoon
      Delight', 63
    'Calypso Mixture', 63
    'Sundance Mix', 63
    'Sundial' Series, 63
Mother of Thyme, 134
  'Albus', 135
  'Coccinea', 135
  'Elfin', 135
  'Pink Chintz', 135
Mountain Ash, 334
Mouse Ear Coreopsis, 193
Mugo Pine, 298
  Dwarf, 299
Mugo Pine
  'Aurea', 299
  'Sunshine', 299
Multiflora Rose, 253
Mum, 77, 204
  Anemone, 205
  Brush, 205
  Button, 205

Daisy, 205
Garden, 204
Hardy, 204
Pompons, 205
Quill, 205
Spider, 205
Spoon, 205
Mum
  'Clara Curtis', 205
  'Duchess of
    Edinburgh', 205
  'Mary Stoker', 205
  'Minngopher', 205
  'Rose Blush', 205
  'Sesquicentennial
    Sun', 205
Muscari armeniacum, 101
Muscari botryoides, 100
Muscari botryoides album, 101
Muscari comosum
  'Plumosum', 101
Musclewood, 349, 362
Nannyberry, 306
Narcissus, 94, 95
Narcissus jonquilla, 95
Narcissus species and
  hybrids, 94
Nasturtium, 64
  'Alaska' Series, 65
  'Whirleybird', 65
New England Aster, 177
  'Alma Potschke', 177
  'Purple Dome', 177
New York Aster, 177
Newport Plum, 366, 367
Nicotiana, 48
Nicotiana alata, 48
Nicotiana langsdorfii
  'Variegata', 49
Nicotiana sylvestris, 49
Northern
  Catalpa, 326
  Lights Azalea, 303
Norway Maple, 120, 361
Oak, 340, 364
  Bur, 365
  Pin, 365
  Red, 365
  Swamp White, 365
  White, 18, 365
Oat Grass, Blue, 152
Oats, Ornamental, 152
Ohio Buckeye, 347
Old-Fashioned Weigela, 308
Onion
  Flowering, 84
  Giant, 84, 85

Ornamental, 84, 85
Opium Poppy, 207
Orange
  Coneflower, 182, 183
  Daylily, 195
  Stonecrop, 219
Orchid, 327
Oriental
  Fountain Grass, 159
  Poppy, 206
    'Allegro', 207
    'Beauty of
      Livermore', 207
Ornamental
  Cherry, 366
  Oats, 152
  Onion, 84, 85
  Plum, 366
  Tobacco, 48
Ornamental Grasses, 148
Orrisroot, 105
Osmunda, 198
Osmunda claytoniana, 199
Ostrich Fern, 198, 199
Ostrya, 349
Ostrya virginiana, 348, 363
Overdam Feather Reed
  Grass, 157
Oyster Plant, 225
Pachysandra, 136
  Japanese, 137
Pachysandra
  'Green Carpet', 137
  'Variegata', 137
Pachysandra procumbens, 137
Pachysandra terminalis, 136
Paeonia hybrids, 208
Pagoda Dogwood, 283
Palabin Lilac, 295
Pampas Grass, 148
Panicum virgatum, 168
  'Hänse Herms', 169
  'Heavy Metal', 169
Pansy, 66
  'Imperial', 67
  'Maxim', 67
  'Second Season', 67
  'Springtime', 67
  'Universal', 67
Papaver orientale, 206
Papaver rhoeas, 207
Papavera somniferum, 207
Paper Birch, 324, 325
Parrot Tulip, 113
Parthenocissus
  quinquefolia, 391
  'Engelmanii', 391

Index

*Parthenocissus
tricuspidata*, 390
Patient Lucy, 54
Pea, 352, 371
PeeGee Hydrangea, 291
Pekin Lilac, 351
Pelargonium × hortorum, 52
Pelargonium peltatum, 53
Pelargonium species, 53
Pennisetum alopecuroides, 159
Pennisetum orientale, 159
Pennisetum setaceum, 158
  'Cupreum', 159
  'Purpureum', 159
  'Rubrum', 159
Penstemon
  'Husker Red', 152
Peony, 113, 208
  Chinese, 208
  Herbaceous, 208
  Hybrid, 208
Perennial
  Fountain Grass, 159
  Rye, 380, 383
  Ryegrass, 376, 384
  Sage, 216, 217
  Salvia, 216
Perennials, 170
Periwinkle, 144
  Madagascar, 58
  Rose, 58
Perovskia atriplicifolia, 214
Petunia, 68
  Grandiflora
    'Daddy' Series, 69
  Multiflora
    'Carpet' Series, 69
    'Wave' Series, 69
Petunia × hybrida, 68
*Philadelphus
coronarius*, 296, 297
Philadelphus × lemoine, 297
Philadelphus microphyllus, 297
Philadelphus × virginalis, 297
  'Glacier', 297
Phlox, 210
  Creeping, 210, 211
  Downy, 211
  Garden, 210, 211
  Hairy, 211
  Moss, 210, 211
  Smooth, 211
  Wild Blue, 211
Phlox
  'David', 211
Phlox divaricata, 211
Phlox glaberrima, 211

Phlox maculata, 211
Phlox paniculata, 211
Phlox pilosa, 211
Phlox subulata, 210, 211
Phylox paniculata, 210
Picea, 374
Picea glauca, 375
  'Conica', 375
Picea omorika, 375
Picea pungens f. *glauca*, 375
Pices abies, 375
Pin Oak, 365
Pine, 298, 368
  Austrian, 369
  Mugo, 298
  Red, 369
  Scotch, 369
  Swiss Mountain, 298
  White, 269, 369
Pinks
  Annual, 34
  Garden, 34
  Indian, 34
  Rainbow, 34
Pinus, 368
Pinus mugo, 298
Pinus mugo mugo, 299
Pinus nigra, 369
Pinus resinosa, 369
Pinus strobus, 369
Pinus sylvestris, 369
PJM Rhododendron, 303
Plantain-Lily, 202
Plum
  Double-Flowering, 367
  Newport, 366, 367
  Ornamental, 366
Poa pratensis, 380
Polyantha, 256
Poppy
  Corn, 207
  Opium, 207
  Oriental, 206
Porcupine Grass, 163
Portulaca grandiflora, 62, 63
Potentilla, 138, 300
  Creeping, 151
  Spring, 138
Potentilla
  'Abbotswood', 301
  'Goldfinger', 301
  'McKay's White', 301
Potentilla fruticosa, 300
Potentilla species, 138
*Potentilla
tabernaemontani*, 139
Potentilla tridentata, 139

Potentilla verna, 139
Prickly Pear Cactus, 228
Prostrate Speedwell, 223
Prunus cerasifera
  'Newport', 367
Prunus × cistena, 367
Prunus maackii, 367
Prunus serotina, 367
Prunus species, 366
Prunus triloba, 367
Prunus virginiana
  'Schubert', 367
Pseudotsuga douglasii, 330
Pseudotsuga menziesii, 330
*Pseudotsuga menziesii
glauca*, 331
Pseudotsuga taxifolia, 330
Pulmonaria, 203
Purple
  Coneflower, 212, 214
    'Magnus', 213
    'White Swan', 213
  Echinacea, 212
  Leaf Sand Cherry, 366
  Moor Grass, 164
  Moor Grass,
    Variegated, 165
  Virgin's Bower, 393
Purpleleaf
  Sand Cherry, 366, 367
  Wintercreeper, 147
Queen Anne's Lace, 120, 343
Queensland Arrowroot, 91
Quercus alba, 365
Quercus bicolor, 365
Quercus macrocarpa, 365
Quercus palustris, 365
Quercus rubra, 365
Quercus species, 364
Quince, 281
Rainbow Pinks, 34
Red
  Cedar, 292, 293, 341
  Elm, 333
  Flame Miscanthus, 163
  Maple, 18, 360, 361, 368
  Oak, 365
  Pine, 369
  Salvia, 70, 71
Redbud, Eastern, 370
Redbud
  'Minnesota Strain', 371
Redosier Dogwood, 283
Redtwig Dogwood, 283
Reed Grass, Feather, 156
Rhododendron, 14, 18, 302
  PJM, 303

Index

Rhododendron species, 302
Rhus aromatica, 286
Rhus odiferous, 286
Rhus typhina, 287
  'Dissecta', 287
  'Laciniata', 287
Ribes alpinum, 268
Ribes odoratum, 269
River Birch, 325
Rock Cotoneaster, 281
Rosa × *hybrida*, 252, 254, 256, 258, 260
Rosa rugosa, 263
Rosa species and hybrids, 262
Rose
  Moss, 62
  Periwinkle, 58
Rose, 14
  Climbing, 252
  Floribunda, 256, 258, 260
  Grandiflora, 253, 258
  Hybrid Tea, 248, 253, 254, 256, 257, 258, 260
  Miniature, 260
  Moss, 62
  Multiflora, 253
  Rugosa, 263
  Shrub, 262
Rosea, 131
Roses, 248
Rough Blazing Star, 201
Rudbeckia fulgida, 183
Rudbeckia fulgida var. *sullivantii*
  'Goldsturm', 183
Rudbeckia hirta, 183
Rudbeckia × *hirta*
  'Chim Chiminee', 183
Rudbeckia maxima, 183
Rudbeckia species, 182
Rudbeckia, Goldsturm, 183
Rugosa Rose, 263
Russian Sage, 212, 214
  'Blue Spire', 215
  'Filigran', 215
  'Login', 215
Rye, Perennial, 380
Ryegrass
  Annual, 385
  Perennial, 376, 384
Saffron Crocus, 93
Sage
  Azure, 214
  Garden, 71
  Mealycup, 71
  Perennial, 216, 217

Russian, 212, 214
Scarlet, 70
White, 174, 175
Salvia, 30, 70, 216, 220
  Blue, 61
  Perennial, 216
  Red, 70, 71
    'Lady in Red', 71
Salvia
  'Carabinere' Series, 71
  'East Friesland', 217
  'Empire' Series, 71
  'Firecracker' Series, 71
  'Mainacht', 217
  'May Night', 157, 217
  'Strata', 71
  'Tricolor', 71
  'Victoria', 71
Salvia farinacea, 71
Salvia officinalis, 71, 217
Salvia species, 216
Salvia splendens, 70
Saucer Magnolia, 359
Scarlet Sage, 70
Scented Geranium, 53
Schizachyrium scoparium, 154
Scilla bifolia, 109
Scilla sibirica, 108
  'Alba', 109
Scotch Pine, 369
Sedum × 'Autumn Joy', 219
Sedum, 218
  'Autumn Joy', 157, 159, 167
  'Vera Jameson', 219
Sedum kamtschaticum, 219
Sedum species, 218
Sedum spurium, 219
Senecio cineraria, 46
Serbian Spruce, 375
Serviceberry, 140, 372
  Allegheny, 373
  Apple, 373
  Downy, 373
  Shadblow, 372, 373
Shasta Daisy, 220
  'Alaska', 221
  'Becky', 221
  'Silver Princess', 221
  'Switzerland', 221
Sheep Fescue, 383
Shiny-Leaf Ginger, 126
Showy
  Crocus, 93
  Mountain Ash, 335
Shrub Rose, 262
  'All that Jazz', 263

  'Carefree Wonder', 263
  'Henry Kelsey', 253
  'John Cabot', 253
  'Starry Night', 263
  'William Baffin', 253, 263
Shrubs, 264
Siberian
  Elm, 333
  Iris, 105, 157
  Squill, 108, 109
    'Spring Beauty', 109
Signet Marigold, 60, 61
  'Lemon Gem', 61
Silver
  Grass, 148, 162
    Chinese, 162, 163
    Japanese, 162
  Maple, 361
  Spike Grass, 166
Silveredge Goutweed, 120
Silvermound
  Artemisia, 174, 175
Slippery Elm, 333
Smooth Phlox, 211
Snapdragon, 72
  Common, 72
  Garden, 72
Snapdragon
  'Floral Carpet' Series, 73
  'Floral Showers' Series, 73
  'Frosted Flames', 73
  'Powy's Pride', 73
  'Rocket' Series, 73
  'Sonnet' Series, 73
Snowdrops, 109
Snowflake, Dwarf
  Minnesota, 295
Snowhill
  Hydrangea, 291, 299
Solenostemon scutellarioides, 42
Sorbus alnifolia, 335
Sorbus americana, 335
Sorbus aucuparia, 334
Sorbus decora, 335
Speckled Alder, 319
Speedwell, 222
  Prostrate, 223
  Spike, 223
  Woolly, 223
Spider
  Cleome, 38, 158
  Flower, 38, 39
Spike, 57, 74, 158
  Grass, 166
    Silver, 166

Index

Speedwell, 223
Spiraea species, 304
Spiraea thunbergii
  'Mt. Fuji', 305
Spiraea × vanhouttei, 305
Spirea, 304
  Bridal Wreath, 299,
    304, 305
  False, 178
  Japanese, 305
  Vanhoutte, 299
Spirea
  'Anthony
    Waterer', 305
  'Froebelii', 305
  'Goldflame', 305
  'Goldmound', 305
Spodiopogon sibiricus, 166
Spotted
  Deadnettle, 124, 125
Spring
  Cinquefoil, 139
  Potentilla, 138
Spruce, 126, 374
  Blue, 336, 337
  Colorado Blue, 330,
    336, 375
  Dwarf Alberta, 375
  Serbian, 375
  White, 375
Spurge
  Allegheny, 137
  Japanese, 136
Squill, 108
  Blue, 108
  Siberian, 108, 109
  Two-leaved, 109
Staghorn Sumac, 287
Standard Dwarf Bearded
  Iris, 105
Star Magnolia, 359
Stonecrop, 218
  Orange, 219
  Two-row, 219
Strawberry, 116
  Barren, 116
  Dry, 116
  False, 117
  Yellow, 116
Sugar Maple, 361
Sulphur Bicolor
  Barrenwort, 119
Sultana, 54
Sumac
  Fragrant, 286, 287
  Staghorn, 287
Summer Lilac, 278

Sun
  Impatiens, 55
  Plant, 62
Sunflower, 76, 169
  Common, 76
  Dwarf, 77
Sunflower
  'Italian White', 77
  'Teddy Bear', 77
  'Valentine', 77
Swamp White Oak, 365
Sweet
  Alyssum, 32
  Autumn Clematis, 393
  Mockorange, 296
  Potato Vine, 397
  William, Wild, 211
  Woodruff, 140
Swiss
  Chard
    'Bright Lites', 27
  Mountain Pine, 298
Switchgrass, 148, 168
  Hänse Herms, 169
  Heavy Metal, 169
Syringa meyeri
  'Palabin', 295
Syringa patula
  'Miss Kim', 295
Syringa pekinensis, 351
Syringa reticulata, 350
Syringa species and
  cultivars, 294
Syringa vulgaris, 295
  'Dappled Dawn', 295
Tagetes erecta, 60, 61
Tagetes patula, 60, 61
Tagetes species, 60
Tagetes tenuifolia, 61
Tall
  Bearded Iris, 105
  Blazing Star, 201
Tamarack, 354, 355
Tamarisk Hydrangea, 167
Tardiva Hydrangea, 167
Tatarian Honeysuckle, 289
Taxus canadensis, 313
Taxus cuspidata, 313
Taxus × media, 313
Taxus species, 312
Techny Arborvitae, 271
Thalia dealbata, 91
Thornapple, 340
Thornless Honey
  Locust, 344
Threadleaf Coreopsis, 84,
  98, 192

Three-Toothed
  Cinquefoil, 138
Thuja occidentalis, 270
  'Techny', 271
Thyme, 134
  Creeping, 134, 135
  Mother of, 134
Thymus angustifolius, 134
Thymus serpyllum, 134
Tickseed, 192, 193
Tiger Lily, 107
Tilia americana, 357
Tilia cordata, 357
Tilia species, 356
Tobacco
  Flowering, 48
  Ornamental, 48
Topaeolum majus, 64
Trees, 314
Tropaeolum peregrinum, 65
Trumpet
  Honeysuckle, 395
  Lily, 88
    'Crimson
      Trumpet', 399
Trumpet Vine, 387, 398
  Yellow, 399
Tsuga canadensis, 342
Tuberous Begonia, 110
  'Non Stop' Series, 111
Tulip, 100, 112
  Lily-flowered, 113
  Parrot, 113
Tulipa species and
  hybrids, 112
Turfgrass, 376
Two-leaved Squill, 109
Ulmus pumila, 333
Ulmus rubra, 333
Ulmus species and
  hybrids, 332
Ulnus parvifolia, 333
Vanhoutte Bridal Wreath
  Spirea, 299
Variegated
  Bishop's Weed, 120
  Hakonechloa, 161
  Miscanthus, 167
  Purple Moor Grass, 165
  Yellow
    Archangel, 125, 142
Verbena, 78
  Brazilian, 79
  Garden, 78
Verbena
  'Imagination', 79
  'Peaches and Cream', 79

Index

'Romance' Series, 79
'Tapien', 79
'Temari', 79
Verbena bonariensis, 75, 79
Verbena × *hybrida*, 78
Vernal Witchhazel, 311
Veronica austriaca subsp.
　teucrium
　'Crater Lake Blue', 223
Veronica, 220, 222
　'Blue Fox', 223
　'Icicle', 223
　'Red Fox', 223
　'Sunny Border Blue', 223
Veronica prostata, 223
Veronica species, 222
Veronica spicata, 223
Veronica spicata subsp.
　incana, 223
Viburnum, 306
　American
Cranberrybush, 307
　Arrowwood, 307
　Cranberrybush, 206
　European
Cranberrybush, 307
　Koreanspice, 307
　Wayfaring, 307
Viburnum
　'Blue Muffin', 307
　'Emerald Triumph', 307
Viburnum carlesii, 307
Viburnum dentatum, 307
Viburnum lantana, 307
Viburnum opulus, 307
Viburnum species, 306
Viburnum trilobum, 307
Vinca, 58, 59, 74, 93, 144
　'Alba', 145
　'Alba Variegata', 145
　'Argenteovariegata', 145
　'Atropurpurea', 145
　'Bowles White', 145
　'Illumination', 145
Vinca minor, 144
Vinca rosea, 58
Vines, 386
Viola tricolor, 67
Viola × *wittrockiana*, 66
Virginia
　Bluebell, 224
　　'Alba', 225
　Creeper, 391
　　Engelmann, 391

Virgin's Bower, 393
　Purple, 393
Waldesteinia fragaroides, 117
Waldsteinia ternata, 116, 117
Washington Hawthorn, 341
Water
　Beech, 363
　Canna, 91
　Lily, 97
　Lily Dahlia, 97
Wax Begonia, 36
Wayfaring Viburnum, 307
Weeping Crabapple, 281
Weigela, 308
　Old-Fashioned, 308
Weigela
　'Bristol Snowflake', 309
　'Java Red', 309
　'Minuet', 309
　'Red Prince', 309
　'Variegata', 309
　'Wine and Roses', 309
Weigela florida, 308, 309
White
　Ash, 320, 321
　　'Autumn
　　　Applause', 321
　　'Autumn Purple', 321
　Cedar, 270, 271
　Fir, 336, 337
　　'Candicans', 337
　Oak, 18, 365
　Pine, 269, 369
　Sage, 174, 175
　Spruce, 375
Wild
　Blue Phlox, 211
　Columbine, 189
　Ginger, 126, 127
　Sweet William, 211
Willow, 41
Willow Tree, 318
Wineleaf
　Cinquefoil, 138, 139
Winged Euonymus, 276
Winter
　Aconite, 109
　King Hawthorn, 341
Wintercreeper, 93, 146, 400
　Big Leaf, 401
　Purpleleaf, 147
Wintercreeper
　Euonymus, 146, 400
Wisteria floribunda, 403

Wisteria macrostachya, 403
Wisteria species, 402
Wisteria, 387, 402
　Chinese, 402
　Japanese, 402, 403
　Kentucky, 402, 403
Witchhazel, 310
　Common, 310
　Vernal, 311
Woodruff, 140, 141
　Sweet, 140
Woolly Speedwell, 223
Wormwood, 174, 175
Yarrow
　'Coronation Gold', 227
Yarrow, 220, 226
　Common, 226, 227
　Fernleaf, 226, 227
Yellow
　Archangel, 142
　Strawberry, 116
　Trumpet Vine, 399
Yew, 9, 312
　Anglojap, 313
　Canadian, 313
Yucca, 13, 84, 228
　'Bright Edge', 229
　'Golden Sword', 229
　'Variegata', 229
Yucca filamentosa, 228
Zantedeschia aethiopica, 88
Zantedeschia albomaculata, 89
Zantedeschia elliottiana, 89
Zebra Grass, 163
Zinnia angustifolia, 81
Zinnia, 28, 80
　Cactus-flowered, 80
　Dahlia-flowered, 80
Zinnia
　'Classic Golden
　　Orange', 81
　'Classic', 81
　'Crystal White', 81
　'Orange Star', 81
　'Peter Pan' Series, 81
　'Profusioon Cherry', 81
　'Profusion Orange', 81
　'Ruffles' Series, 81
　'Thumbelina' Series, 81
Zinnia elegans, 80
Zinnia haageana, 81
Zinnia linearis, 81
Zonal Geranium, 52
Zoysia, 376

MELINDA MYERS, best known for her common-sense and practical approach to gardening, has over twenty years of horticultural experience in both hands-on and instructional settings. She is a Certified Arborist and Horticultural Instructor at Milwaukee Area Technical College, where she teaches students preparing to work in the field of landscape horticulture. Outside the classroom, Myers shares her expertise through a variety of media. She has hosted the "Plant Doctor Radio Show" on WTMJ since 1982. She hosted Wisconsin Lawn and Garden, a weekly show on PBS, from 1996 to 1999. She hosted "Yardworks," a nationally syndicated yard care and garden show, and has scripted and hosted various other cable gardening programs.

Myers is also an accomplished garden writer. She has written a bi-monthly column, "Gardeners' Questions," for the Milwaukee Journal since 1986, and has been a contributing editor and columnist for Birds & Blooms Magazine, a publication with 2 million subscribers throughout the United States and Canada, since 1996. Myers has written several books, including *The Garden Book for Wisconsin, My Wisconsin Garden: A Gardener's Journal, Month-By-Month Gardening in Minnesota,* and *Minnesota Horticultural Society's Minnesota Gardener's Guide.*

Her thirteen years experience at the University of Wisconsin Extension service allowed her to work with backyard, community, and master gardeners throughout Wisconsin. As Milwaukee's Assistant City Forester, Myers helped manage the street tree, boulevards, and green spaces for the city. She has worked with the Young Adult Conservation Corps supervising crews that maintain University of Wisconsin urban test gardens and provide trail repair and other conservation work. Myers has been a member of the Wisconsin Arborist Association since 1979, has chaired the Arbor Day Committee Chair since 1987, and is a past president. Since 1985 she has been a member of the International Society of Arboriculture, and serves as the Arbor Day Committee Liaison to Wisconsin. Currently she heads her local committee for the "Harvest for the Hungry" program, a part of the GWAA Plant-A-Row for the Hungry initiative. A horticultural consultant to numerous community and beautification groups, Melinda began the Master Garden Program in Milwaukee County.

For her work and media presence Myers has received recognition and numerous awards including the 1998 Garden Communicator's Award from the American Nursery and Landscape Association and the 1998 Quill and Trowel Award from the Garden Writers Association of America.

CHUCK LEVINE is a professional horticulturist and a teacher of horticulture and botany for the Minnesota State Horticulture Society, Intermediate School District #287, and Hennepin Technical College. Chuck's personal garden is an acre of urban paradise and has been featured in the *Minneapolis Star Tribune* and on several garden tours. He is a member of The Garden Writer's Association of America, the American Vocational Association, and the City of Roseville Community Arboretum Advisory Council. He serves on the Minnesota State Horticultural Society's Board of Directors and Executive Committee. Chuck has developed and implemented a curriculum on vocational plant production for the Hennepin Country Corrections Facility in Plymouth, Minnesota. He has worked as a horticulture specialist for the Chicago Botanic Garden and the Minnesota Extension Service. Chuck has appeared as a garden expert on radio and television and has been published in the *Northern Gardener, Chicago Tribune, Garden Magazine,* and *Tropical Fish Hobbyist.*

DATE DUE
